ZOMBIEPOWDER.

Vol. 3
PIERCE ME STANDING IN THE
FIREGARDEN

Story & Art by
Tite Kubo

*On this gravestone three steps from the sun,
we don't even know why we continue to spin.*

CHARAC TERS

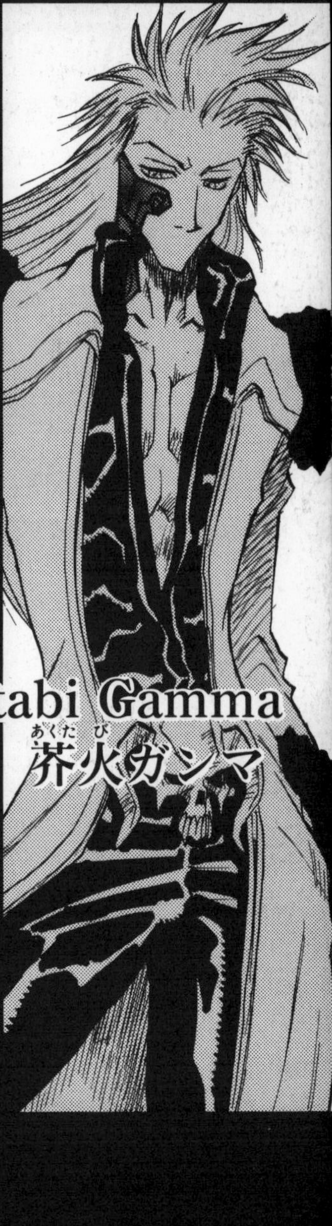

Akutabi Gamma
芥火(あくたび)ガンマ

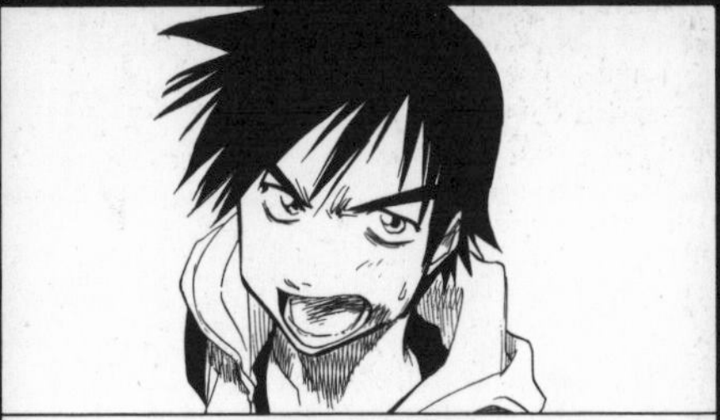

Elwood
エルウッド

R Y

But the Rings are dangerous…and alive. Arriving in a small town, the Powder Hunters discover that a Ring exists inside Emilio, the younger brother of Wolfina, a muckraking journalist. Fusing with his flesh, the Ring has put Emilio into a coma while it slowly devours his life force. Balmunk the Mystic, the ringmaster of a deadly circus troupe, steals Emilio's body in order to extract the precious Ring…by ripping off his head…

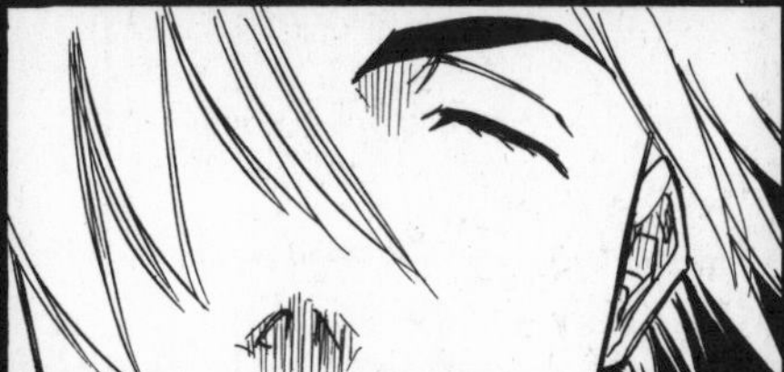

Emilio
エミリオ

CHARAC
TERS

Wolfina
ウルフィーナ

C.T.Smith
C.T.スミス

S T O

The Rings of the Dead: the world's only source
of "Zombie Powder," a substance said to be able
to raise the dead and give the living eternal life.
In the badlands of blood and smoke, no one is
more feared than the "Powder Hunters"…
reckless souls such as Gamma, C.T. Smith and
Elwood, who are willing to risk their own lives
in pursuit of the dream.

Balmunk
バルムンク

ZOMBIEPOWDER.
Vol. 3
PIERCE ME STANDING IN THE FIREGARDEN

CONTENTS

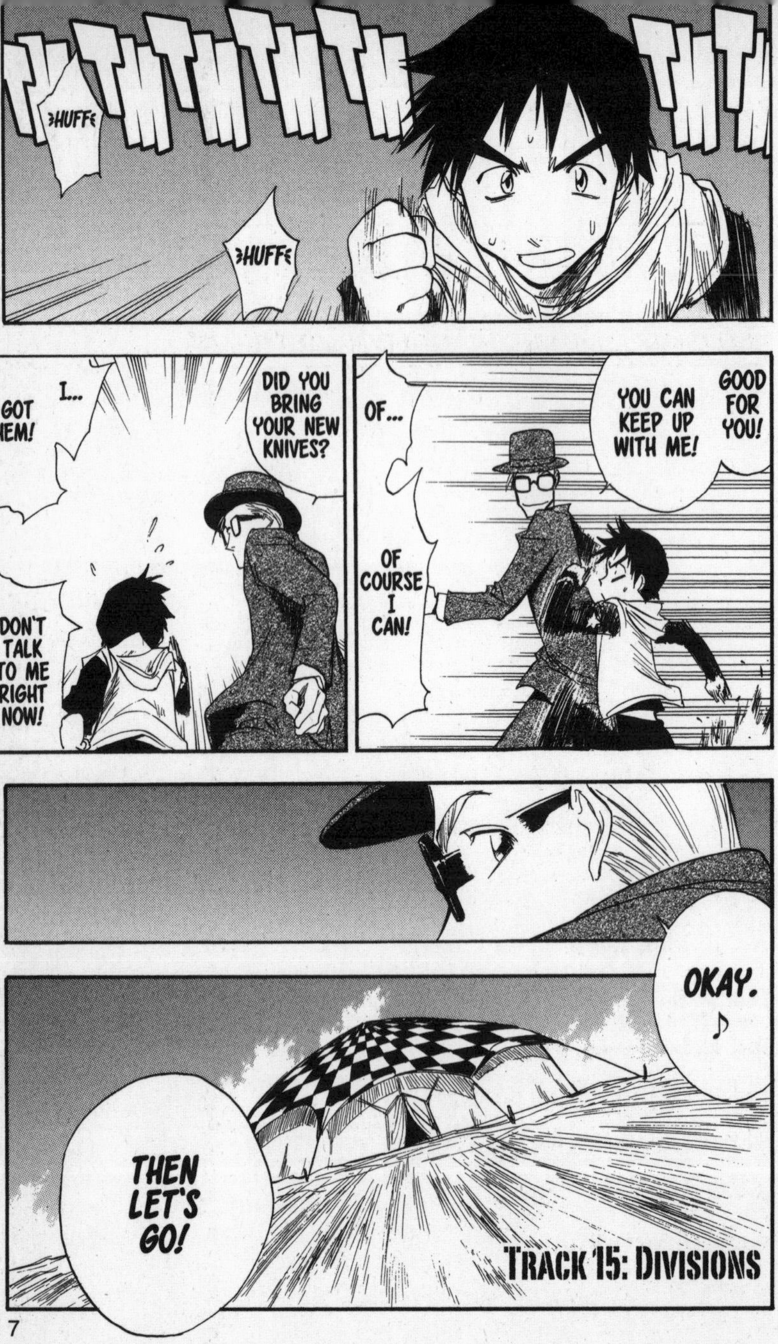
HUFF
HUFF
GOOD FOR YOU!
YOU CAN KEEP UP WITH ME!
OF...
OF COURSE I CAN!
DID YOU BRING YOUR NEW KNIVES?
I...
I GOT THEM!
DON'T TALK TO ME RIGHT NOW!
OKAY. ♪
THEN LET'S GO!
TRACK 15: DIVISIONS

ZOMBIEPOWDER.

Track 15: Divisions

READ THIS WAY

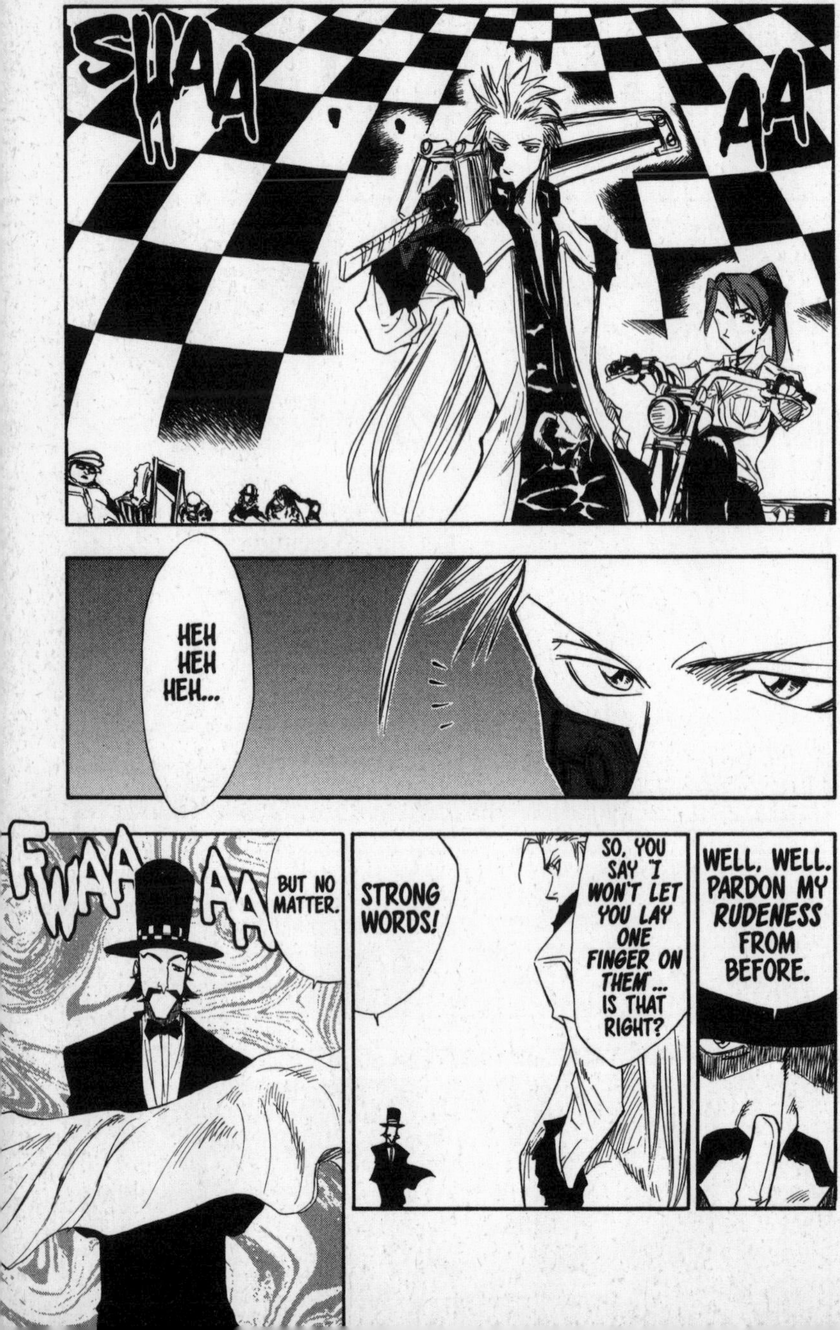
SHAA
AA
HEH HEH HEH...
WELL, WELL. PARDON MY RUDENESS FROM BEFORE.
SO, YOU SAY "I WON'T LET YOU LAY ONE FINGER ON THEM"... IS THAT RIGHT?
STRONG WORDS!
BUT NO MATTER.
FWAA
AA

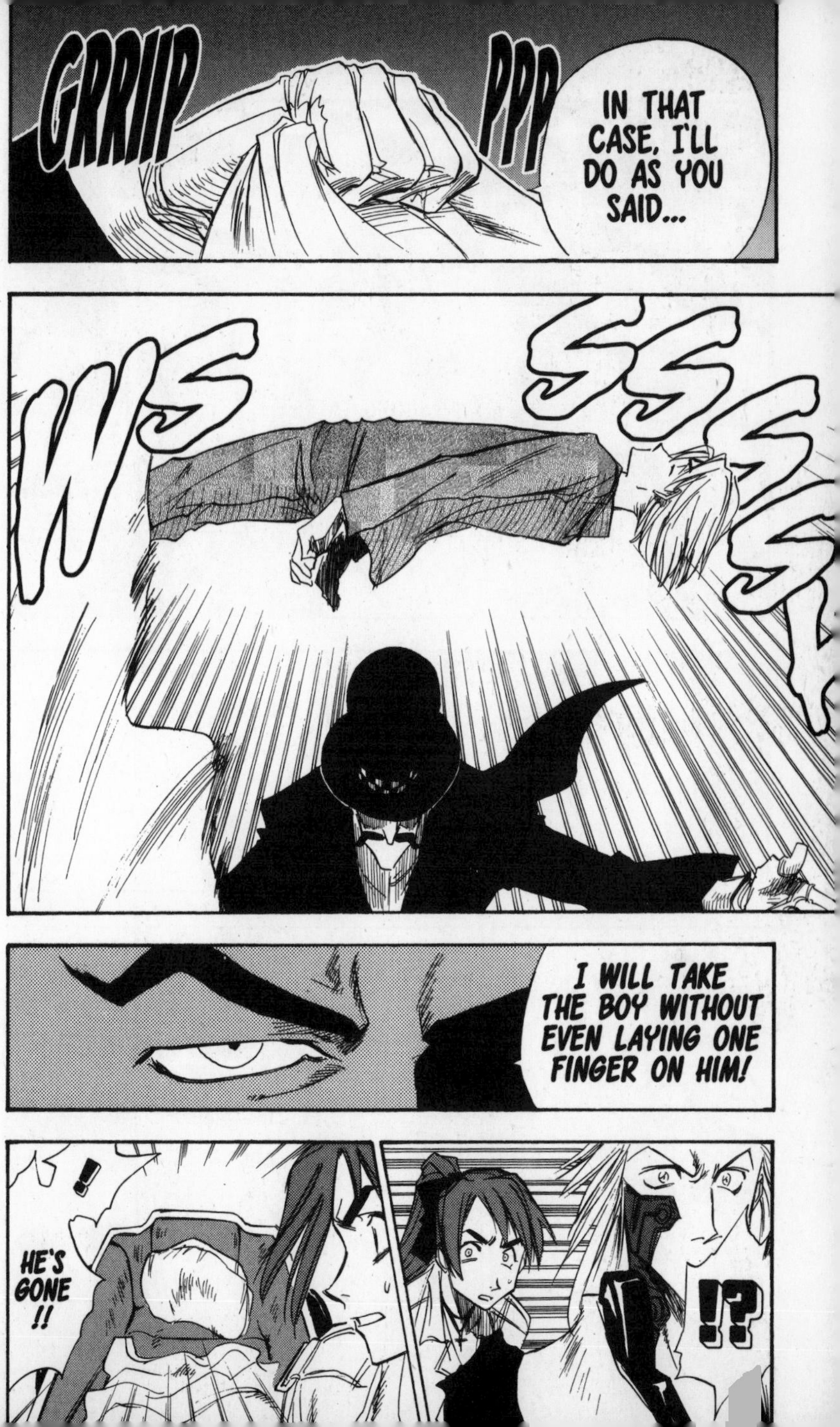
GRRIIP
PPP
IN THAT CASE, I'LL DO AS YOU SAID...
WS
SSSH
I WILL TAKE THE BOY WITHOUT EVEN LAYING ONE FINGER ON HIM!
!?
!
HE'S GONE !!

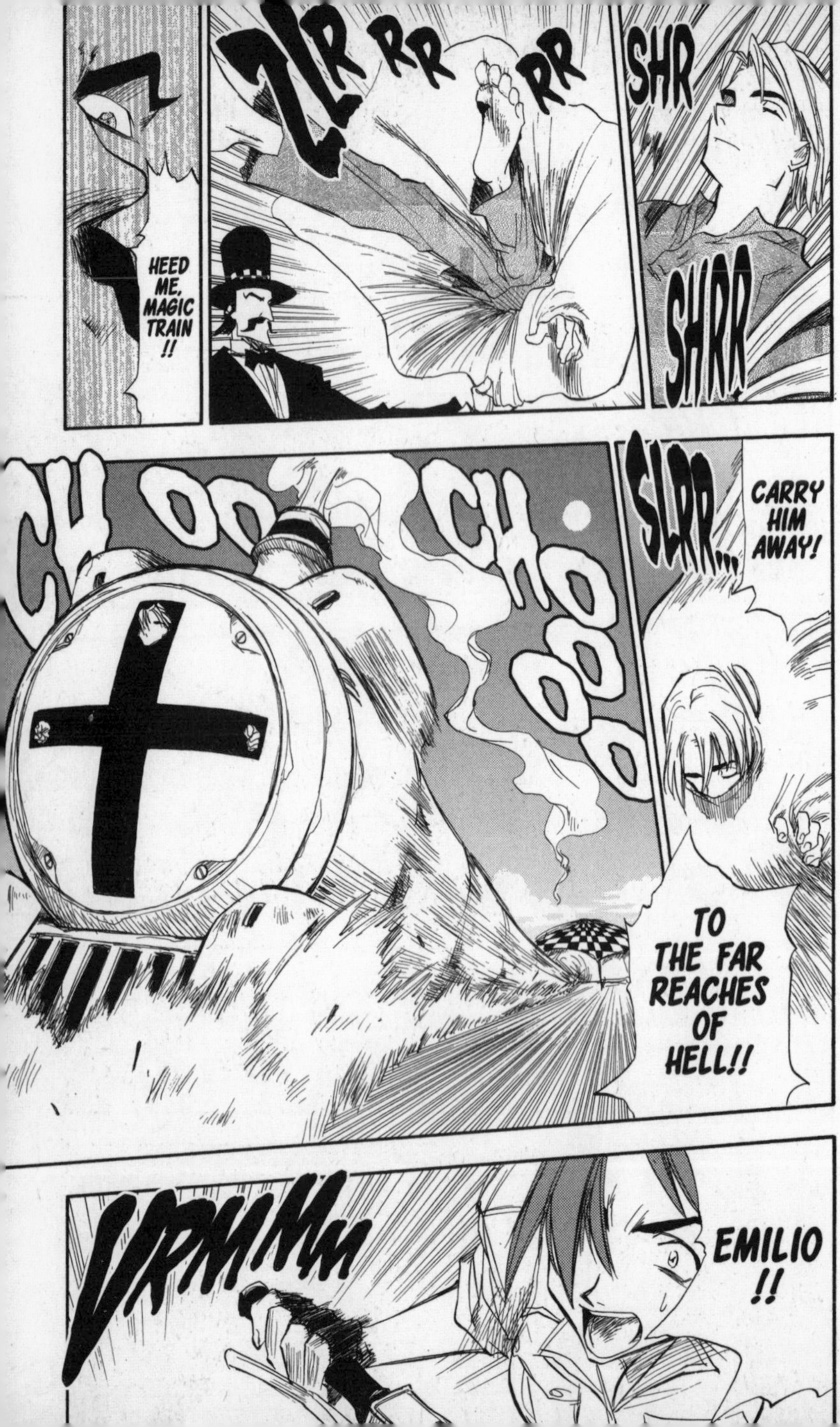
SHR
SHRR
ZIR RR RR
HEED ME, MAGIC TRAIN!!
SLRR...
CARRY HIM AWAY!
TO THE FAR REACHES OF HELL!!
CHOO
CHOOOOO
VRMMM
EMILIO!!

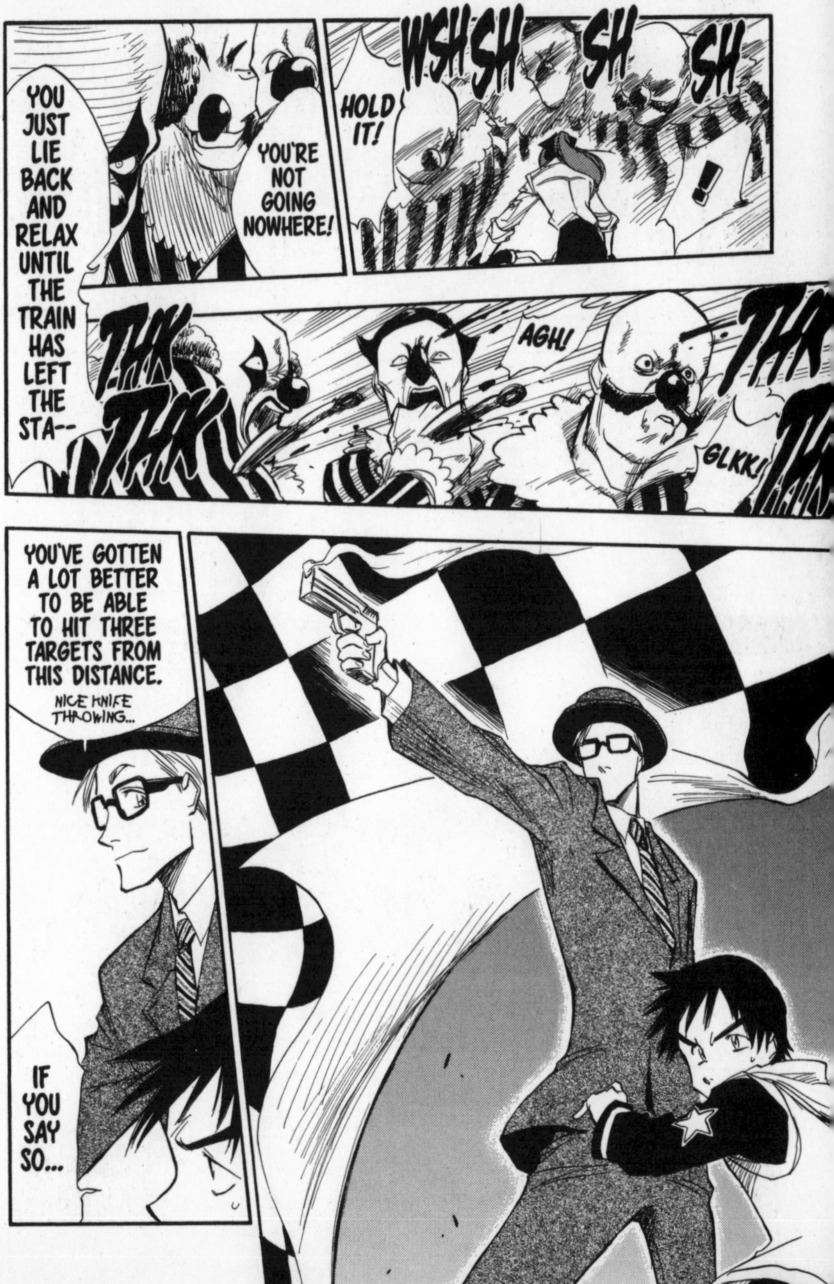
WSH SH SH SH
HOLD IT!
!
YOU'RE NOT GOING NOWHERE!
YOU JUST LIE BACK AND RELAX UNTIL THE TRAIN HAS LEFT THE STA--
THK THK
GLKK!
AGH!
THK THK
YOU'VE GOTTEN A LOT BETTER TO BE ABLE TO HIT THREE TARGETS FROM THIS DISTANCE.
NICE KNIFE THROWING...
IF YOU SAY SO...

READ THIS WAY

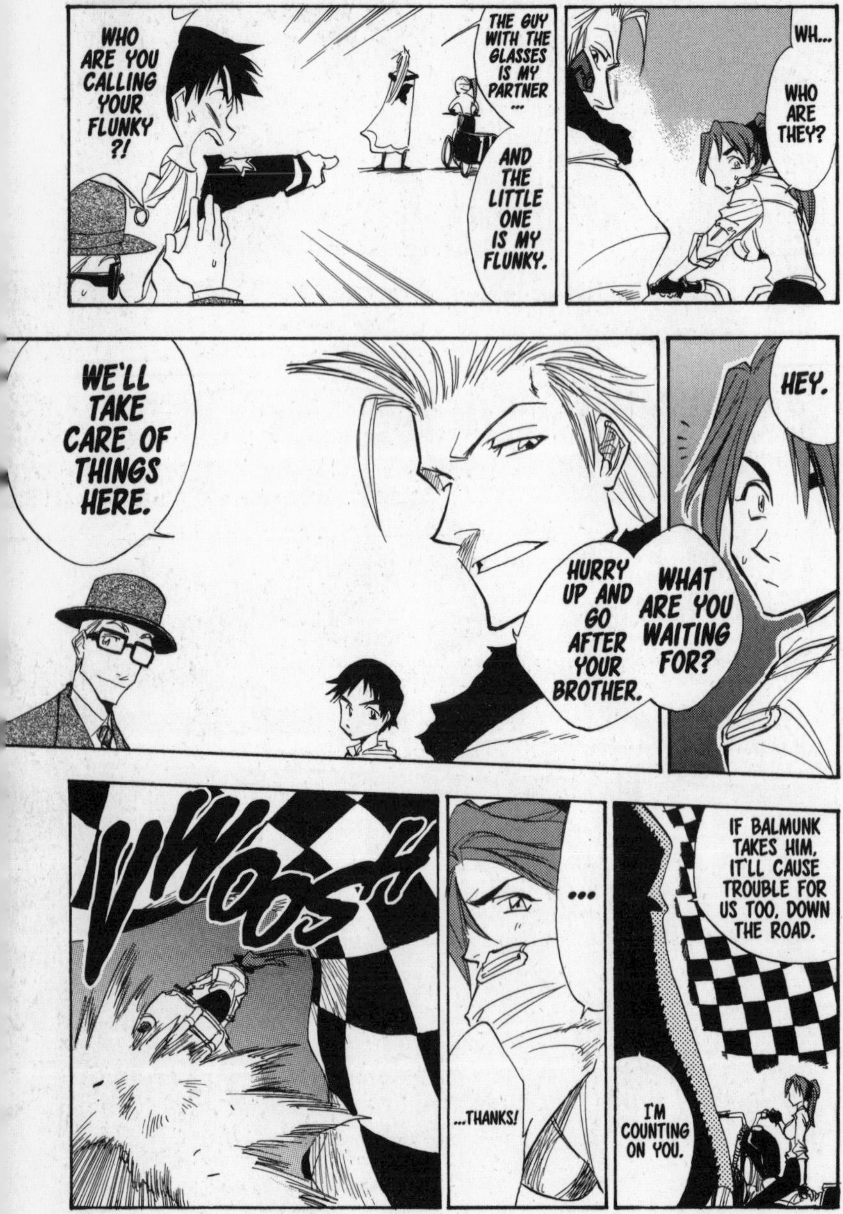

WH...
WHO ARE THEY?
THE GUY WITH THE GLASSES IS MY PARTNER ...
AND THE LITTLE ONE IS MY FLUNKY.
WHO ARE YOU CALLING YOUR FLUNKY?!
HEY.
WHAT ARE YOU WAITING FOR?
HURRY UP AND GO AFTER YOUR BROTHER.
WE'LL TAKE CARE OF THINGS HERE.
IF BALMUNK TAKES HIM, IT'LL CAUSE TROUBLE FOR US TOO, DOWN THE ROAD.
I'M COUNTING ON YOU.
...
...THANKS!
Woosh

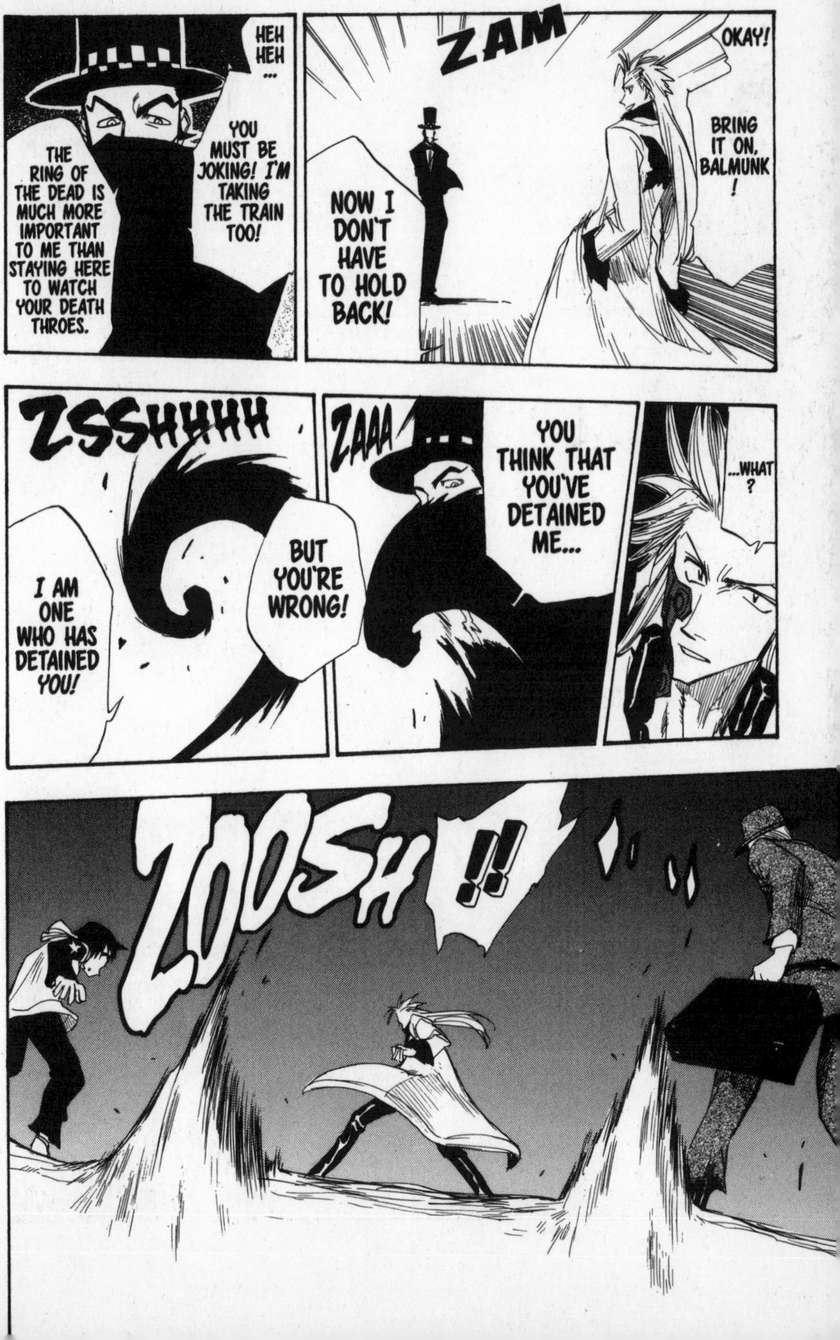
ZAM
OKAY!
BRING IT ON, BALMUNK!
NOW I DON'T HAVE TO HOLD BACK!
HEH HEH...
YOU MUST BE JOKING! I'M TAKING THE TRAIN TOO!
THE RING OF THE DEAD IS MUCH MORE IMPORTANT TO ME THAN STAYING HERE TO WATCH YOUR DEATH THROES.
...WHAT?
ZAAA
YOU THINK THAT YOU'VE DETAINED ME...
BUT YOU'RE WRONG!
ZSSHHHH
I AM ONE WHO HAS DETAINED YOU!
ZOOSH!!

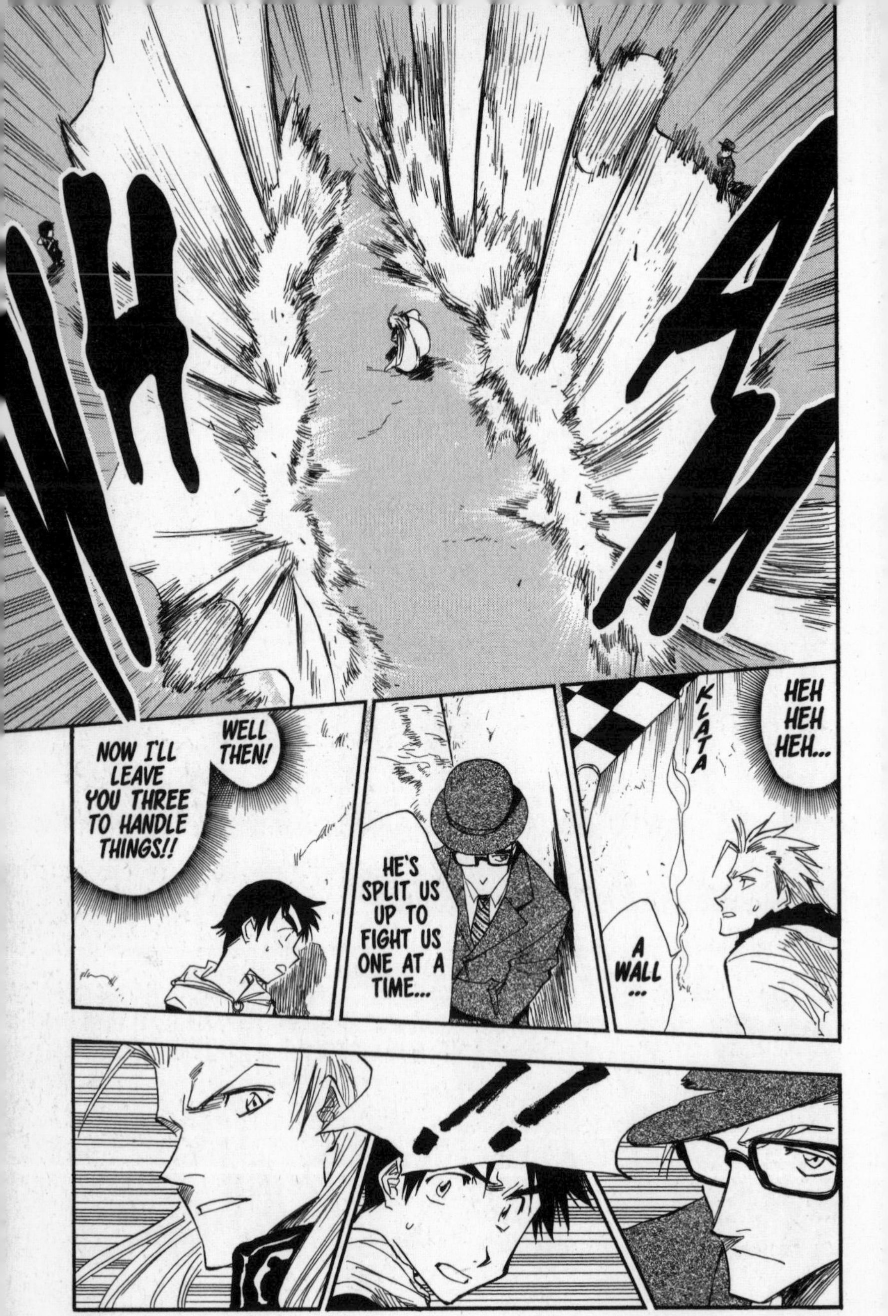
WHAM
HEH HEH HEH...
KLATA
A WALL ...
HE'S SPLIT US UP TO FIGHT US ONE AT A TIME...
WELL THEN!
NOW I'LL LEAVE YOU THREE TO HANDLE THINGS!!
!!

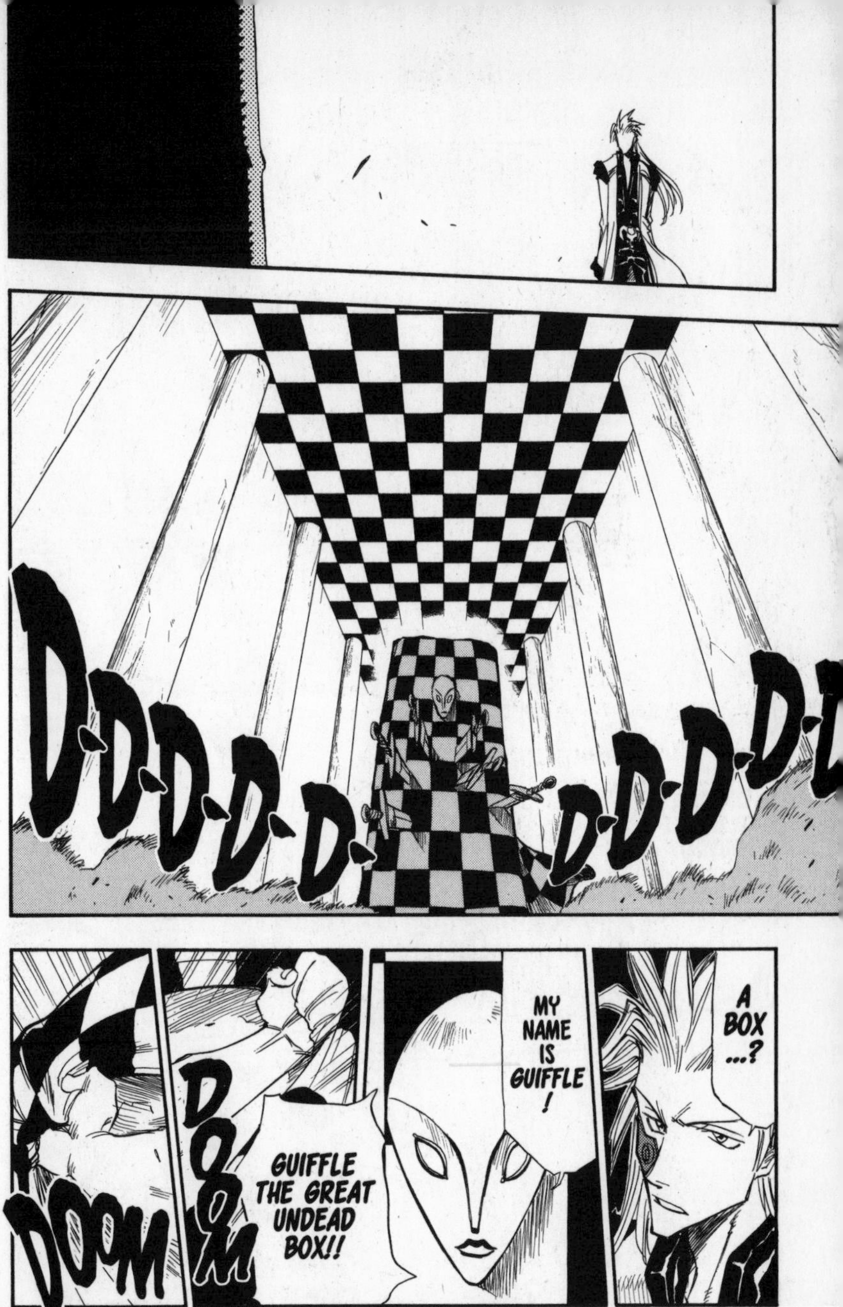
D-D-D-D-D-D-D-D-D-D-D-D-D
A BOX ...?
MY NAME IS GUIFFLE!
GUIFFLE THE GREAT UNDEAD BOX!!
DOOM
DOOM

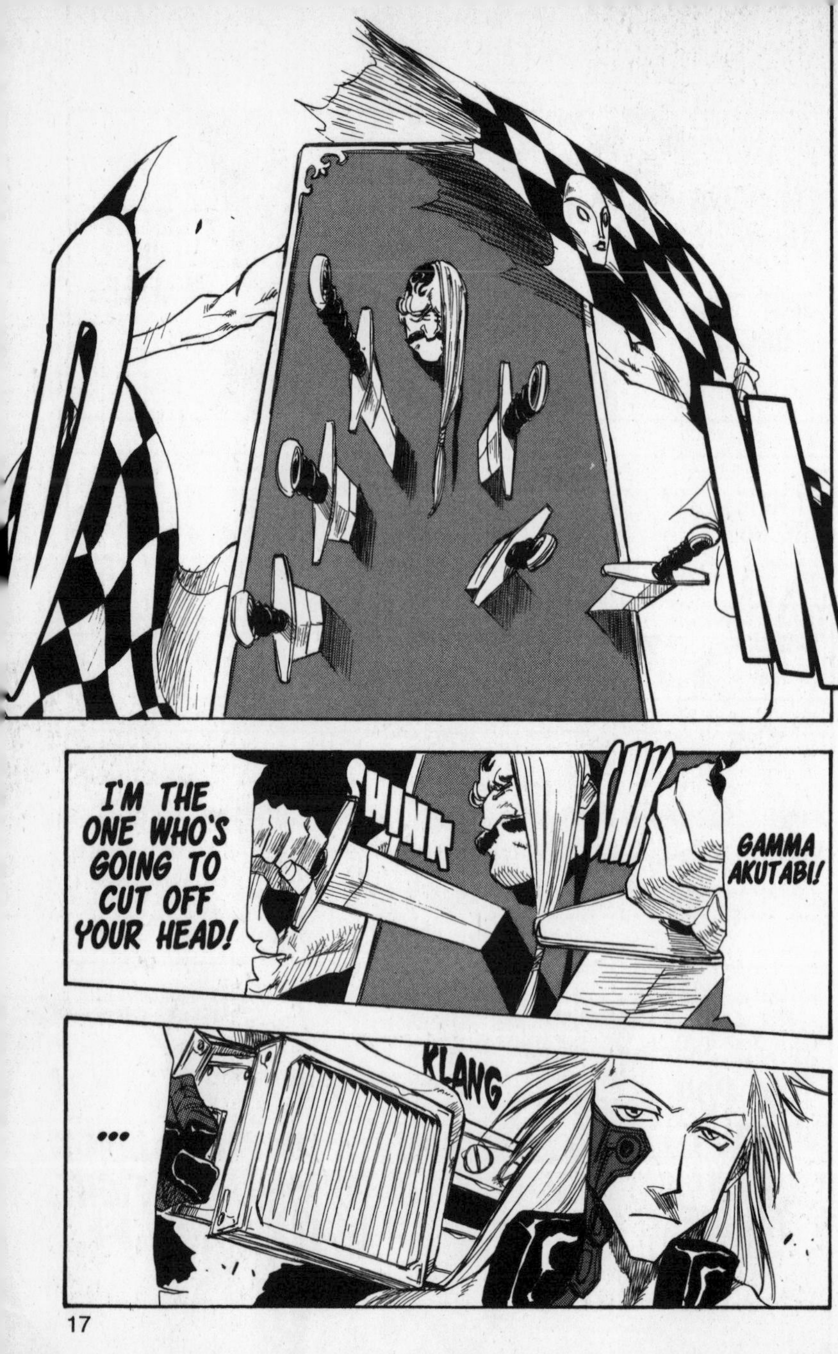
GAMMA AKUTABI!
SHINK
I'M THE ONE WHO'S GOING TO CUT OFF YOUR HEAD!
KLANG
...

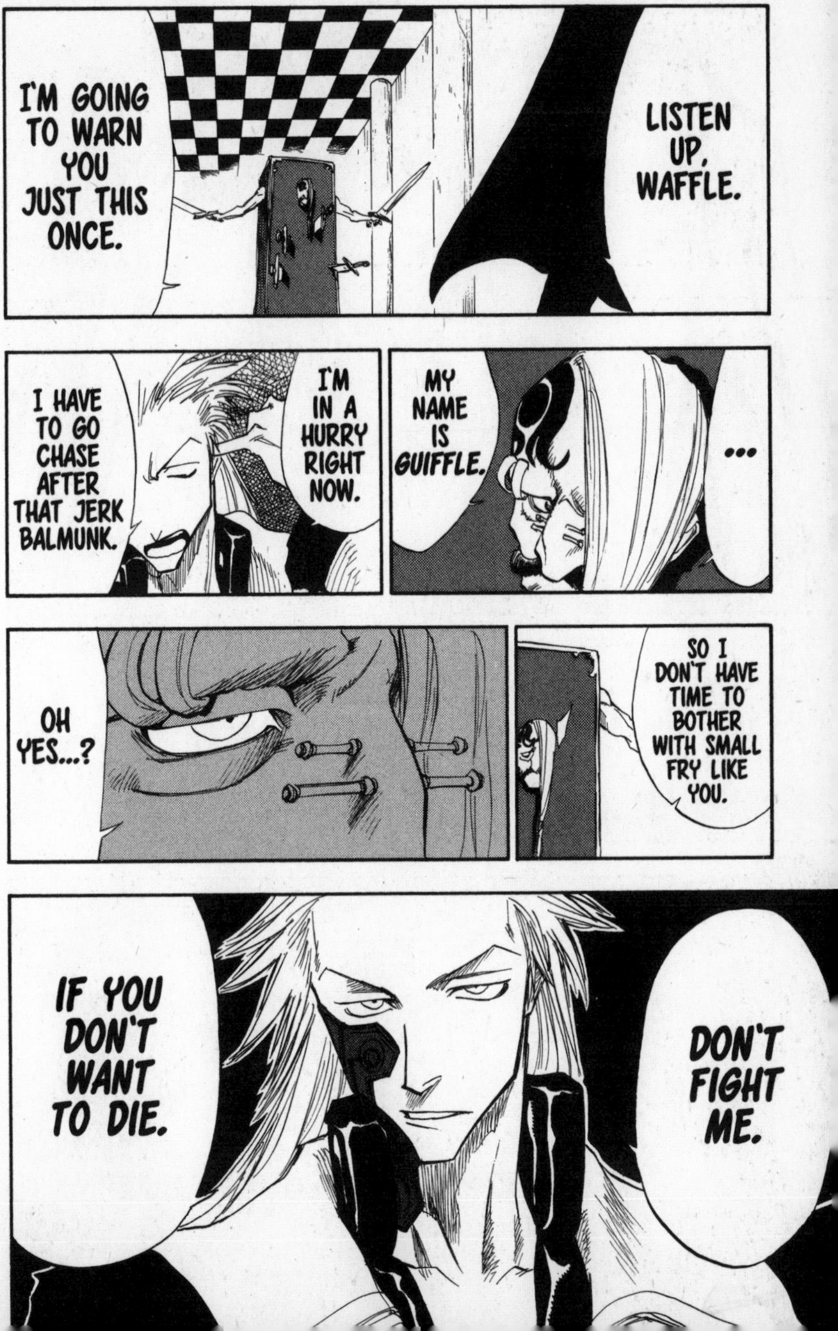
LISTEN UP, WAFFLE.
I'M GOING TO WARN YOU JUST THIS ONCE.
...
MY NAME IS GUIFFLE.
I'M IN A HURRY RIGHT NOW.
I HAVE TO GO CHASE AFTER THAT JERK BALMUNK.
SO I DON'T HAVE TIME TO BOTHER WITH SMALL FRY LIKE YOU.
OH YES...?
DON'T FIGHT ME.
IF YOU DON'T WANT TO DIE.

READ THIS WAY

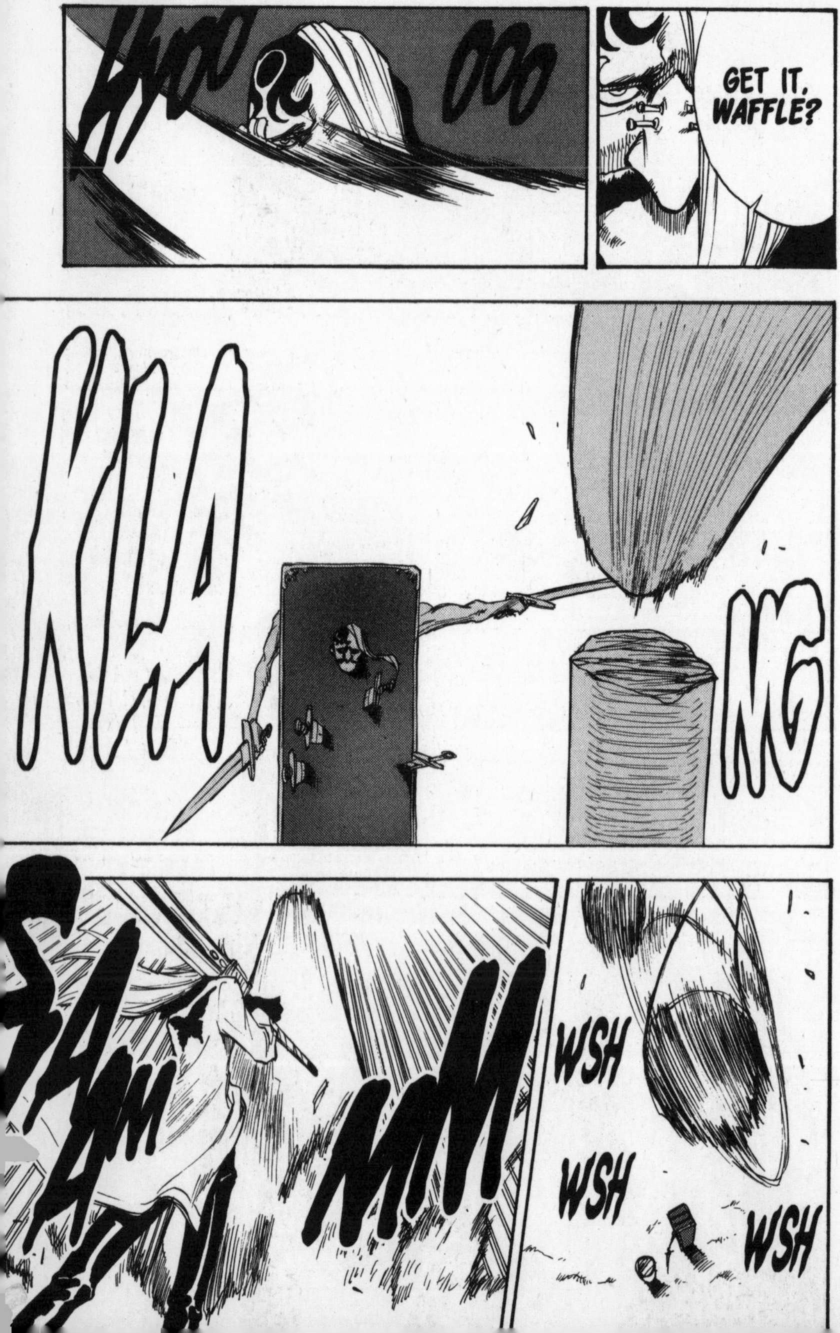
GET IT, WAFFLE?
HYOOOOOO
KLANG
WSH
WSH
WSH

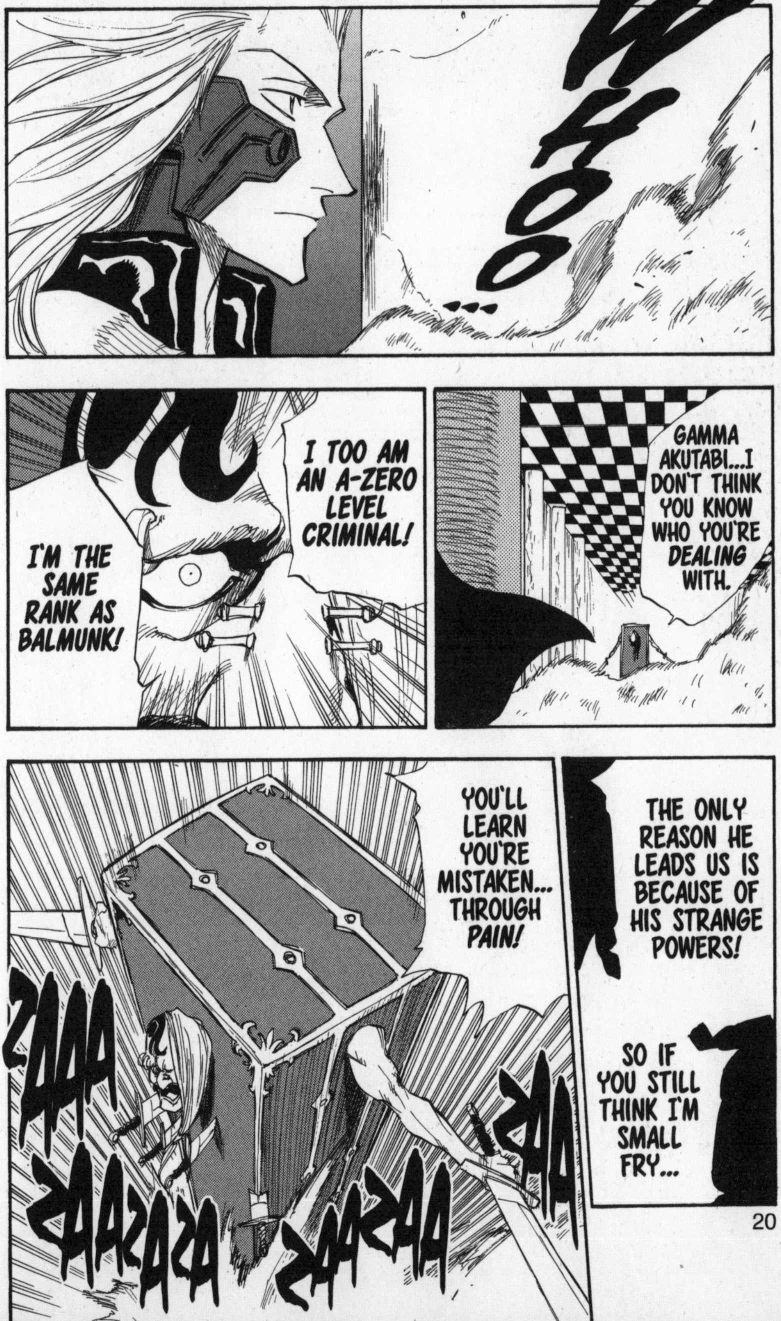
WHOOOO...
GAMMA AKUTABI...I DON'T THINK YOU KNOW WHO YOU'RE DEALING WITH.
I TOO AM AN A-ZERO LEVEL CRIMINAL!
I'M THE SAME RANK AS BALMUNK!
THE ONLY REASON HE LEADS US IS BECAUSE OF HIS STRANGE POWERS!
SO IF YOU STILL THINK I'M SMALL FRY...
YOU'LL LEARN YOU'RE MISTAKEN... THROUGH PAIN!

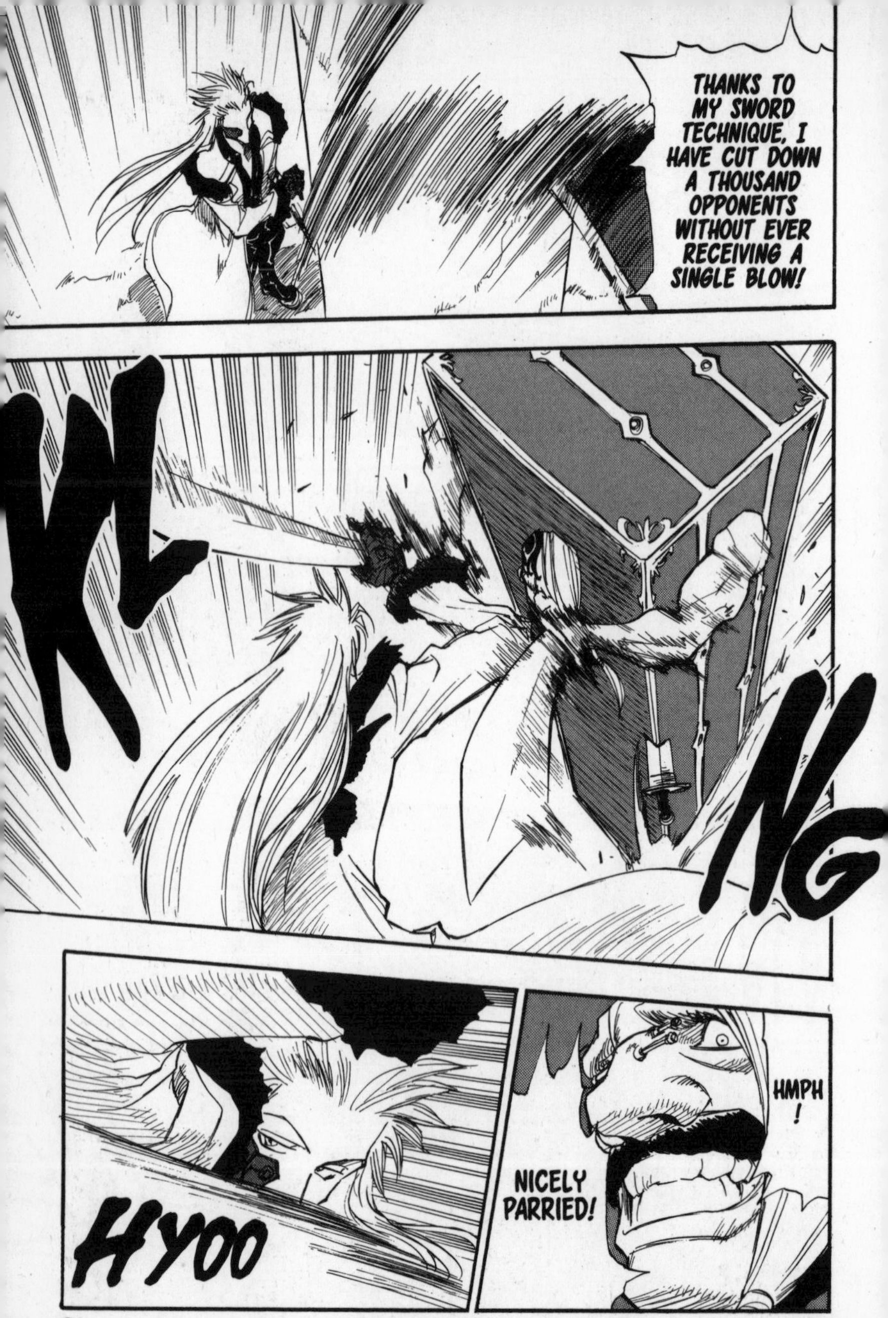
THANKS TO MY SWORD TECHNIQUE, I HAVE CUT DOWN A THOUSAND OPPONENTS WITHOUT EVER RECEIVING A SINGLE BLOW!
KL
NG
HMPH!
NICELY PARRIED!
HYOO

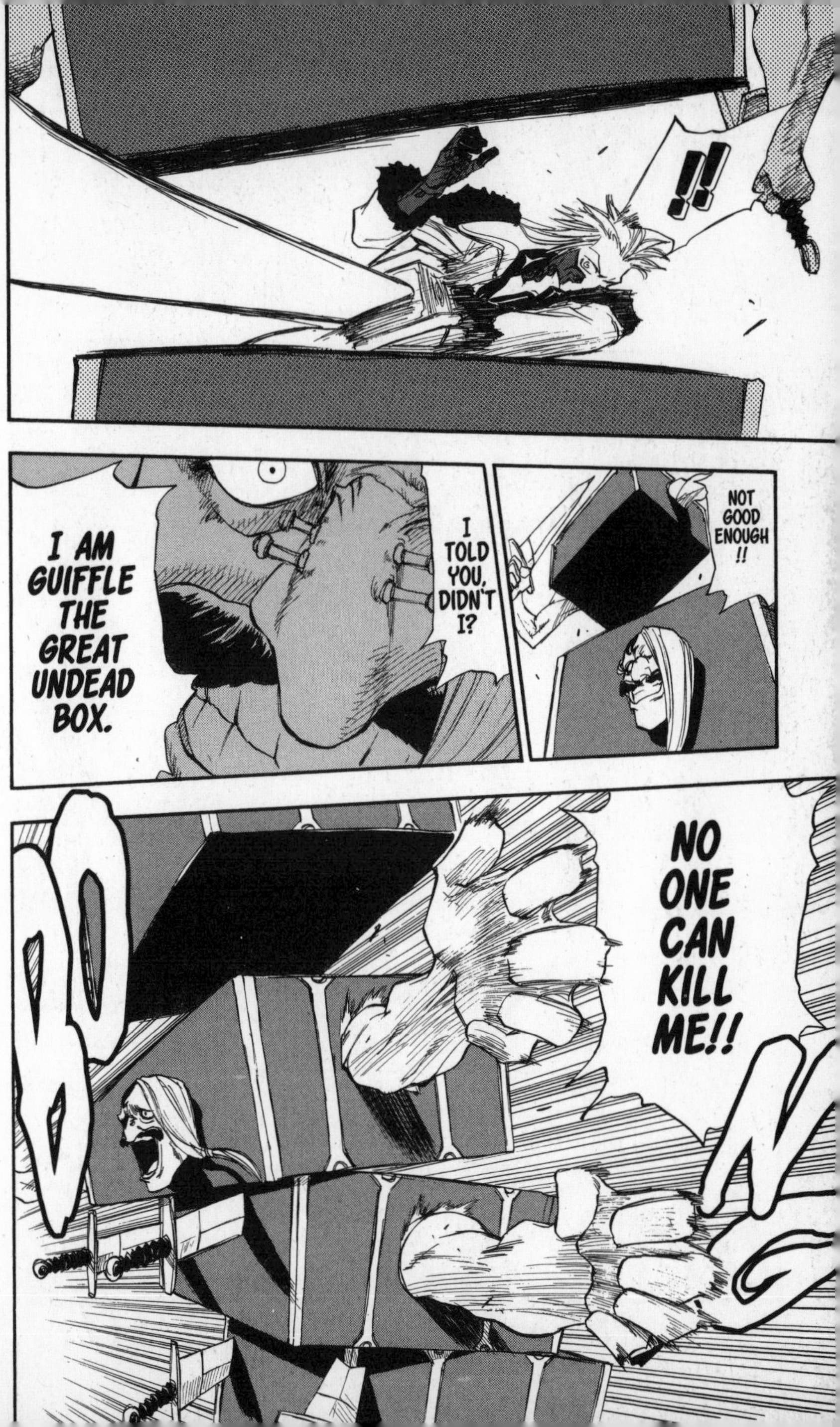
!!
NOT GOOD ENOUGH!!
I TOLD YOU, DIDN'T I?
I AM GUIFFLE THE GREAT UNDEAD BOX.
NO ONE CAN KILL ME!!

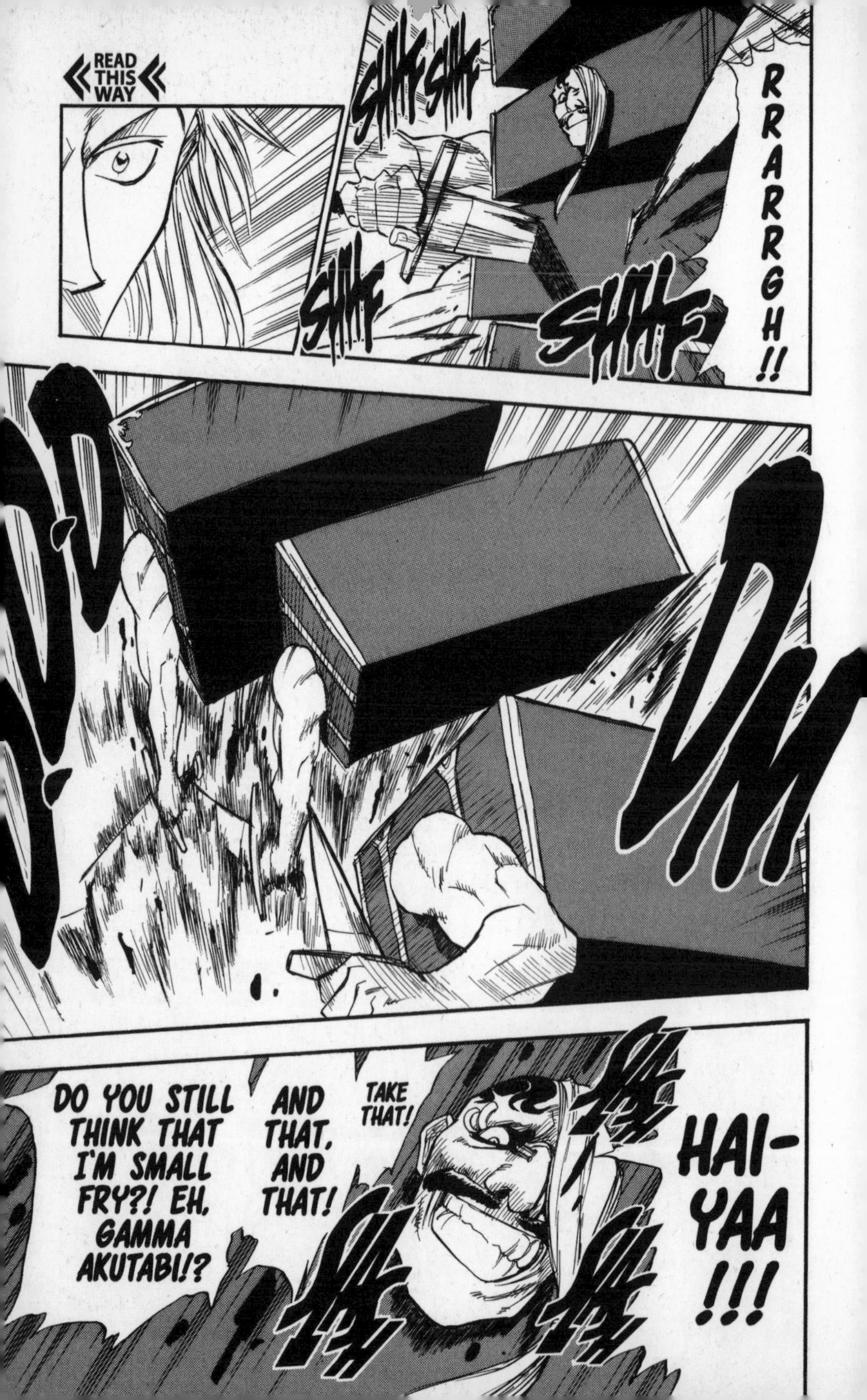

READ THIS WAY
RRARRRGH!!
SHFF SHFF
SHFF
SHFF
HAI-YAA!!!
TAKE THAT!
AND THAT, AND THAT!
DO YOU STILL THINK THAT I'M SMALL FRY?! EH, GAMMA AKUTABI!?

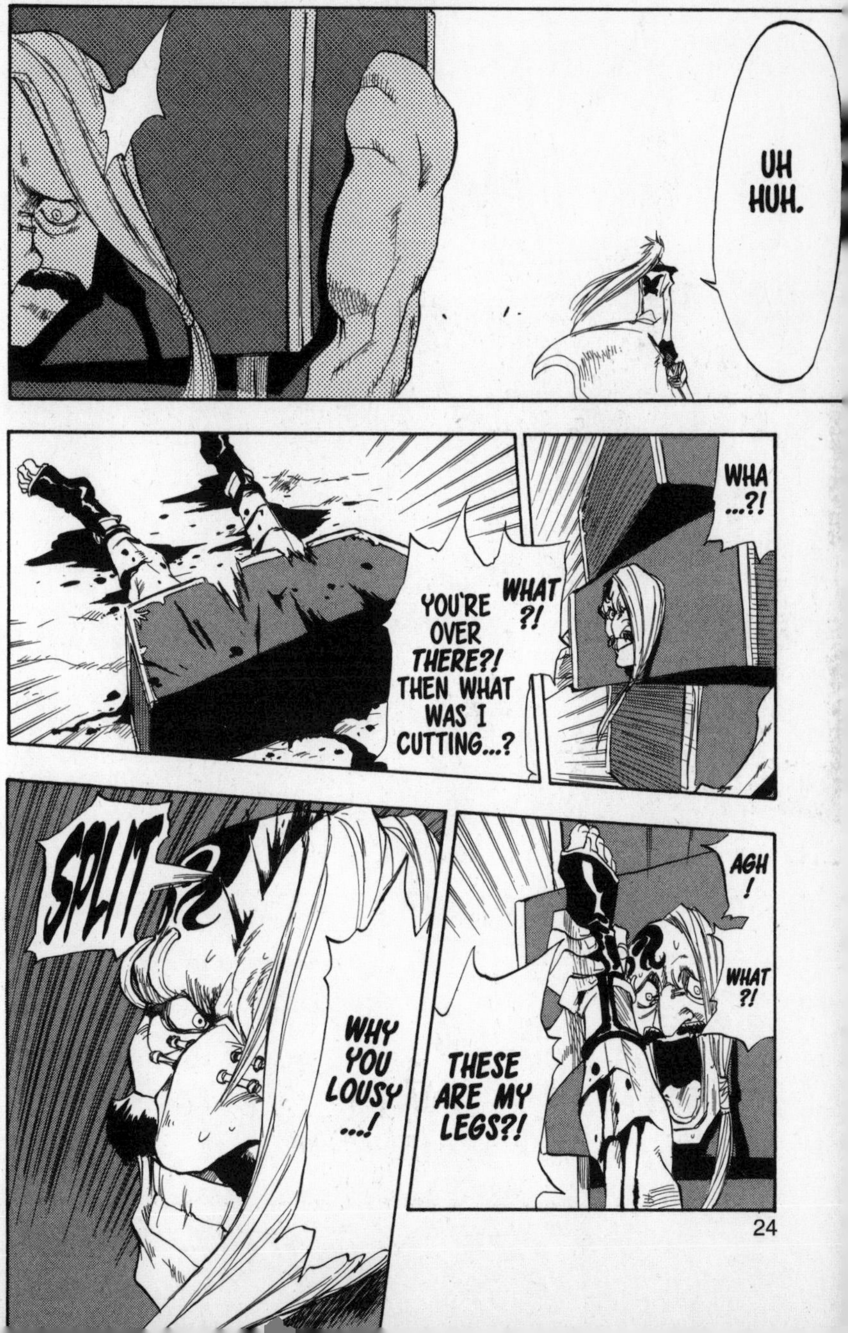
UH HUH.
WHA ...?!
WHAT ?!
YOU'RE OVER THERE?! THEN WHAT WAS I CUTTING...?
AGH!
WHAT ?!
THESE ARE MY LEGS?!
SPLIT
WHY YOU LOUSY ...!

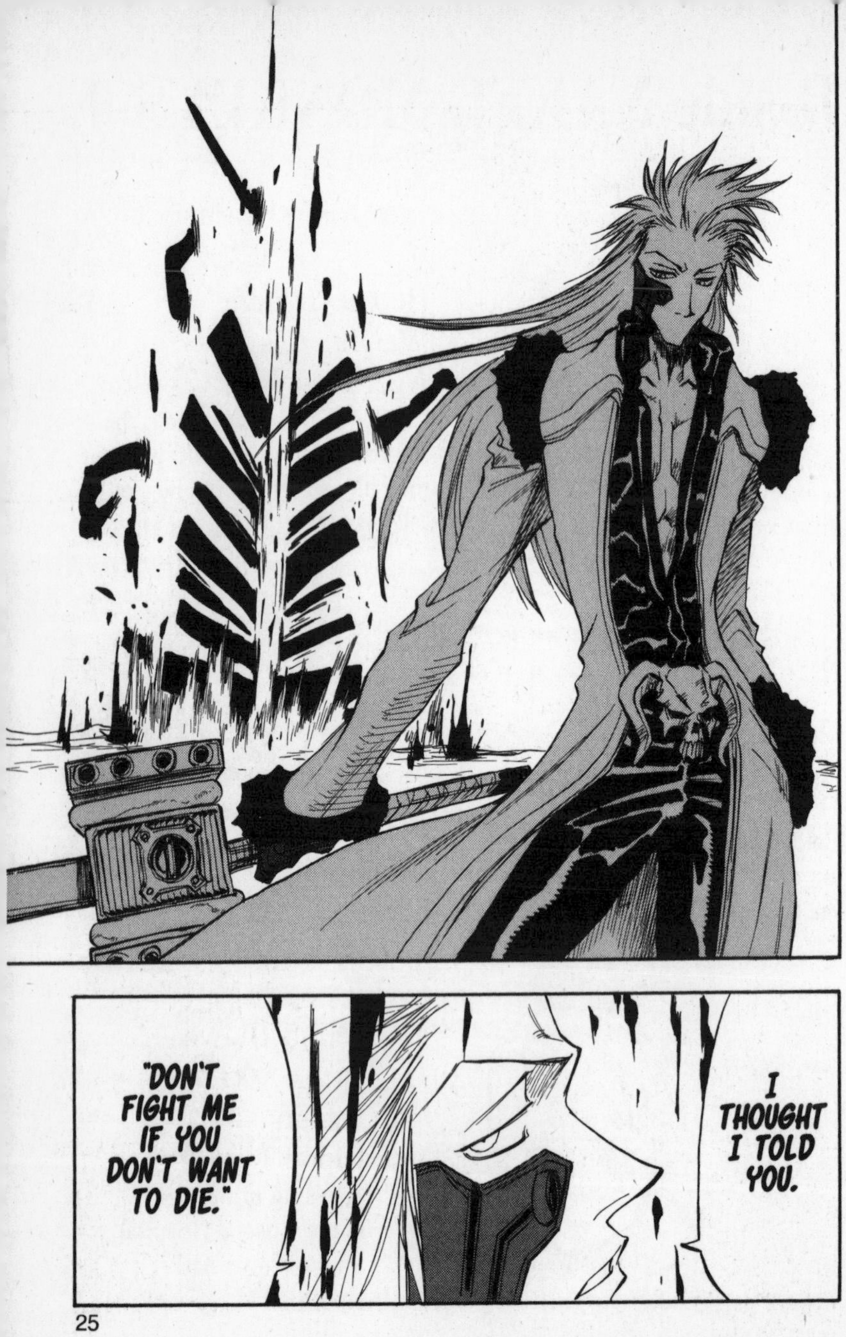
I THOUGHT I TOLD YOU.
"DON'T FIGHT ME IF YOU DON'T WANT TO DIE."

B-side NAKED MONKEYS 9.

Antonio Scamandero
アントニオ・スカマンデロ

Height: 168 cm
Weight: 70 kg
Age: 28
Leader of the desert gang, the Snods. The 28-year old with the nice hairdo…hold on, he's only 28?! By the way, he's a virgin.

Sandra Silverstone
サンドラ・シルヴァーストーン

Date of Birth: 6/18
Age: 24
The girl who was rescued from Calder's place. I had to make a ton of changes to the scene when she was being tortured.

Nina Blowse
ニナ・ブロウズ
Age: 6
Blood Type: BO
A young orphan girl at the Roscoe Hospital. She loves stuffed animals.

Track 16: Flamediver

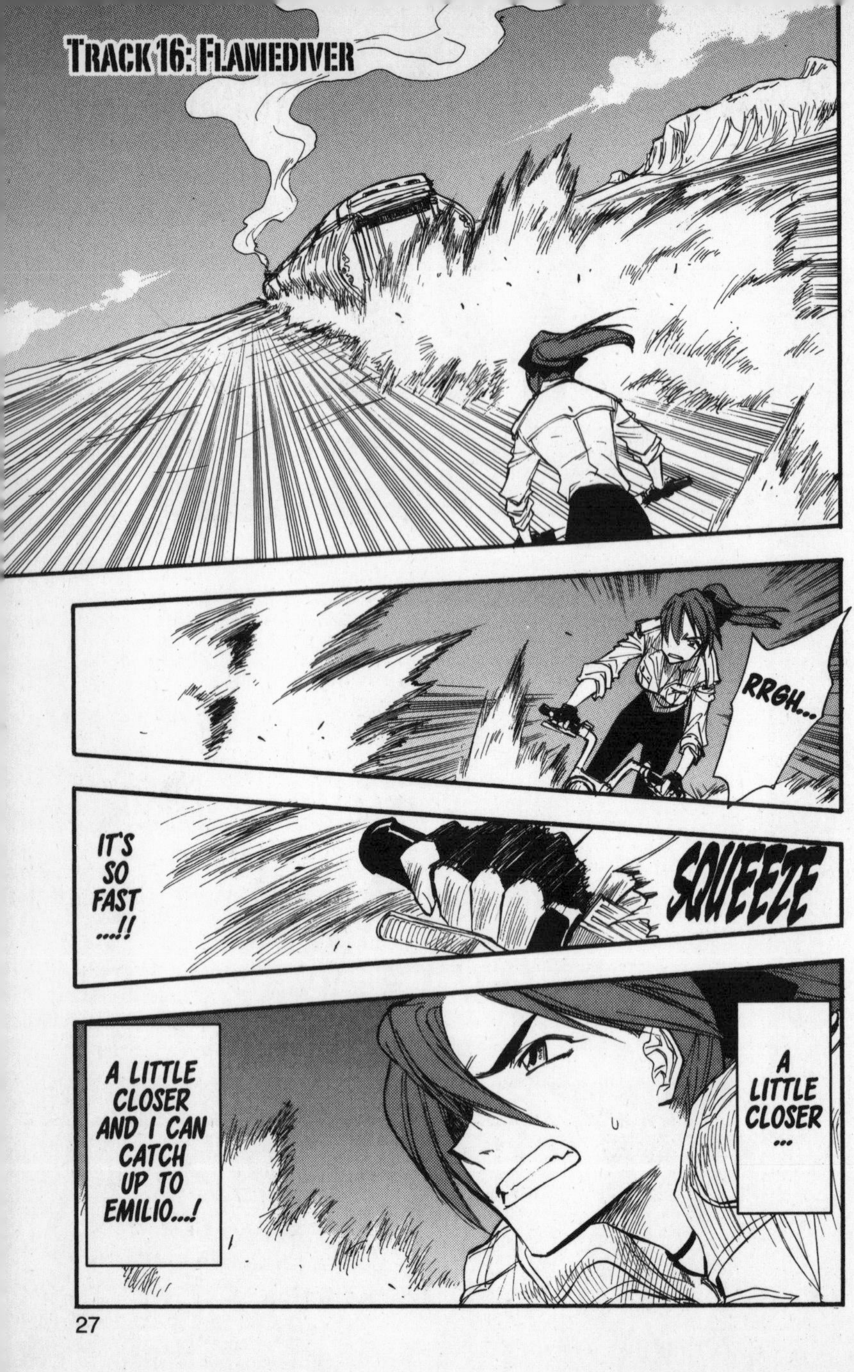

RRGH...
SQUEEZE
IT'S SO FAST ...!!
A LITTLE CLOSER ...
A LITTLE CLOSER AND I CAN CATCH UP TO EMILIO...!

TRACK 16: FLAMEDIVER

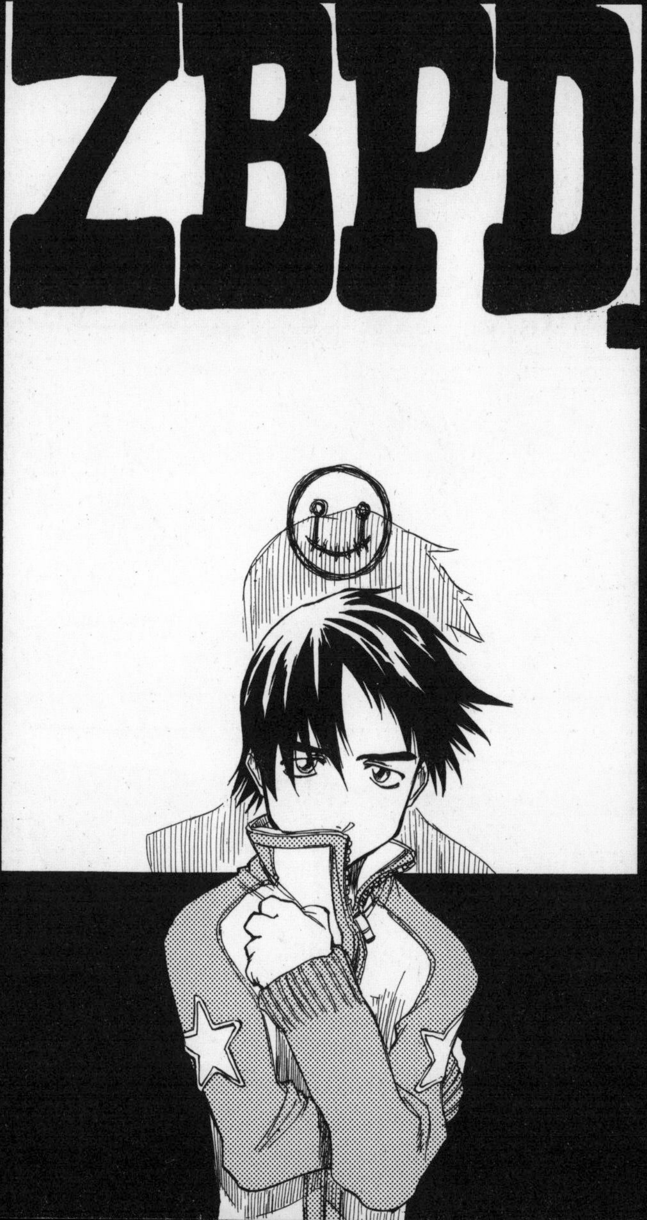
ZBPD.

READ THIS WAY

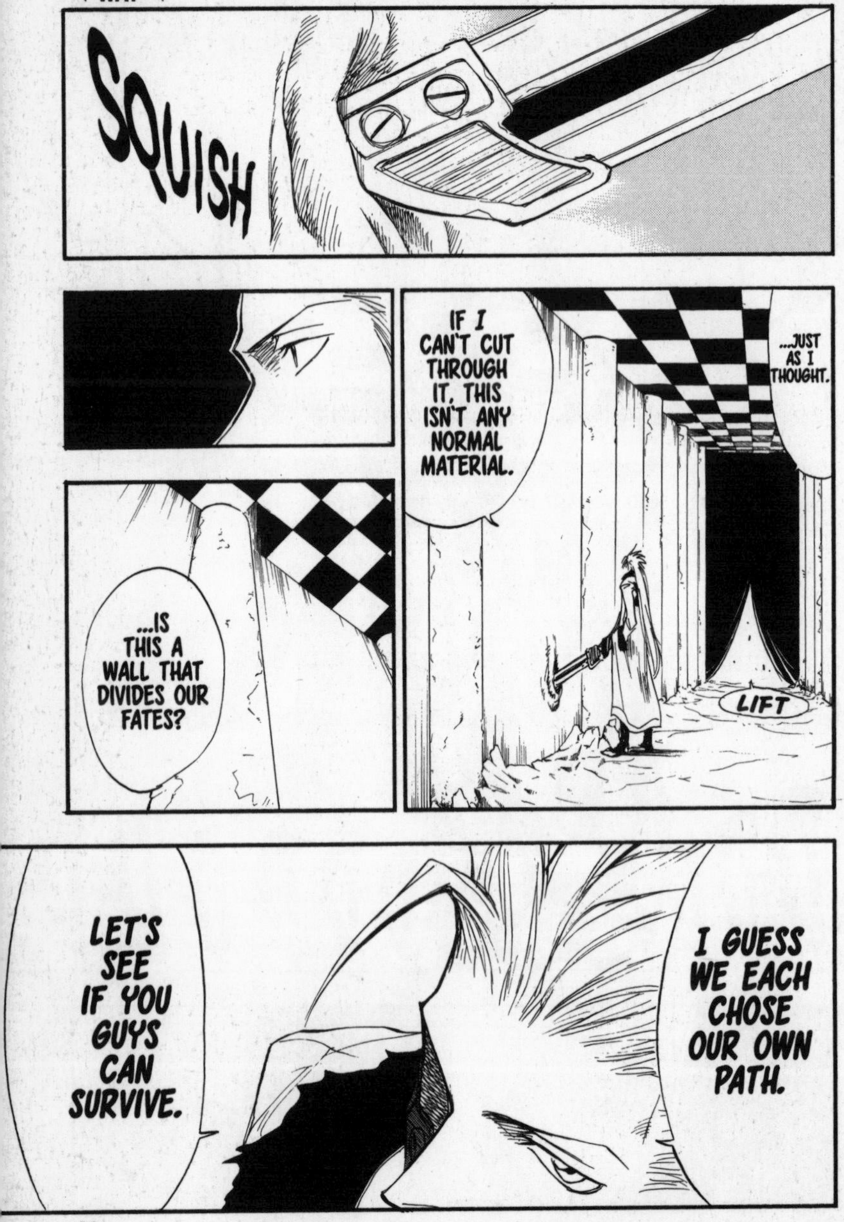
SQUISH
...JUST AS I THOUGHT.
IF I CAN'T CUT THROUGH IT, THIS ISN'T ANY NORMAL MATERIAL.
LIFT
...IS THIS A WALL THAT DIVIDES OUR FATES?
I GUESS WE EACH CHOSE OUR OWN PATH.
LET'S SEE IF YOU GUYS CAN SURVIVE.

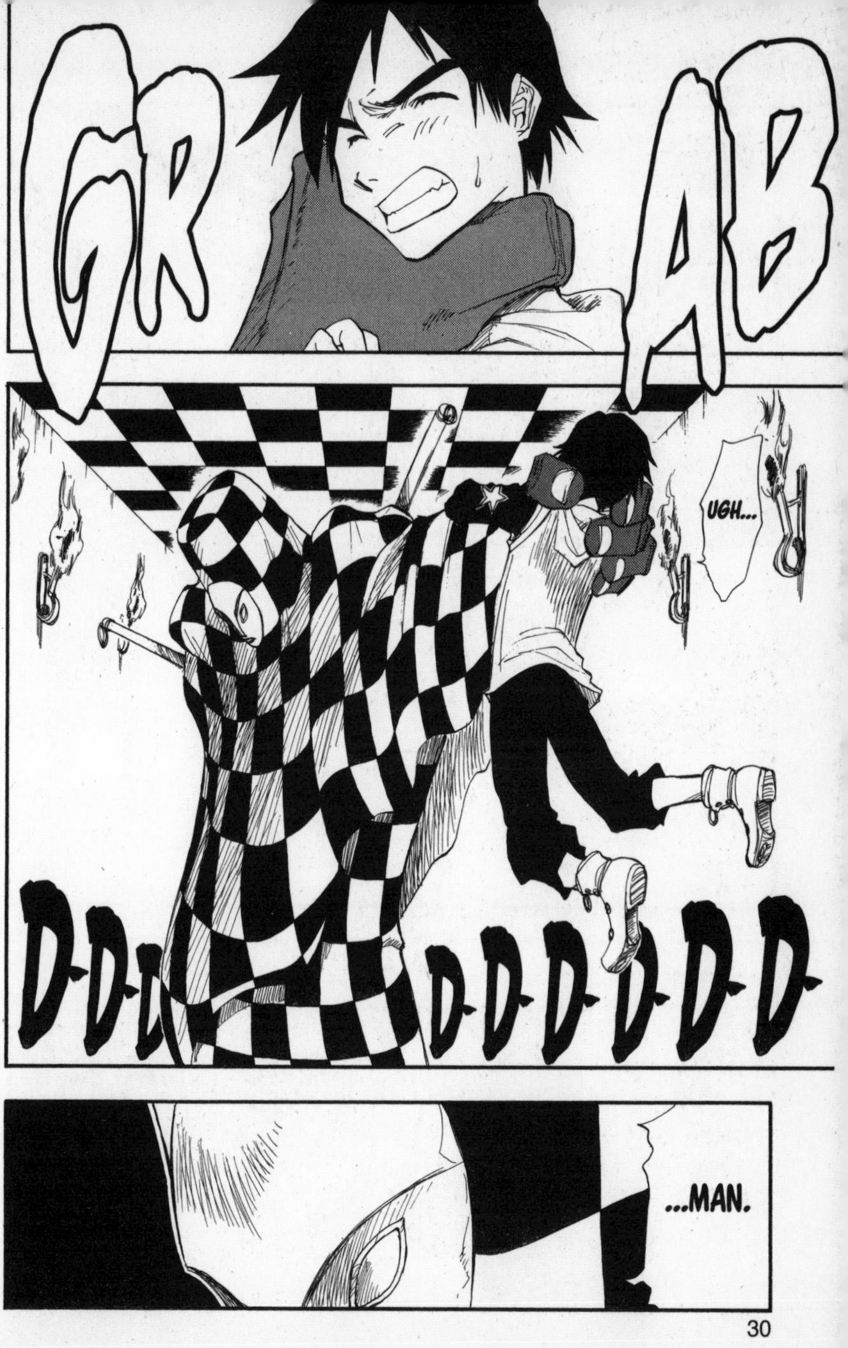
GRAB
UGH...
D-D-D D-D-D-D-D-D
...MAN.

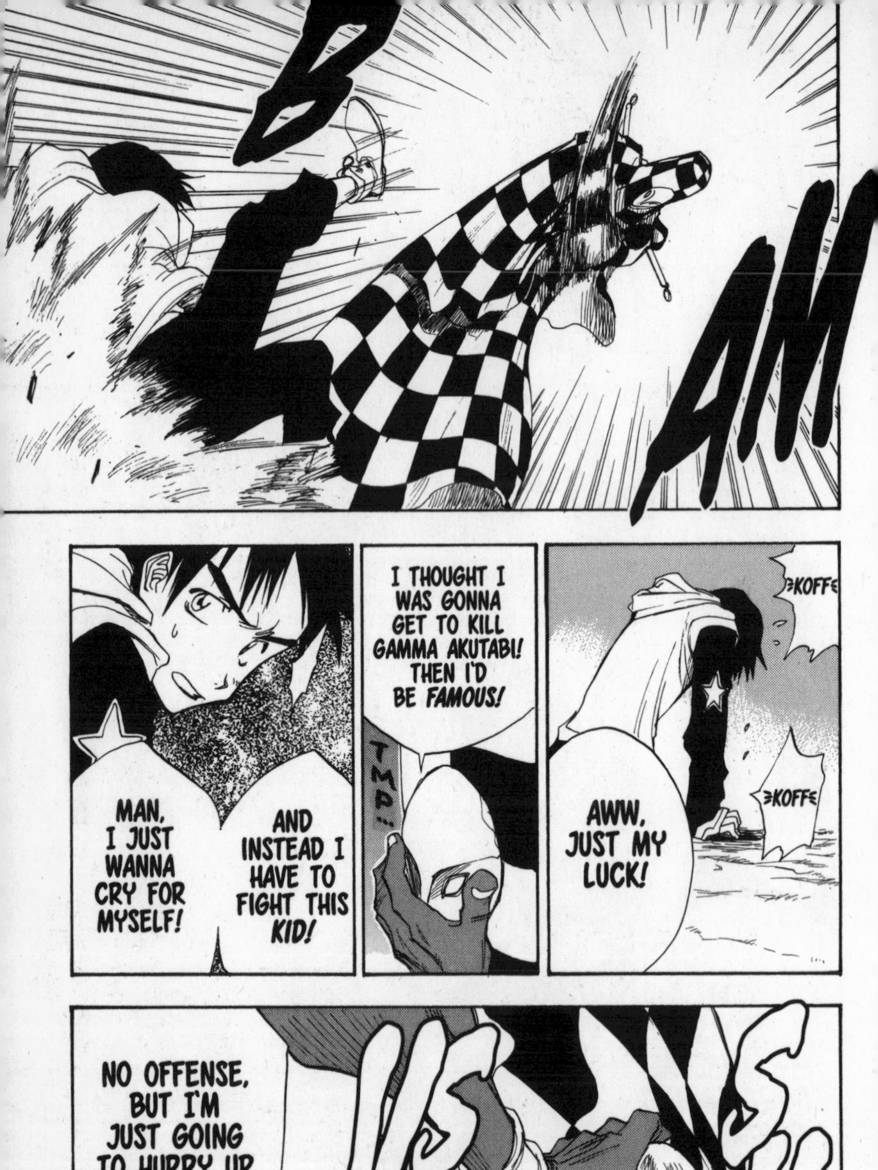
BAM
ƎKOFFƐ
ƎKOFFƐ
AWW, JUST MY LUCK!
I THOUGHT I WAS GONNA GET TO KILL GAMMA AKUTABI! THEN I'D BE *FAMOUS!*
TMP...
AND INSTEAD I HAVE TO FIGHT THIS *KID!*
MAN, I JUST WANNA CRY FOR MYSELF!
NO OFFENSE, BUT I'M JUST GOING TO HURRY UP AND GET THIS OVER WITH.

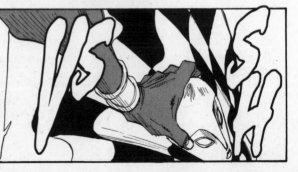

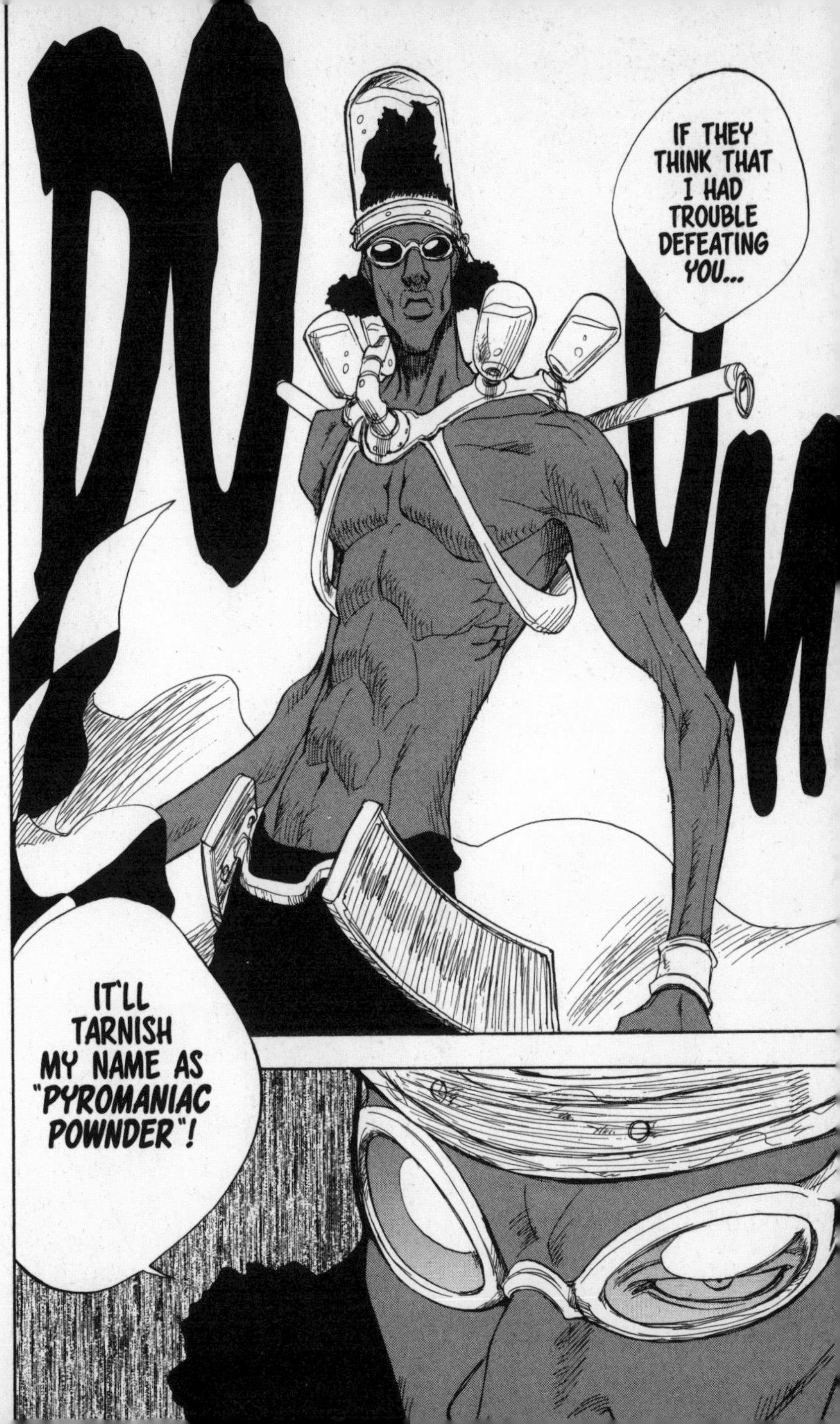
DOOM
IF THEY THINK THAT I HAD TROUBLE DEFEATING YOU...
IT'LL TARNISH MY NAME AS "PYROMANIAC POWNDER"!

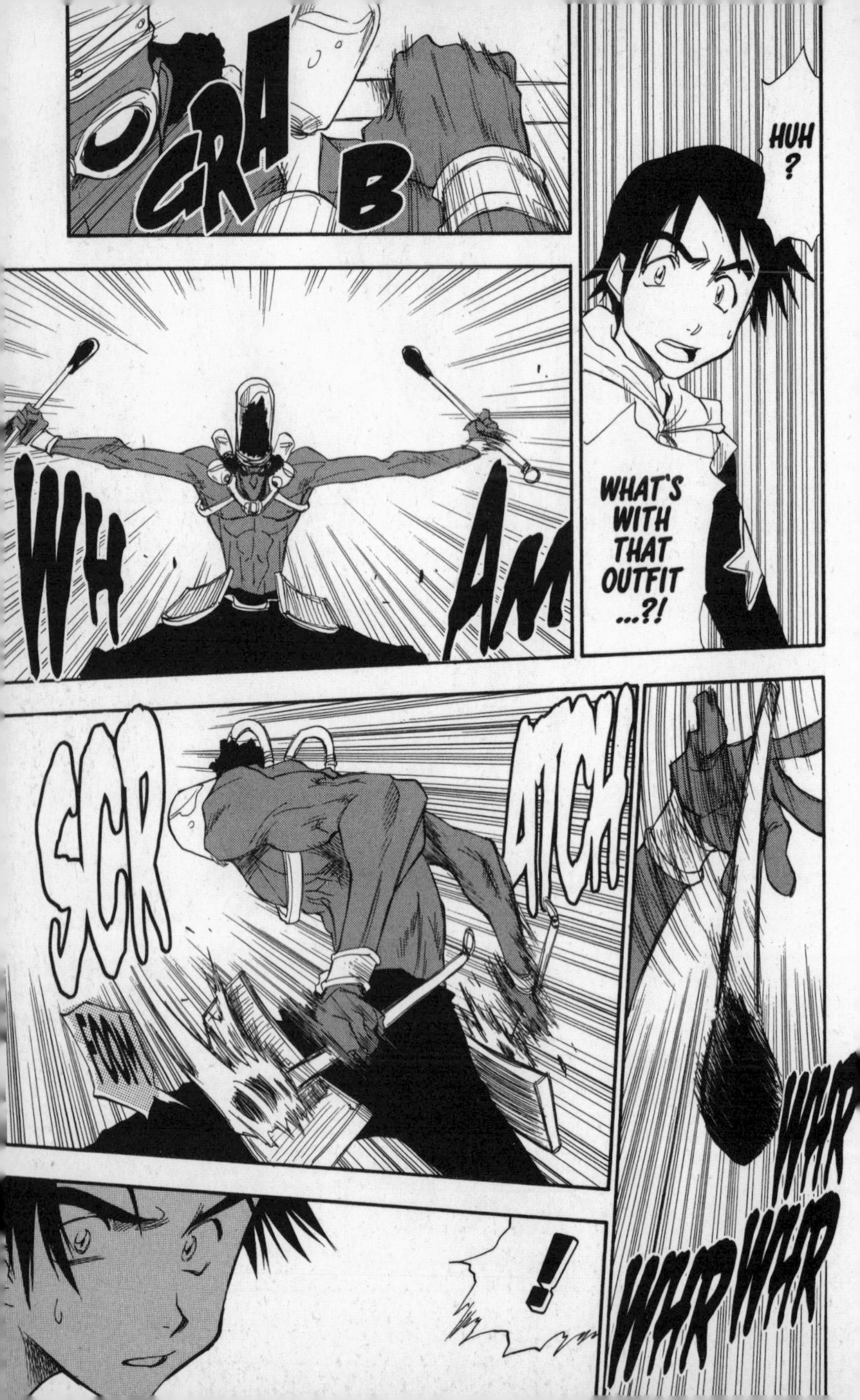
HUH?
WHAT'S WITH THAT OUTFIT ...?!
GRAB
WHAM
WHR WHR WHR
SCRATCH
FOOM
!

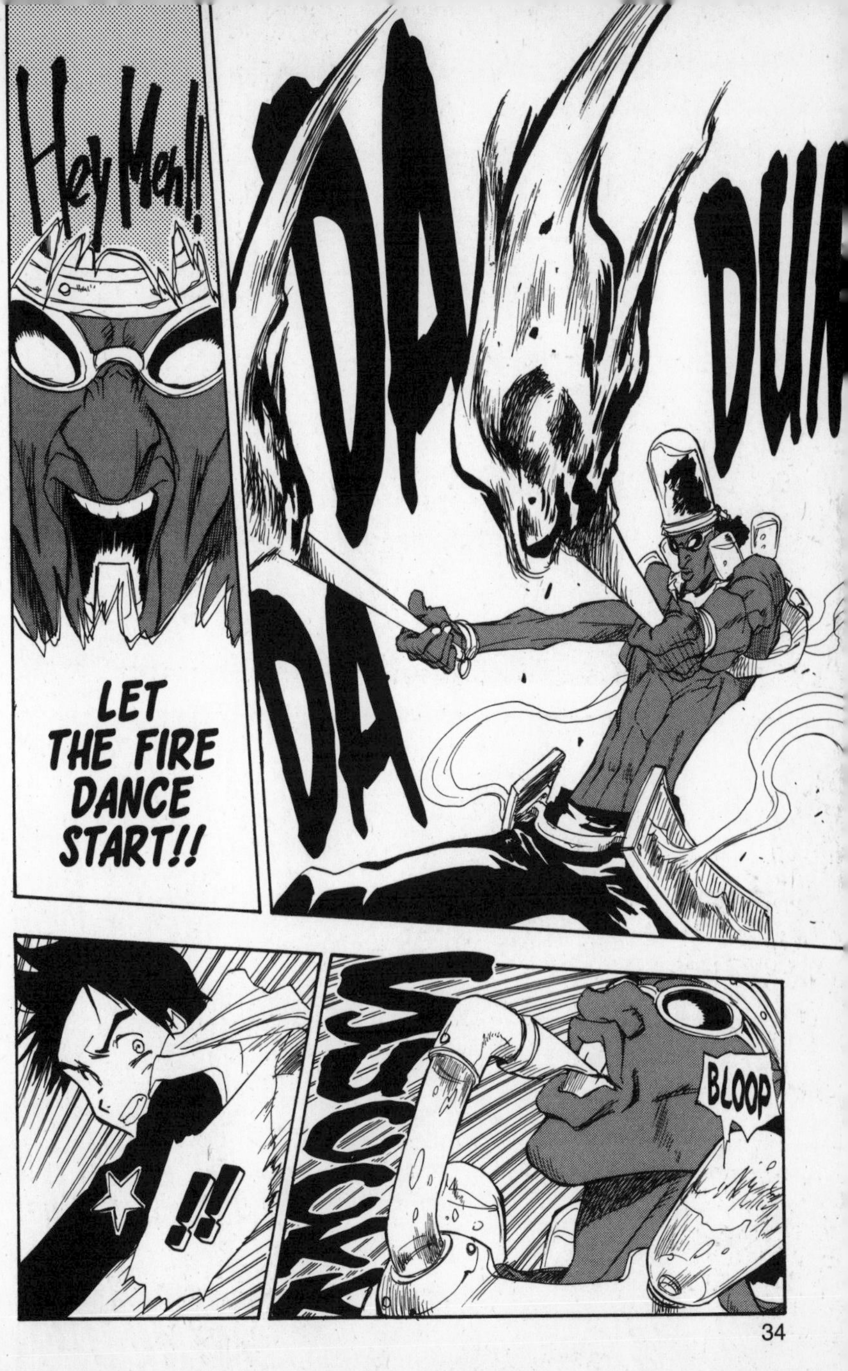
DA
DA
DUN
Hey Men!!
LET THE FIRE DANCE START!!
BLOOP
!!

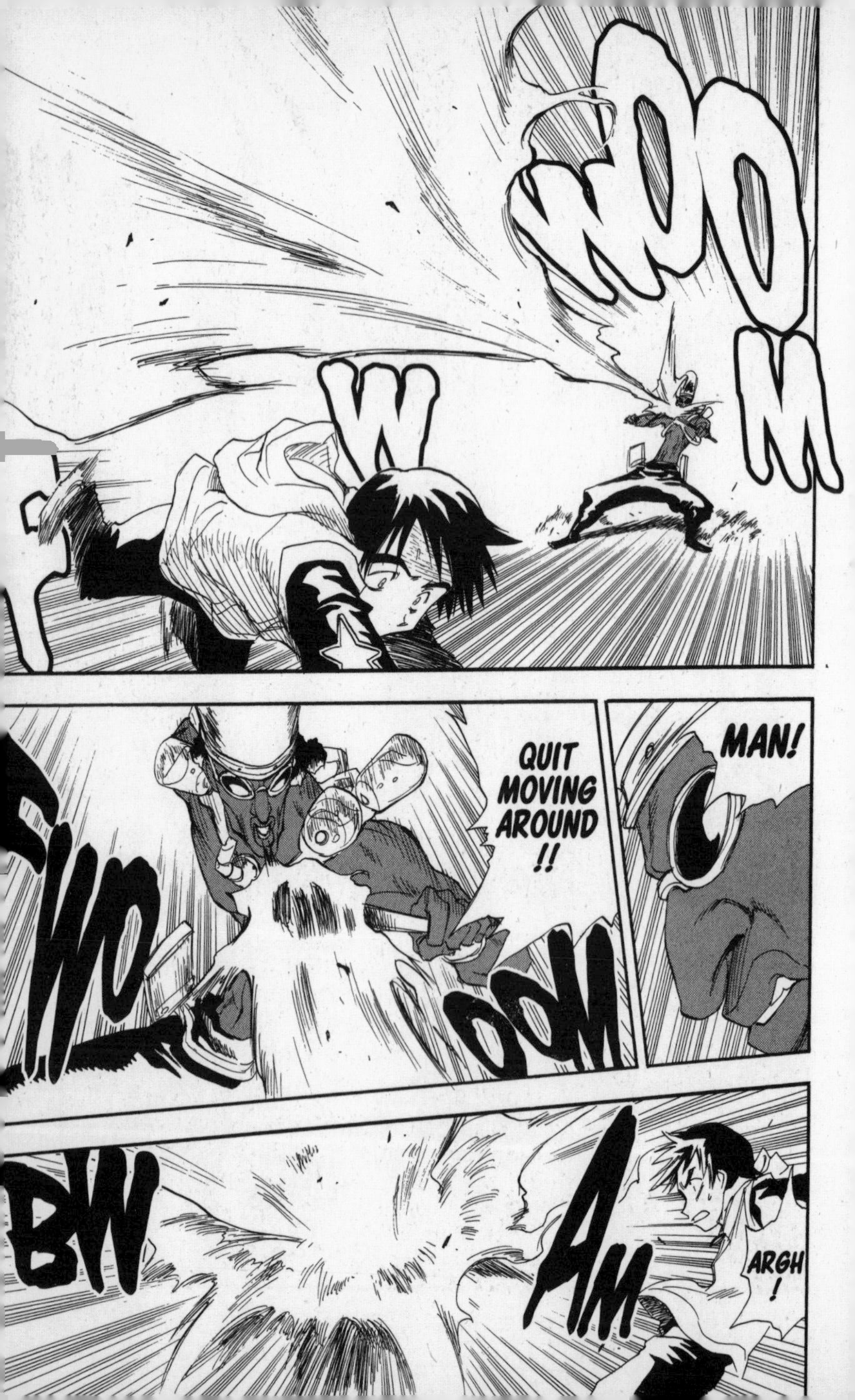
MAN!
QUIT MOVING AROUND !!
ARGH !

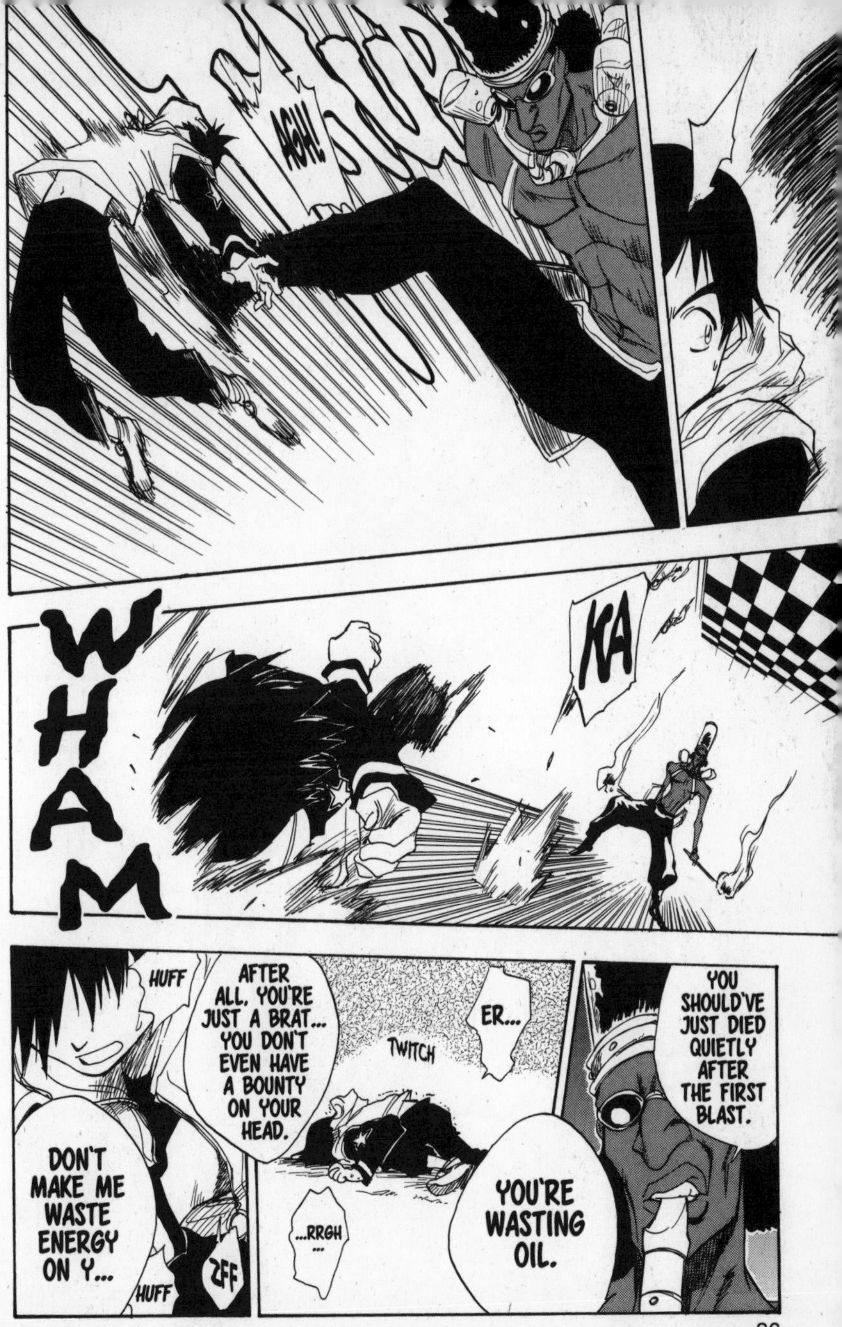
AGH!
KA
WHAM
YOU SHOULD'VE JUST DIED QUIETLY AFTER THE FIRST BLAST.
YOU'RE WASTING OIL.
ER...
TWITCH
...RRGH ...
HUFF
AFTER ALL, YOU'RE JUST A BRAT... YOU DON'T EVEN HAVE A BOUNTY ON YOUR HEAD.
DON'T MAKE ME WASTE ENERGY ON Y...
ZFF
HUFF

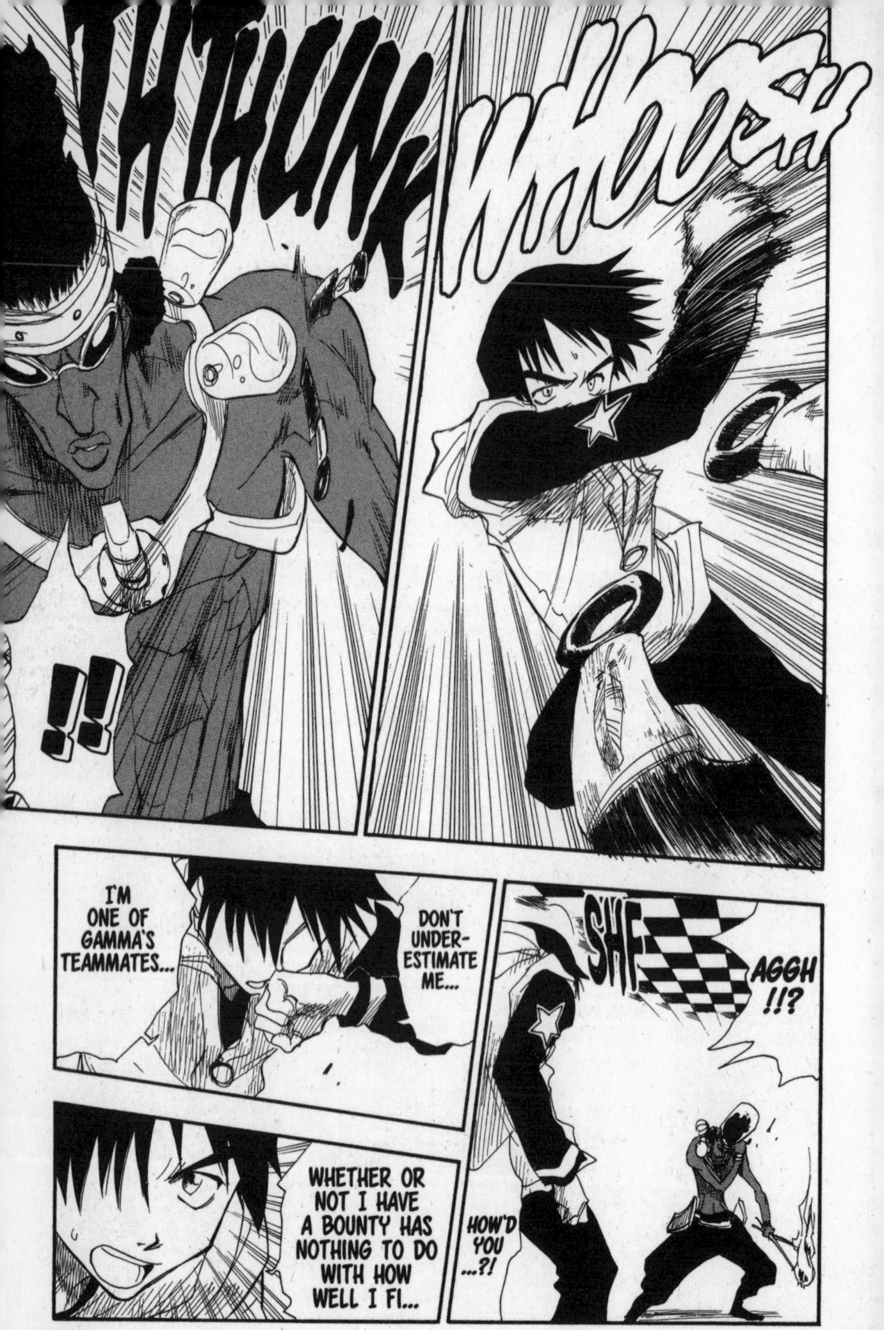
!!
SHF
AGGH !!?
HOW'D YOU ...?!
DON'T UNDER-ESTIMATE ME...
I'M ONE OF GAMMA'S TEAMMATES...
WHETHER OR NOT I HAVE A BOUNTY HAS NOTHING TO DO WITH HOW WELL I FI...

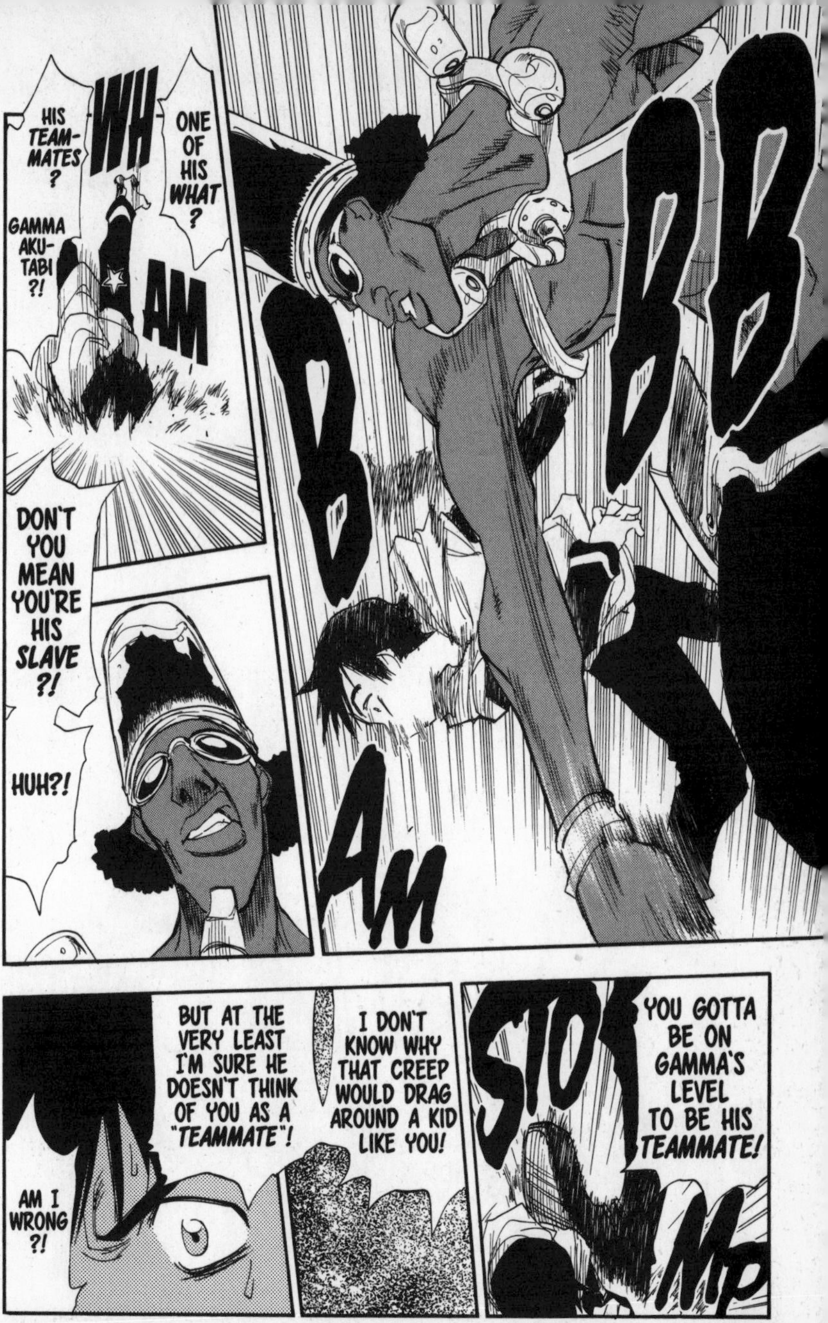
BBB
AM
ONE OF HIS WHAT?
HIS TEAM-MATES?
WH
AM
GAMMA AKU-TABI?!
DON'T YOU MEAN YOU'RE HIS SLAVE?!
HUH?!
YOU GOTTA BE ON GAMMA'S LEVEL TO BE HIS TEAMMATE!
STO
MP
I DON'T KNOW WHY THAT CREEP WOULD DRAG AROUND A KID LIKE YOU!
BUT AT THE VERY LEAST I'M SURE HE DOESN'T THINK OF YOU AS A "TEAMMATE"!
AM I WRONG?!

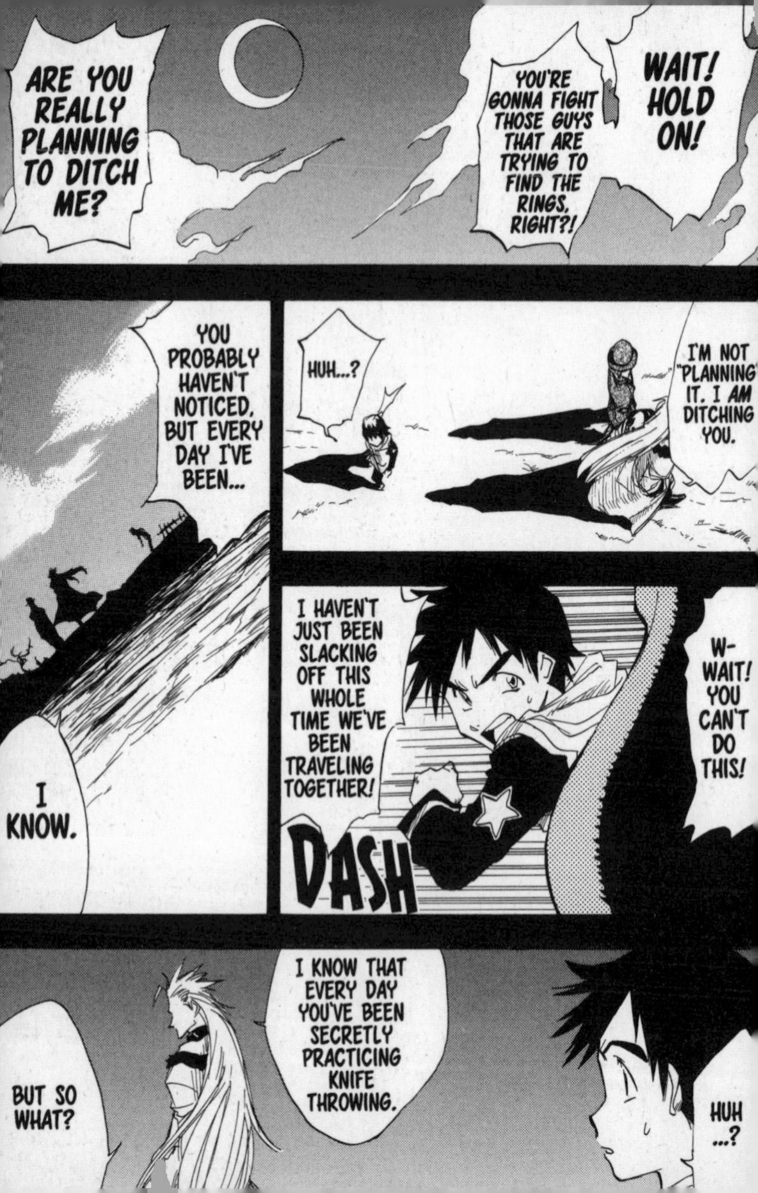
WAIT! HOLD ON!
YOU'RE GONNA FIGHT THOSE GUYS THAT ARE TRYING TO FIND THE RINGS, RIGHT?!
ARE YOU REALLY PLANNING TO DITCH ME?
I'M NOT "PLANNING" IT. I *AM* DITCHING YOU.
HUH...?
W-WAIT! YOU CAN'T DO THIS!
I HAVEN'T JUST BEEN SLACKING OFF THIS WHOLE TIME WE'VE BEEN TRAVELING TOGETHER!
DASH
YOU PROBABLY HAVEN'T NOTICED, BUT EVERY DAY I'VE BEEN...
I KNOW.
HUH ...?
I KNOW THAT EVERY DAY YOU'VE BEEN SECRETLY PRACTICING KNIFE THROWING.
BUT SO WHAT?

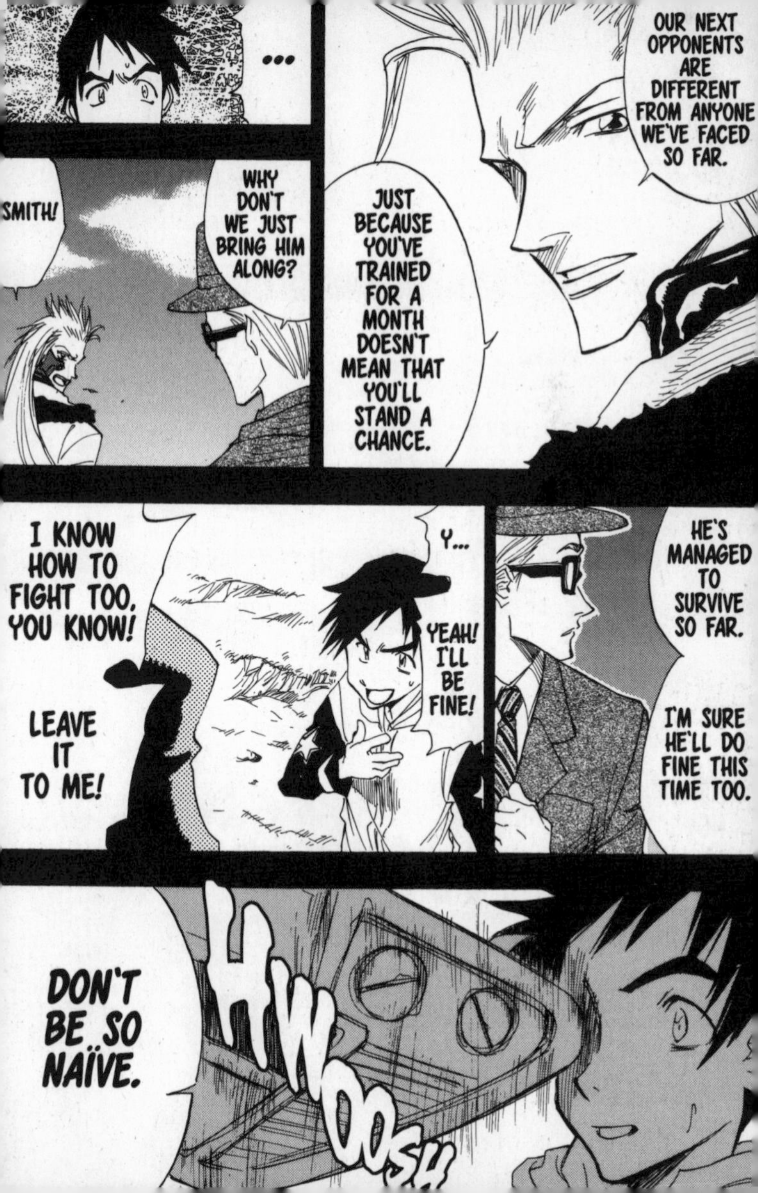
OUR NEXT OPPONENTS ARE DIFFERENT FROM ANYONE WE'VE FACED SO FAR.
JUST BECAUSE YOU'VE TRAINED FOR A MONTH DOESN'T MEAN THAT YOU'LL STAND A CHANCE.
...
WHY DON'T WE JUST BRING HIM ALONG?
SMITH!
HE'S MANAGED TO SURVIVE SO FAR.
I'M SURE HE'LL DO FINE THIS TIME TOO.
Y...
YEAH! I'LL BE FINE!
I KNOW HOW TO FIGHT TOO, YOU KNOW!
LEAVE IT TO ME!
HWOOSH
DON'T BE SO NAÏVE.

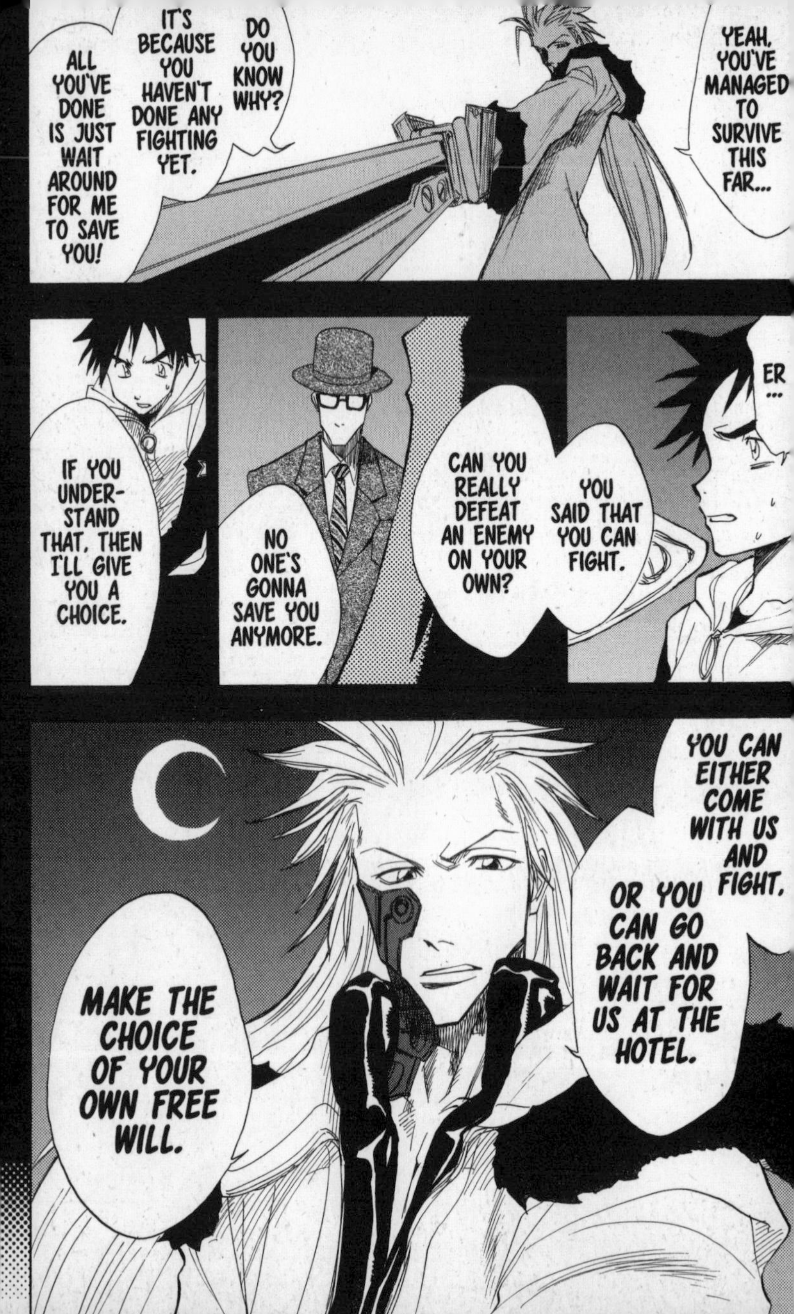
YEAH, YOU'VE MANAGED TO SURVIVE THIS FAR...
DO YOU KNOW WHY?
IT'S BECAUSE YOU HAVEN'T DONE ANY FIGHTING YET.
ALL YOU'VE DONE IS JUST WAIT AROUND FOR ME TO SAVE YOU!
ER...
YOU SAID THAT YOU CAN FIGHT.
CAN YOU REALLY DEFEAT AN ENEMY ON YOUR OWN?
NO ONE'S GONNA SAVE YOU ANYMORE.
IF YOU UNDER-STAND THAT, THEN I'LL GIVE YOU A CHOICE.
YOU CAN EITHER COME WITH US AND FIGHT,
OR YOU CAN GO BACK AND WAIT FOR US AT THE HOTEL.
MAKE THE CHOICE OF YOUR OWN FREE WILL.

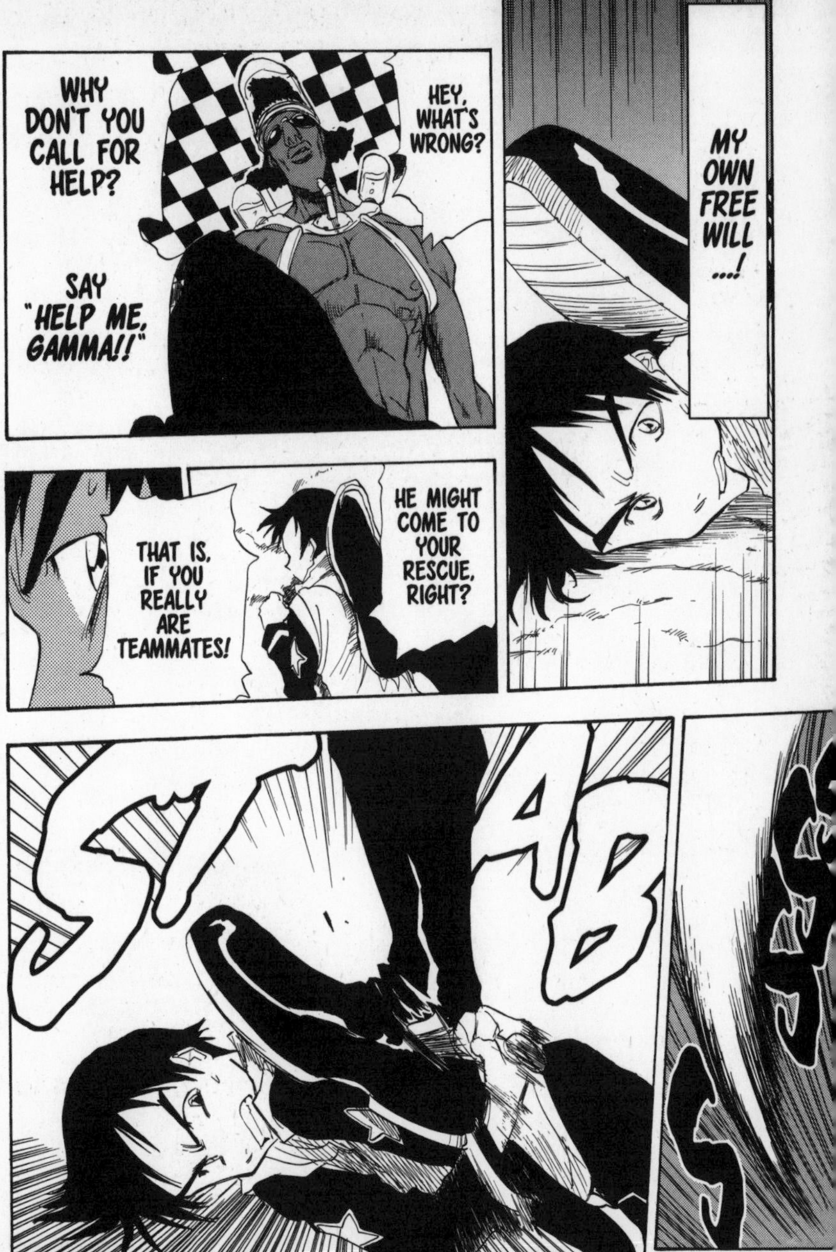
MY OWN FREE WILL ...!
HEY, WHAT'S WRONG?
WHY DON'T YOU CALL FOR HELP?
SAY "HELP ME, GAMMA!!"
HE MIGHT COME TO YOUR RESCUE, RIGHT?
THAT IS, IF YOU REALLY ARE TEAMMATES!
STAB

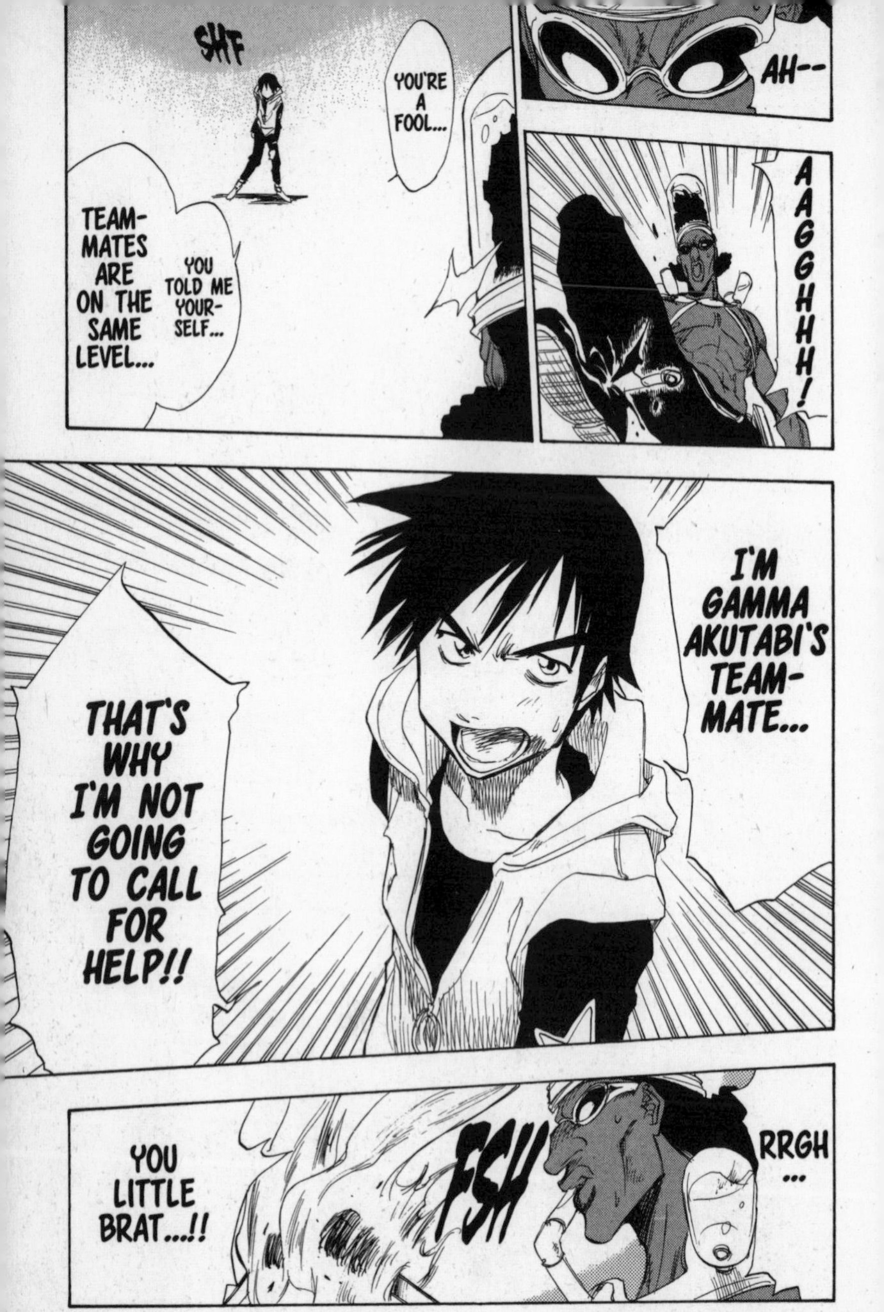
AH--
AAGGHHH!
YOU'RE A FOOL...
SHF
YOU TOLD ME YOURSELF...
TEAMMATES ARE ON THE SAME LEVEL...
I'M GAMMA AKUTABI'S TEAMMATE...
THAT'S WHY I'M NOT GOING TO CALL FOR HELP!!
RRGH...
FSH
YOU LITTLE BRAT...!!

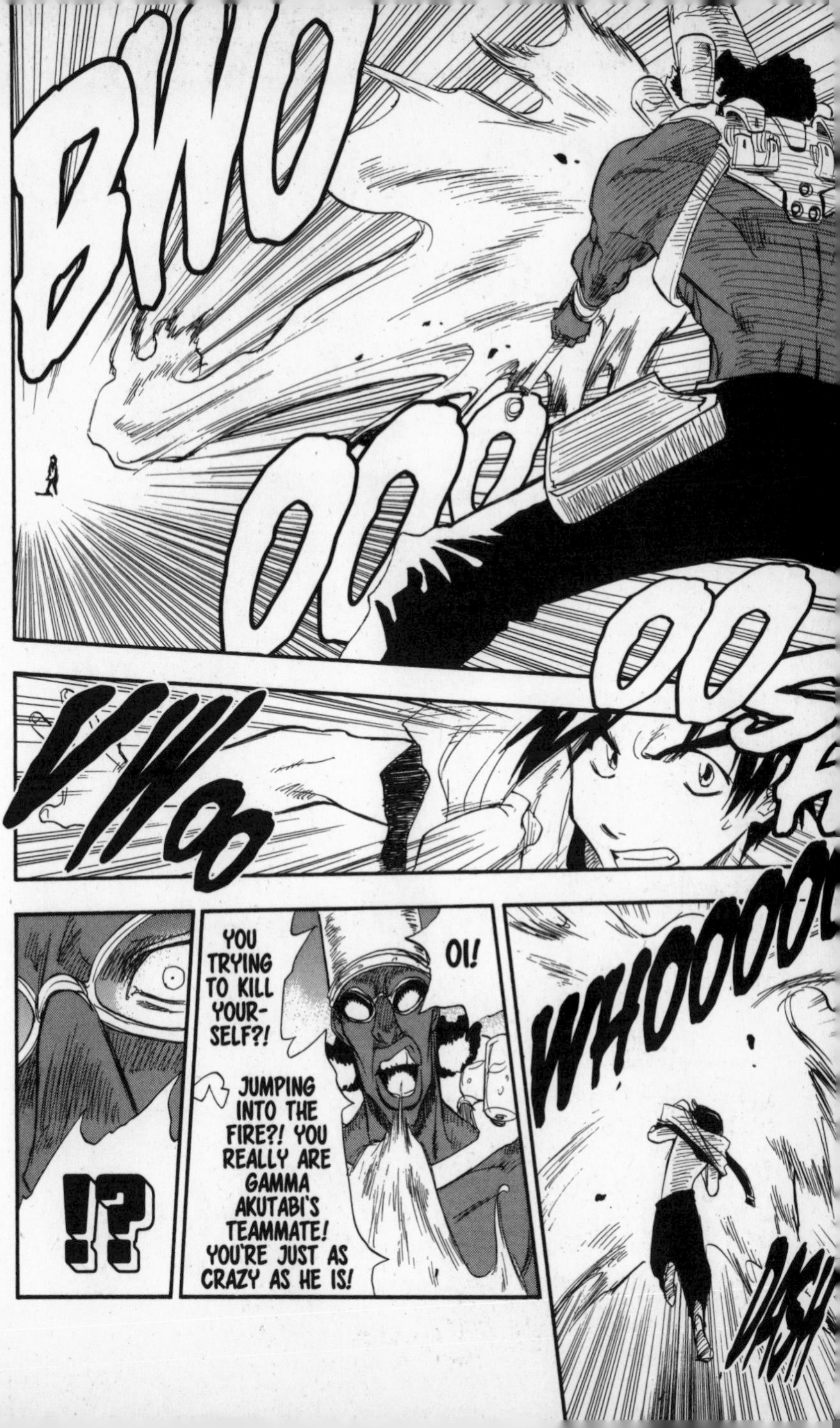
BWOOOOOOO
VWOO
WHOOOOO
OI!
YOU TRYING TO KILL YOURSELF?!
JUMPING INTO THE FIRE?! YOU REALLY ARE GAMMA AKUTABI'S TEAMMATE! YOU'RE JUST AS CRAZY AS HE IS!
DASH
!?

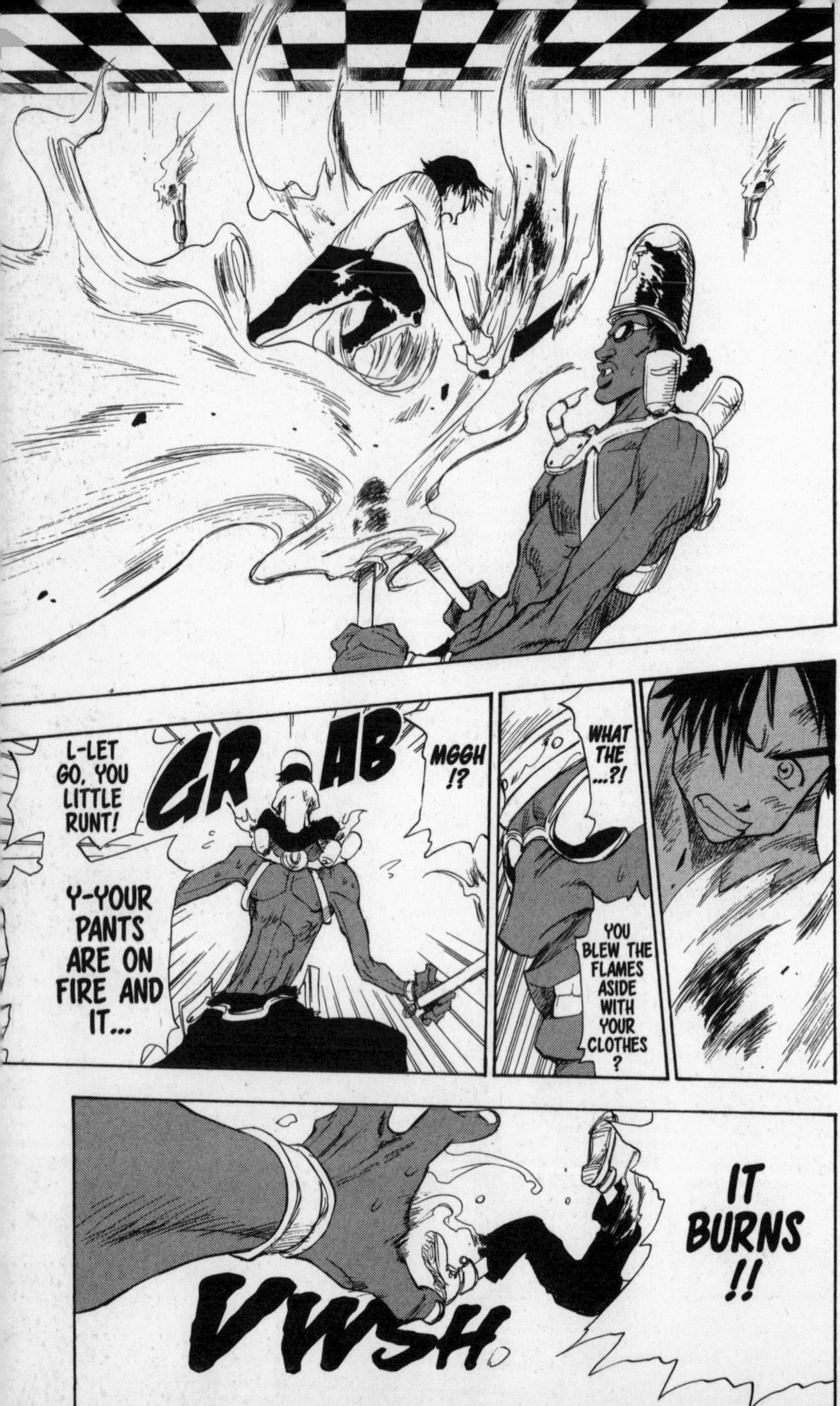
WHAT THE ...?!
YOU BLEW THE FLAMES ASIDE WITH YOUR CLOTHES?
MGGH !?
GRAB
L-LET GO, YOU LITTLE RUNT!
Y-YOUR PANTS ARE ON FIRE AND IT...
IT BURNS !!
VWSH

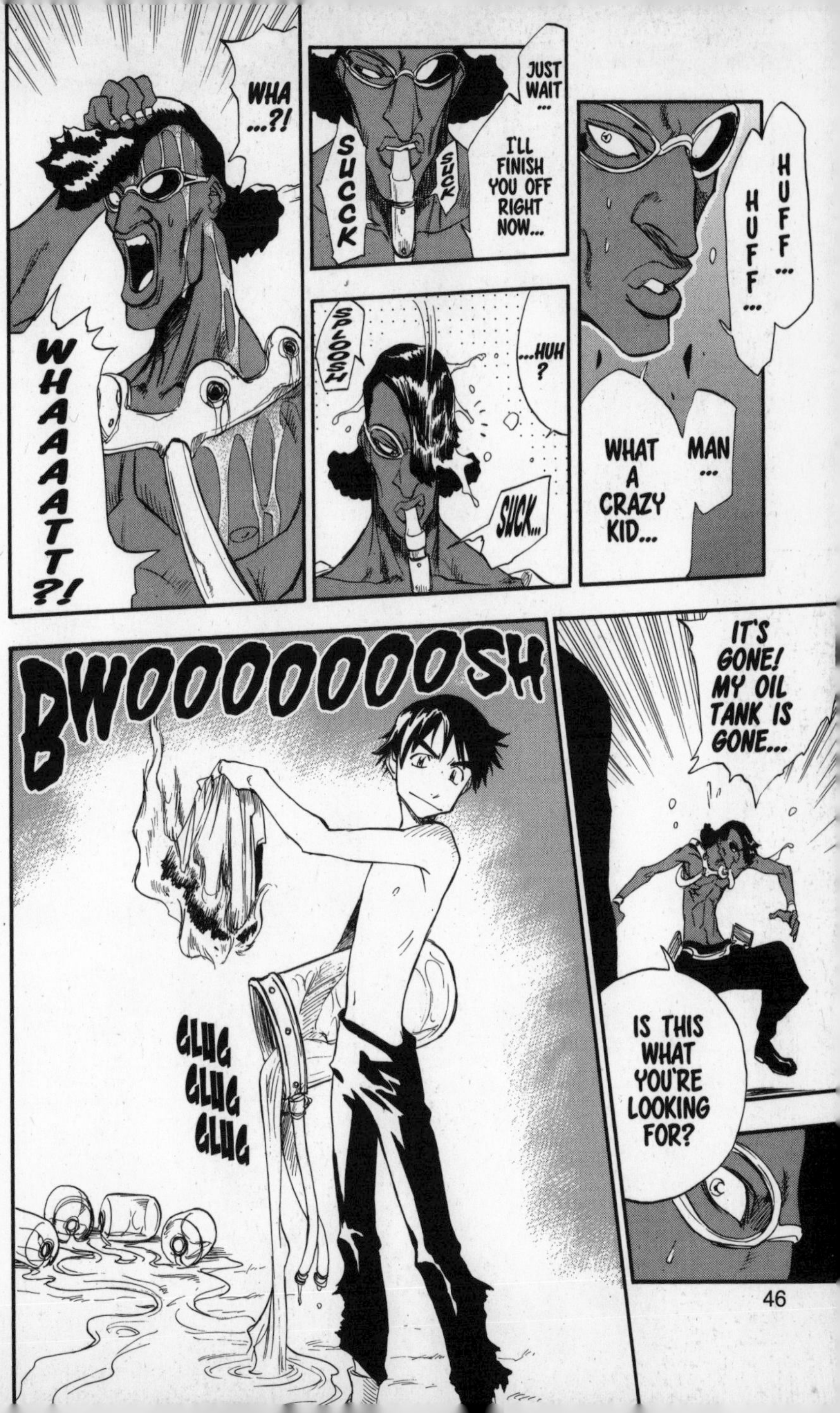
HUFF...
HUFF...
MAN...
WHAT A CRAZY KID...
JUST WAIT...
SUCK
SUCCK
I'LL FINISH YOU OFF RIGHT NOW...
...HUH?
SPLOOSH
SUCK...
WHA...?!
WHAAAAATT?!
IT'S GONE! MY OIL TANK IS GONE...
IS THIS WHAT YOU'RE LOOKING FOR?
BWOOOOOOOOSH
GLUG GLUG GLUG

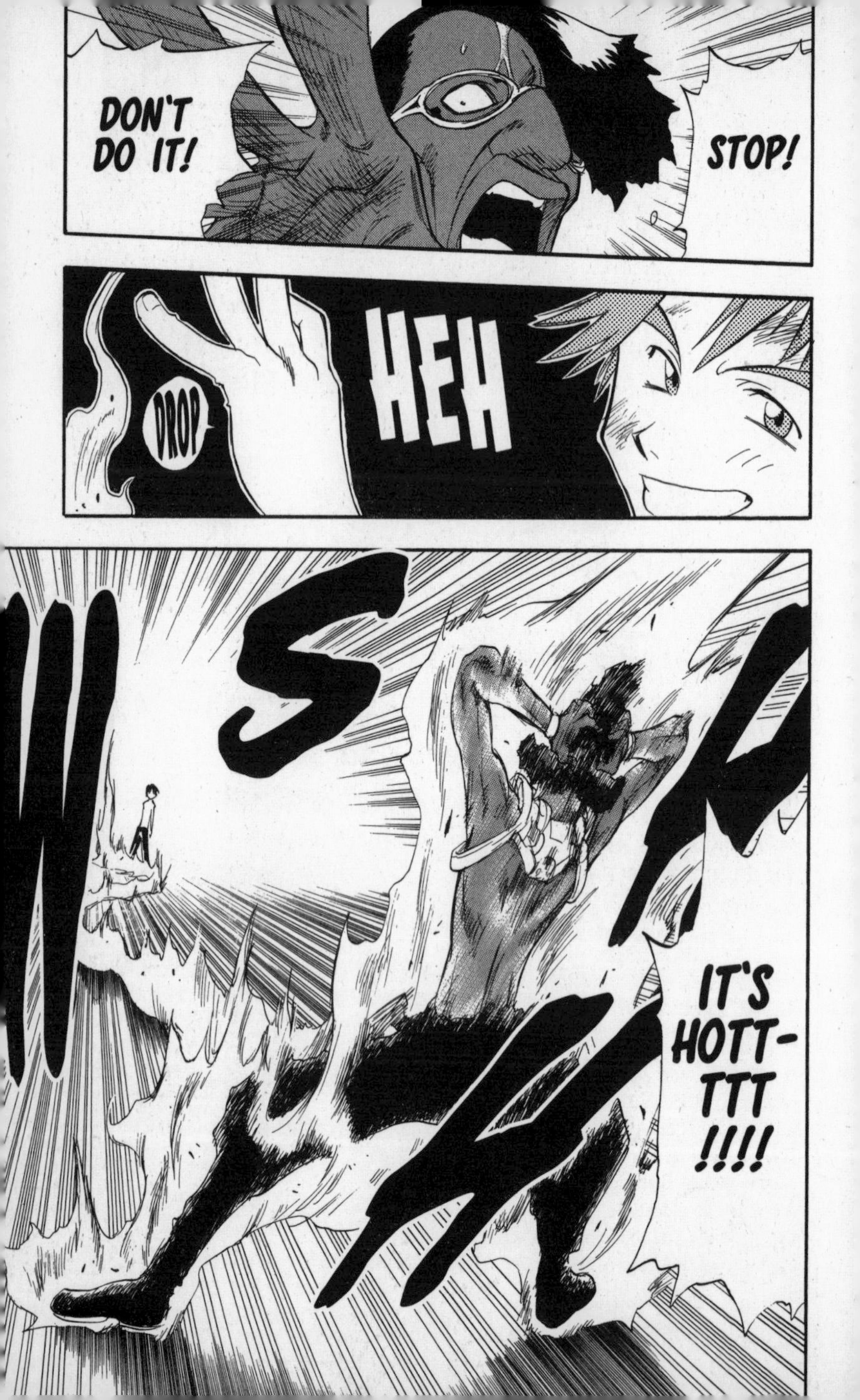
STOP!
DON'T DO IT!
HEH
DROP
IT'S HOTT-TTT!!!!

B-side NAKED MONKEYS 10.

Vaultwatch Brothers
ヴォールトウォッチ

The brothers that guarded the vault at Calder's place. By the way, the one on the left is the older brother and the one on the right is the younger brother.

Birks Decarlo

Height: 169cm
Weight: 62kg
Blood Type: O

Bernard Decarlo

Height: 176cm
Weight: 60kg
Blood Type: AB

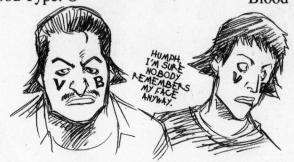

HUMPH, I'M SURE NOBODY REMEMBERS MY FACE ANYWAY.

Guiffle "The Great Undead Box"
ギッフル・"ザ・グレイト・アンデッド・ボックス"

Real Name:
Height: unknown
Weight: unknown
Date of Birth: 1/23
Age: 42
Blood Type: AB

This unfortunate middle-aged man had the shortest life span of all the major troupe members. When he's inside the box, the position of his head looks weird no matter how you look at him. That's his solitary "charm point." But this is what he looks like when he gets out of the box. Yes…I know…no one wants to see any more of this guy!

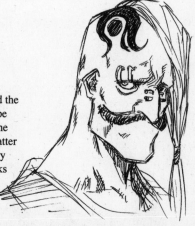

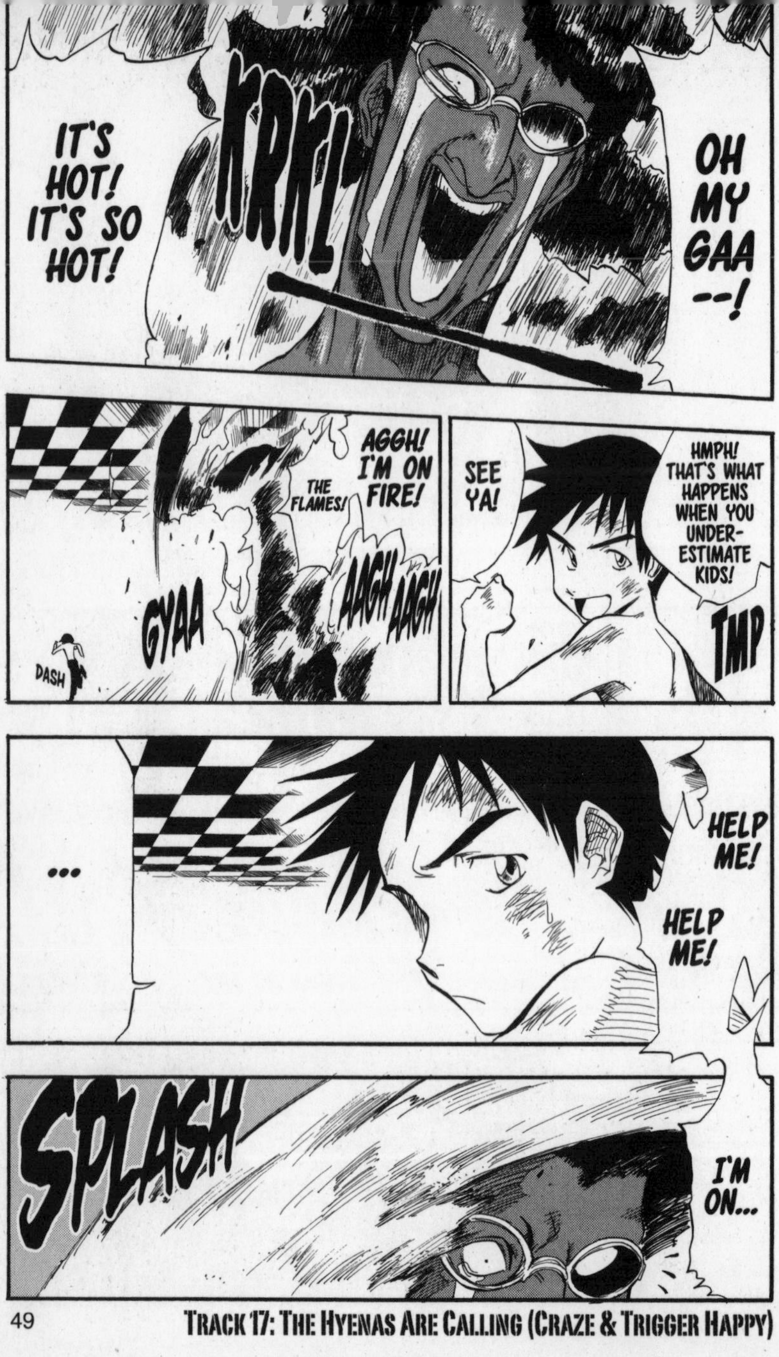
OH MY GAA--!
IT'S HOT! IT'S SO HOT!
HMPH! THAT'S WHAT HAPPENS WHEN YOU UNDER-ESTIMATE KIDS!
TMP
SEE YA!
AGGH! I'M ON FIRE!
THE FLAMES!
AAGH AAGH
GYAA
DASH
HELP ME!
HELP ME!
...
I'M ON...
SPLASH

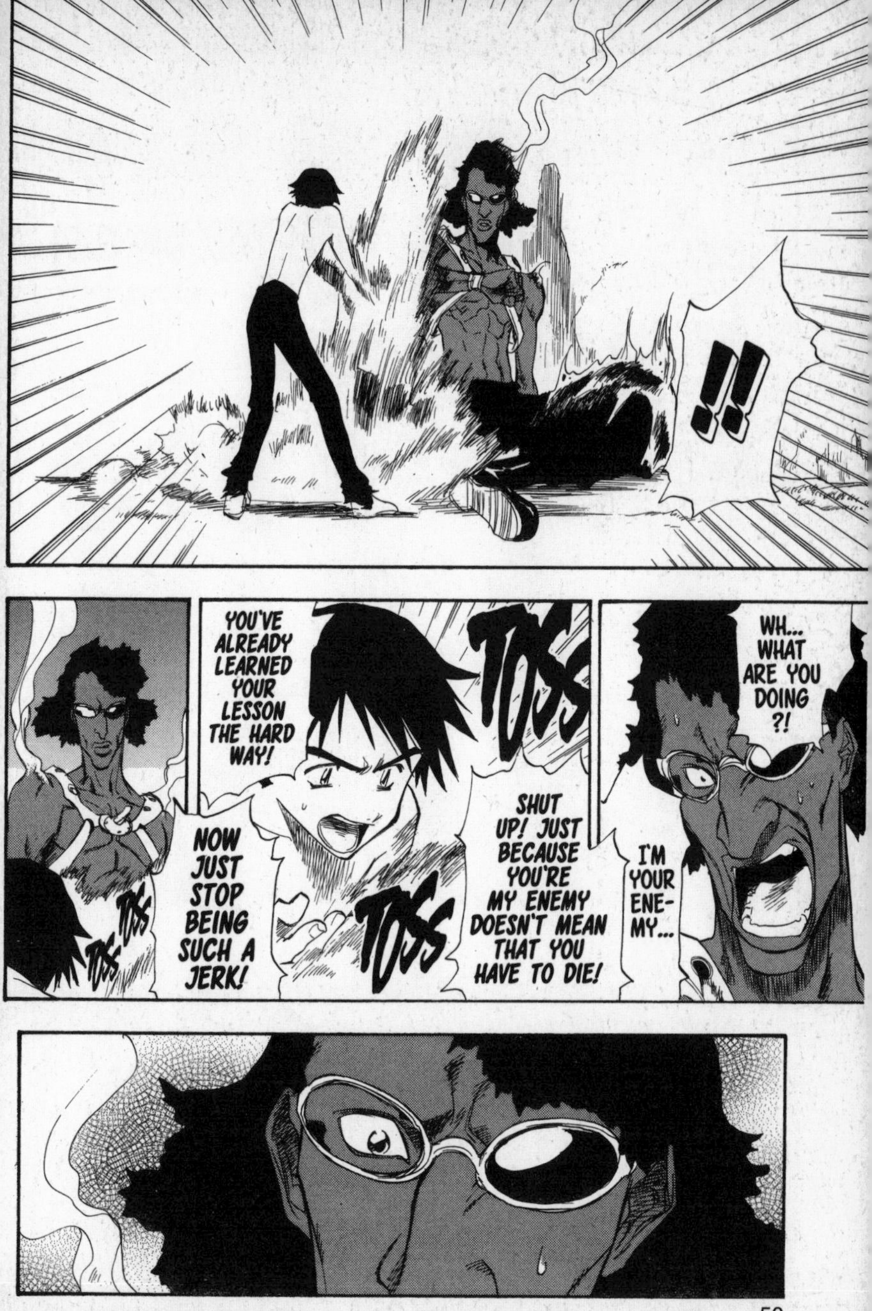
!!
WH... WHAT ARE YOU DOING ?!
I'M YOUR ENE-MY...
TOSS
SHUT UP! JUST BECAUSE YOU'RE MY ENEMY DOESN'T MEAN THAT YOU HAVE TO DIE!
YOU'VE ALREADY LEARNED YOUR LESSON THE HARD WAY!
TOSS
NOW JUST STOP BEING SUCH A JERK!
TOSS
TOSS

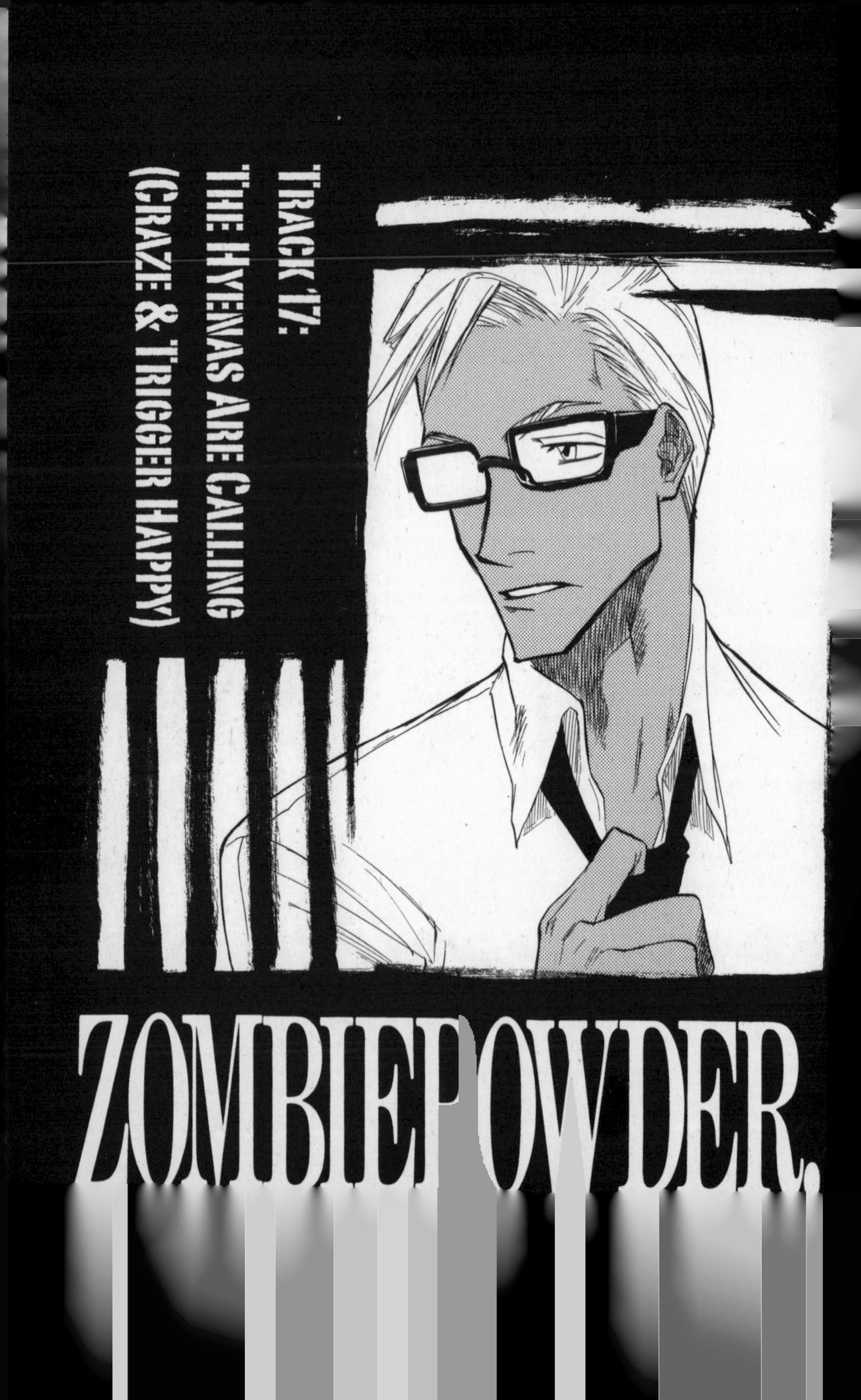
TRACK 17: THE HYENAS ARE CALLING (CRAZE & TRIGGER HAPPY)
ZOMBIEPOWDER.

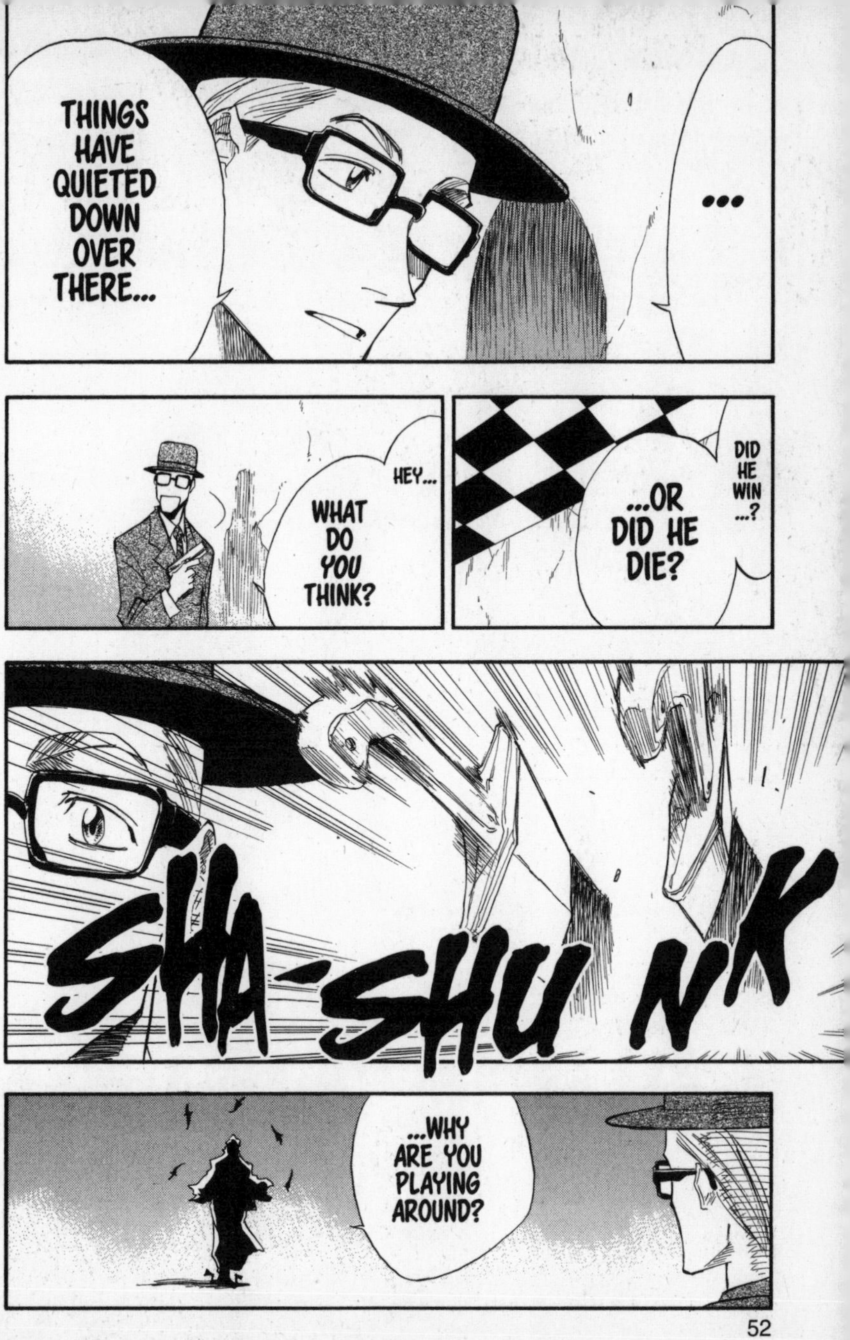
...
THINGS HAVE QUIETED DOWN OVER THERE...
DID HE WIN...?
...OR DID HE DIE?
HEY...
WHAT DO YOU THINK?
SHA-SHUNK
...WHY ARE YOU PLAYING AROUND?

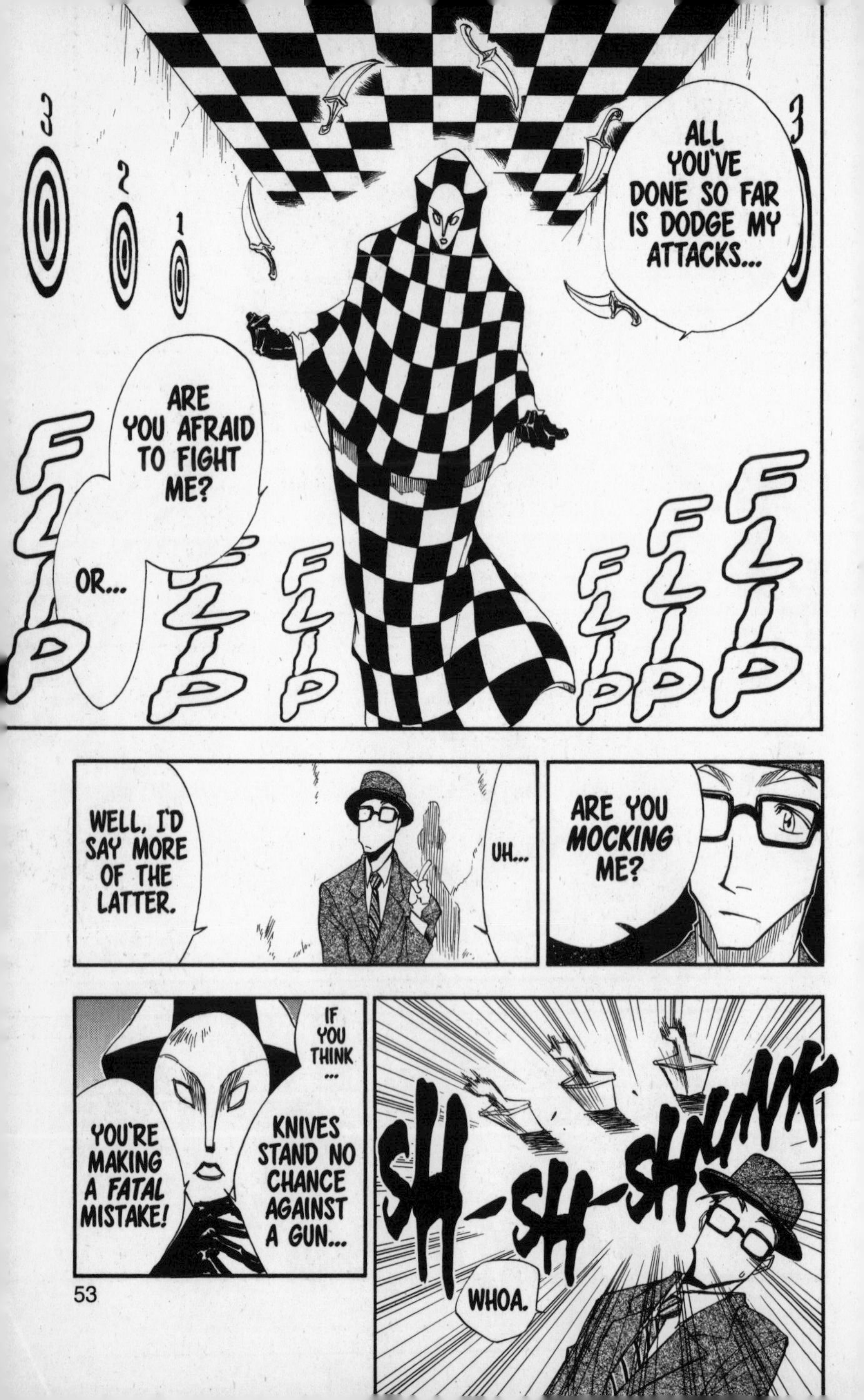
3
3
2
1
ALL YOU'VE DONE SO FAR IS DODGE MY ATTACKS...
ARE YOU AFRAID TO FIGHT ME?
OR...
FLIP FLIP FLIP FLIP FLIP FLIP FLIP
ARE YOU MOCKING ME?
UH...
WELL, I'D SAY MORE OF THE LATTER.
SH-SH-SHUNK
WHOA.
IF YOU THINK...
KNIVES STAND NO CHANCE AGAINST A GUN...
YOU'RE MAKING A FATAL MISTAKE!

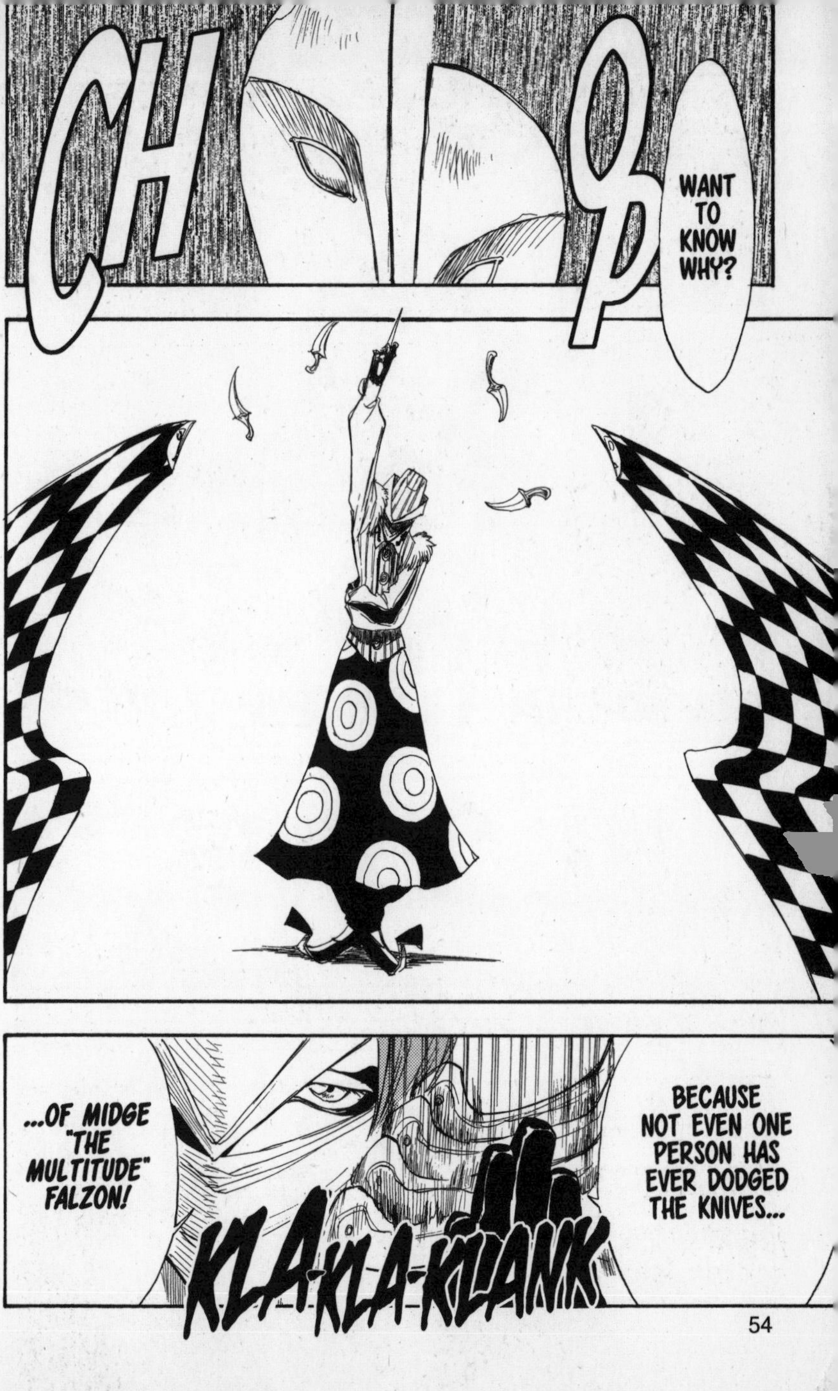
CHOP
WANT TO KNOW WHY?
BECAUSE NOT EVEN ONE PERSON HAS EVER DODGED THE KNIVES...
...OF MIDGE "THE MULTITUDE" FALZON!
KLA-KLA-KLANK

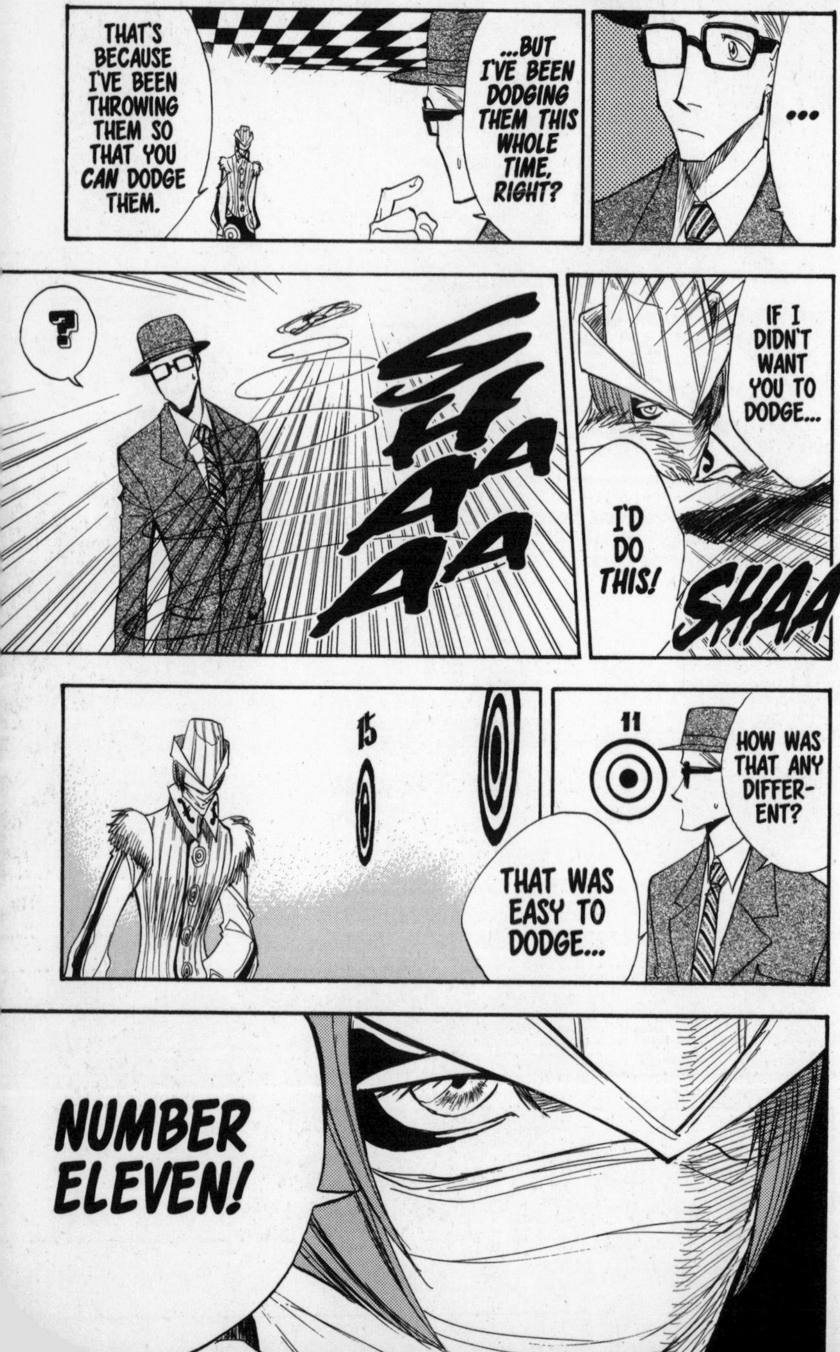
...
...BUT I'VE BEEN DODGING THEM THIS WHOLE TIME, RIGHT?
THAT'S BECAUSE I'VE BEEN THROWING THEM SO THAT YOU CAN DODGE THEM.
IF I DIDN'T WANT YOU TO DODGE...
I'D DO THIS!
SHAA
?
SHAAAAA
11
HOW WAS THAT ANY DIFFER-ENT?
THAT WAS EASY TO DODGE...
15
NUMBER ELEVEN!

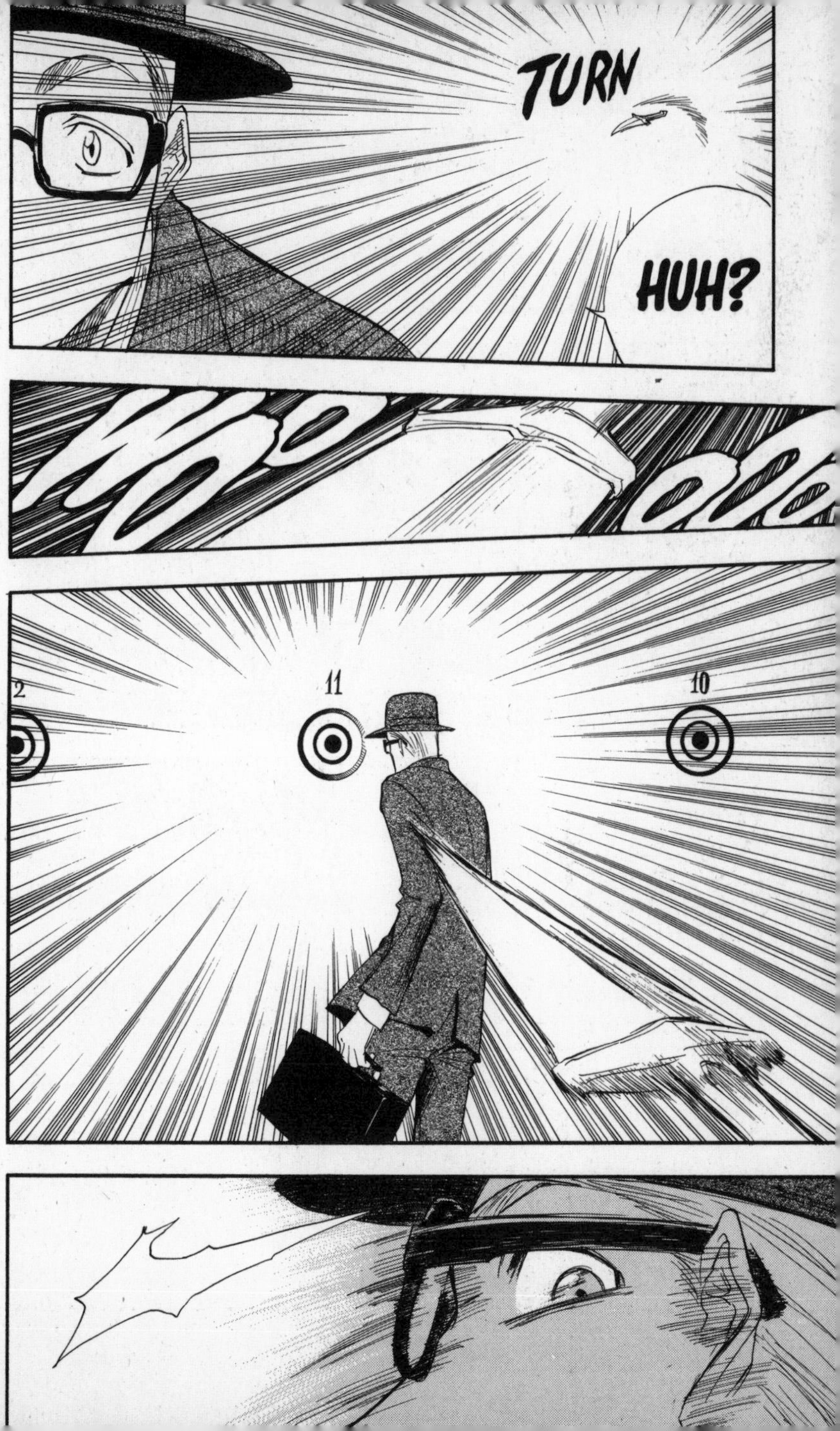
TURN
HUH?
11
10

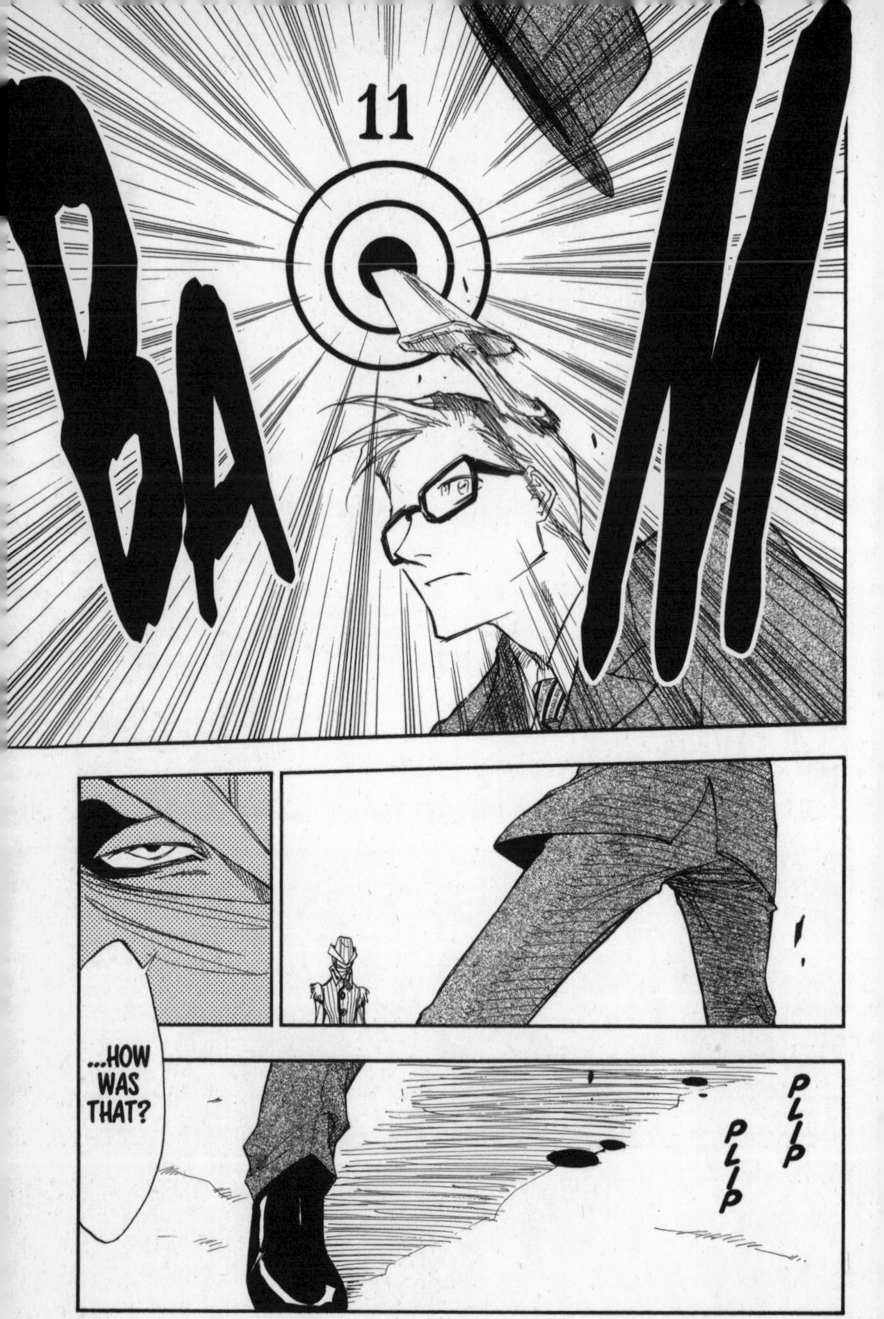
11
BAM
...HOW WAS THAT?
PLIP PLIP

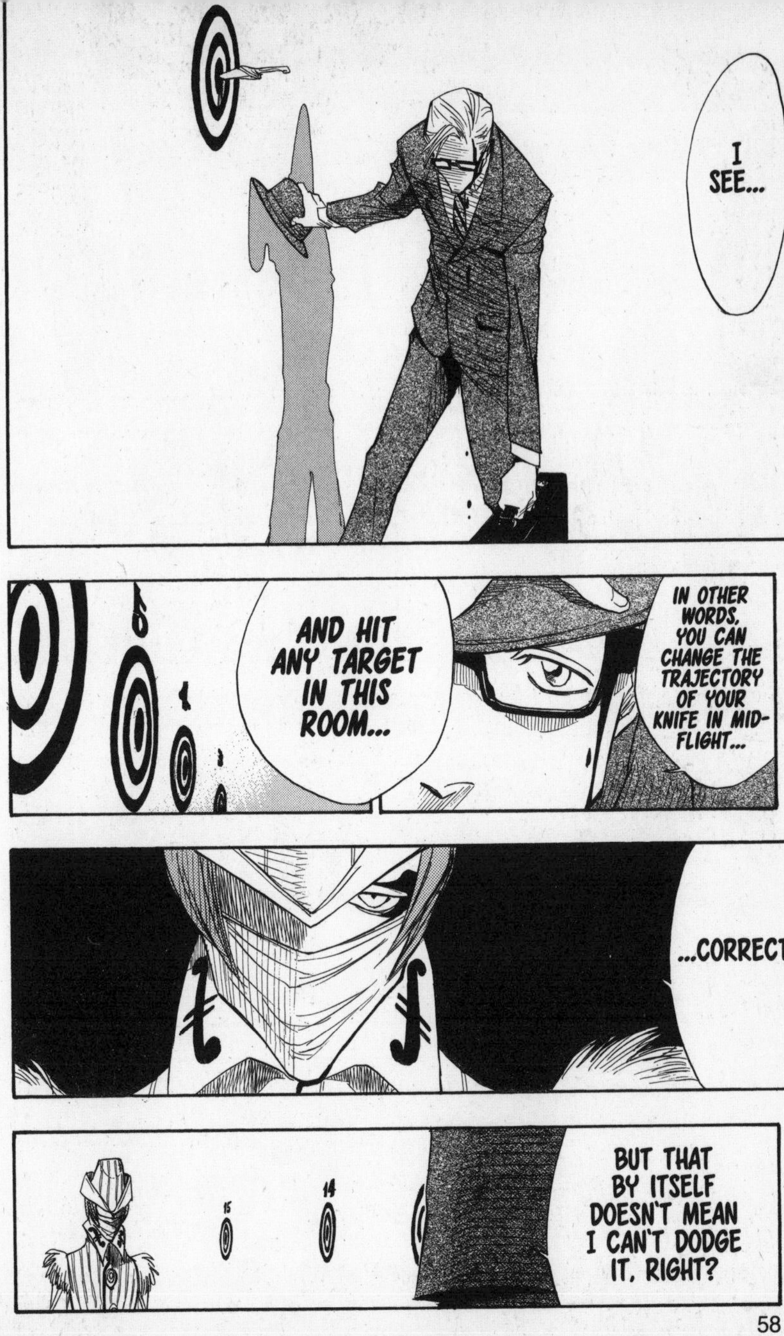
I SEE...
IN OTHER WORDS, YOU CAN CHANGE THE TRAJECTORY OF YOUR KNIFE IN MID-FLIGHT...
AND HIT ANY TARGET IN THIS ROOM...
...CORRECT.
BUT THAT BY ITSELF DOESN'T MEAN I CAN'T DODGE IT, RIGHT?

READ THIS WAY

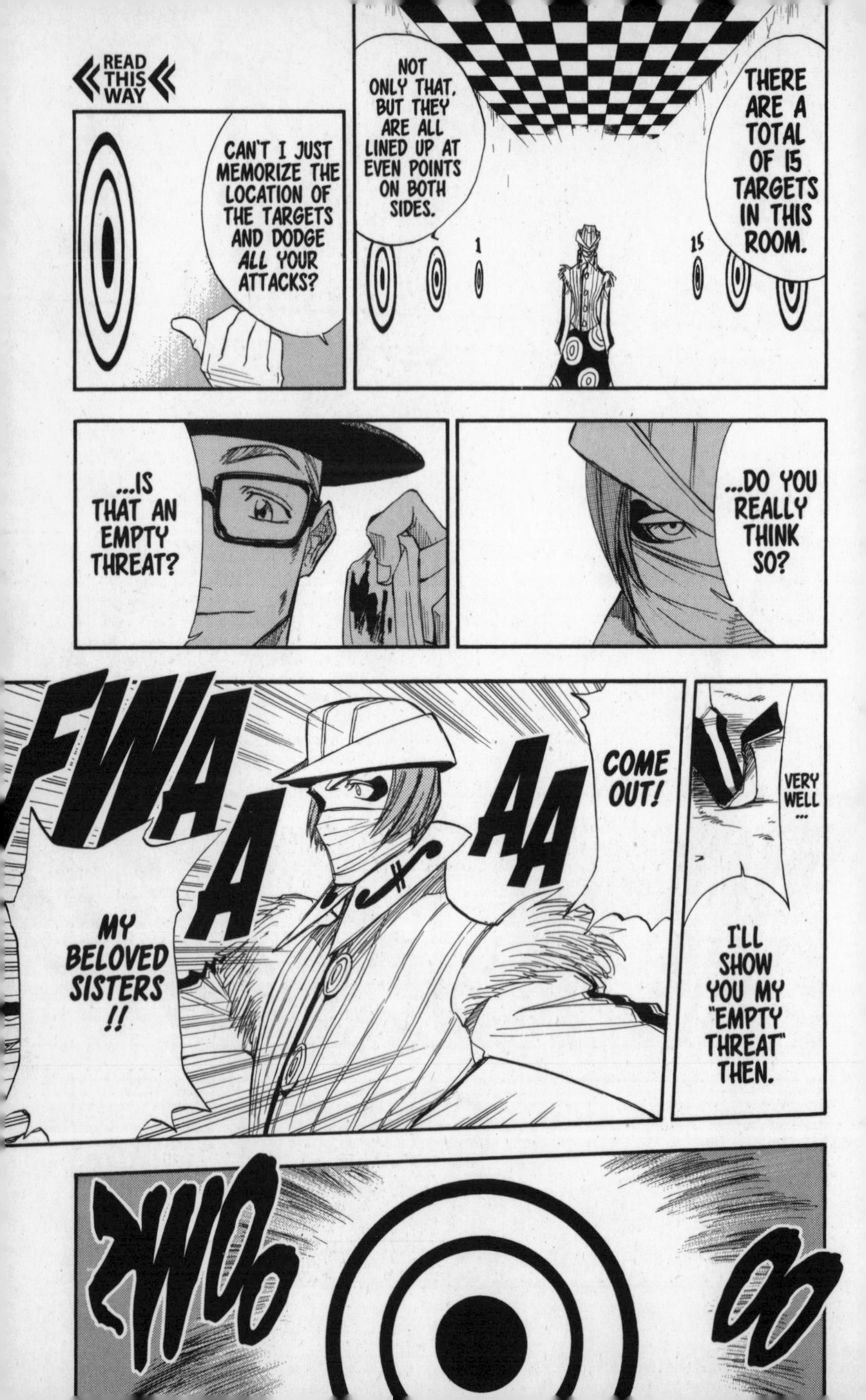

THERE ARE A TOTAL OF 15 TARGETS IN THIS ROOM.
NOT ONLY THAT, BUT THEY ARE ALL LINED UP AT EVEN POINTS ON BOTH SIDES.
15
1
CAN'T I JUST MEMORIZE THE LOCATION OF THE TARGETS AND DODGE ALL YOUR ATTACKS?
...DO YOU REALLY THINK SO?
...IS THAT AN EMPTY THREAT?
VERY WELL...
I'LL SHOW YOU MY "EMPTY THREAT" THEN.
COME OUT!
FWAAAA
MY BELOVED SISTERS!!

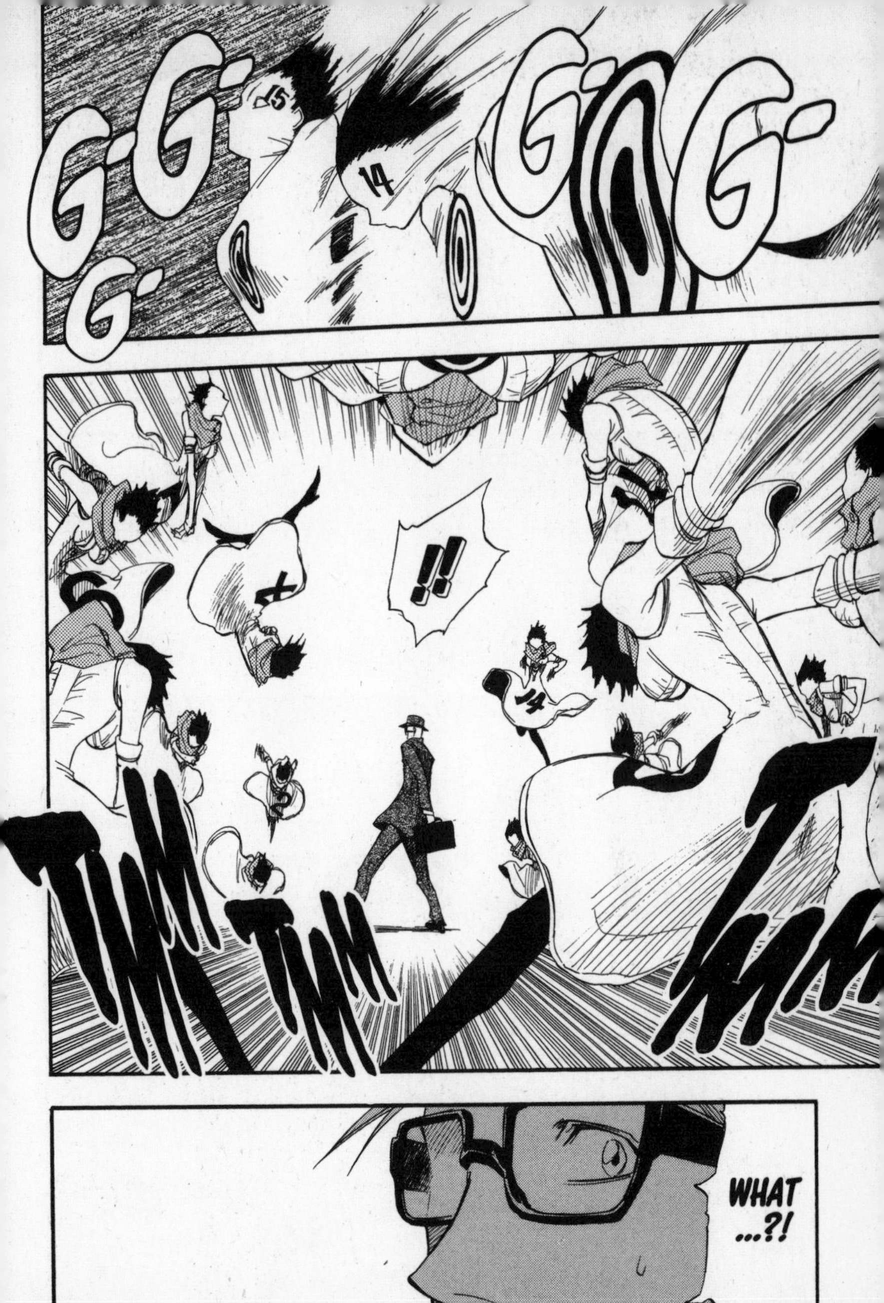
G-G-G-
!!
WHAT ...?!

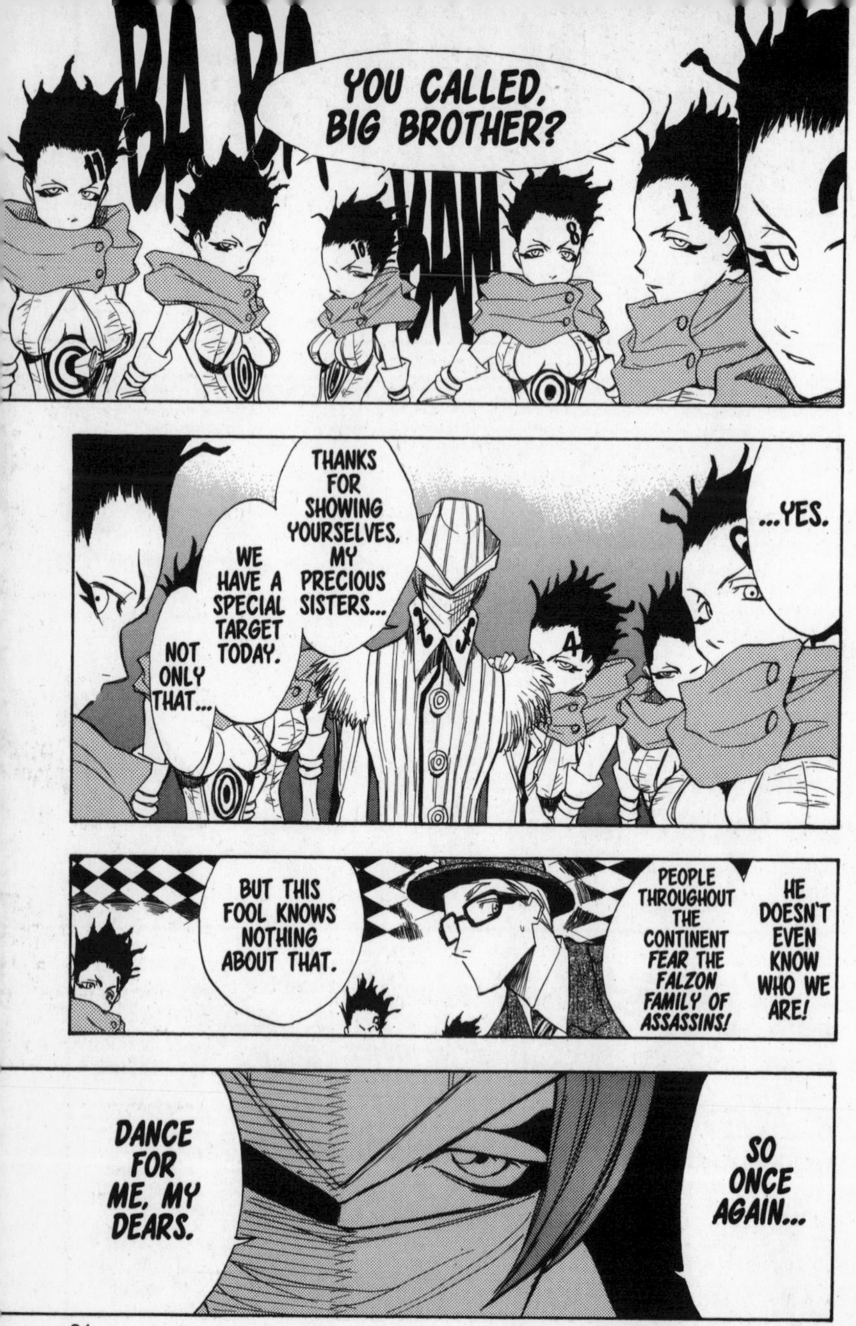
YOU CALLED, BIG BROTHER?
...YES.
THANKS FOR SHOWING YOURSELVES, MY PRECIOUS SISTERS...
WE HAVE A SPECIAL TARGET TODAY.
NOT ONLY THAT...
HE DOESN'T EVEN KNOW WHO WE ARE!
PEOPLE THROUGHOUT THE CONTINENT FEAR THE FALZON FAMILY OF ASSASSINS!
BUT THIS FOOL KNOWS NOTHING ABOUT THAT.
SO ONCE AGAIN...
DANCE FOR ME, MY DEARS.

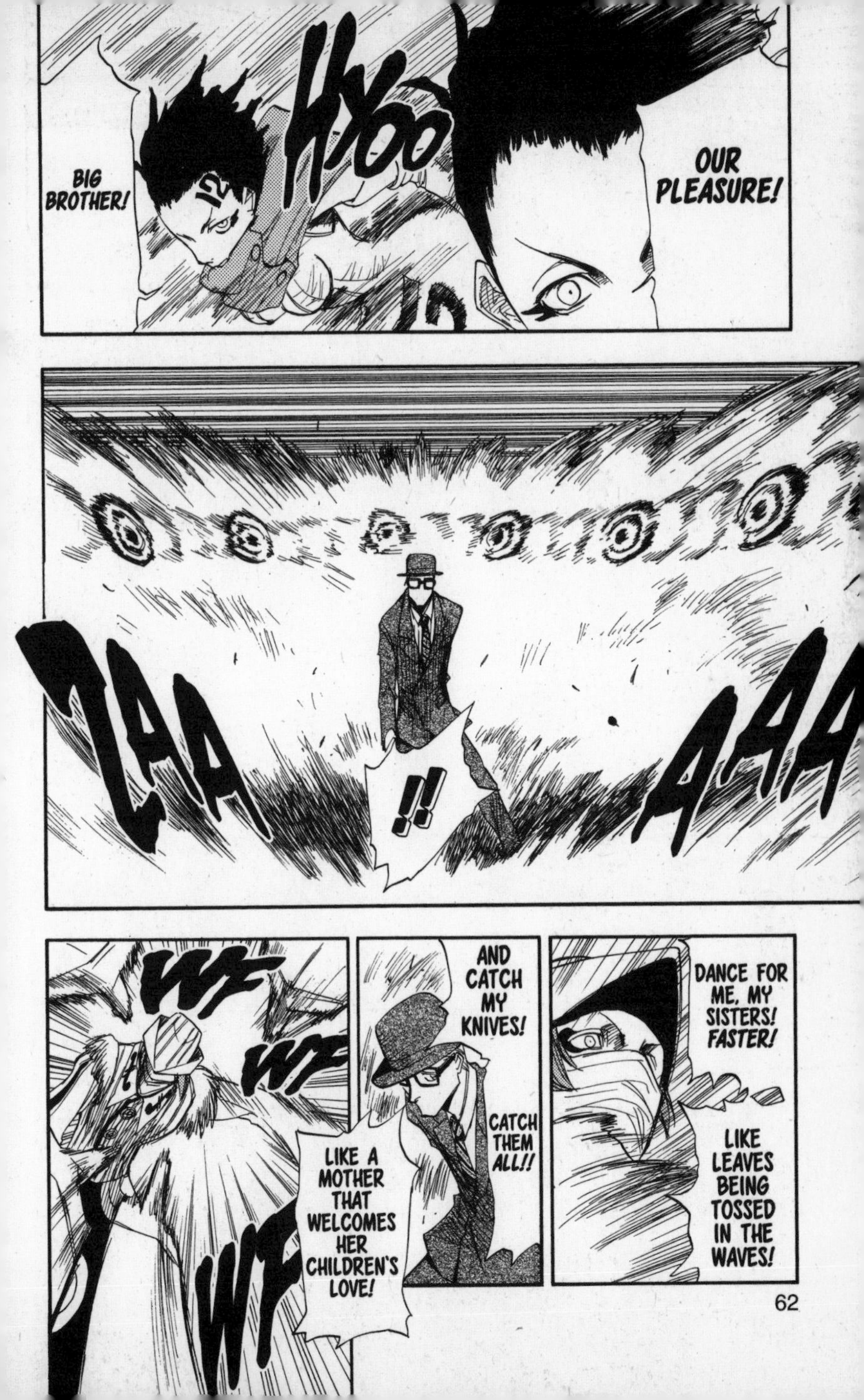
OUR PLEASURE!
HYOO
BIG BROTHER!
ZAAAAA
!!
DANCE FOR ME, MY SISTERS! FASTER!
LIKE LEAVES BEING TOSSED IN THE WAVES!
AND CATCH MY KNIVES!
CATCH THEM ALL!!
LIKE A MOTHER THAT WELCOMES HER CHILDREN'S LOVE!
WF
WF
WF

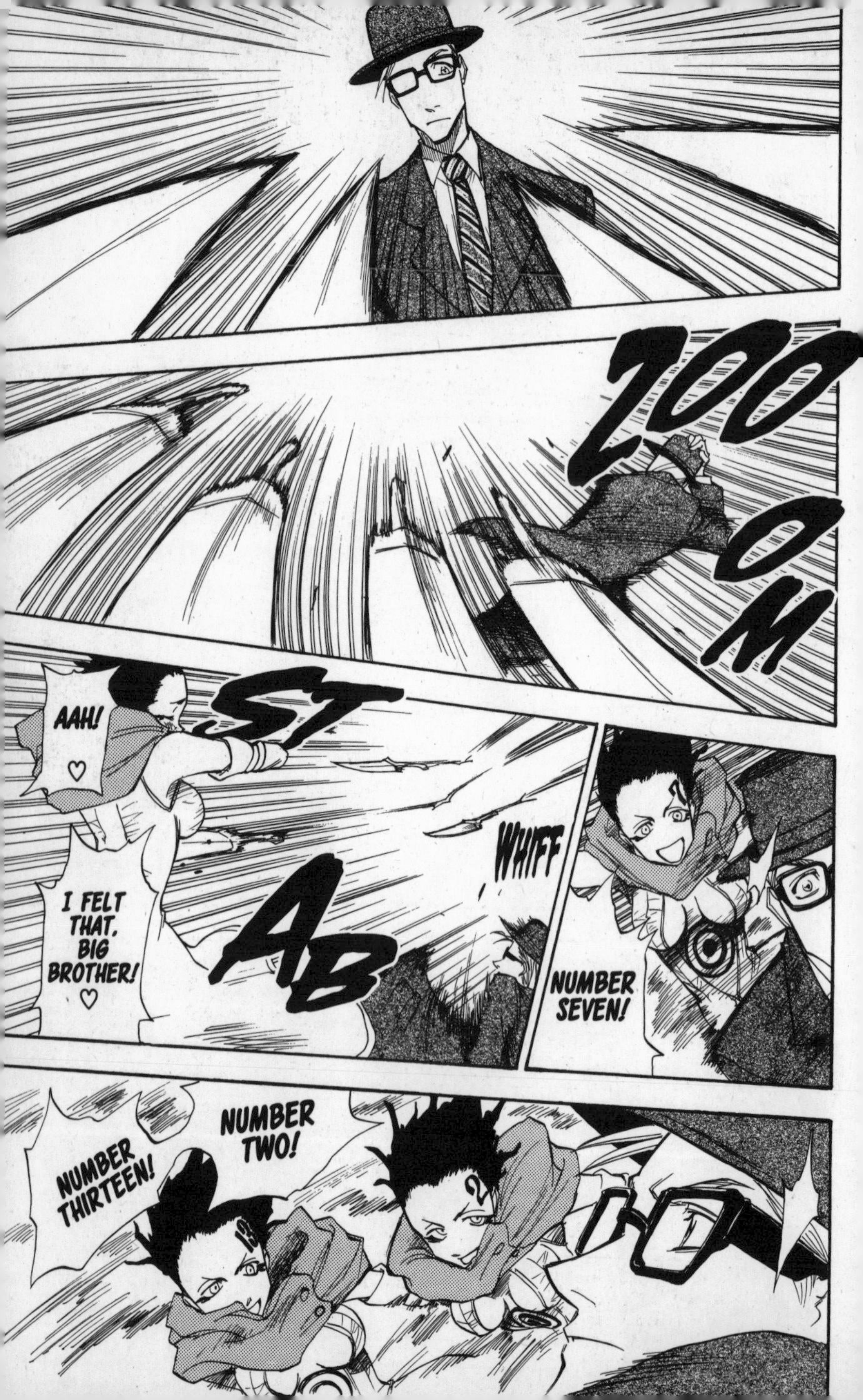
ZOOOM
NUMBER SEVEN!
ST
AAH! ♡
WHIFF
AB
I FELT THAT, BIG BROTHER! ♡
NUMBER TWO!
NUMBER THIRTEEN!

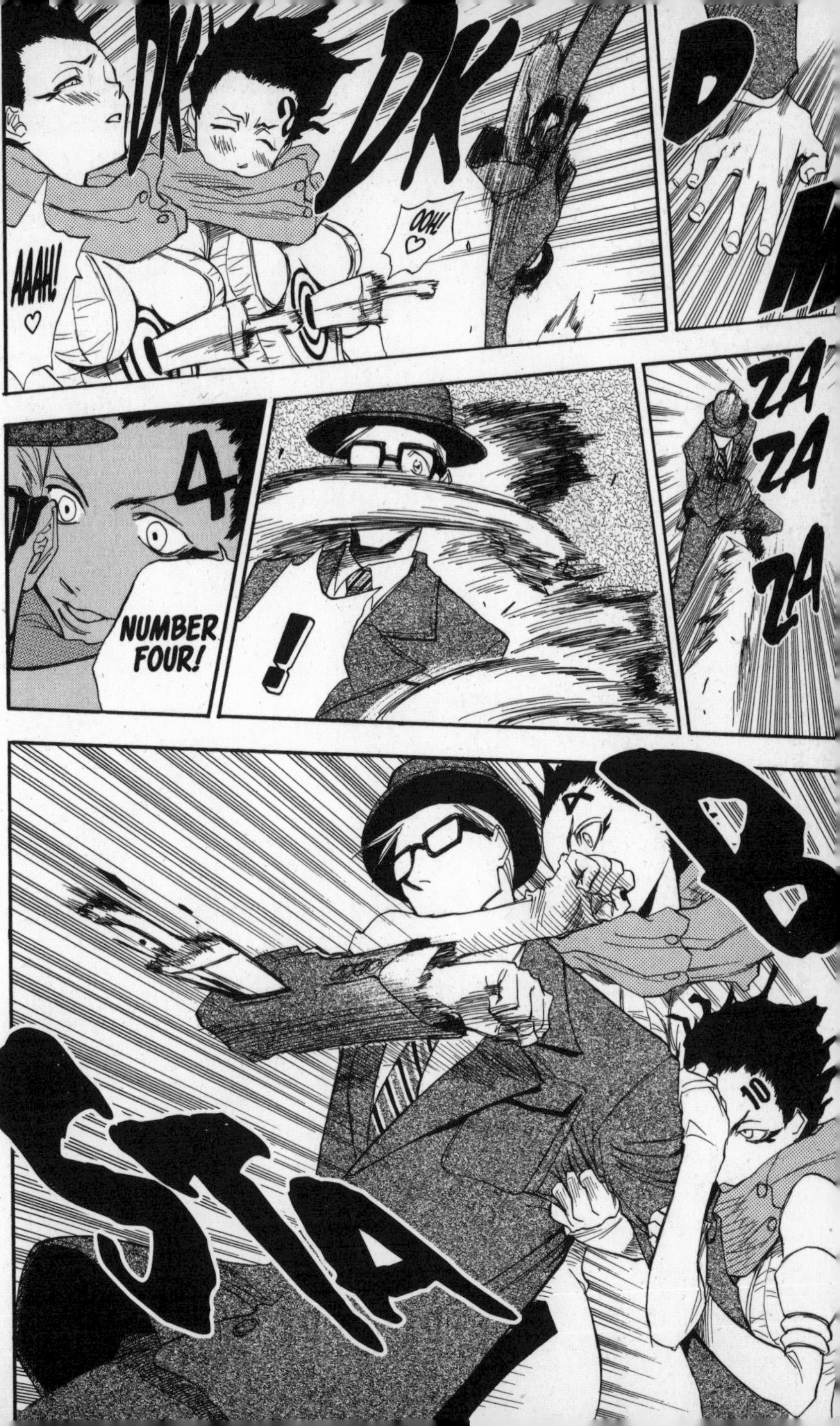

DM
DK
DK
OOH! ♡
AAAH! ♡
ZA ZA ZA ZA
!
NUMBER FOUR!
B
STA

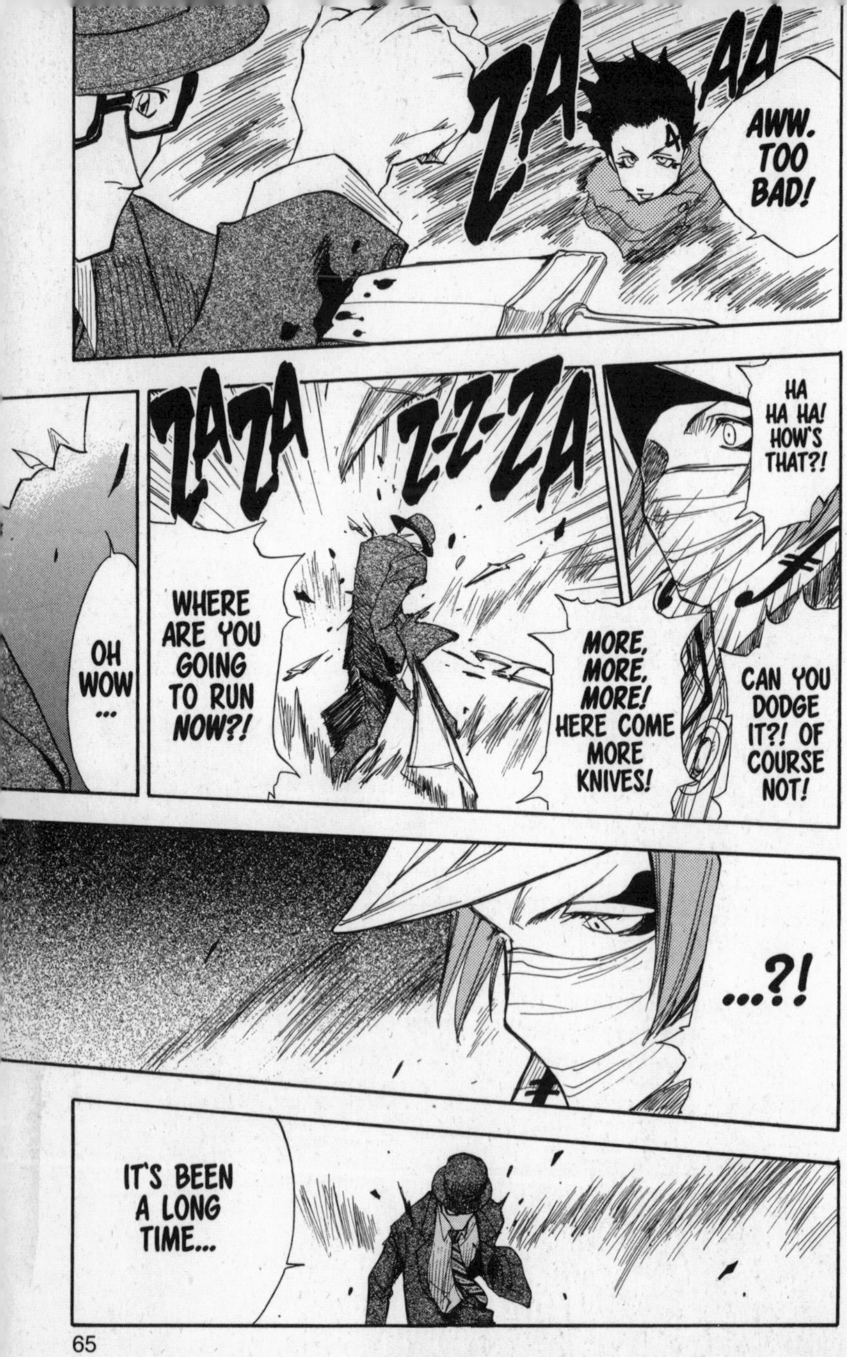
ZA-AA
AWW. TOO BAD!
HA HA HA! HOW'S THAT?!
CAN YOU DODGE IT?! OF COURSE NOT!
ZAZA
Z-Z-ZA
MORE, MORE, MORE! HERE COME MORE KNIVES!
WHERE ARE YOU GOING TO RUN NOW?!
OH WOW...
...?!
IT'S BEEN A LONG TIME...

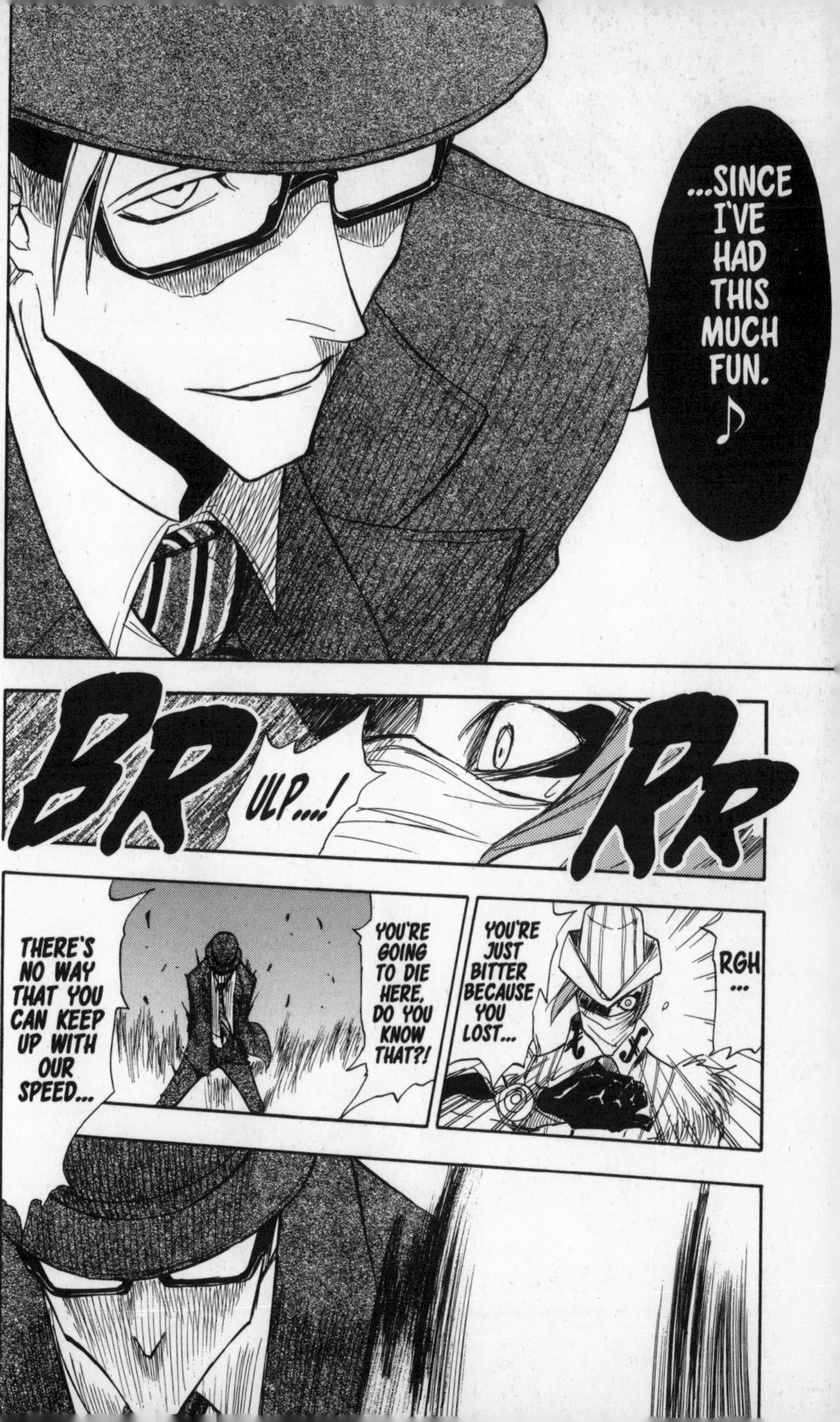
...SINCE I'VE HAD THIS MUCH FUN. ♪
BR RR
ULP...!
RGH ...
YOU'RE JUST BITTER BECAUSE YOU LOST...
YOU'RE GOING TO DIE HERE, DO YOU KNOW THAT?!
THERE'S NO WAY THAT YOU CAN KEEP UP WITH OUR SPEED...

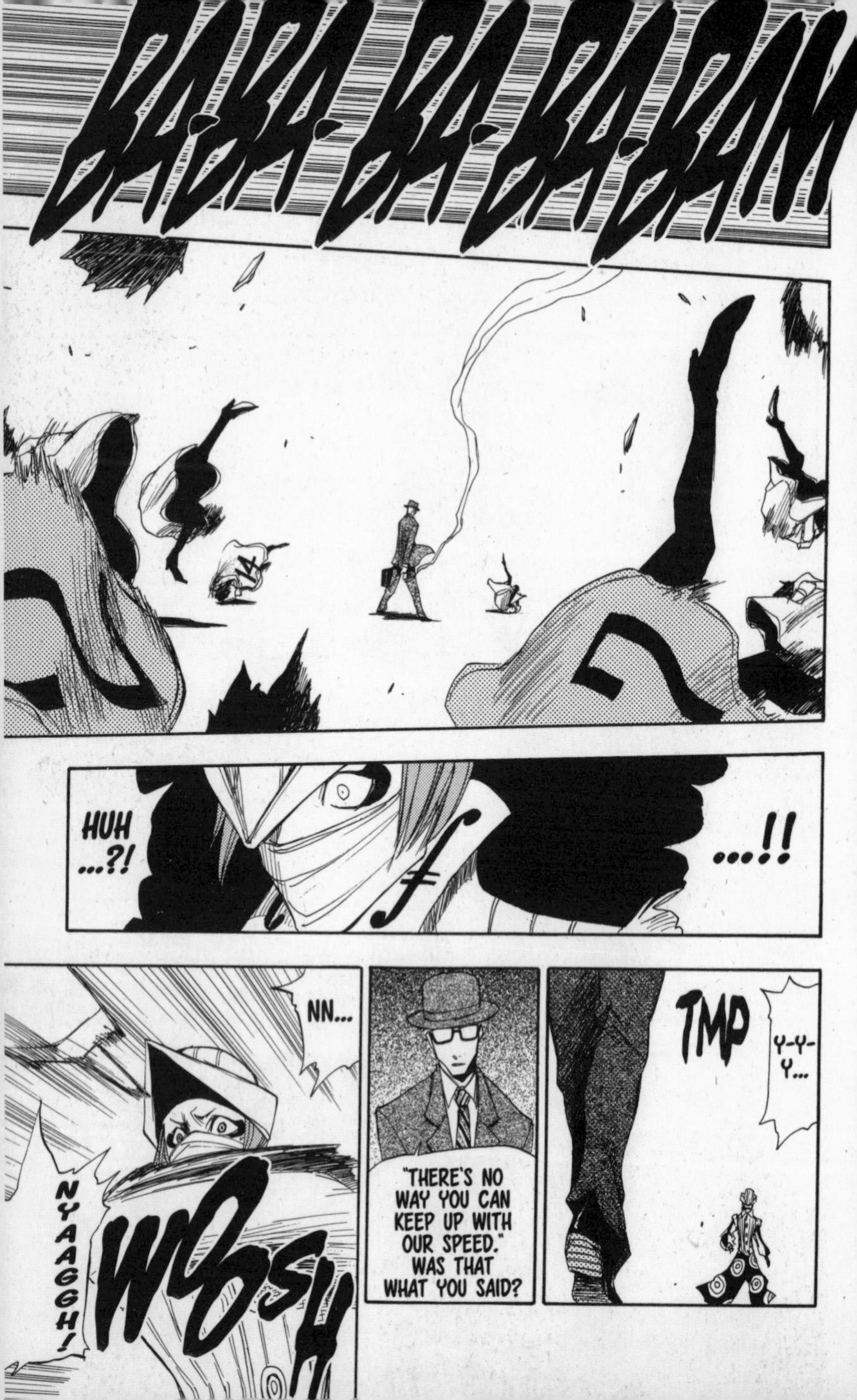
BABA-BA-BABAM
...!!
HUH ...?!
TMP
Y-Y-Y...
"THERE'S NO WAY YOU CAN KEEP UP WITH OUR SPEED." WAS THAT WHAT YOU SAID?
NN...
NYAAAGGH!
WOSH

THIS...

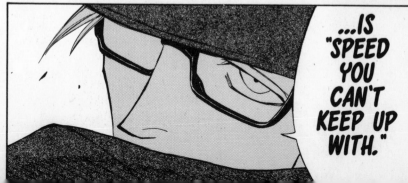

...IS "SPEED YOU CAN'T KEEP UP WITH."

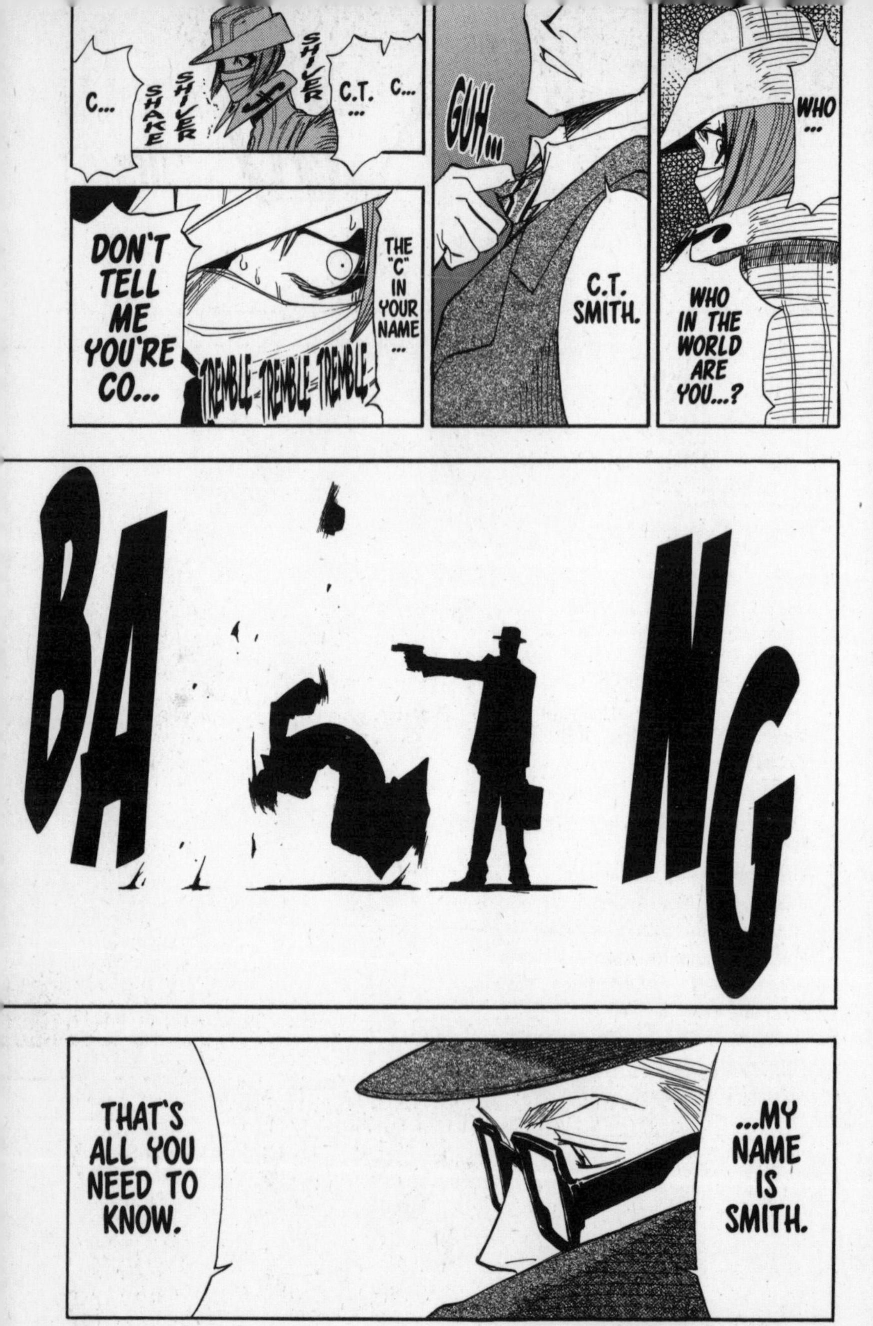
WHO ...
WHO IN THE WORLD ARE YOU...?
GUH...
C.T. SMITH.
C...
C.T. ...
SHIVER
SHIVER
SHAKE
C...
THE "C" IN YOUR NAME ...
DON'T TELL ME YOU'RE CO...
TREMBLE TREMBLE TREMBLE
BANG
...MY NAME IS SMITH.
THAT'S ALL YOU NEED TO KNOW.

B-side NAKED MONKEYS 11.

"Pyromaniac" Pownder
"パイロマニア" パウンダー

Real Name:
Lechris Pownder Rescher
Height: 208cm
Weight: 102kg
Date of Birth: 8/17
Age: 26
Blood Type: BO
Hometown:
Port Bisckes, Gayne

A fire-eater from Port Bisckes in Gayne. His full name is Lechris Pownder Rescher. He's the No. 3 member of the Balmunk circus troupe. He's one of its top performers, and also has a lot of common sense. He likes kids and takes good care of his subordinates. He was the only person who opposed fighting Gamma and his crew when he found out that there was a child involved. (Due to page constraints this plot point wasn't included.) His hobby is to look through picture books of animals. His favorite things are ping pong and green asparagus. He is close friends with Gringo "The Neck Chopper," a guillotine performer. He hates the assistant ringmaster, Falzon.

Track 18: The Evergreen Birdcage (Append Selfdemonizer Mix)

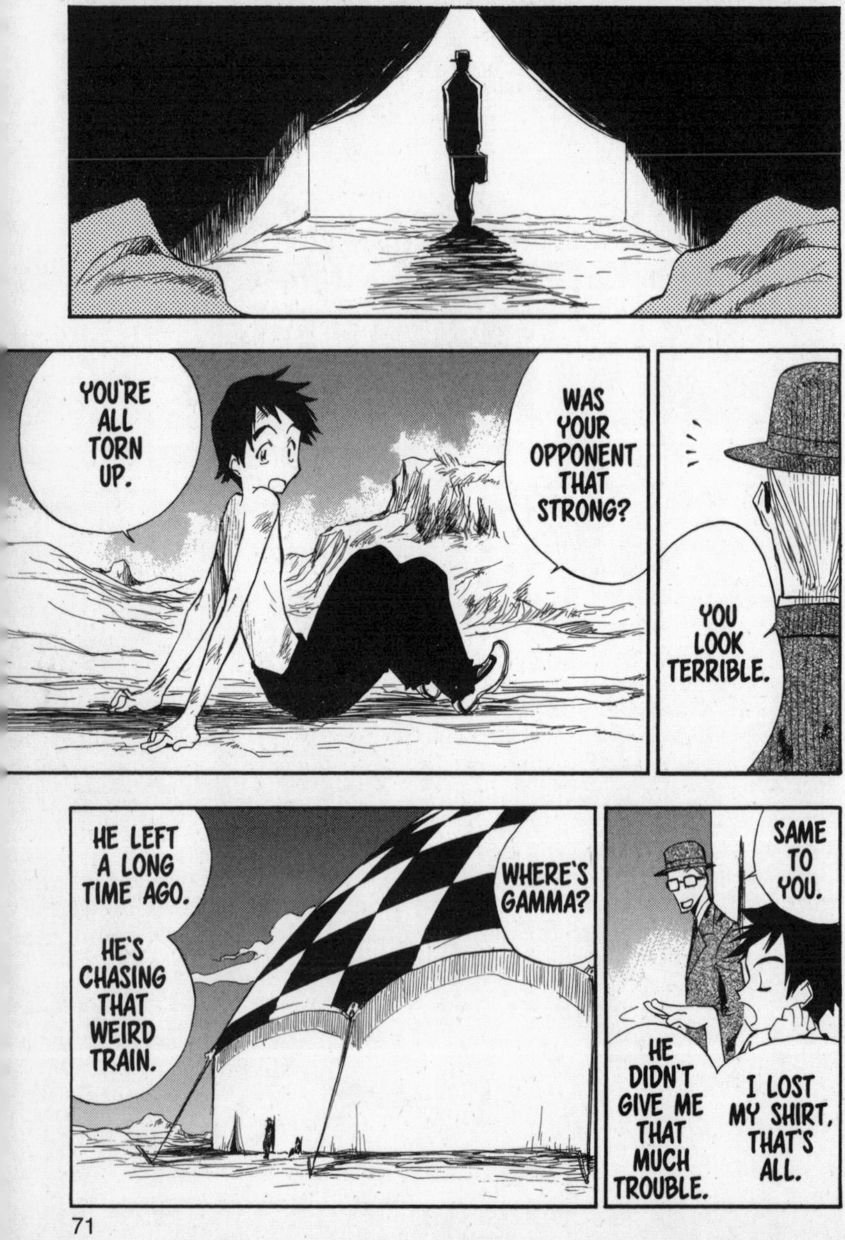
YOU LOOK TERRIBLE.
WAS YOUR OPPONENT THAT STRONG?
YOU'RE ALL TORN UP.
SAME TO YOU.
I LOST MY SHIRT, THAT'S ALL.
HE DIDN'T GIVE ME THAT MUCH TROUBLE.
WHERE'S GAMMA?
HE LEFT A LONG TIME AGO.
HE'S CHASING THAT WEIRD TRAIN.

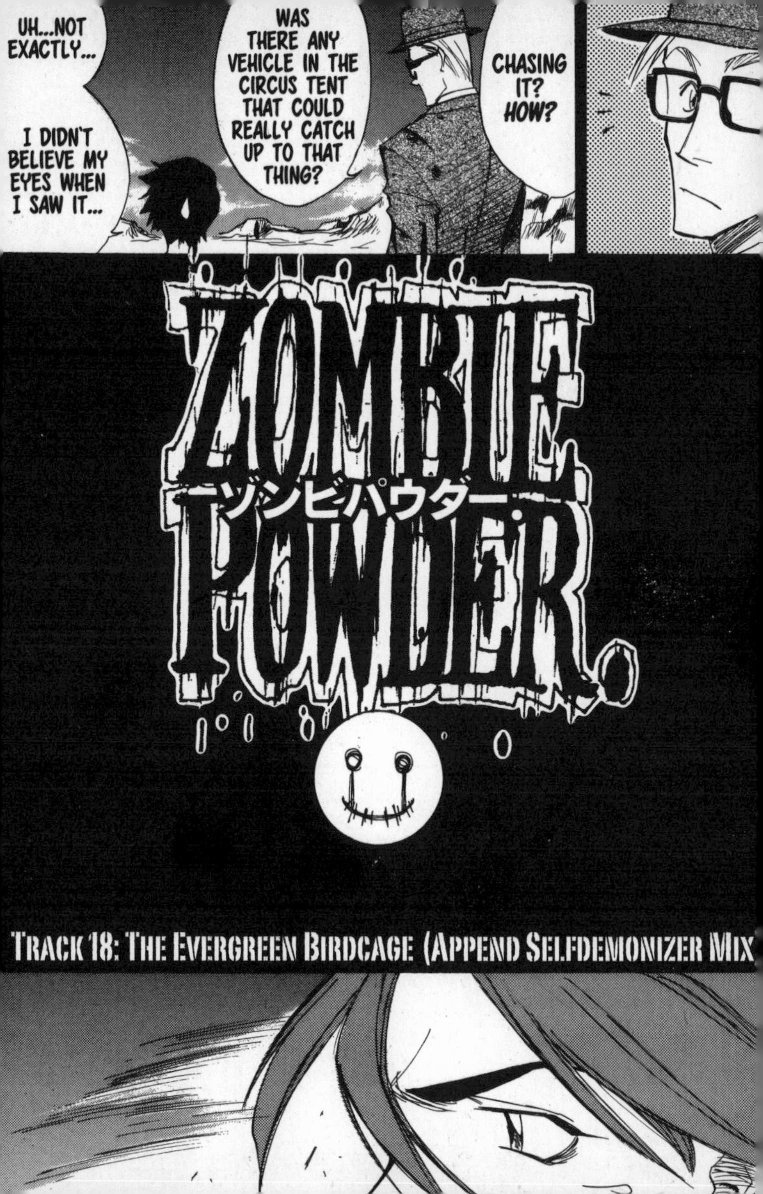
CHASING IT? HOW?
WAS THERE ANY VEHICLE IN THE CIRCUS TENT THAT COULD REALLY CATCH UP TO THAT THING?
UH...NOT EXACTLY...
I DIDN'T BELIEVE MY EYES WHEN I SAW IT...
ZOMBIE POWDER.
ゾンビパウダー
TRACK 18: THE EVERGREEN BIRDCAGE (APPEND SELFDEMONIZER MIX

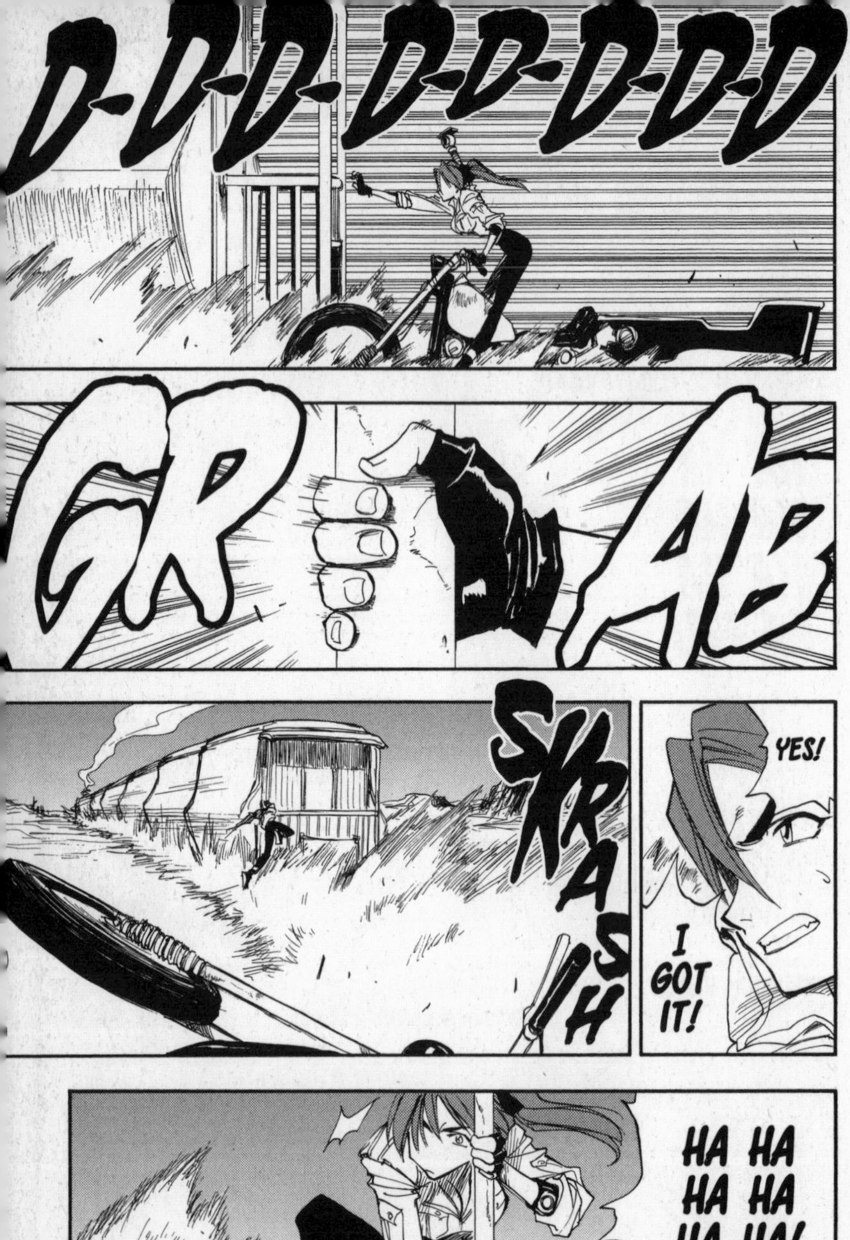
D-D-D-D-D-D-D-D-D
GRAB
YES!
I GOT IT!
SKRASH
HA HA HA HA HA HA!

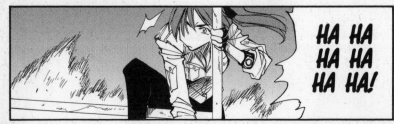

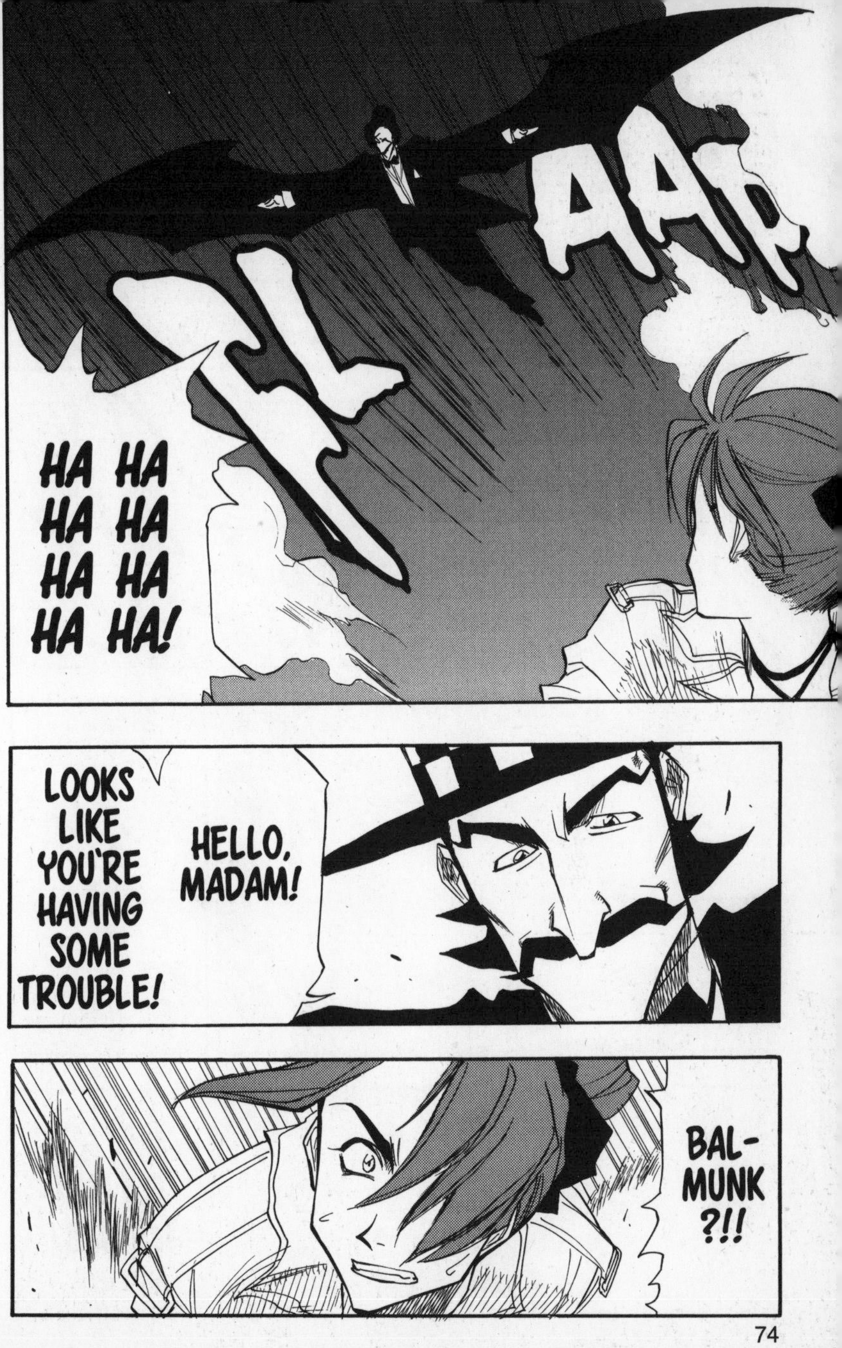
HA HA
HA HA
HA HA
HA HA!
HELLO, MADAM!
LOOKS LIKE YOU'RE HAVING SOME TROUBLE!
BAL-MUNK?!!

READ THIS WAY

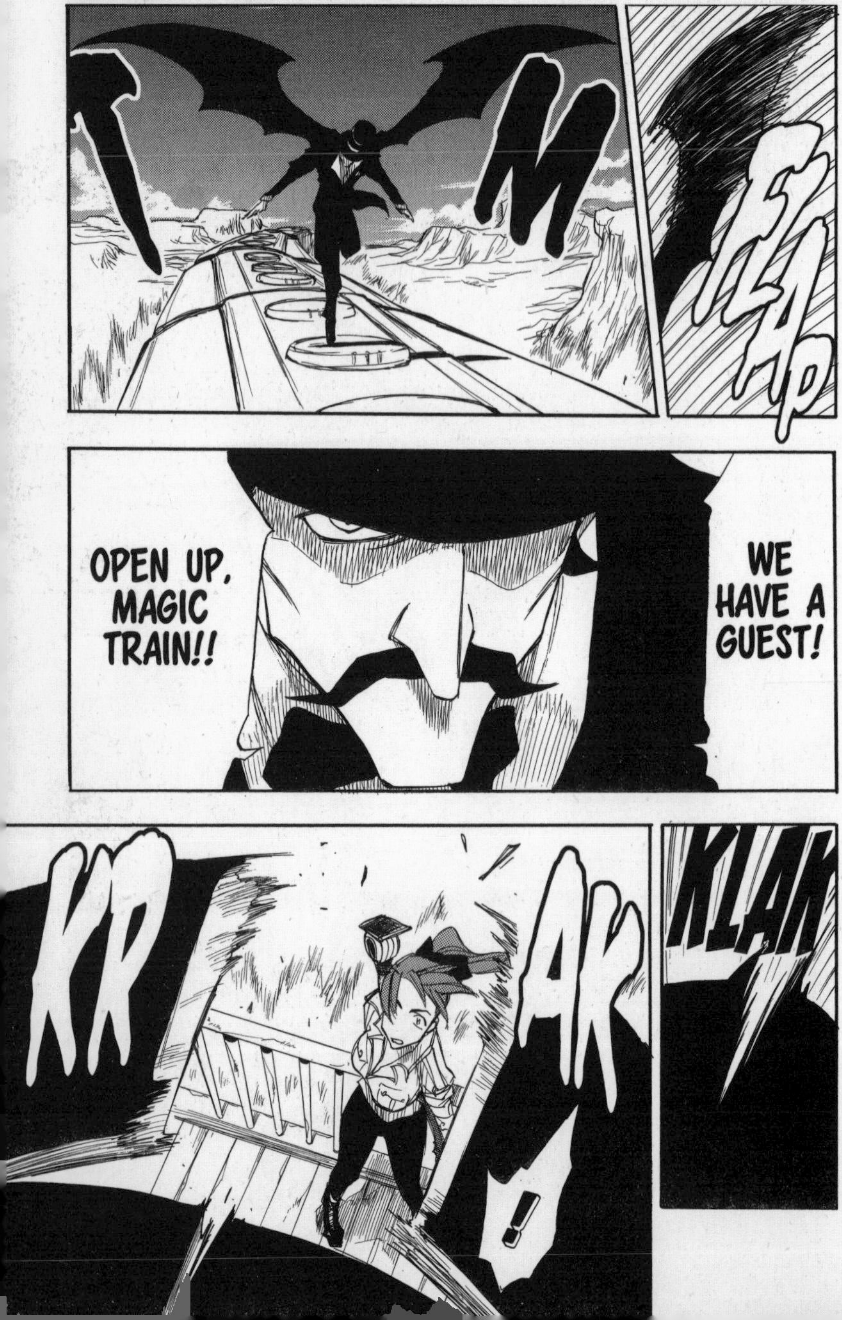
FLAP
WE HAVE A GUEST!
OPEN UP, MAGIC TRAIN!!
KLAK
KRAK!

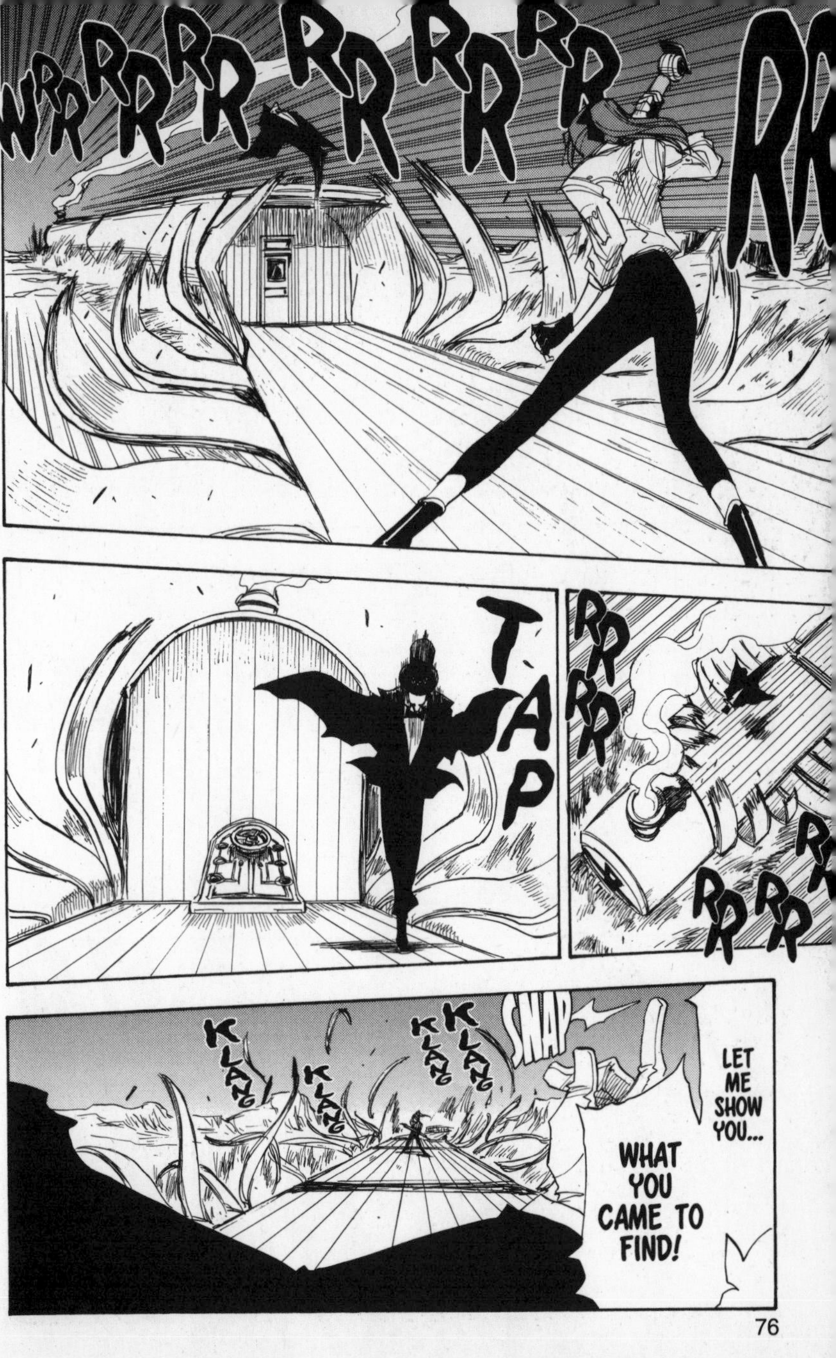
WRRRRRRRRRRRRRRRR
RRRR
RRRRR
TAP
LET ME SHOW YOU...
WHAT YOU CAME TO FIND!
SNAP
KLANG
KLANG
KLANG
KLANG

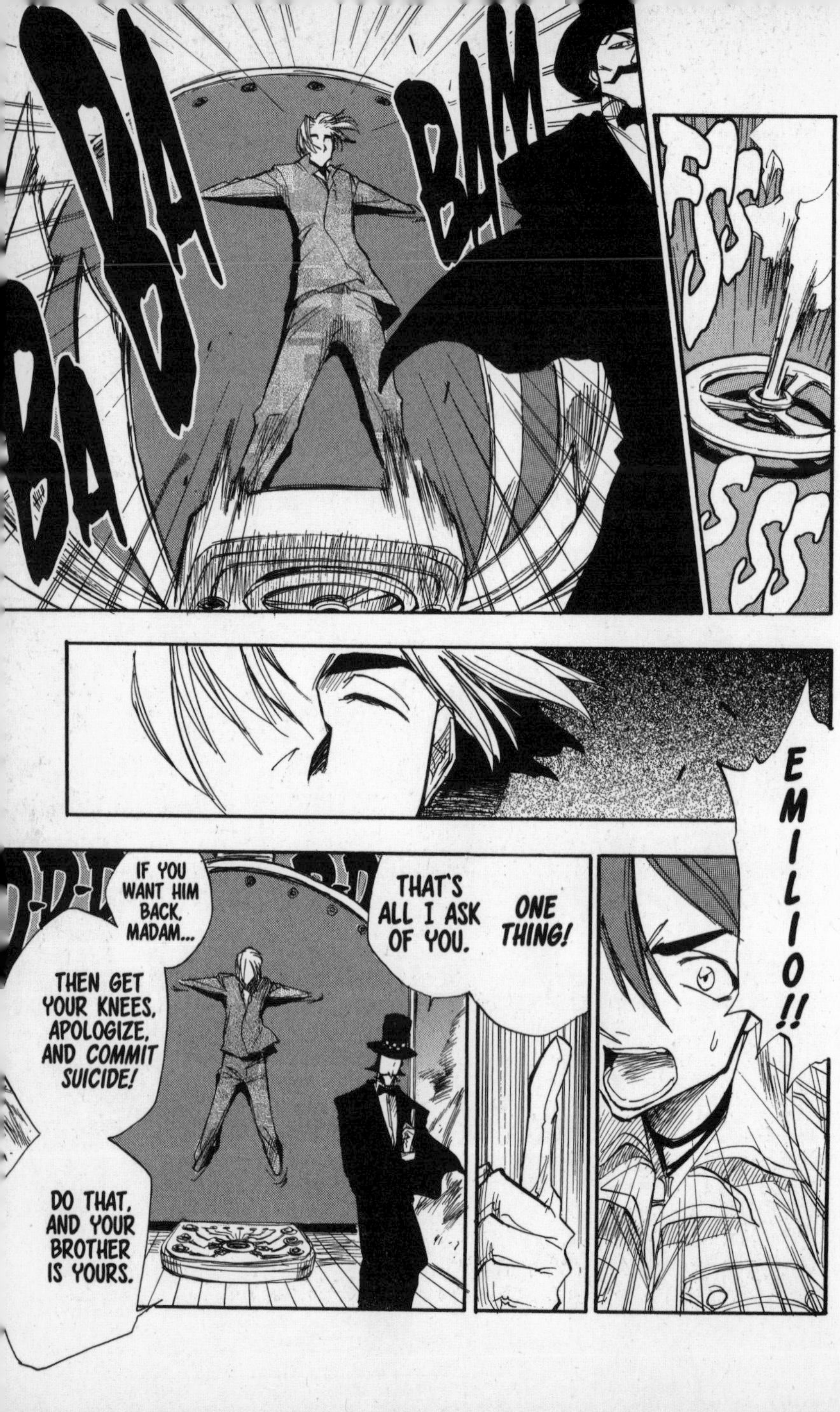
BABA
BAM
EMILIO!!
ONE THING!
THAT'S ALL I ASK OF YOU.
IF YOU WANT HIM BACK, MADAM...
THEN GET YOUR KNEES, APOLOGIZE, AND COMMIT SUICIDE!
DO THAT, AND YOUR BROTHER IS YOURS.

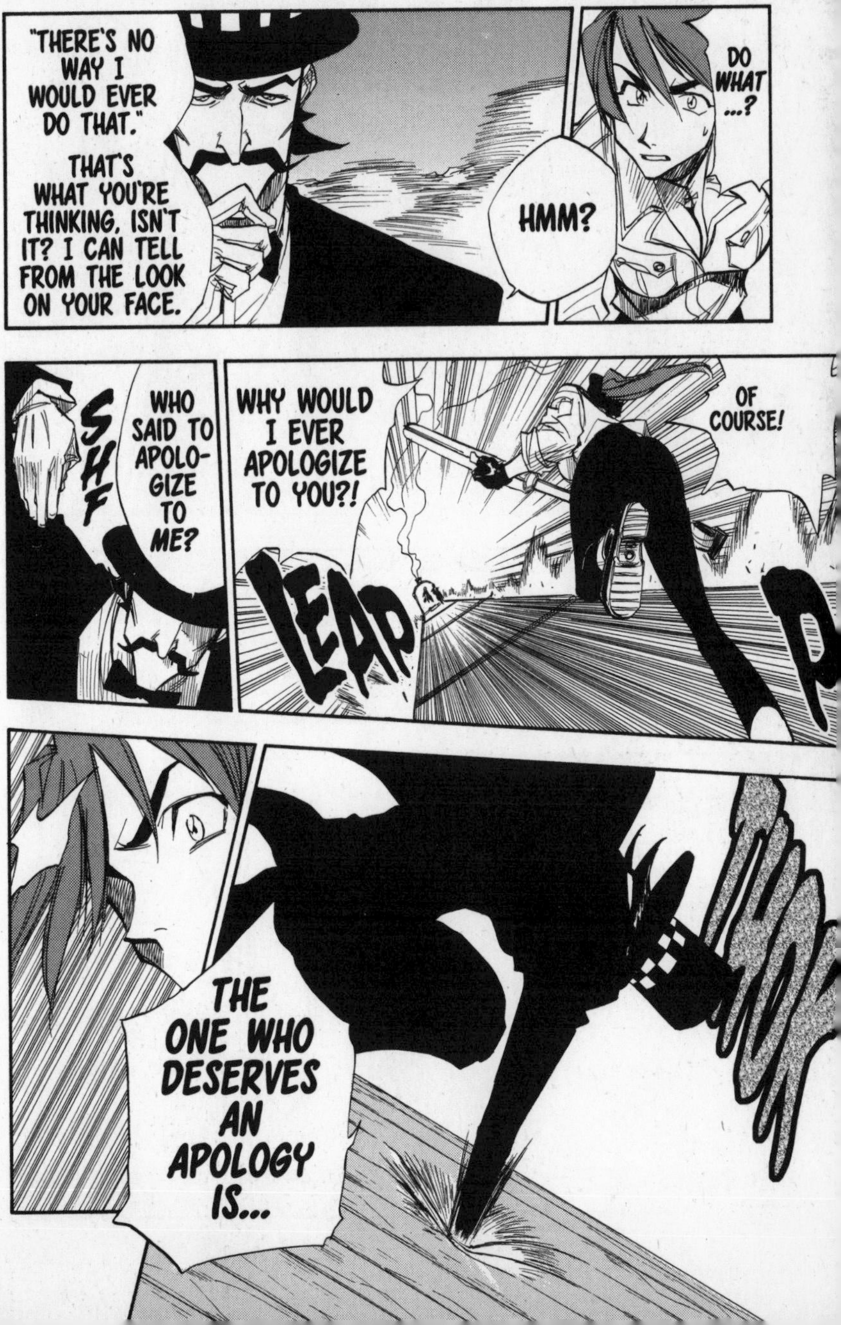
DO WHAT ...?
HMM?
"THERE'S NO WAY I WOULD EVER DO THAT."
THAT'S WHAT YOU'RE THINKING, ISN'T IT? I CAN TELL FROM THE LOOK ON YOUR FACE.
OF COURSE!
WHY WOULD I EVER APOLOGIZE TO YOU?!
LEAP
SHF
WHO SAID TO APOLO-GIZE TO ME?
THE ONE WHO DESERVES AN APOLOGY IS...

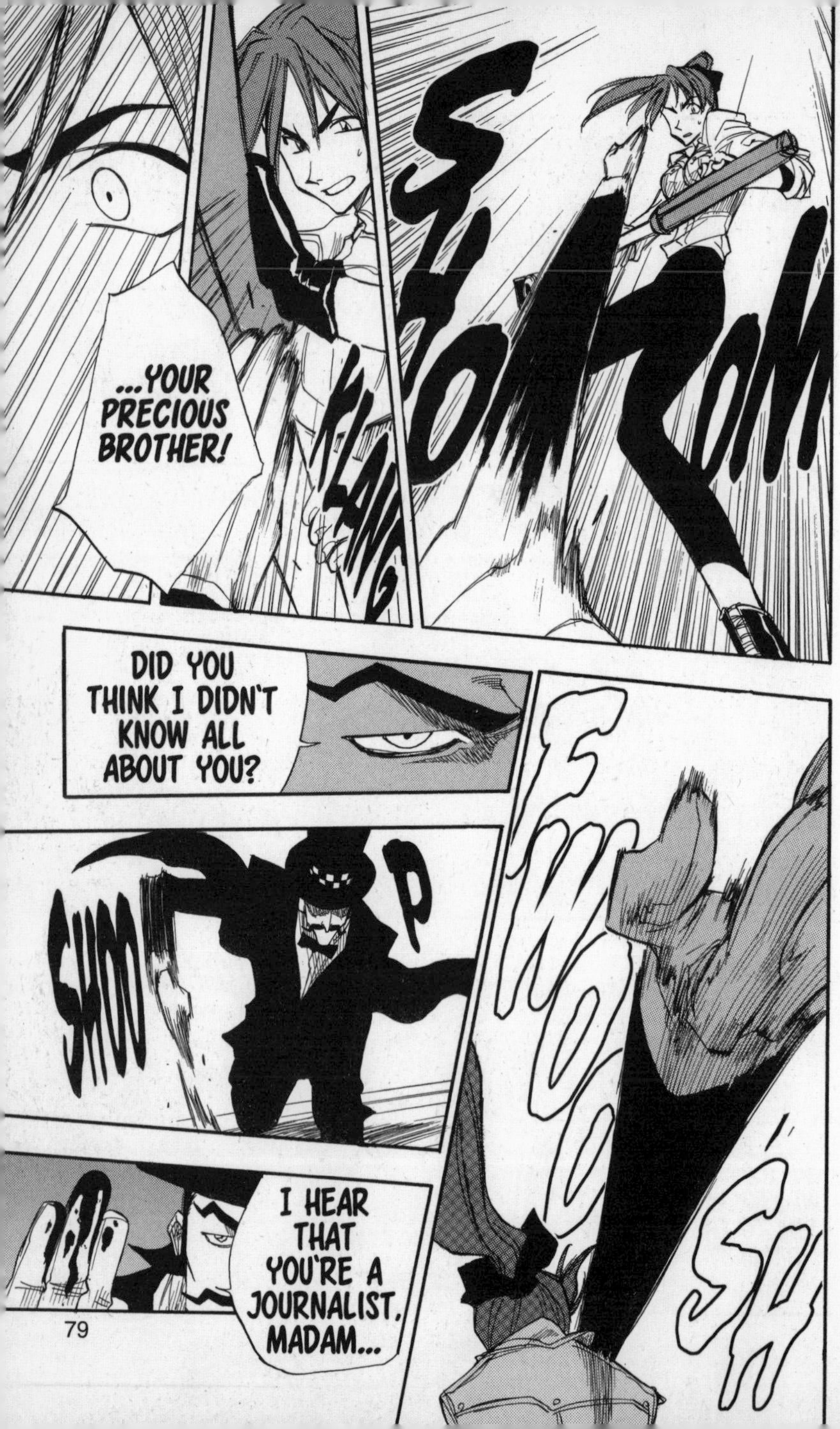
KLANG
...YOUR PRECIOUS BROTHER!
DID YOU THINK I DIDN'T KNOW ALL ABOUT YOU?
SHOOP
I HEAR THAT YOU'RE A JOURNALIST, MADAM...

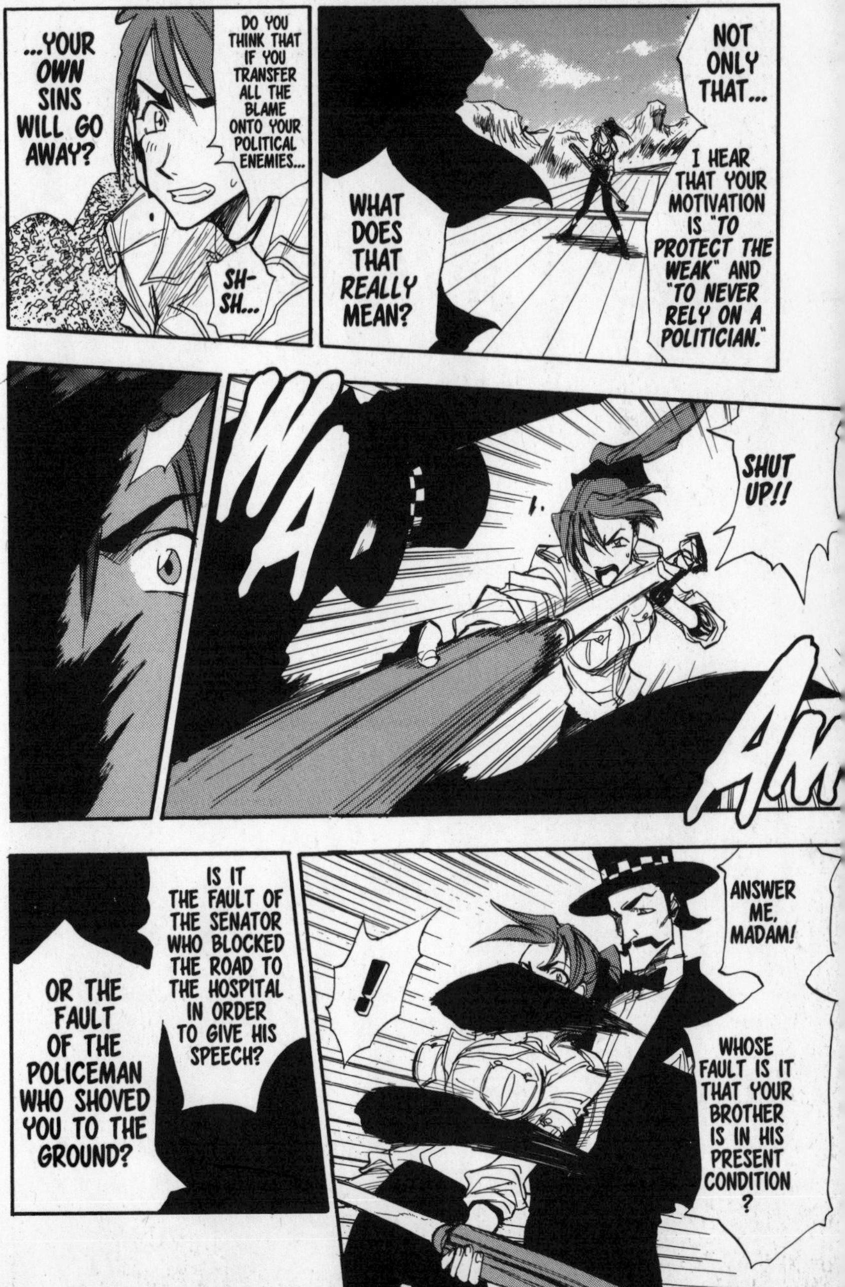
NOT ONLY THAT...
I HEAR THAT YOUR MOTIVATION IS "TO PROTECT THE WEAK" AND "TO NEVER RELY ON A POLITICIAN."
WHAT DOES THAT REALLY MEAN?
DO YOU THINK THAT IF YOU TRANSFER ALL THE BLAME ONTO YOUR POLITICAL ENEMIES...
...YOUR OWN SINS WILL GO AWAY?
SH-SH...
SHUT UP!!
ANSWER ME, MADAM!
!
WHOSE FAULT IS IT THAT YOUR BROTHER IS IN HIS PRESENT CONDITION?
IS IT THE FAULT OF THE SENATOR WHO BLOCKED THE ROAD TO THE HOSPITAL IN ORDER TO GIVE HIS SPEECH?
OR THE FAULT OF THE POLICEMAN WHO SHOVED YOU TO THE GROUND?

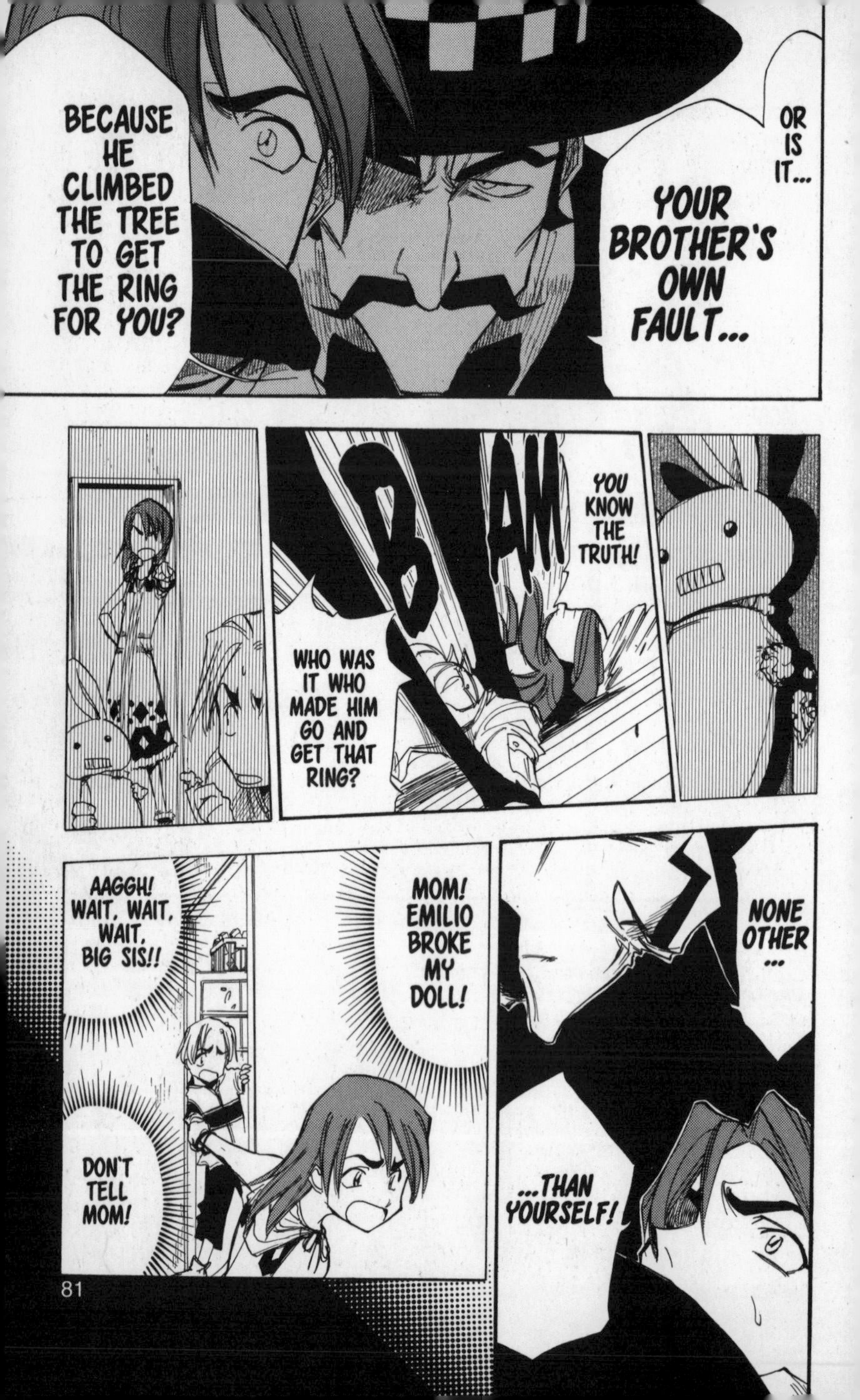
OR IS IT...
YOUR BROTHER'S OWN FAULT...
BECAUSE HE CLIMBED THE TREE TO GET THE RING FOR YOU?
BAM
YOU KNOW THE TRUTH!
WHO WAS IT WHO MADE HIM GO AND GET THAT RING?
NONE OTHER...
...THAN YOURSELF!
MOM! EMILIO BROKE MY DOLL!
AAGGH! WAIT, WAIT, WAIT, BIG SIS!!
DON'T TELL MOM!

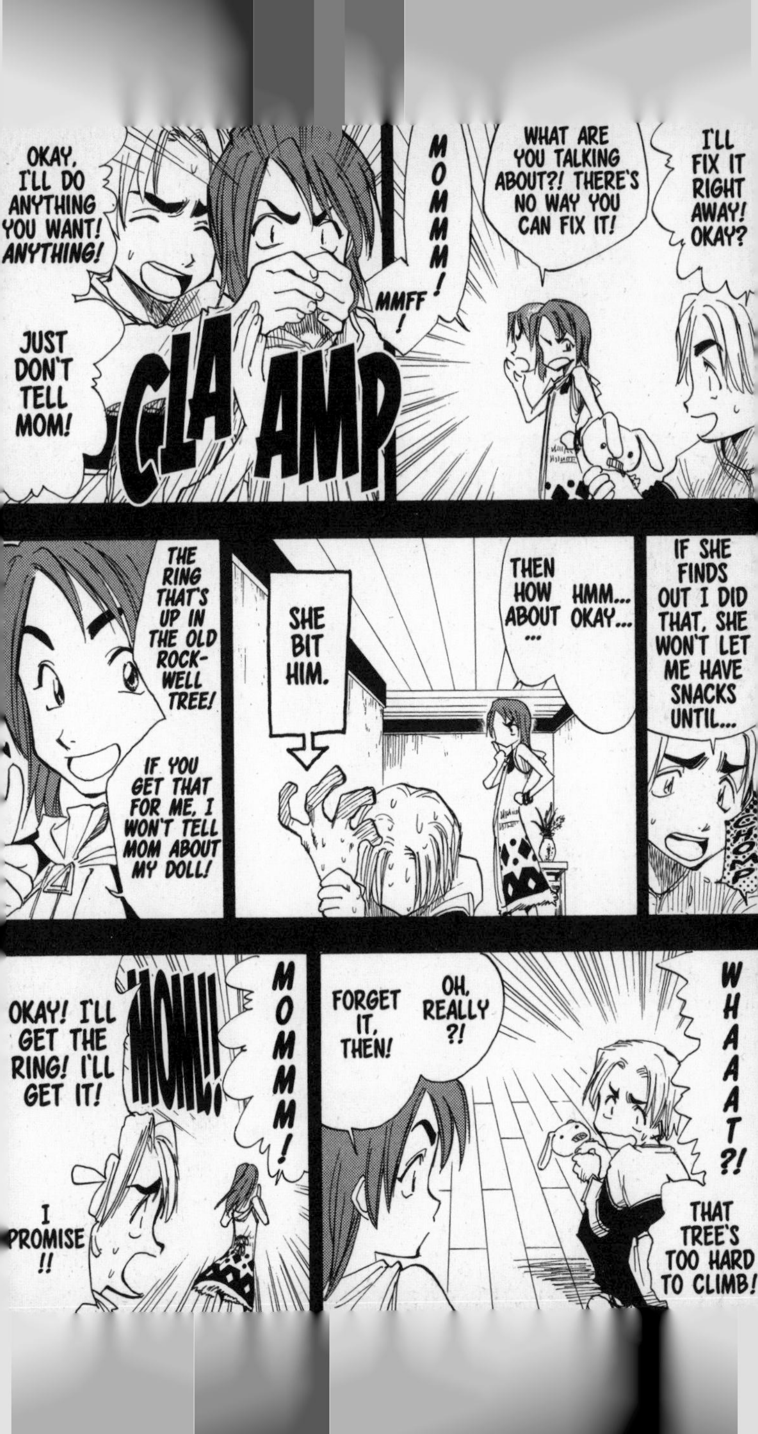
I'LL FIX IT RIGHT AWAY! OKAY?
WHAT ARE YOU TALKING ABOUT?! THERE'S NO WAY YOU CAN FIX IT!
MOMMMM!
MMFF!
OKAY, I'LL DO ANYTHING YOU WANT! ANYTHING!
JUST DON'T TELL MOM!
CLA AMP
IF SHE FINDS OUT I DID THAT, SHE WON'T LET ME HAVE SNACKS UNTIL...
CHOMP
HMM... OKAY...
THEN HOW ABOUT ...
SHE BIT HIM.
THE RING THAT'S UP IN THE OLD ROCK-WELL TREE!
IF YOU GET THAT FOR ME, I WON'T TELL MOM ABOUT MY DOLL!
WHAAAAT?!
THAT TREE'S TOO HARD TO CLIMB!
OH, REALLY?!
FORGET IT, THEN!
MOMMMM!
MOM!!
OKAY! I'LL GET THE RING! I'LL GET IT!
I PROMISE!!

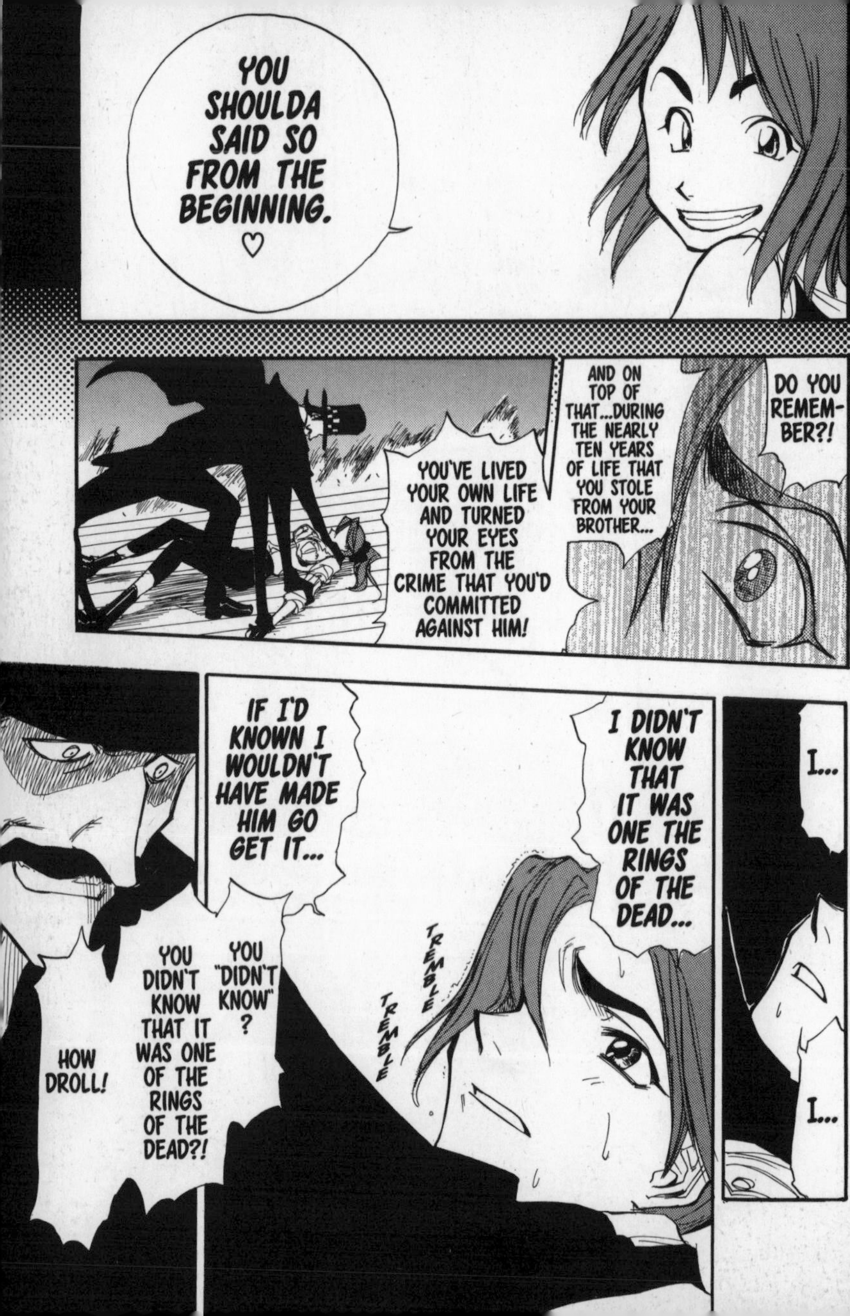
YOU SHOULDA SAID SO FROM THE BEGINNING. ♡
DO YOU REMEMBER?!
AND ON TOP OF THAT...DURING THE NEARLY TEN YEARS OF LIFE THAT YOU STOLE FROM YOUR BROTHER...
YOU'VE LIVED YOUR OWN LIFE AND TURNED YOUR EYES FROM THE CRIME THAT YOU'D COMMITTED AGAINST HIM!
I...
I...
I DIDN'T KNOW THAT IT WAS ONE THE RINGS OF THE DEAD...
IF I'D KNOWN I WOULDN'T HAVE MADE HIM GO GET IT...
TREMBLE
TREMBLE
YOU "DIDN'T KNOW"?
YOU DIDN'T KNOW THAT IT WAS ONE OF THE RINGS OF THE DEAD?!
HOW DROLL!

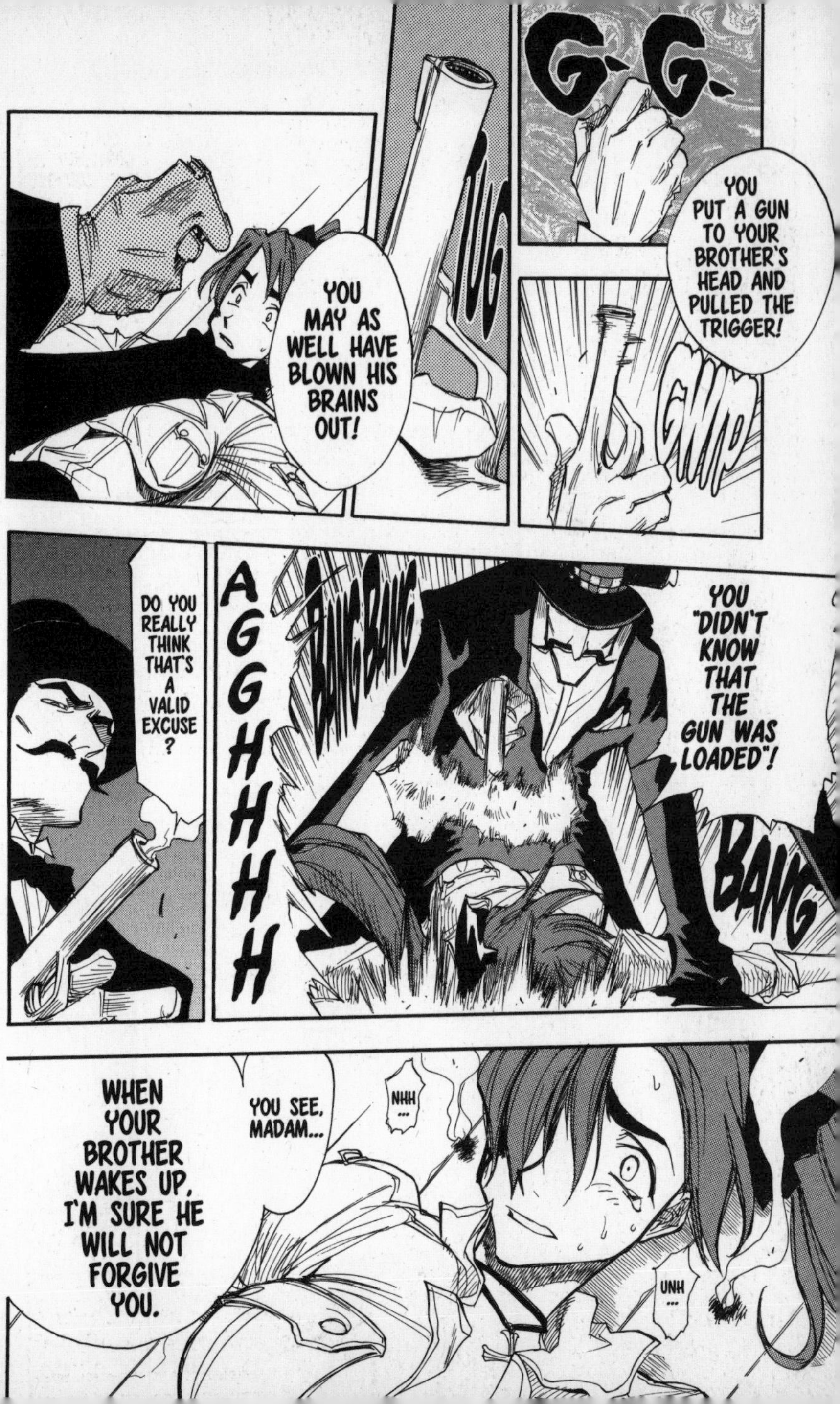
G-G-
YOU PUT A GUN TO YOUR BROTHER'S HEAD AND PULLED THE TRIGGER!
GMP
TUG
YOU MAY AS WELL HAVE BLOWN HIS BRAINS OUT!
YOU "DIDN'T KNOW THAT THE GUN WAS LOADED"!
BANG
BANG BANG
AGGHHHHH
DO YOU REALLY THINK THAT'S A VALID EXCUSE?
NHH...
UNH...
YOU SEE, MADAM...
WHEN YOUR BROTHER WAKES UP, I'M SURE HE WILL NOT FORGIVE YOU.

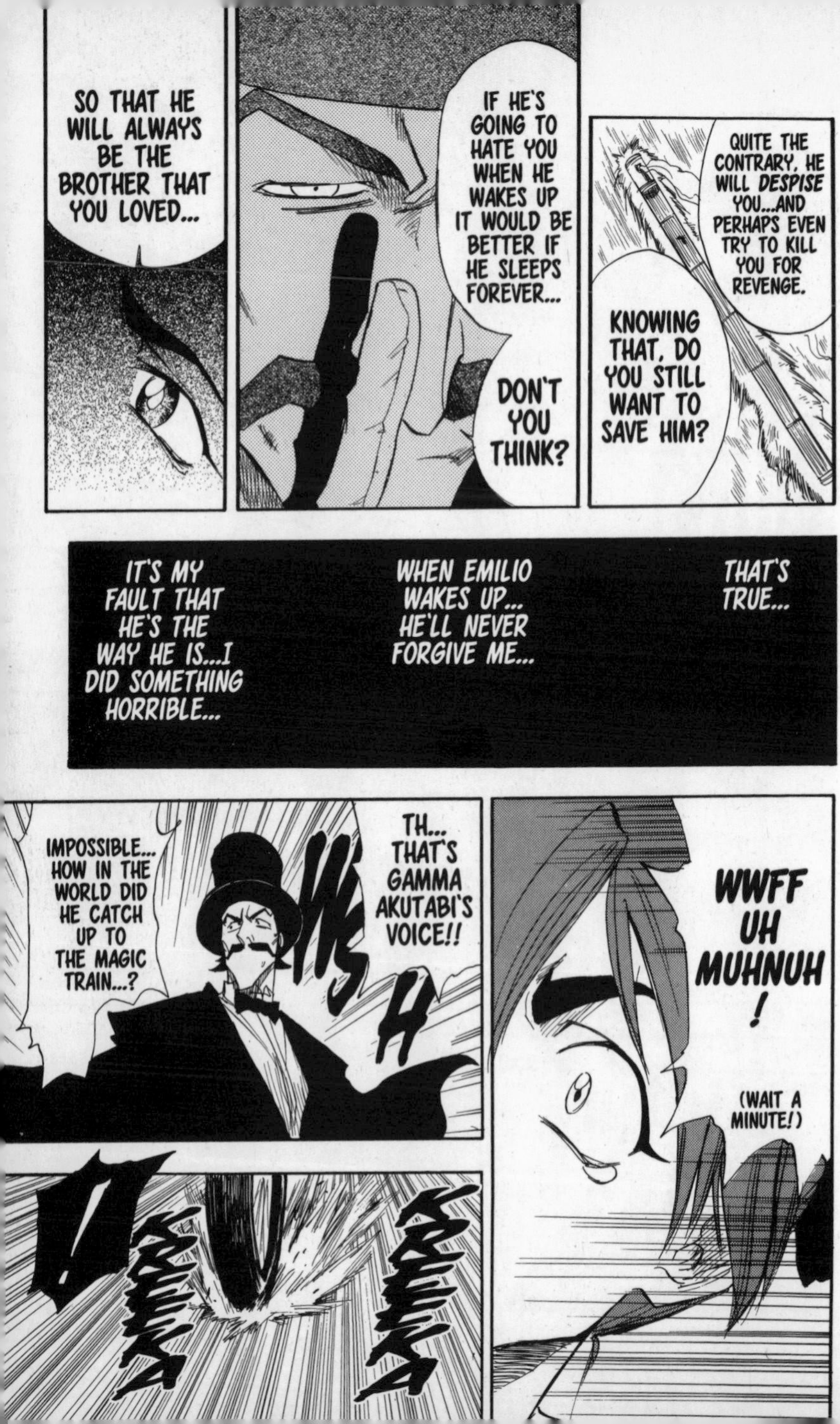
QUITE THE CONTRARY, HE WILL DESPISE YOU...AND PERHAPS EVEN TRY TO KILL YOU FOR REVENGE.
KNOWING THAT, DO YOU STILL WANT TO SAVE HIM?
IF HE'S GOING TO HATE YOU WHEN HE WAKES UP IT WOULD BE BETTER IF HE SLEEPS FOREVER...
DON'T YOU THINK?
SO THAT HE WILL ALWAYS BE THE BROTHER THAT YOU LOVED...
THAT'S TRUE...
WHEN EMILIO WAKES UP... HE'LL NEVER FORGIVE ME...
IT'S MY FAULT THAT HE'S THE WAY HE IS...I DID SOMETHING HORRIBLE...
WWFF UH MUHNUH!
(WAIT A MINUTE!)
TH... THAT'S GAMMA AKUTABI'S VOICE!!
IMPOSSIBLE... HOW IN THE WORLD DID HE CATCH UP TO THE MAGIC TRAIN...?

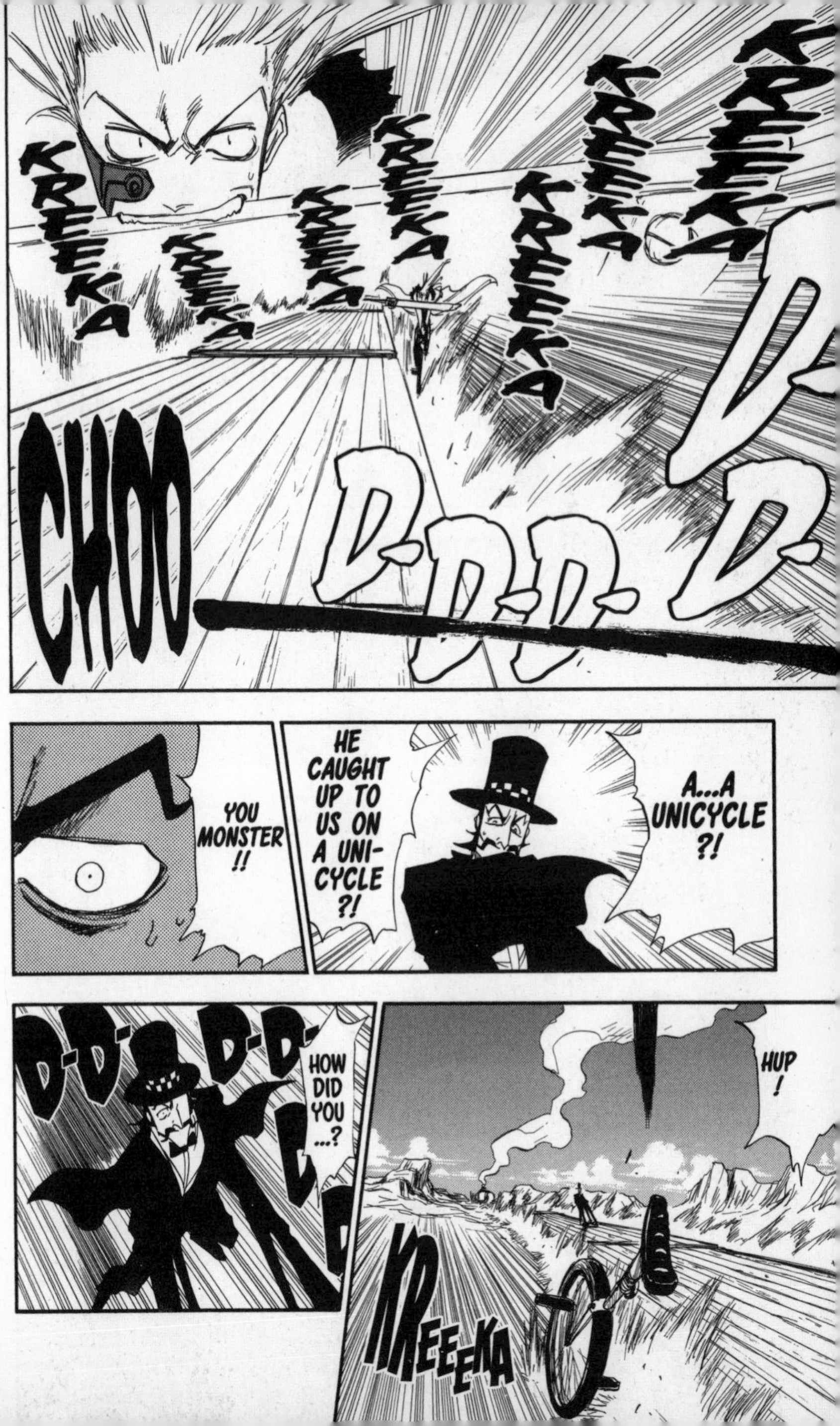
KREEKA
KREEKA
KREEKA
KREEKA
KREEKA
KREEKA
KREEKA
D-D-D-D-D
CHOO
A...A UNICYCLE ?!
HE CAUGHT UP TO US ON A UNI-CYCLE ?!
YOU MONSTER !!
HUP !
KREEEKA
HOW DID YOU ...?
D-D-D-D-D

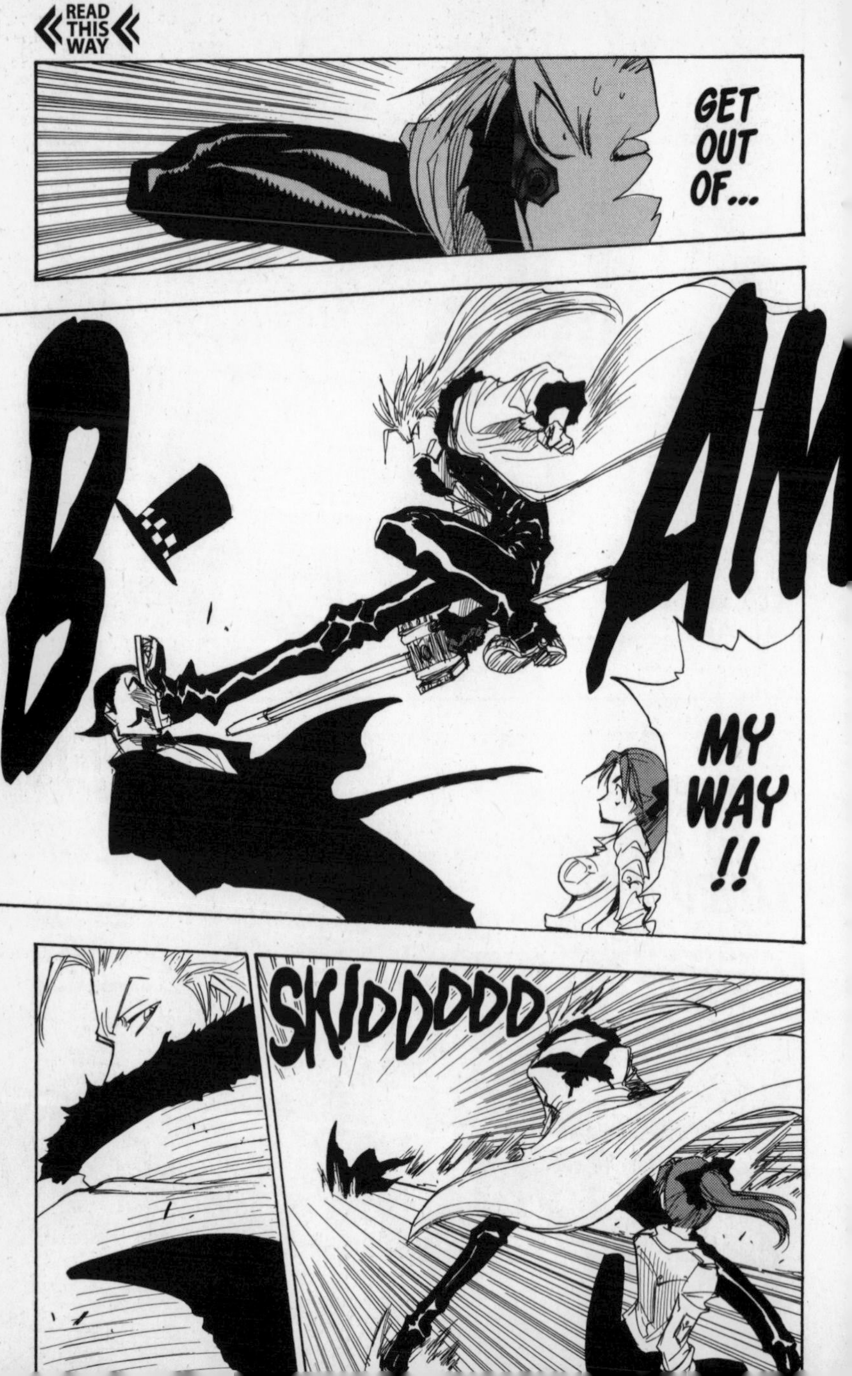
READ THIS WAY
GET OUT OF...
B-AM
MY WAY !!
SKIDDDDD

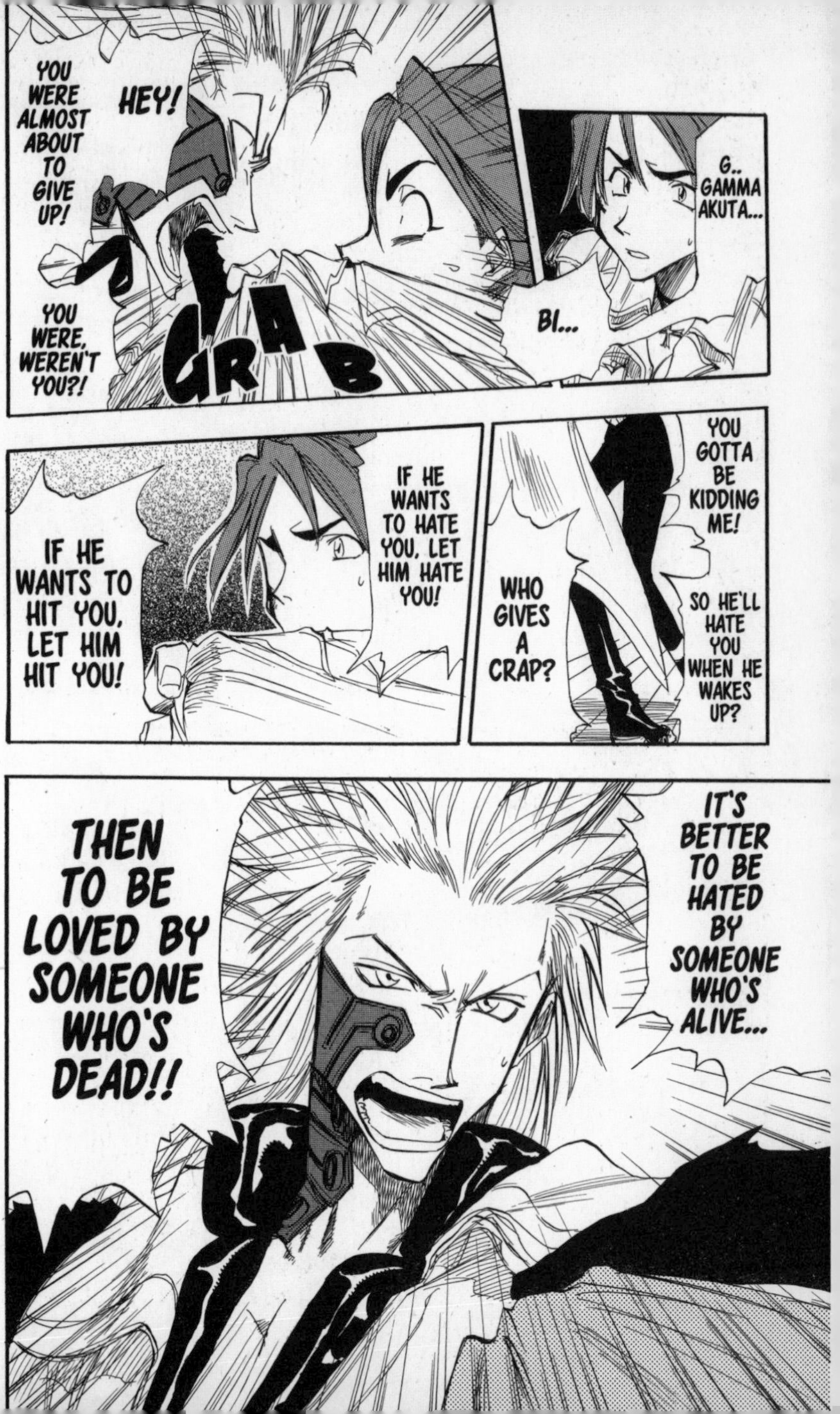
G.. GAMMA AKUTA...
BI...
HEY!
YOU WERE ALMOST ABOUT TO GIVE UP!
GRAB
YOU WERE, WEREN'T YOU?!
YOU GOTTA BE KIDDING ME!
SO HE'LL HATE YOU WHEN HE WAKES UP?
WHO GIVES A CRAP?
IF HE WANTS TO HATE YOU, LET HIM HATE YOU!
IF HE WANTS TO HIT YOU, LET HIM HIT YOU!
IT'S BETTER TO BE HATED BY SOMEONE WHO'S ALIVE...
THEN TO BE LOVED BY SOMEONE WHO'S DEAD!!

READ THIS WAY

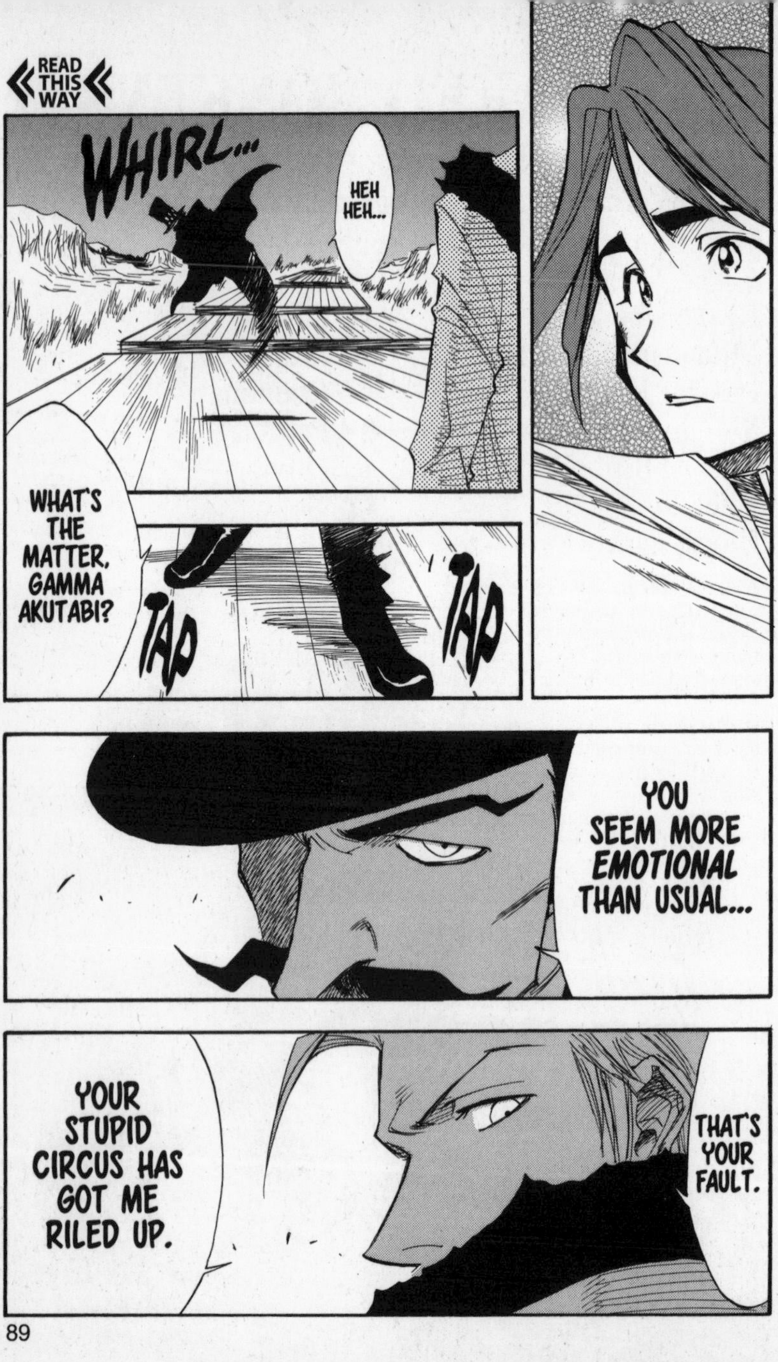
HEH HEH...
WHIRL...
WHAT'S THE MATTER, GAMMA AKUTABI?
TAP
TAP
YOU SEEM MORE *EMOTIONAL* THAN USUAL...
THAT'S YOUR FAULT.
YOUR STUPID CIRCUS HAS GOT ME RILED UP.

B-side NAKED MONKEYS 12.

Midge "The Multitude" Falzon & Falzon Sisters #(ナンバー) 1~15

ミッジ "ザ・マルチチュード" ファルゾン&ファルゾン・シスターズ#(ナンバー) 1~15

Real Name:
Milan Gerald Falzon
Height: 177 cm
Weight: 62 kg
Date of Birth: 7/28
Age: 28
Blood Type: O

Assistant ringmaster of the Balmunk Circus Troupe. His full name is Milan Gerald Falzon. Despite the fact that he wears a mask, is a sexual pervert, and is almost as crazy as Balmunk, he was for some reason the most popular character among female readers. Is a person's face the most important thing in the world after all? He lives with his 15 sisters who all have the same face and the same style of clothing. By the way, his sisters' names are listed to the right.

1 Scheela
2 Rina
3 Quentina
4 Patricia
5 Olivia
6 Nora
7 Lolita
8 Kistia
9 Juriana
10 Illva
11 Hestia
12 Geordina
13 Fiscana
14 Ewrina
15 Dorianna

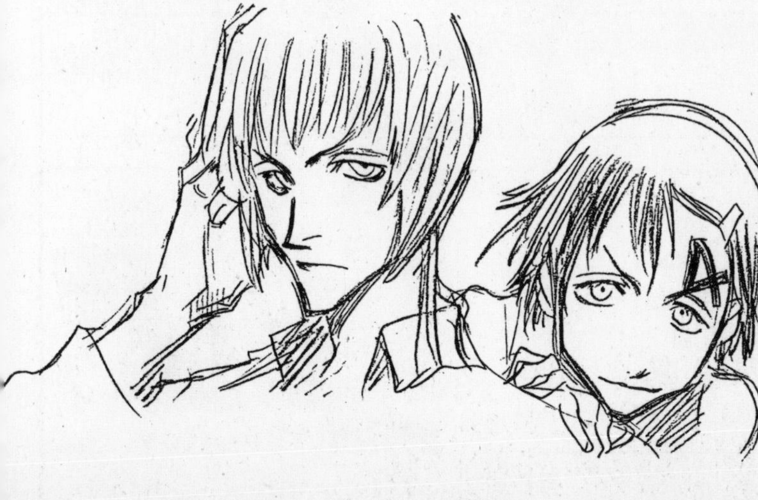

Track 19: Excoriated the Black Butterfly

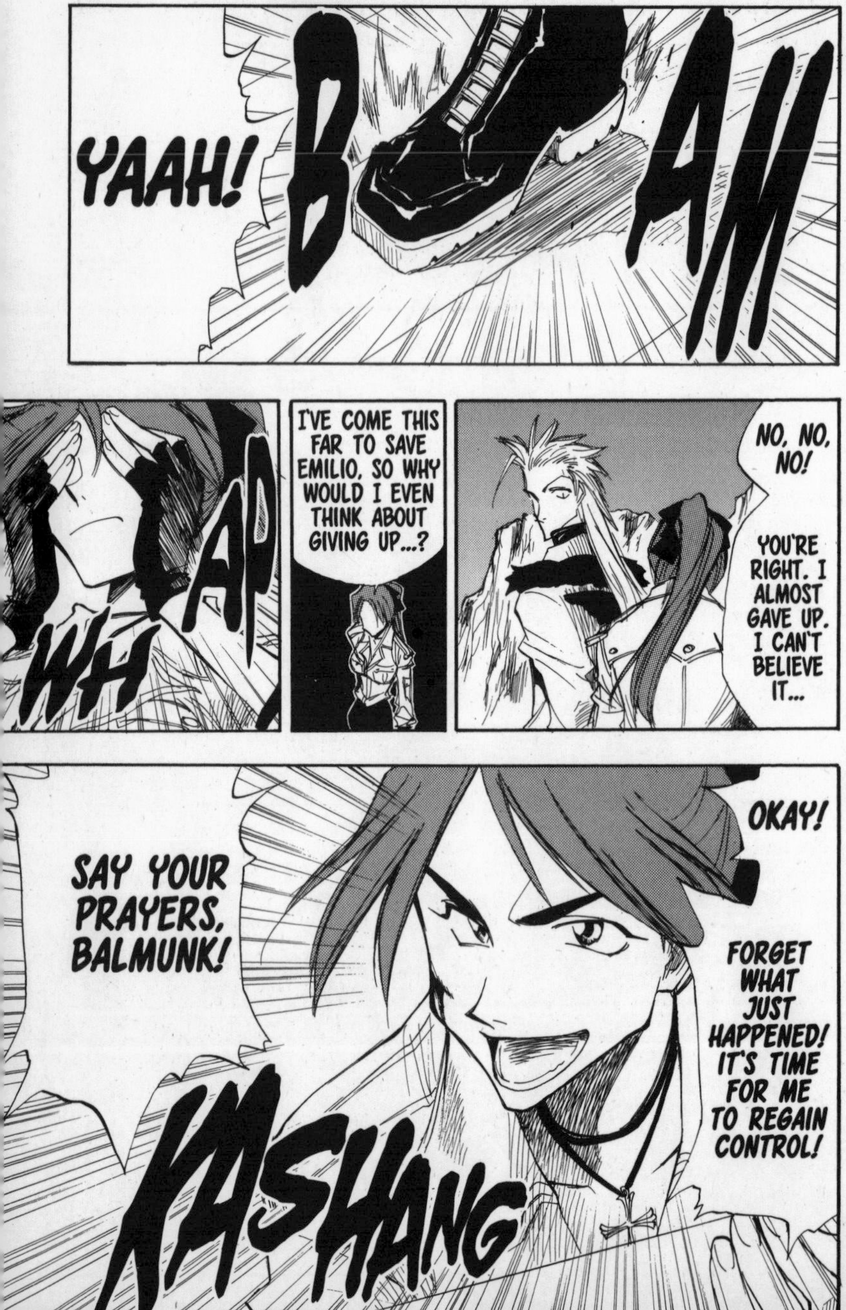
YAAH!
BAM
NO, NO, NO!
YOU'RE RIGHT. I ALMOST GAVE UP. I CAN'T BELIEVE IT...
I'VE COME THIS FAR TO SAVE EMILIO, SO WHY WOULD I EVEN THINK ABOUT GIVING UP...?
WHAP
OKAY!
FORGET WHAT JUST HAPPENED! IT'S TIME FOR ME TO REGAIN CONTROL!
SAY YOUR PRAYERS, BALMUNK!
KASHANG

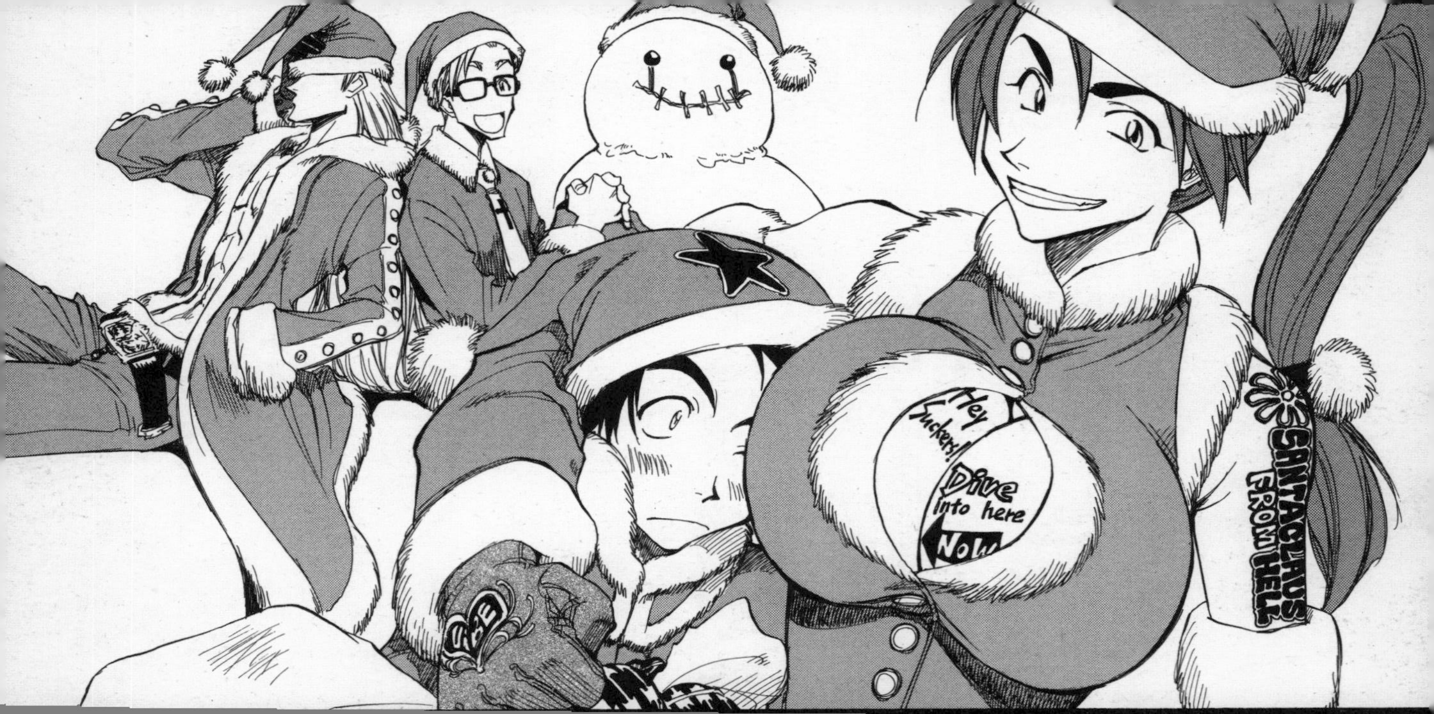
Hey Suckers!
Dive into here
Now
SANTACLAUS FROM HELL

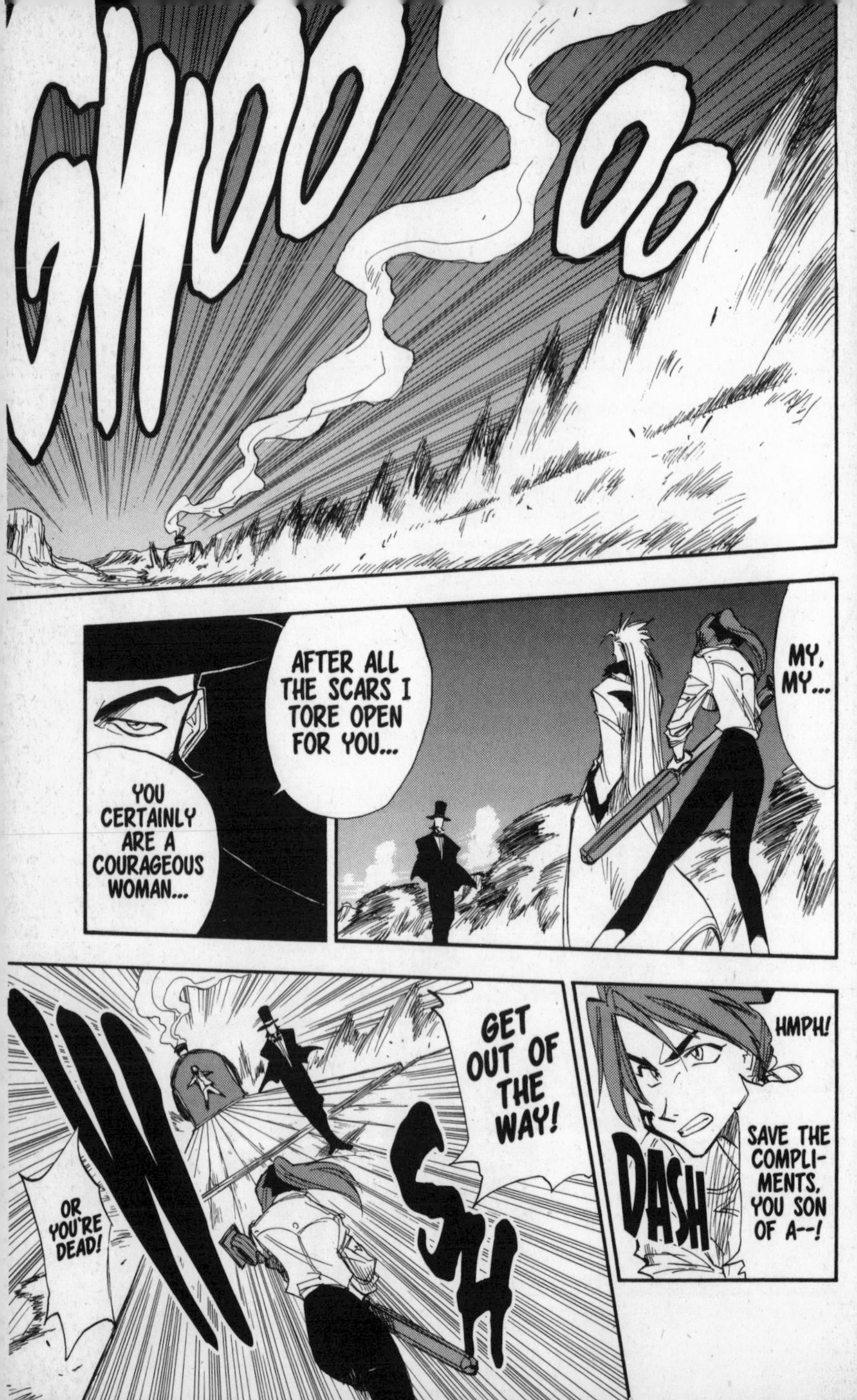
SWOOO-OO
MY, MY...
AFTER ALL THE SCARS I TORE OPEN FOR YOU...
YOU CERTAINLY ARE A COURAGEOUS WOMAN...
HMPH!
DASH
SAVE THE COMPLI-MENTS, YOU SON OF A--!
GET OUT OF THE WAY!
WSH
OR YOU'RE DEAD!

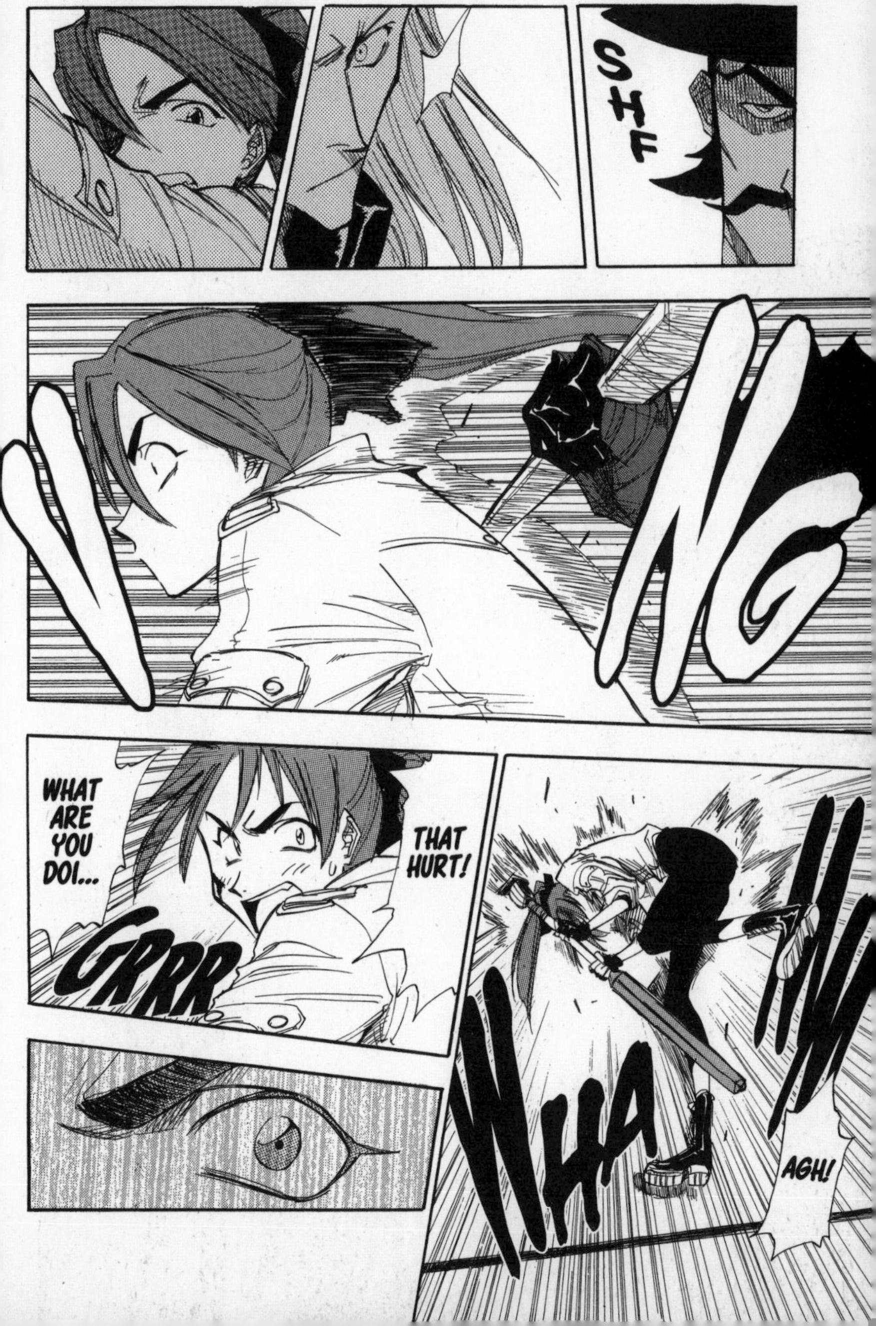
SHF
WHAM
AGH!
WHAT ARE YOU DOI...
THAT HURT!
GRRR

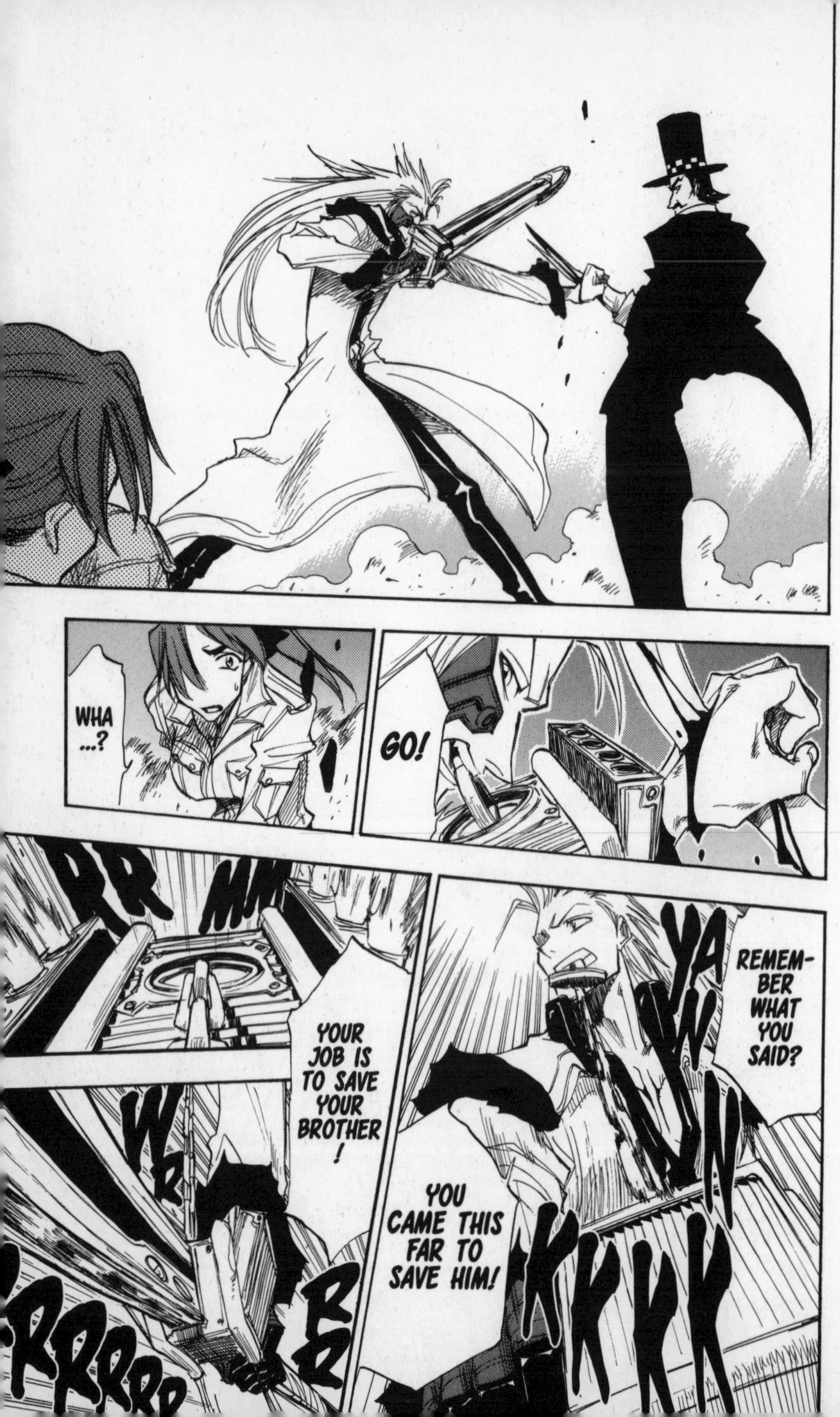
GO!
WHA ...?
REMEMBER WHAT YOU SAID?
YOUR JOB IS TO SAVE YOUR BROTHER!
YOU CAME THIS FAR TO SAVE HIM!

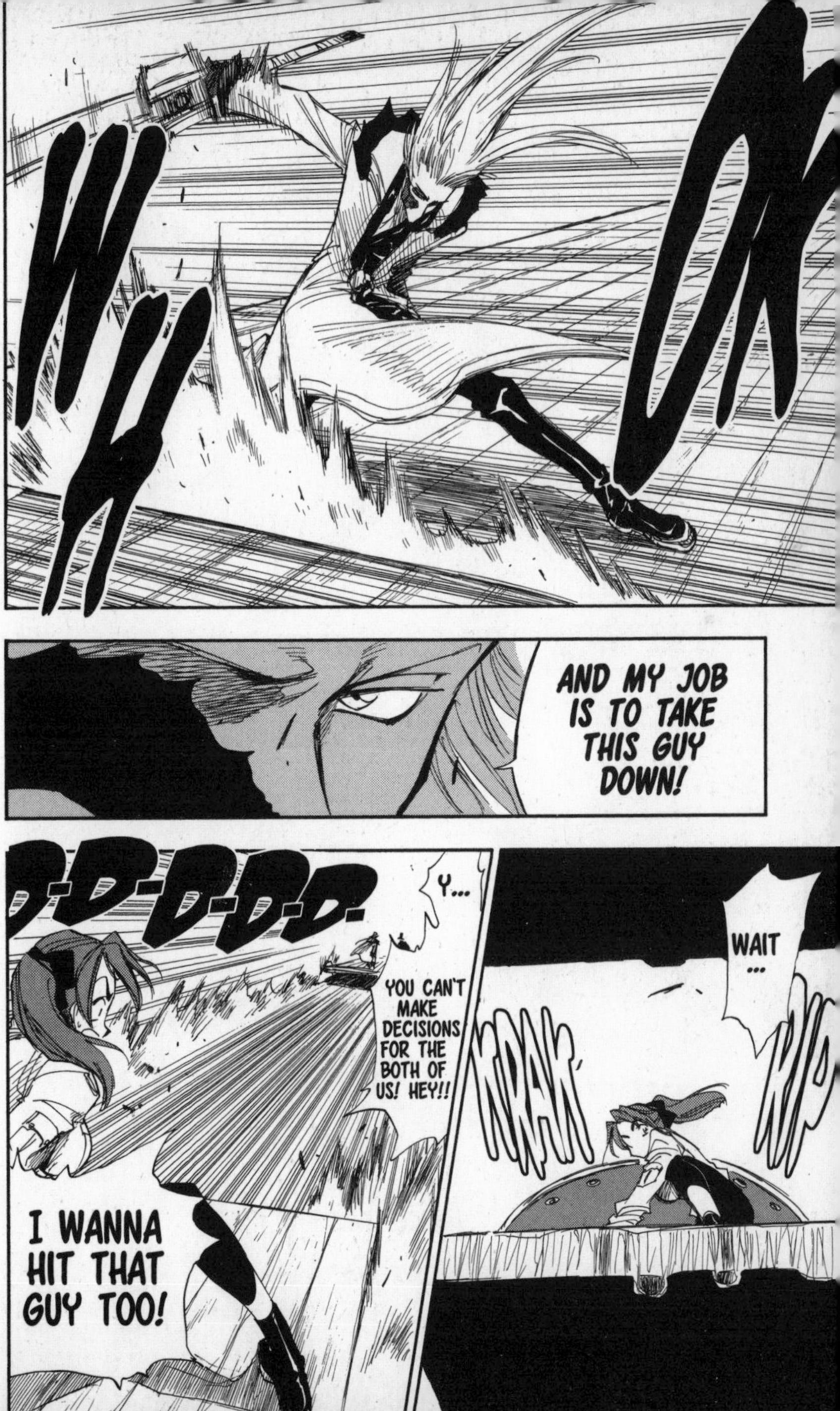
AND MY JOB IS TO TAKE THIS GUY DOWN!
WAIT ...
KRAK
Y...
YOU CAN'T MAKE DECISIONS FOR THE BOTH OF US! HEY!!
I WANNA HIT THAT GUY TOO!

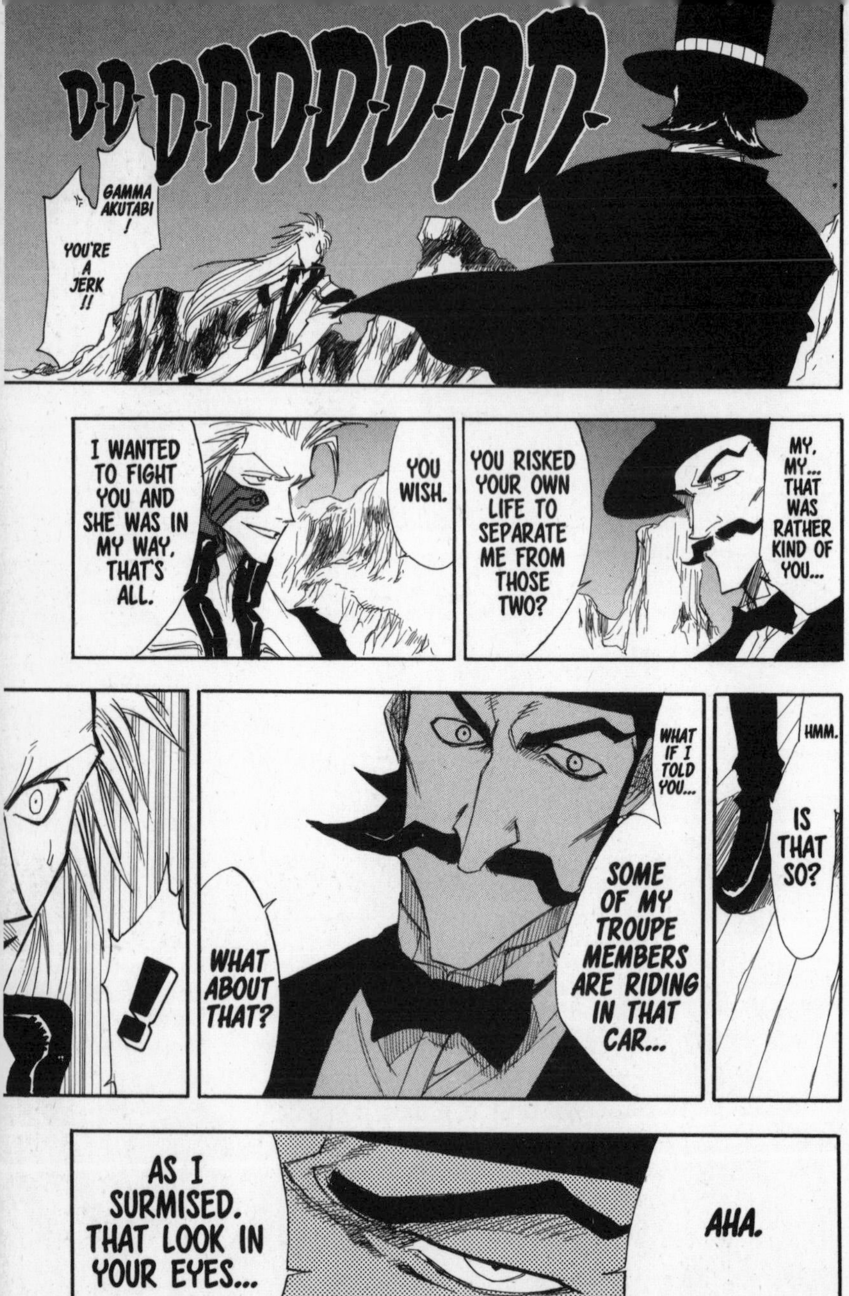
D-D-D-D-D-D-D-D-D
GAMMA AKUTABI!
YOU'RE A JERK!!
MY, MY... THAT WAS RATHER KIND OF YOU...
YOU RISKED YOUR OWN LIFE TO SEPARATE ME FROM THOSE TWO?
YOU WISH.
I WANTED TO FIGHT YOU AND SHE WAS IN MY WAY, THAT'S ALL.
HMM.
IS THAT SO?
WHAT IF I TOLD YOU...
SOME OF MY TROUPE MEMBERS ARE RIDING IN THAT CAR...
WHAT ABOUT THAT?
!
AHA.
AS I SURMISED. THAT LOOK IN YOUR EYES...

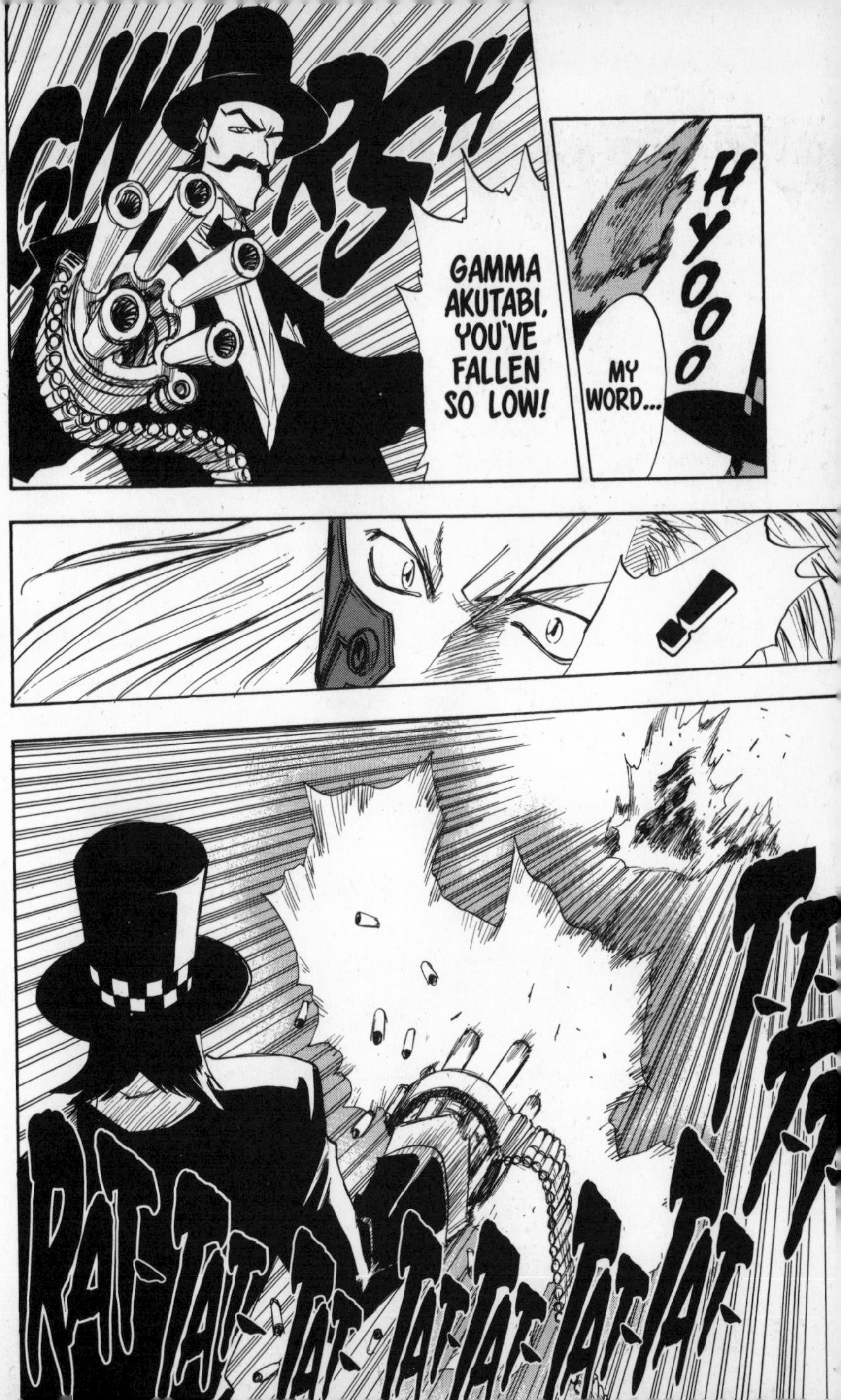
HYOOO
MY WORD...
GAMMA AKUTABI, YOU'VE FALLEN SO LOW!
!
RAT-TAT-TAT-TAT-TAT-TAT-TAT

READ THIS WAY

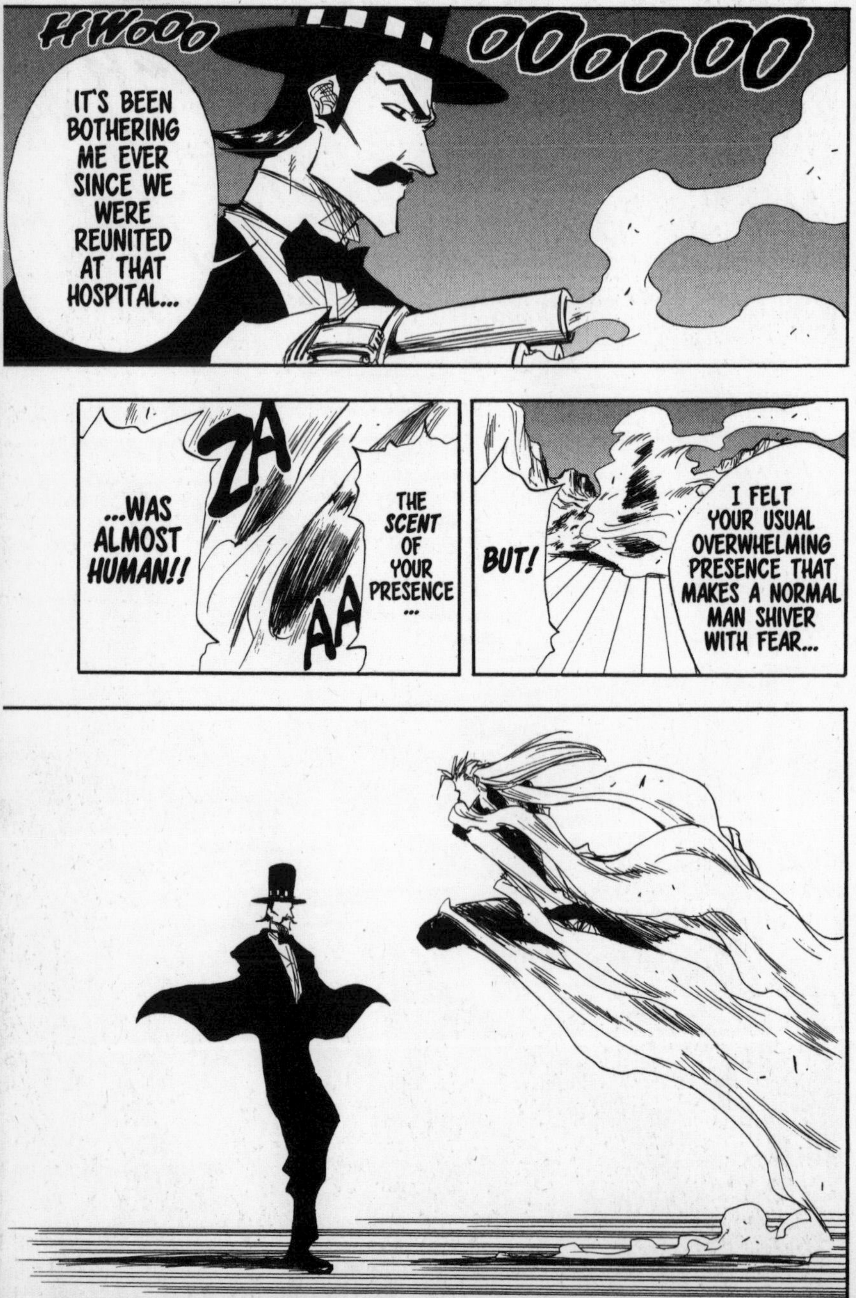
HWOOOOOOOOO
IT'S BEEN BOTHERING ME EVER SINCE WE WERE REUNITED AT THAT HOSPITAL...
I FELT YOUR USUAL OVERWHELMING PRESENCE THAT MAKES A NORMAL MAN SHIVER WITH FEAR...
BUT!
THE SCENT OF YOUR PRESENCE...
ZAAA
...WAS ALMOST HUMAN!!

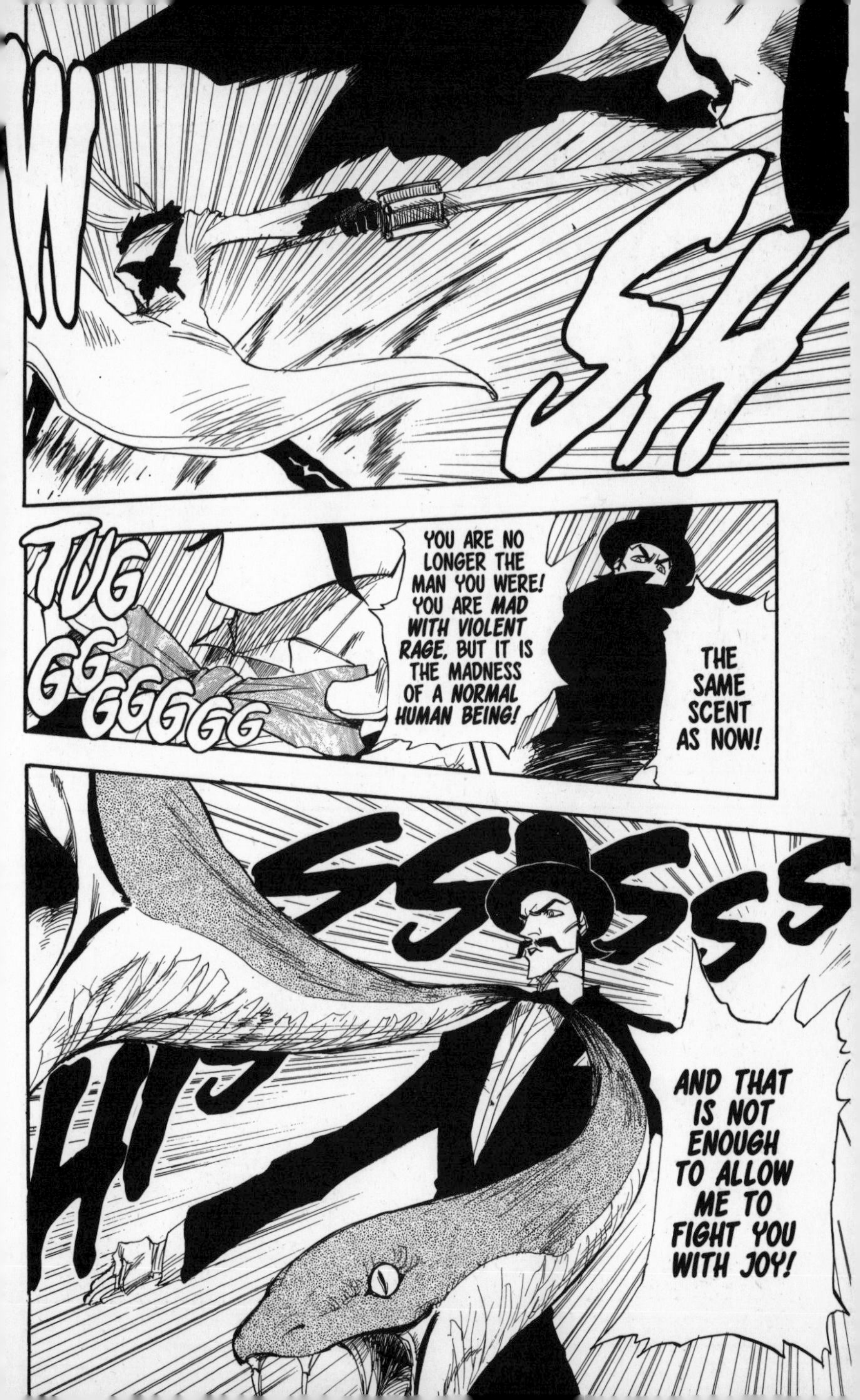
THE SAME SCENT AS NOW!
YOU ARE NO LONGER THE MAN YOU WERE! YOU ARE *MAD* WITH VIOLENT RAGE, BUT IT IS THE MADNESS OF A *NORMAL* HUMAN BEING!
TUGGGGGGGG
SSSSSS
AND THAT IS NOT ENOUGH TO ALLOW ME TO FIGHT YOU WITH JOY!

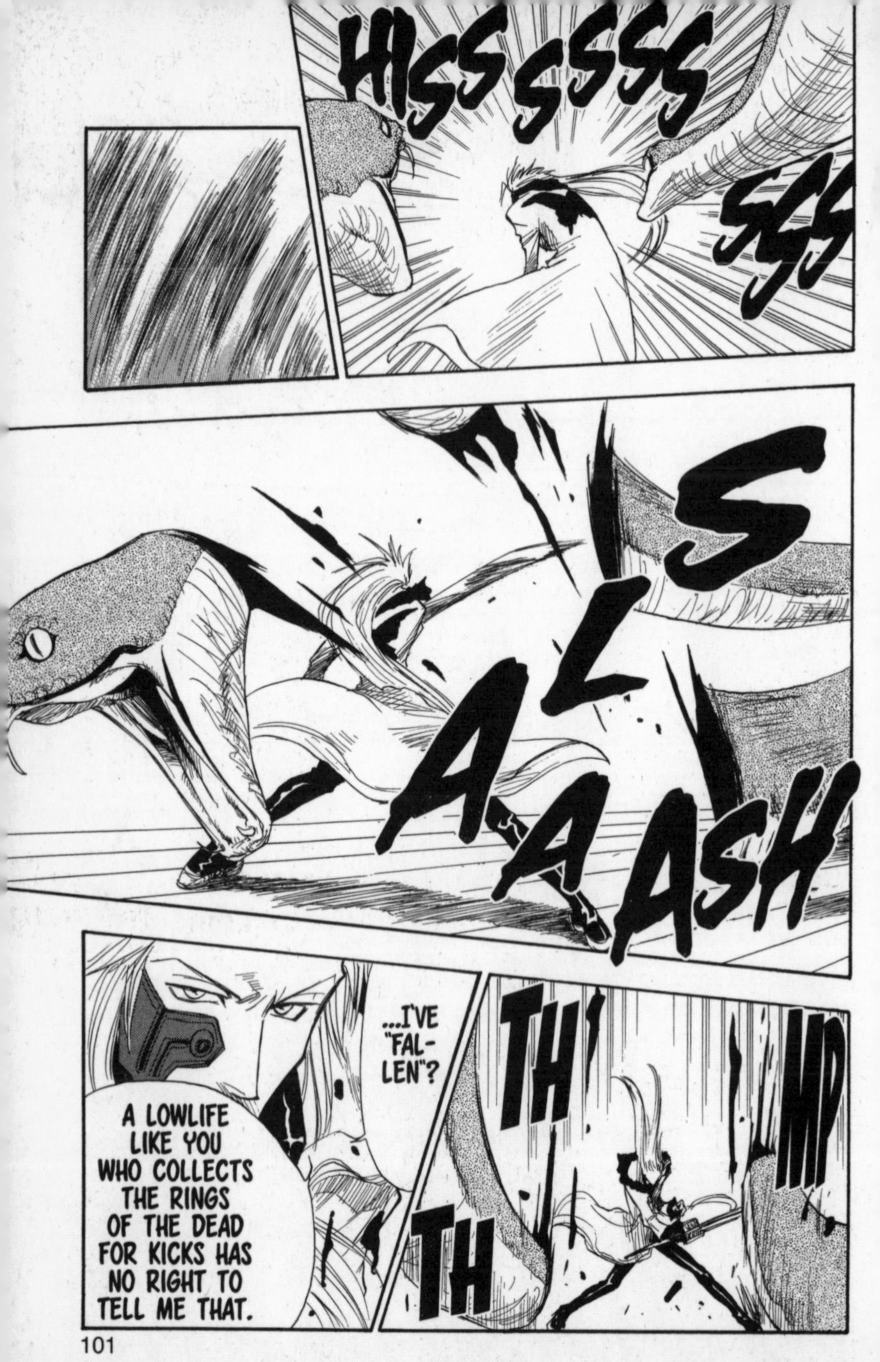
HISSSSSSS
SSS
SLAAASH
TH MP
TH
...I'VE "FAL-LEN"?
A LOWLIFE LIKE YOU WHO COLLECTS THE RINGS OF THE DEAD FOR KICKS HAS NO RIGHT TO TELL ME THAT.

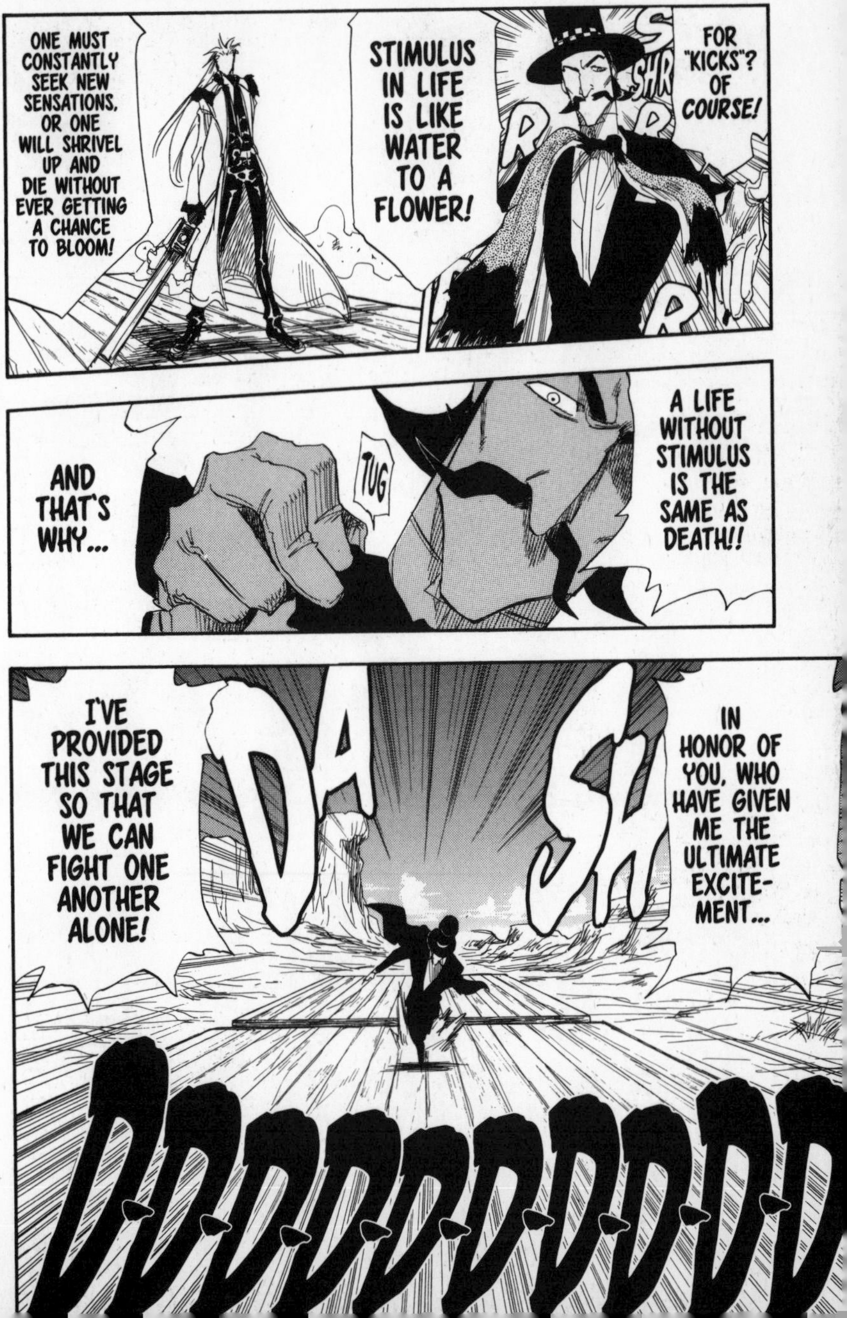
FOR "KICKS"? OF COURSE!
SHR
STIMULUS IN LIFE IS LIKE WATER TO A FLOWER!
ONE MUST CONSTANTLY SEEK NEW SENSATIONS, OR ONE WILL SHRIVEL UP AND DIE WITHOUT EVER GETTING A CHANCE TO BLOOM!
A LIFE WITHOUT STIMULUS IS THE SAME AS DEATH!!
TUG
AND THAT'S WHY...
IN HONOR OF YOU, WHO HAVE GIVEN ME THE ULTIMATE EXCITEMENT...
DASH
I'VE PROVIDED THIS STAGE SO THAT WE CAN FIGHT ONE ANOTHER ALONE!
DDDDDDDDDD

READ THIS WAY

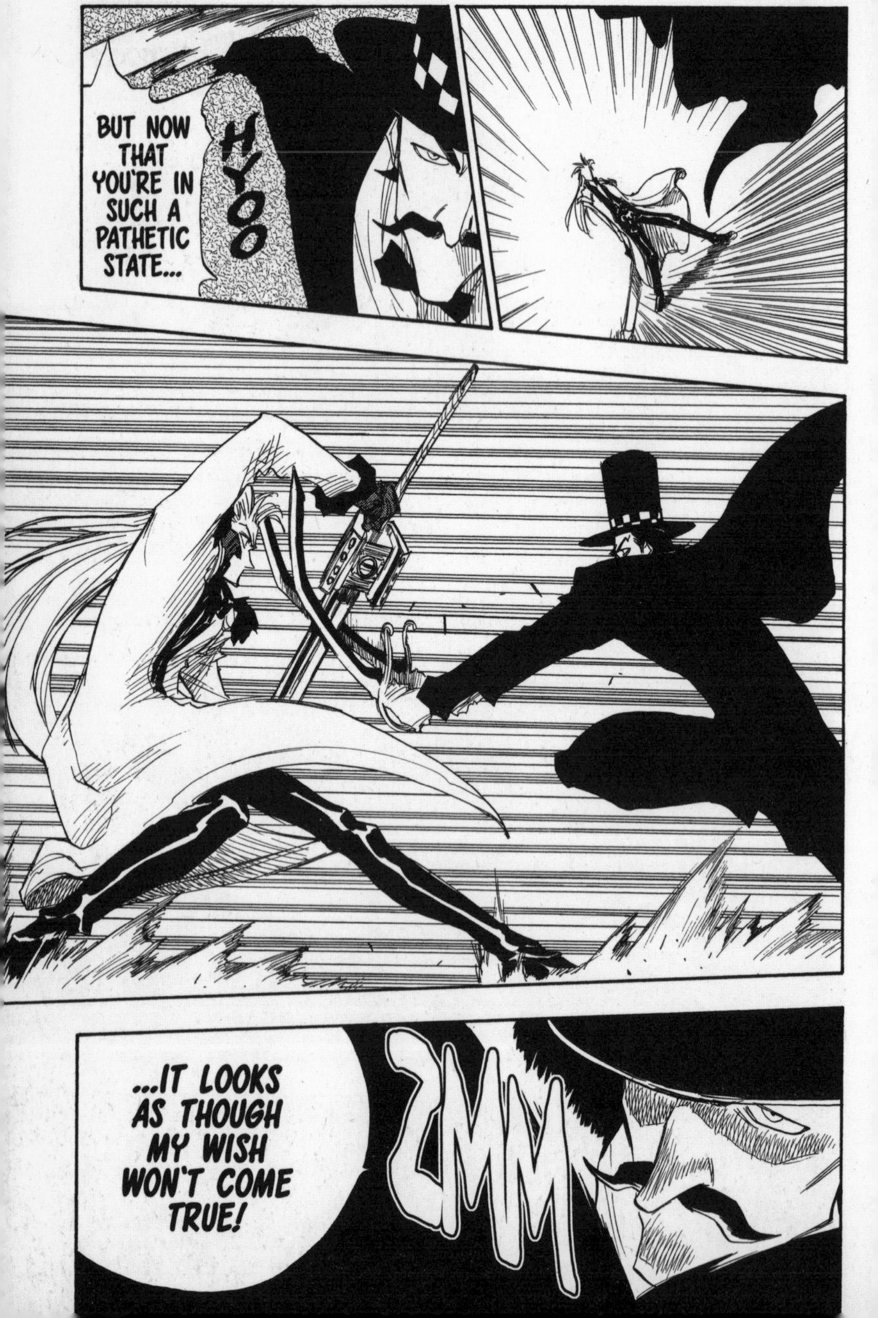
HYOO
BUT NOW THAT YOU'RE IN SUCH A PATHETIC STATE...
ZMM
...IT LOOKS AS THOUGH MY WISH WON'T COME TRUE!

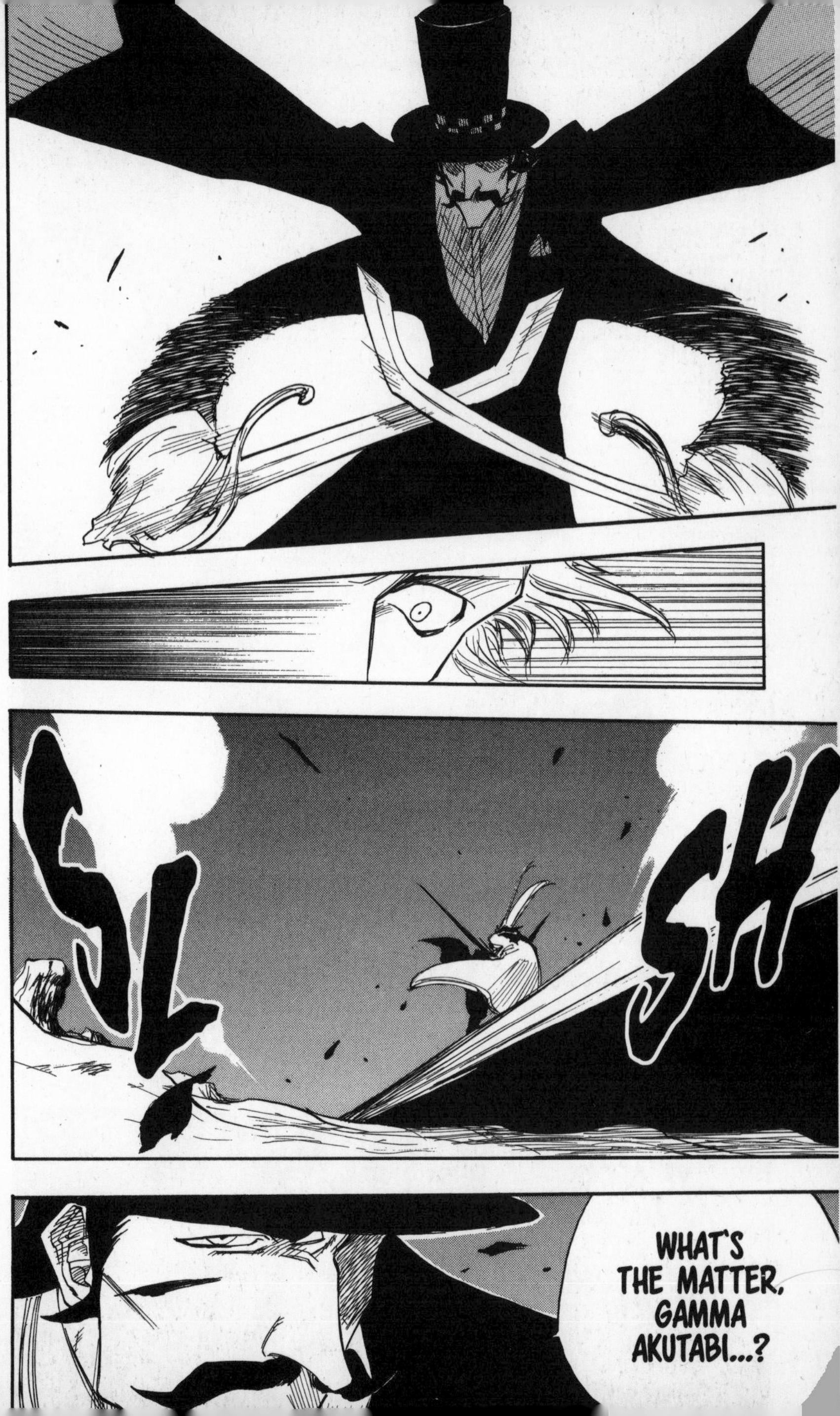
SLSH
WHAT'S THE MATTER, GAMMA AKUTABI...?

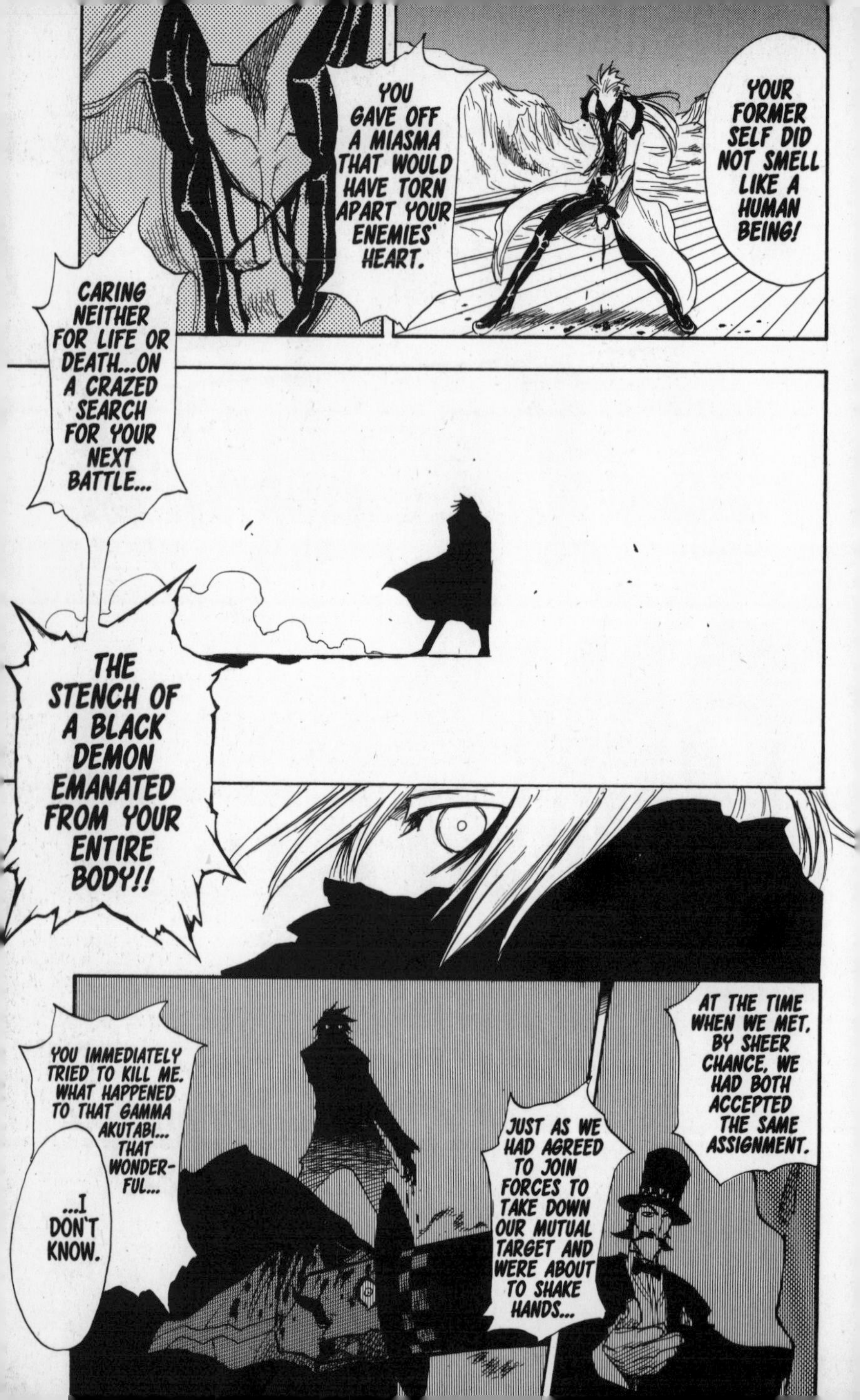
YOUR FORMER SELF DID NOT SMELL LIKE A HUMAN BEING!
YOU GAVE OFF A MIASMA THAT WOULD HAVE TORN APART YOUR ENEMIES' HEART.
CARING NEITHER FOR LIFE OR DEATH...ON A CRAZED SEARCH FOR YOUR NEXT BATTLE...
THE STENCH OF A BLACK DEMON EMANATED FROM YOUR ENTIRE BODY!!
AT THE TIME WHEN WE MET, BY SHEER CHANCE, WE HAD BOTH ACCEPTED THE SAME ASSIGNMENT.
JUST AS WE HAD AGREED TO JOIN FORCES TO TAKE DOWN OUR MUTUAL TARGET AND WERE ABOUT TO SHAKE HANDS...
YOU IMMEDIATELY TRIED TO KILL ME. WHAT HAPPENED TO THAT GAMMA AKUTABI... THAT WONDERFUL...
...I DON'T KNOW.

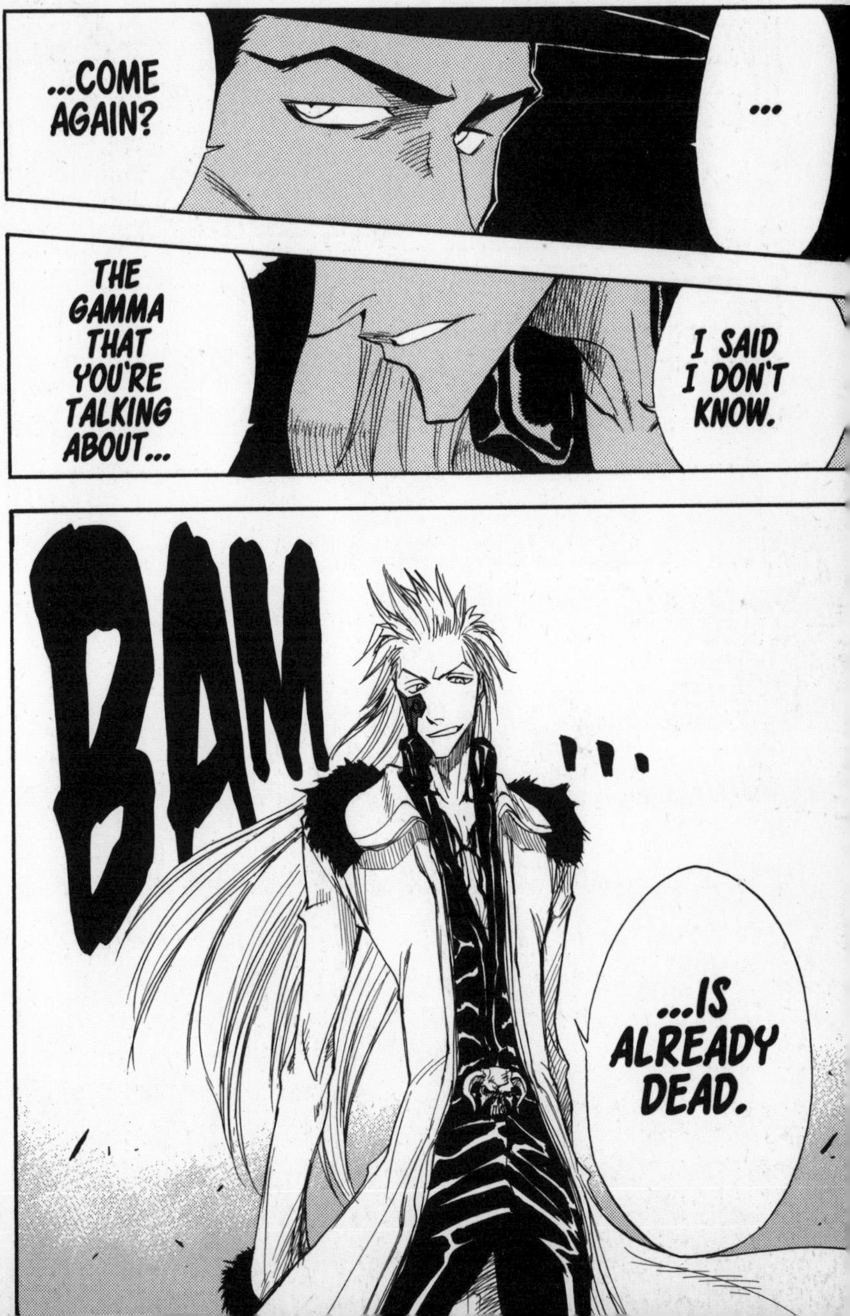
...
...COME AGAIN?
I SAID I DON'T KNOW.
THE GAMMA THAT YOU'RE TALKING ABOUT...
BAM...
...IS ALREADY DEAD.

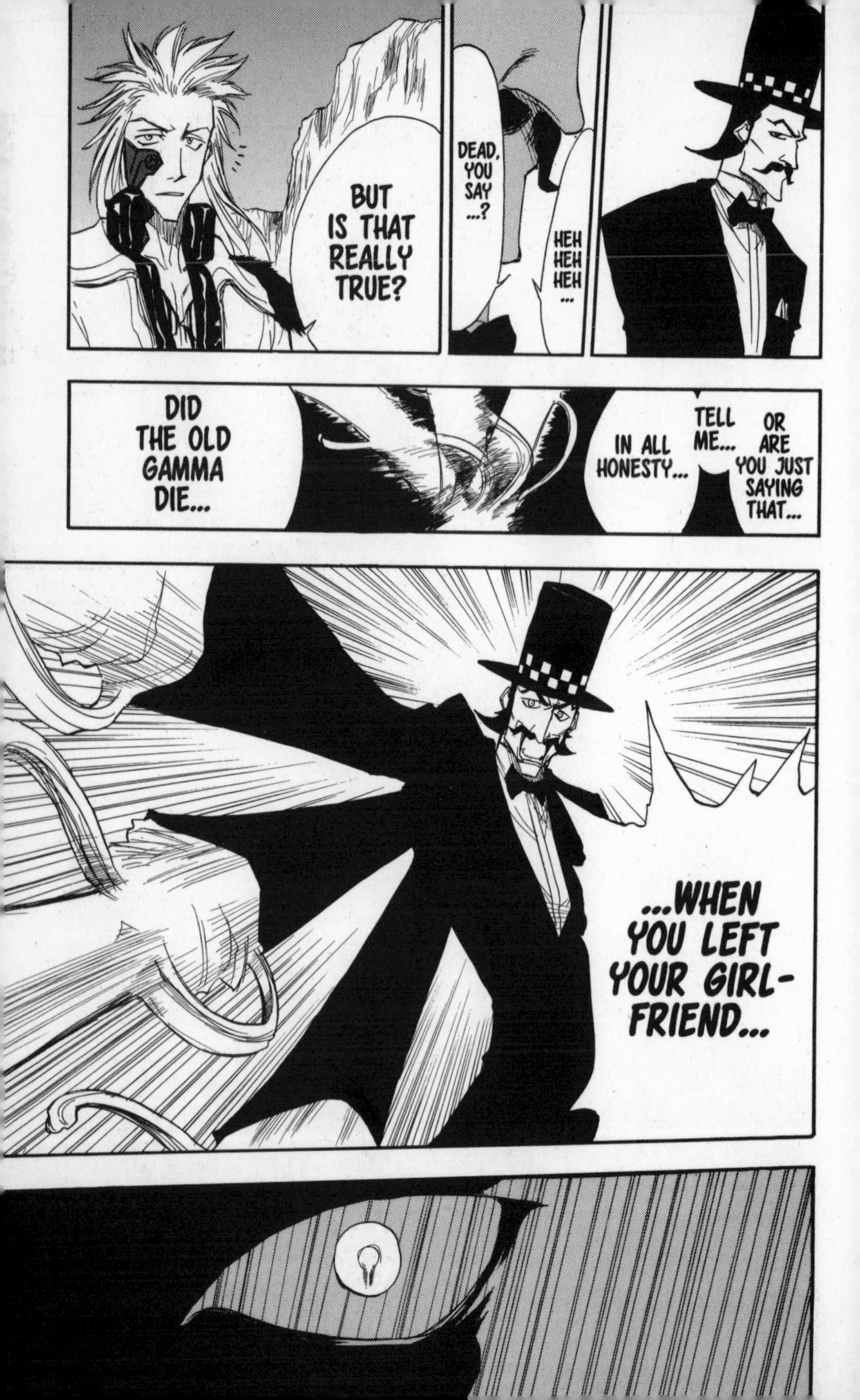
DEAD, YOU SAY ...?
HEH HEH HEH ...
BUT IS THAT REALLY TRUE?
OR ARE YOU JUST SAYING THAT...
TELL ME...
IN ALL HONESTY...
DID THE OLD GAMMA DIE...
...WHEN YOU LEFT YOUR GIRL-FRIEND...

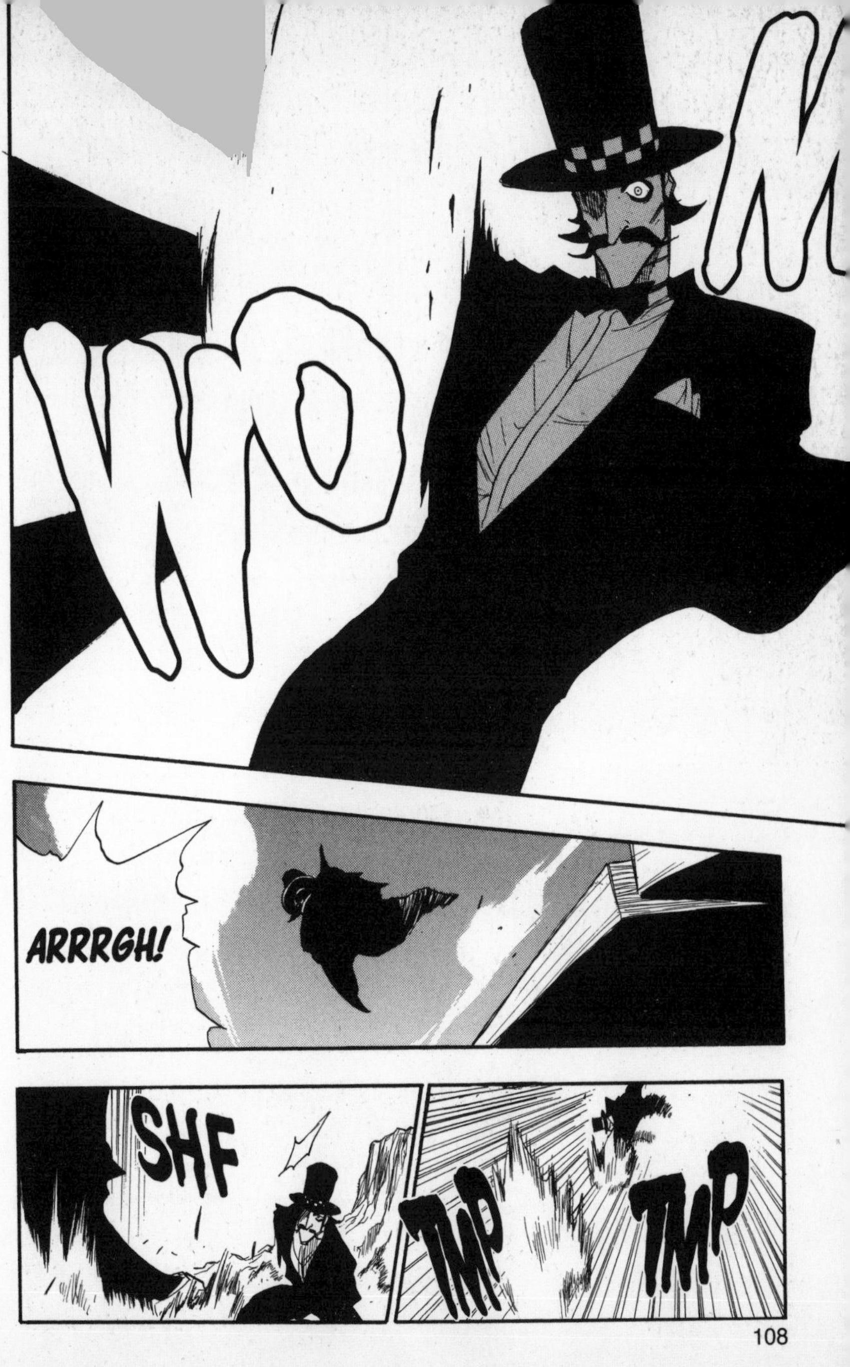
WOM
ARRRGH!
TMP TMP
SHF

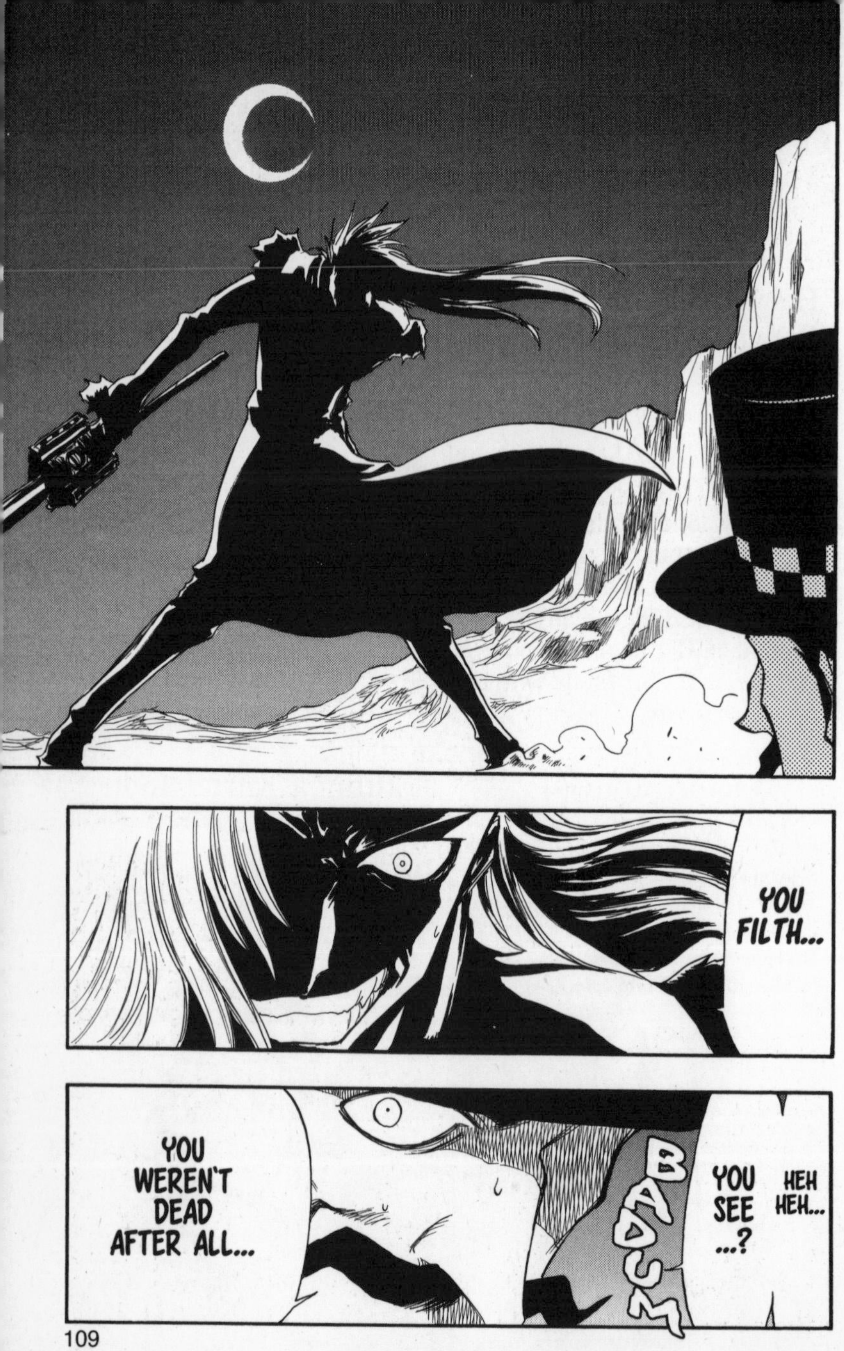
YOU FILTH...
HEH HEH...
YOU SEE ...?
BADUM
YOU WEREN'T DEAD AFTER ALL...

B-side NAKED MONKEYS 13.

Luka−Lughca
ルカ＝ルカ

Height: 149cm
Weight: 37kg
Date of Birth: 12/14
Age: 12
Blood Type: AO

An acrobat from the Balmunk circus
troupe. A lot of readers think that
she's a boy, but she's actually a girl.
Don't tell her that her breasts are
small because she's really sensitive
about that. Her favorite food is lasagna.
Her dream for the future is to become
Pownder's wife.

Victor Mougen
ビクトル・ムーゲン

A juggler and Luka-Lughca's partner.
The most affable and well-educated of
the entire troupe. And the least talkative.
His name wasn't even mentioned but I
just had to include him here.

Julinoa Kartelainen
ユリノア・カーテライネン

A nurse who works at the Roscoe
hospital. She's a hard-working 21-
year-old from the north country.

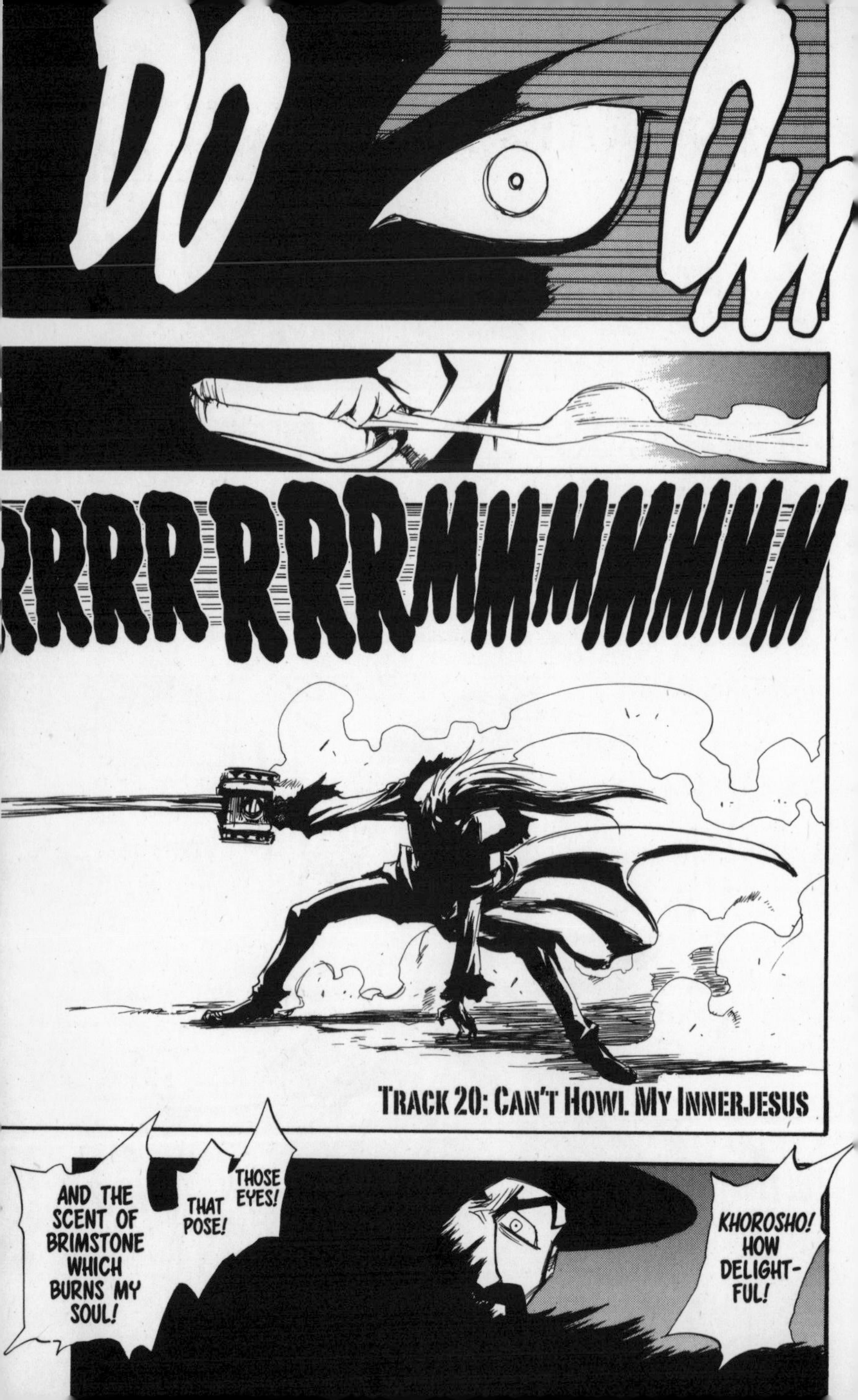
DOOM
RRRRRRRMMMMMMMMMM
TRACK 20: CAN'T HOWL MY INNERJESUS
KHOROSHO! HOW DELIGHT-FUL!
THOSE EYES!
THAT POSE!
AND THE SCENT OF BRIMSTONE WHICH BURNS MY SOUL!

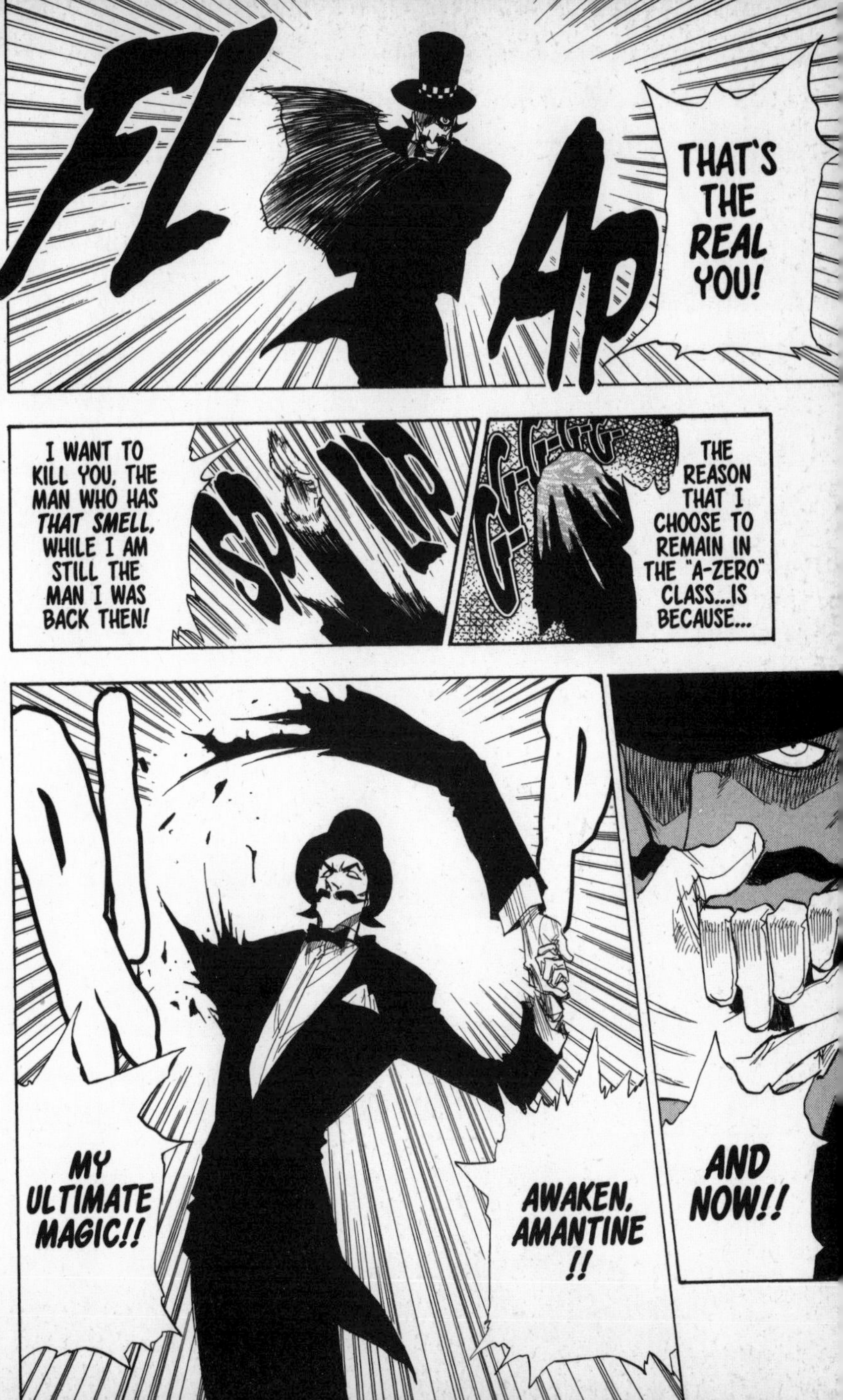
THAT'S THE REAL YOU!
FLAP
THE REASON THAT I CHOOSE TO REMAIN IN THE "A-ZERO" CLASS...IS BECAUSE...
I WANT TO KILL YOU, THE MAN WHO HAS *THAT SMELL,* WHILE I AM STILL THE MAN I WAS BACK THEN!
AND NOW!!
AWAKEN, AMANTINE!!
MY ULTIMATE MAGIC!!

TRACK 20: CAN'T HOWL MY INNERJESUS

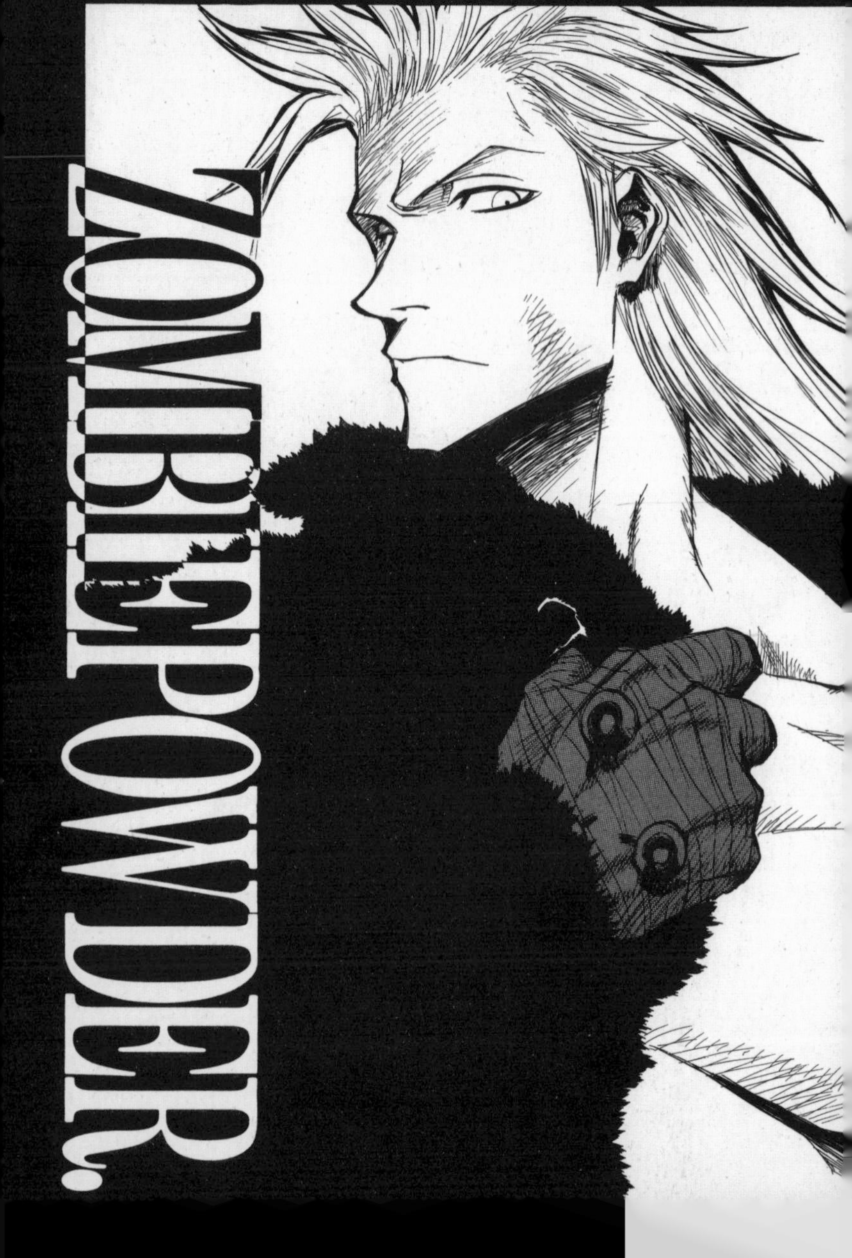
ZOMBIEPOWDER.

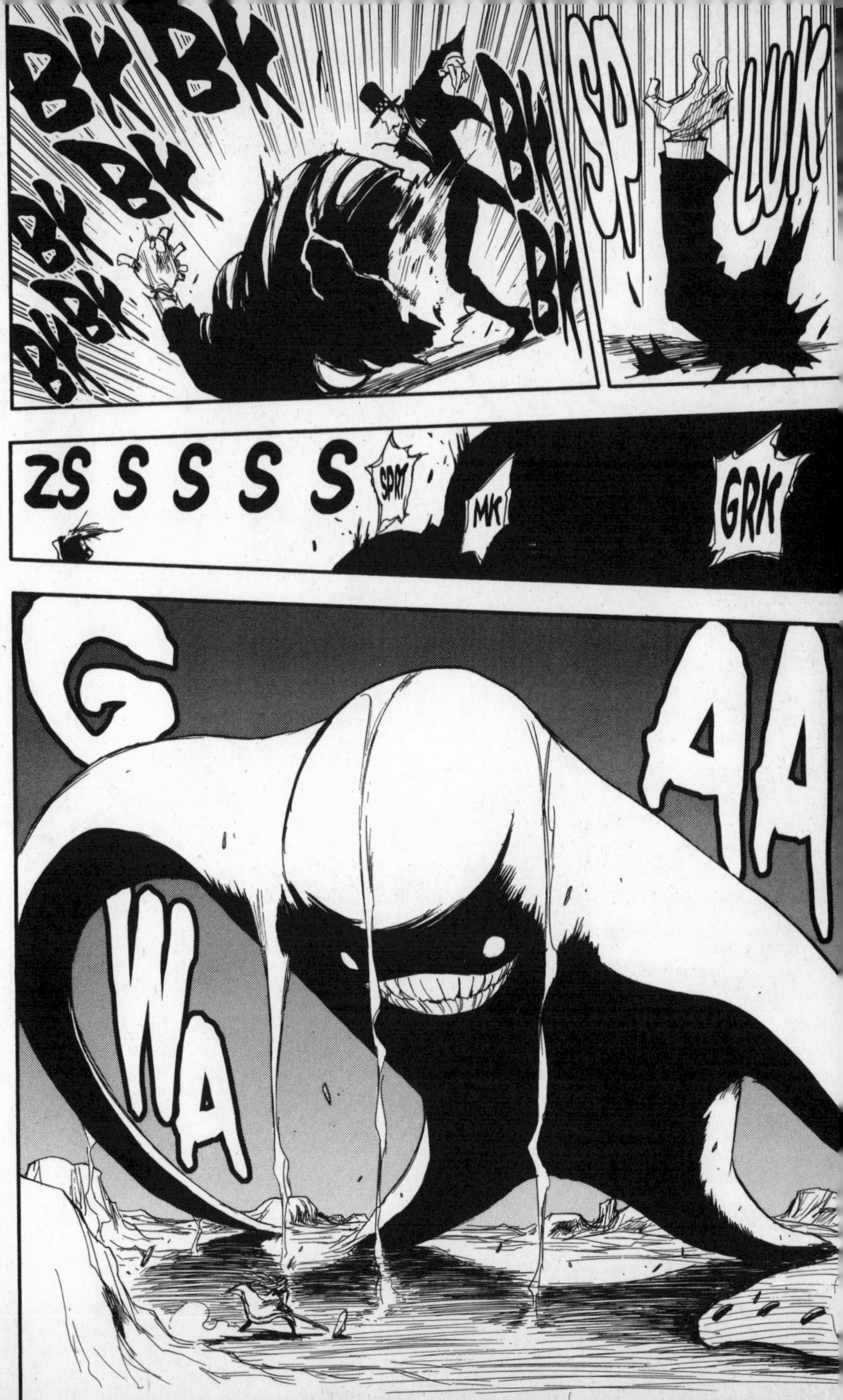
SP
LUK
BKBK
BKBK
BKBKBKBK
BK BK BK
GRK
MK
SPRT
ZS S S S S
G
WAA
AA

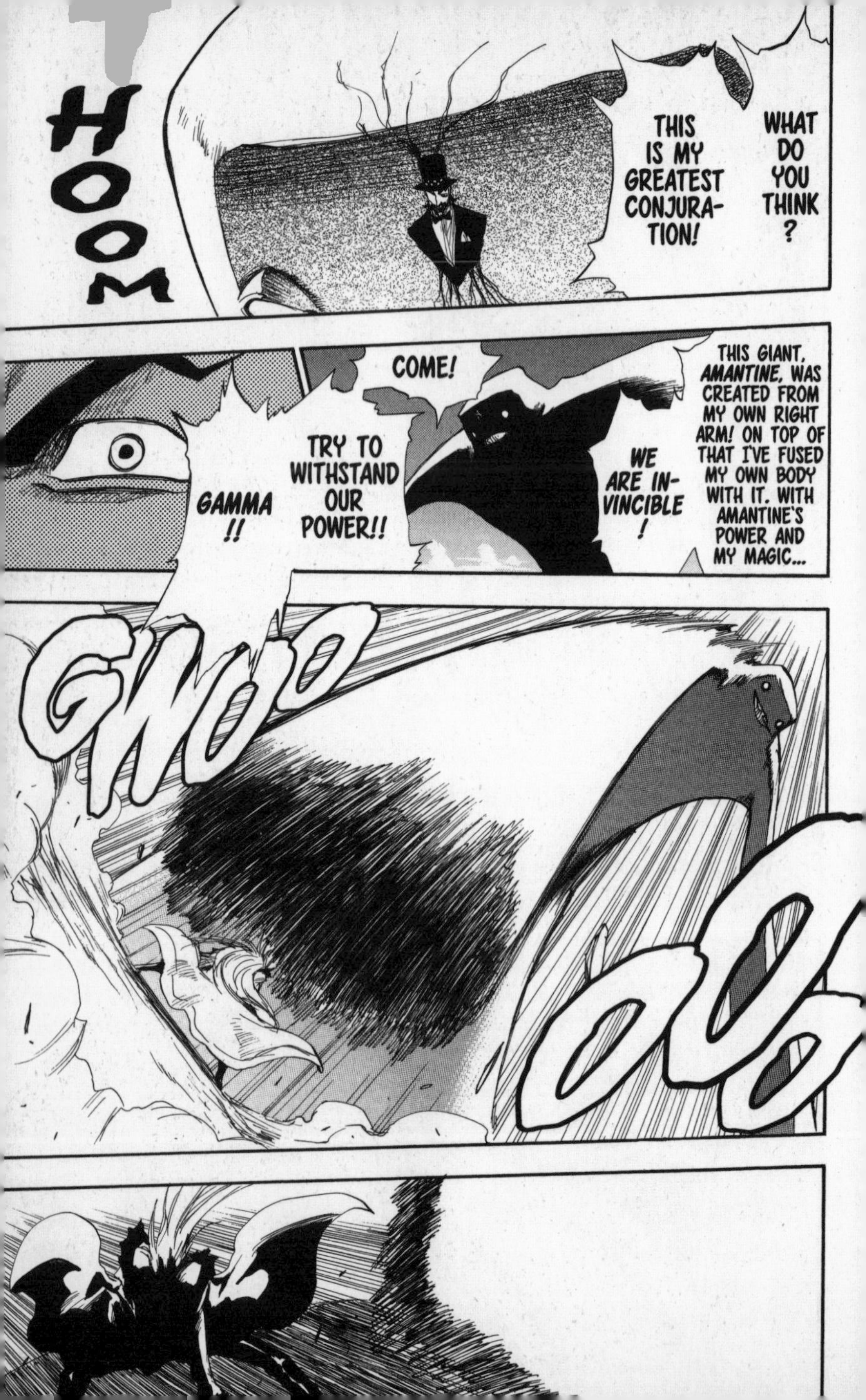
WHAT DO YOU THINK?
THIS IS MY GREATEST CONJURA-TION!
HOOM
THIS GIANT, AMANTINE, WAS CREATED FROM MY OWN RIGHT ARM! ON TOP OF THAT I'VE FUSED MY OWN BODY WITH IT. WITH AMANTINE'S POWER AND MY MAGIC...
WE ARE IN-VINCIBLE!
COME!
TRY TO WITHSTAND OUR POWER!!
GAMMA!!
GWOO

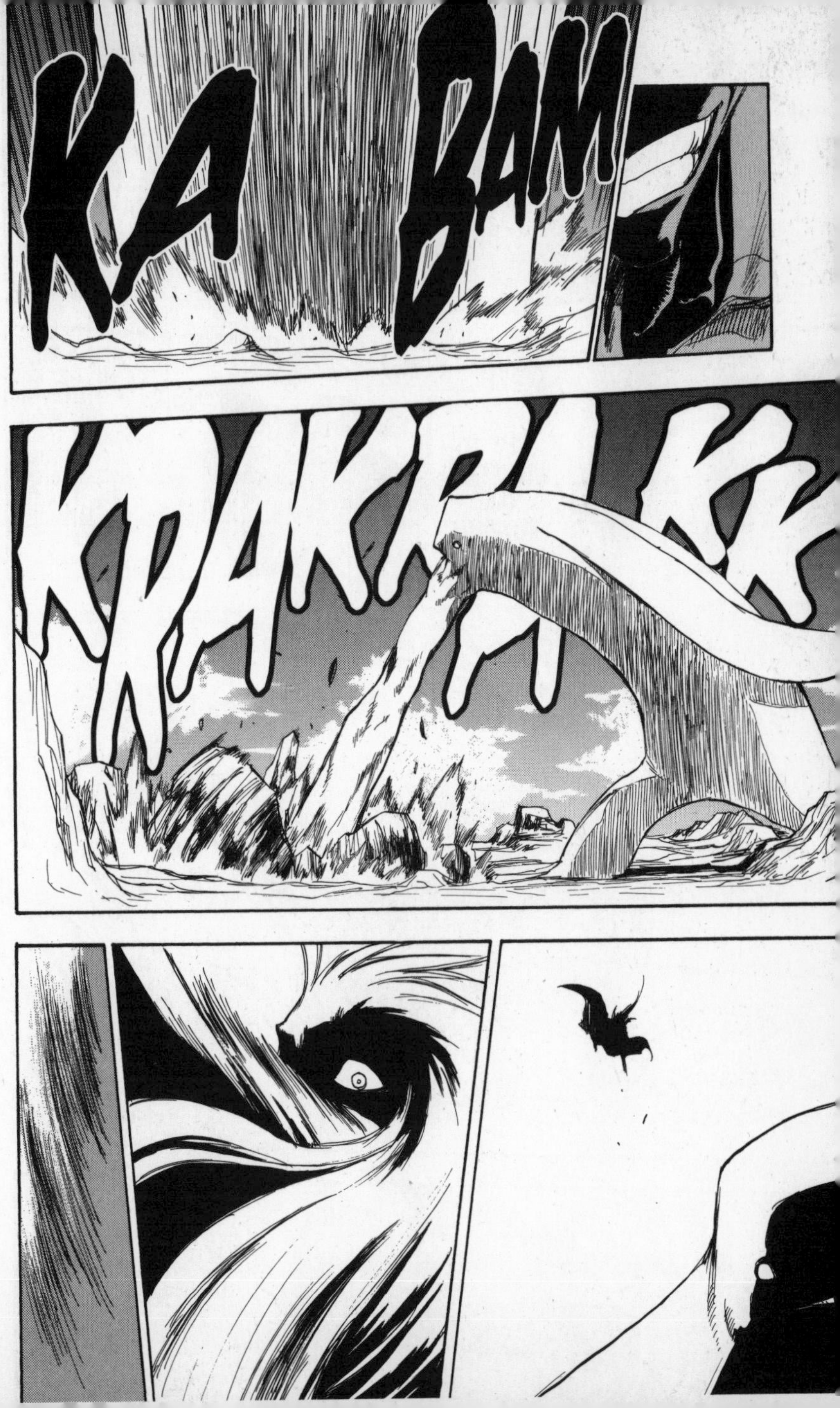
KA BAM

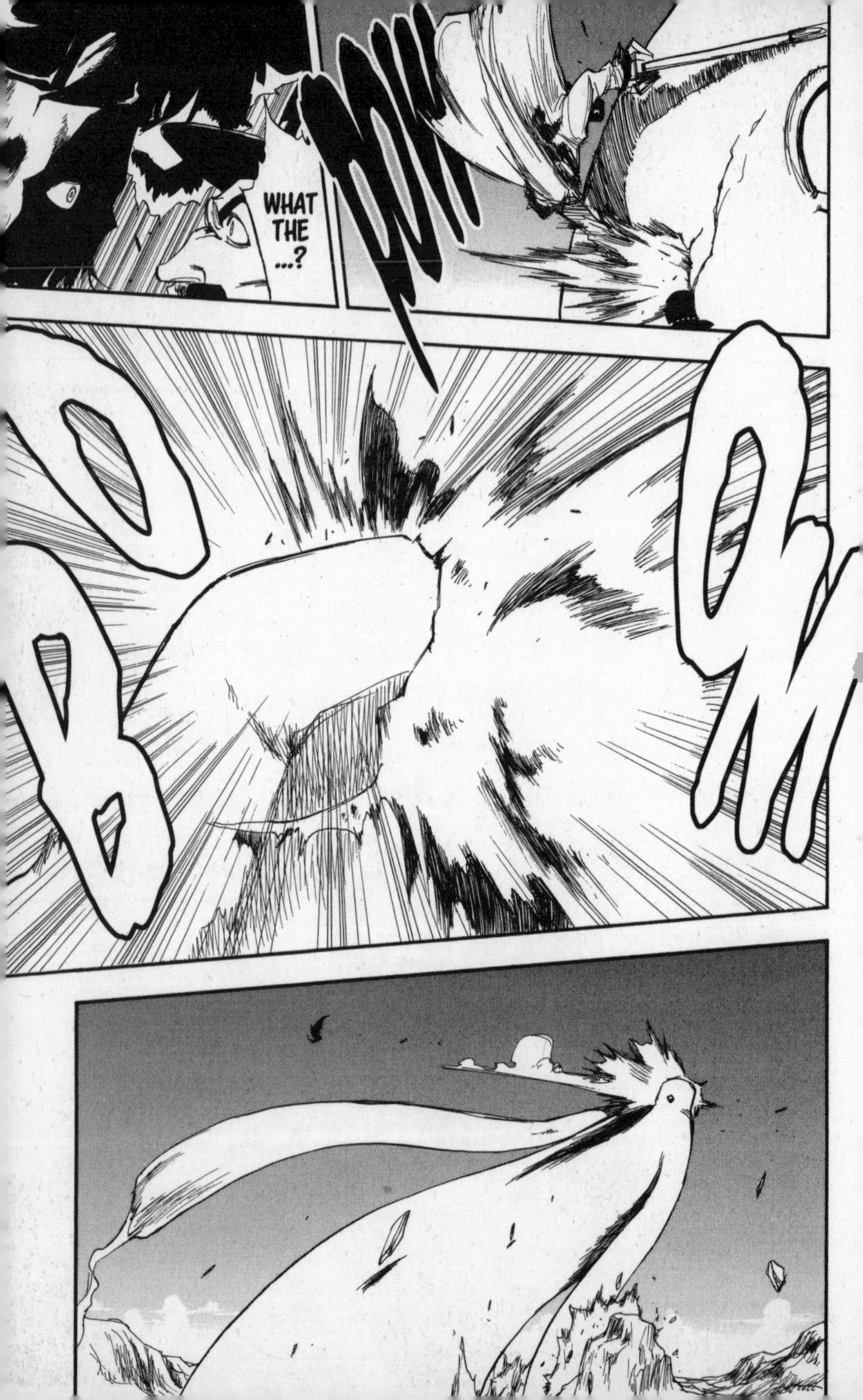
WHAT THE ...?

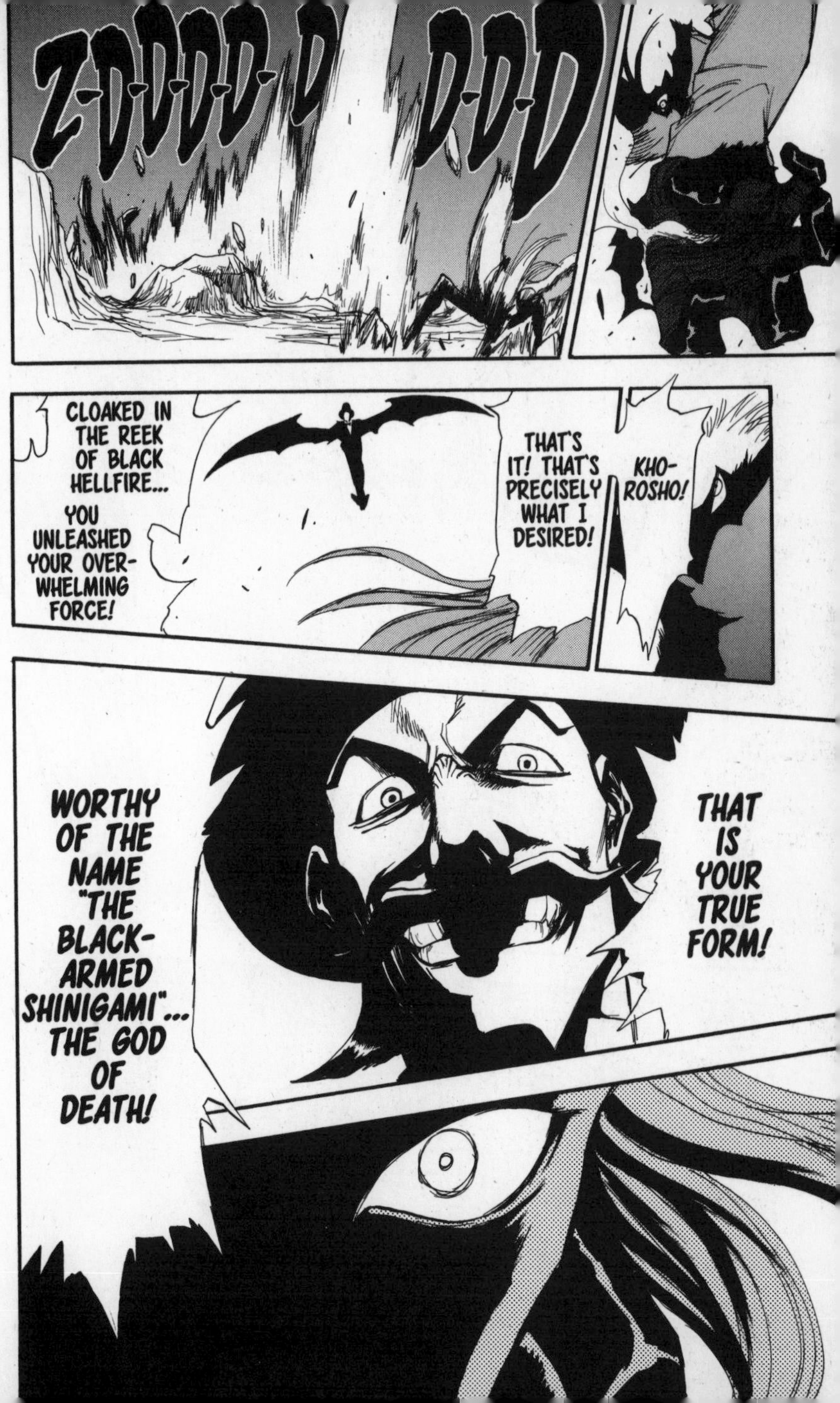
Z-D-D-D-D-D
D-D-D
KHO-ROSHO!
THAT'S IT! THAT'S PRECISELY WHAT I DESIRED!
CLOAKED IN THE REEK OF BLACK HELLFIRE...
YOU UNLEASHED YOUR OVER-WHELMING FORCE!
THAT IS YOUR TRUE FORM!
WORTHY OF THE NAME "THE BLACK-ARMED SHINIGAMI"... THE GOD OF DEATH!

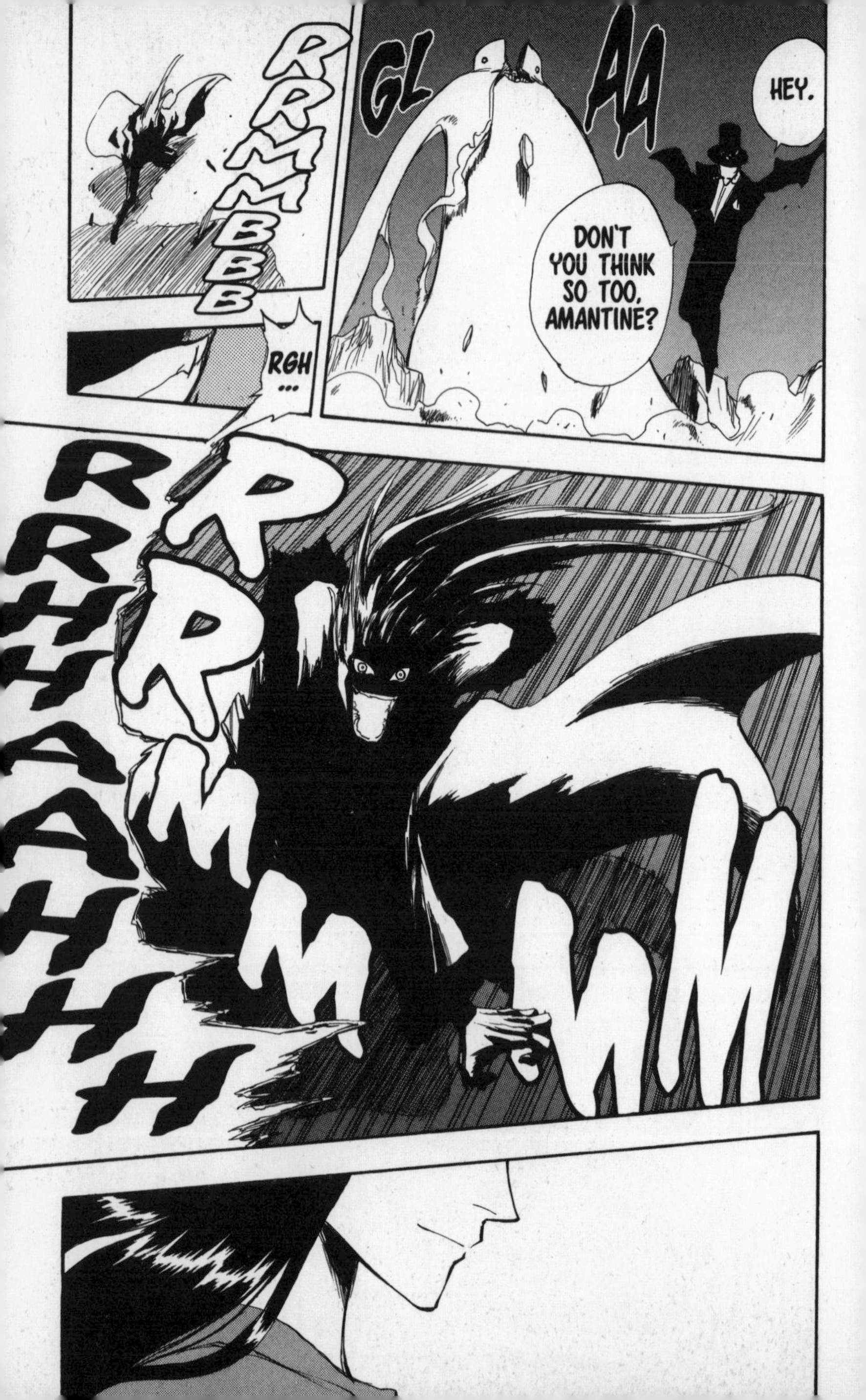
HEY.
DON'T YOU THINK SO TOO, AMANTINE?
GL AA
RRMMBBB
RGH...
RRMMMM
RRHHAAHHH

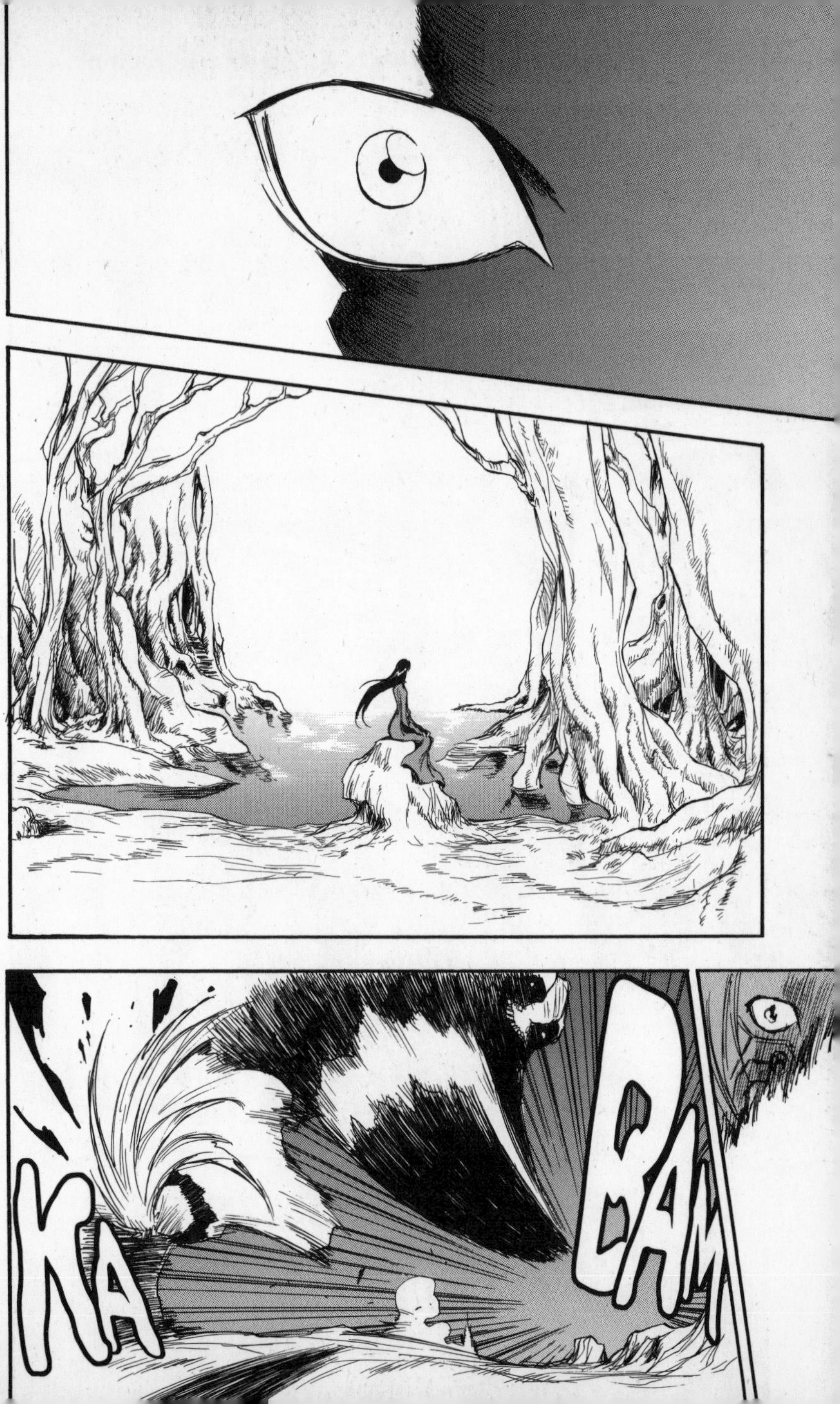
KA
DAM

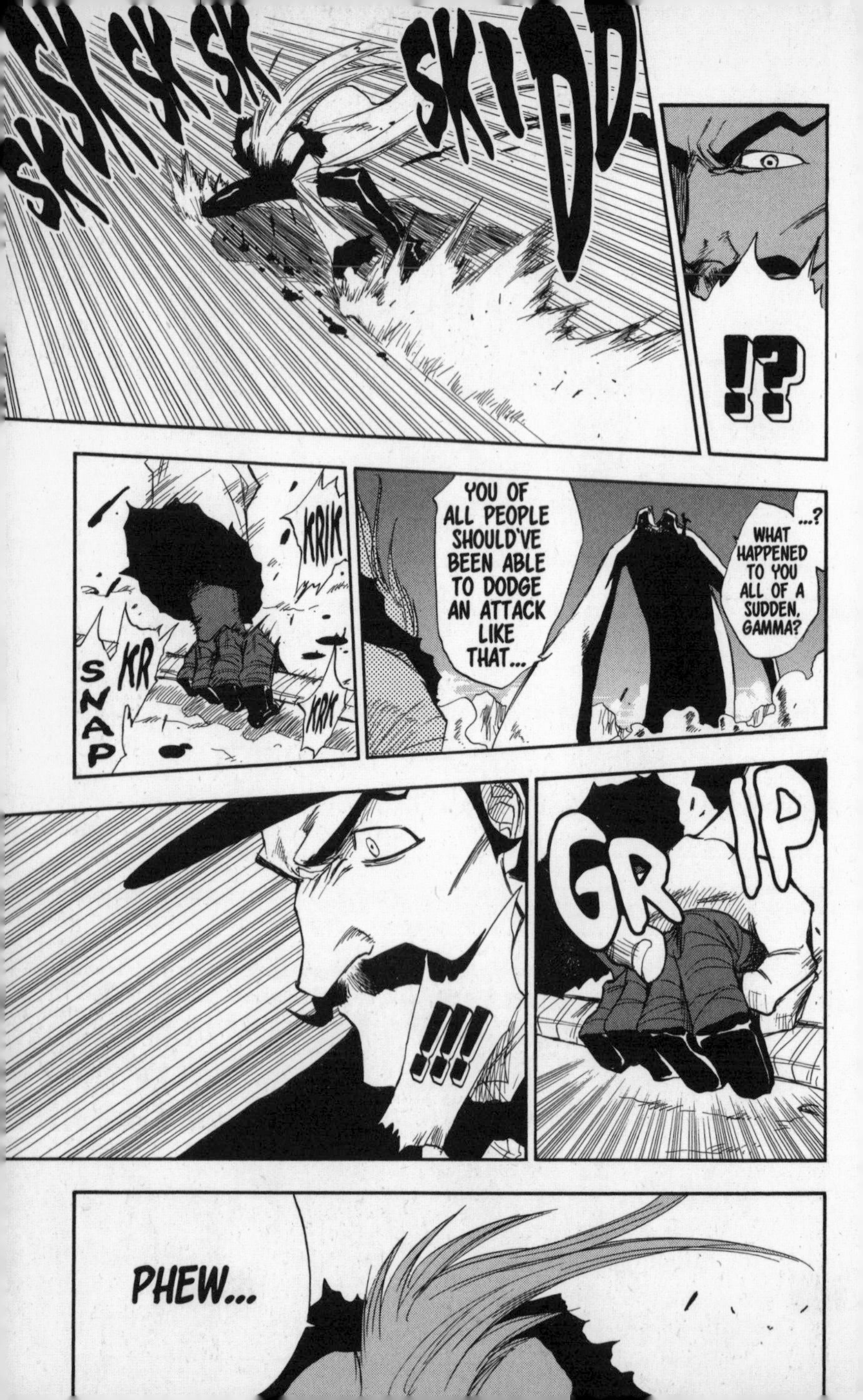
!?
SK SK SK SK
SKIDD
...?
WHAT HAPPENED TO YOU ALL OF A SUDDEN, GAMMA?
YOU OF ALL PEOPLE SHOULD'VE BEEN ABLE TO DODGE AN ATTACK LIKE THAT...
KRIK
KR
SNAP
KRK
GRIP
!!!
PHEW...

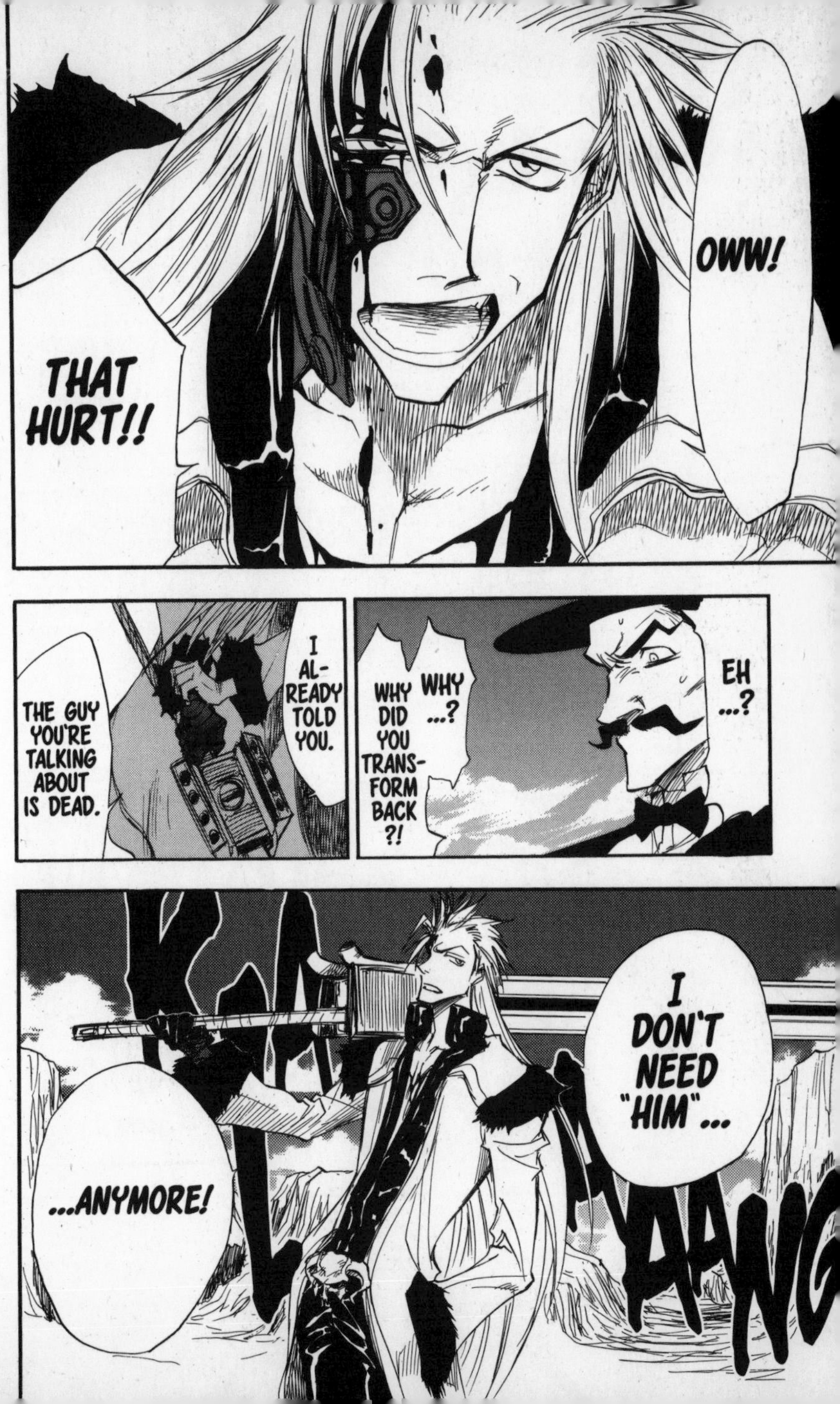
OWW!
THAT HURT!!
EH ...?
WHY ...?
WHY DID YOU TRANS-FORM BACK ?!
I AL-READY TOLD YOU.
THE GUY YOU'RE TALKING ABOUT IS DEAD.
I DON'T NEED "HIM"...
...ANYMORE!

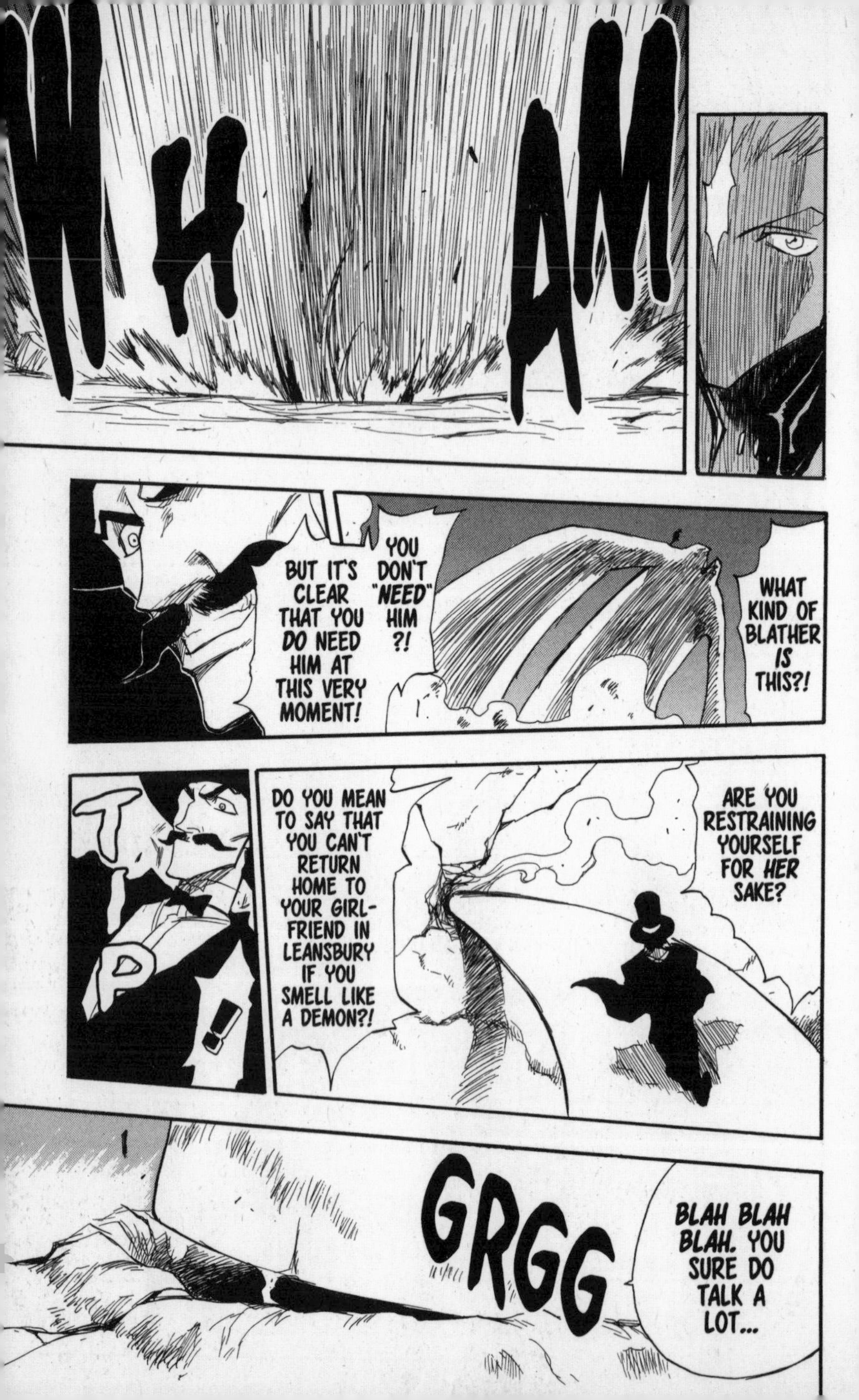
WHHAM
WHAT KIND OF BLATHER IS THIS?!
YOU DON'T "NEED" HIM ?!
BUT IT'S CLEAR THAT YOU DO NEED HIM AT THIS VERY MOMENT!
ARE YOU RESTRAINING YOURSELF FOR HER SAKE?
DO YOU MEAN TO SAY THAT YOU CAN'T RETURN HOME TO YOUR GIRL-FRIEND IN LEANSBURY IF YOU SMELL LIKE A DEMON?!
TP
!
BLAH BLAH BLAH. YOU SURE DO TALK A LOT...
GRGG

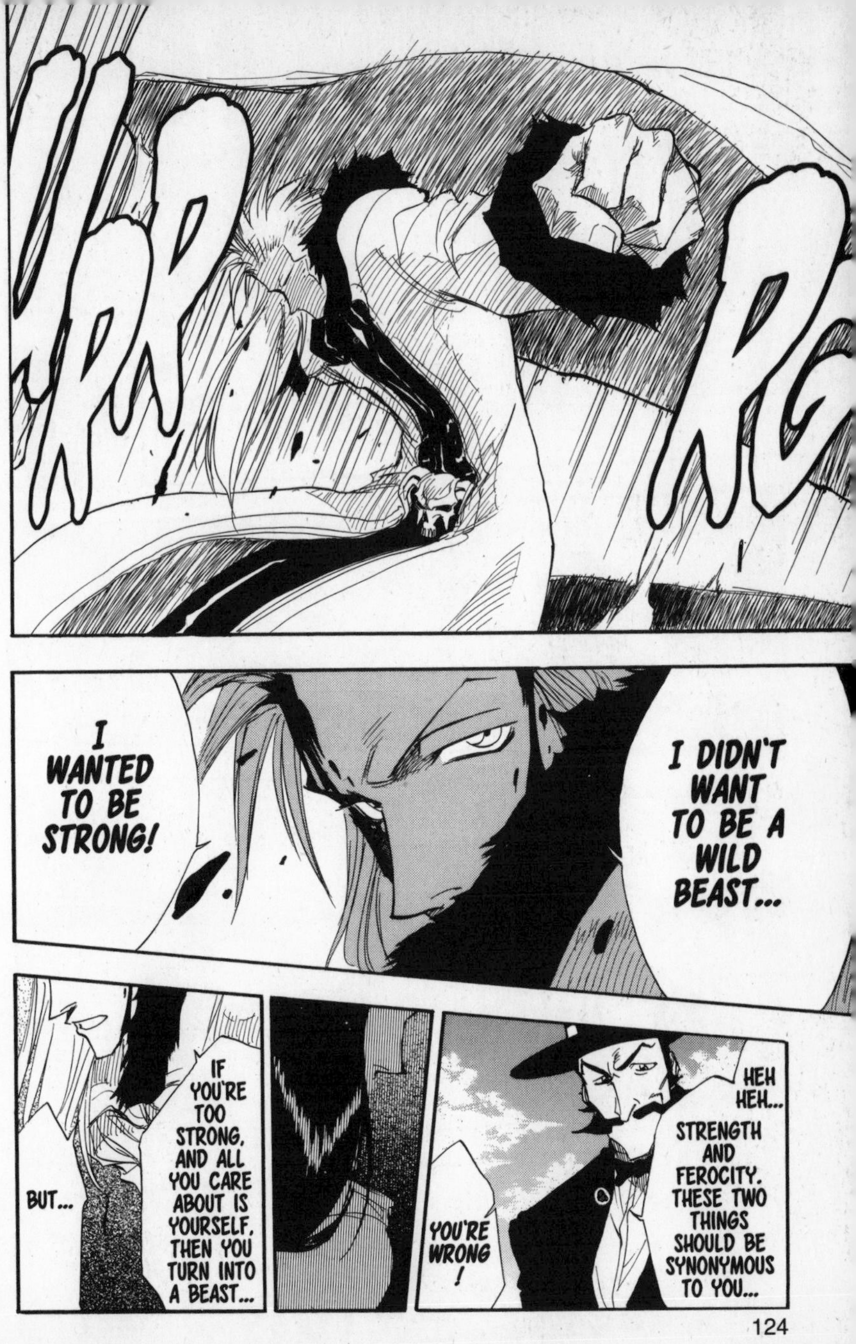
I DIDN'T WANT TO BE A WILD BEAST...
I WANTED TO BE STRONG!
HEH HEH...
STRENGTH AND FEROCITY. THESE TWO THINGS SHOULD BE SYNONYMOUS TO YOU...
YOU'RE WRONG!
IF YOU'RE TOO STRONG, AND ALL YOU CARE ABOUT IS YOURSELF, THEN YOU TURN INTO A BEAST...
BUT...

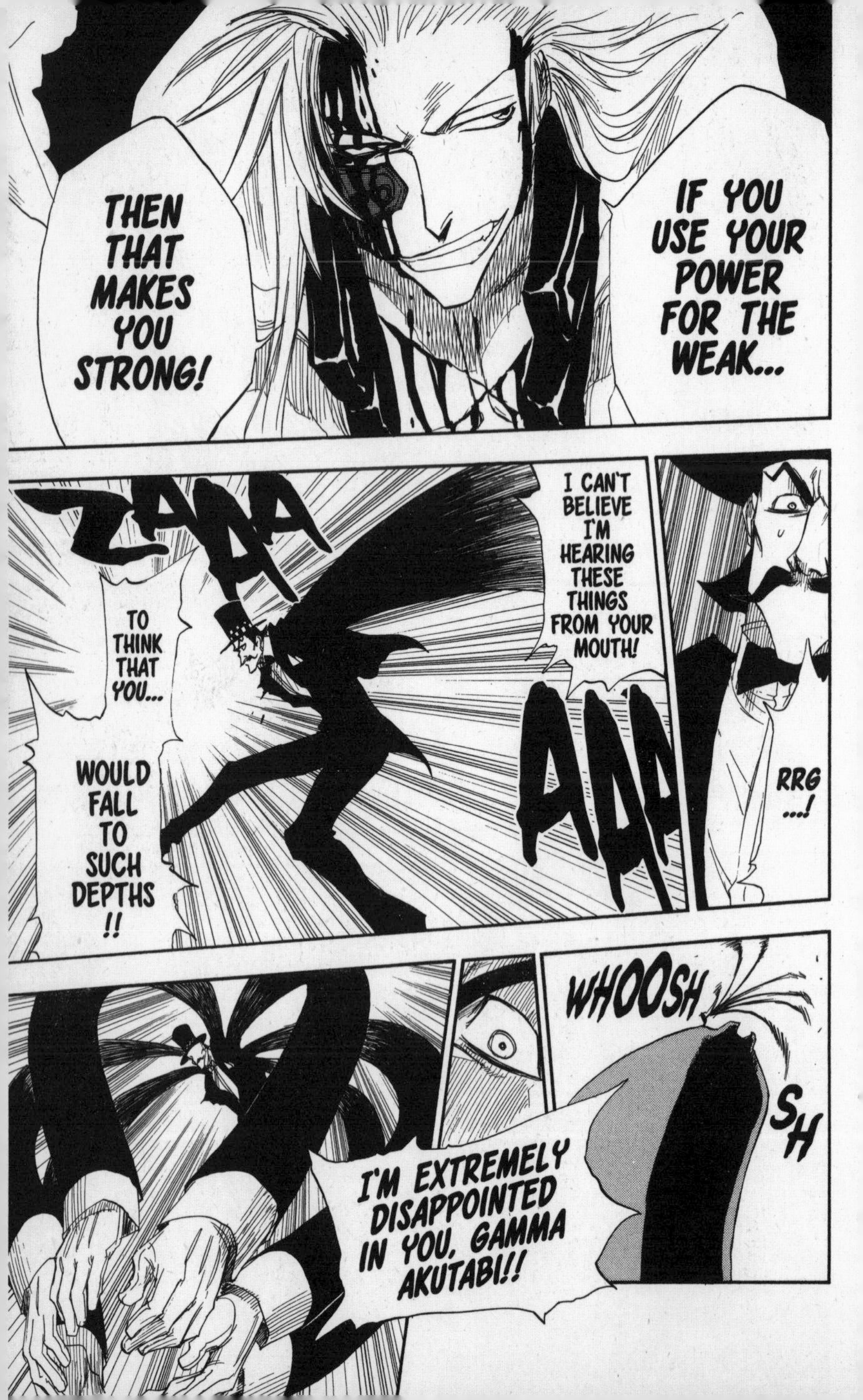
IF YOU USE YOUR POWER FOR THE WEAK...
THEN THAT MAKES YOU STRONG!
RRG ...!
I CAN'T BELIEVE I'M HEARING THESE THINGS FROM YOUR MOUTH!
ZAAA
AAA
TO THINK THAT YOU...
WOULD FALL TO SUCH DEPTHS!!
WHOOSH
SH
I'M EXTREMELY DISAPPOINTED IN YOU, GAMMA AKUTABI!!

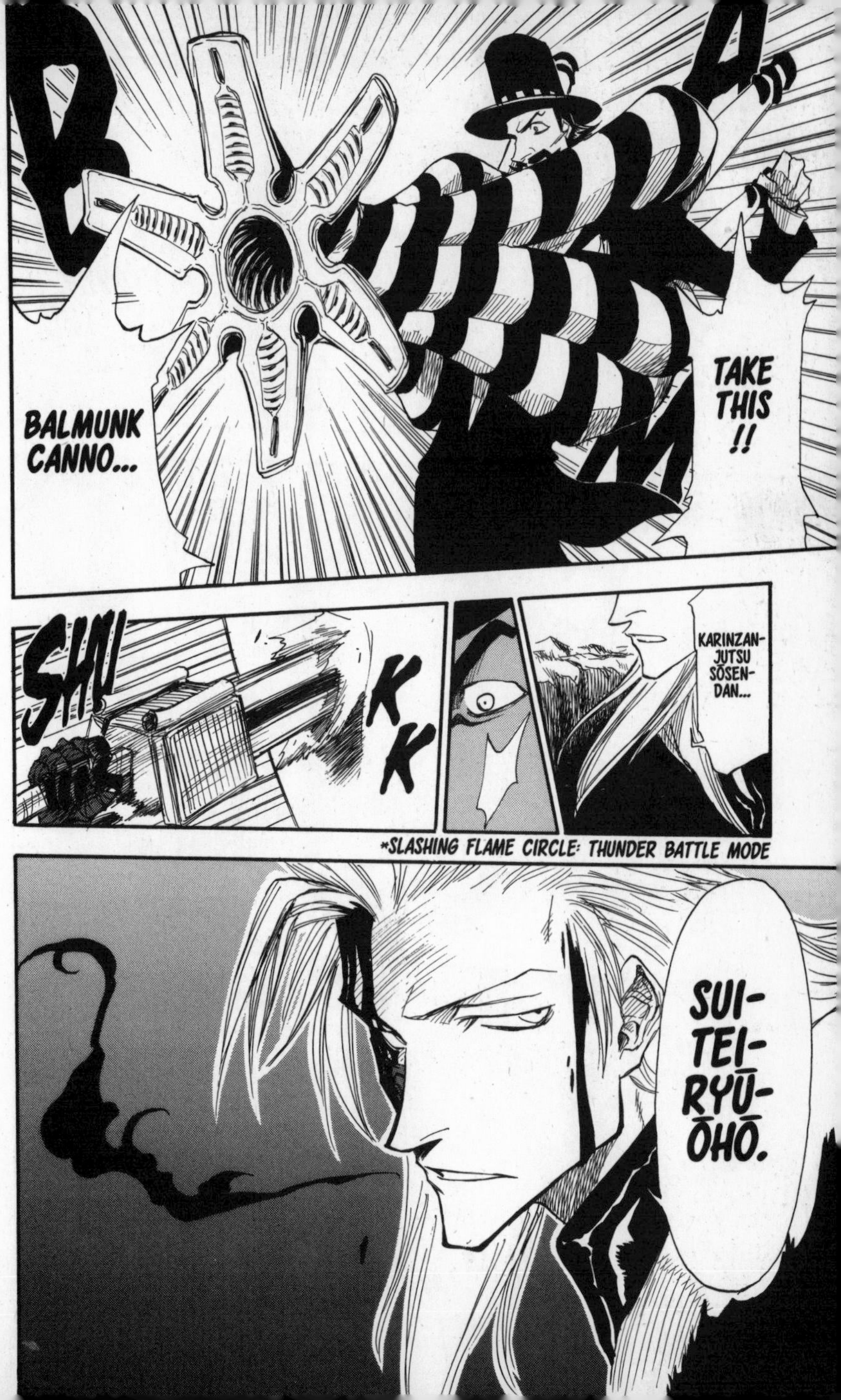
BA
TAKE THIS!!
BALMUNK CANNO...
KARINZAN-JUTSU SŌSEN-DAN...
SHU
KK
*SLASHING FLAME CIRCLE: THUNDER BATTLE MODE
SUI-TEI-RYŪ-ŌHŌ.

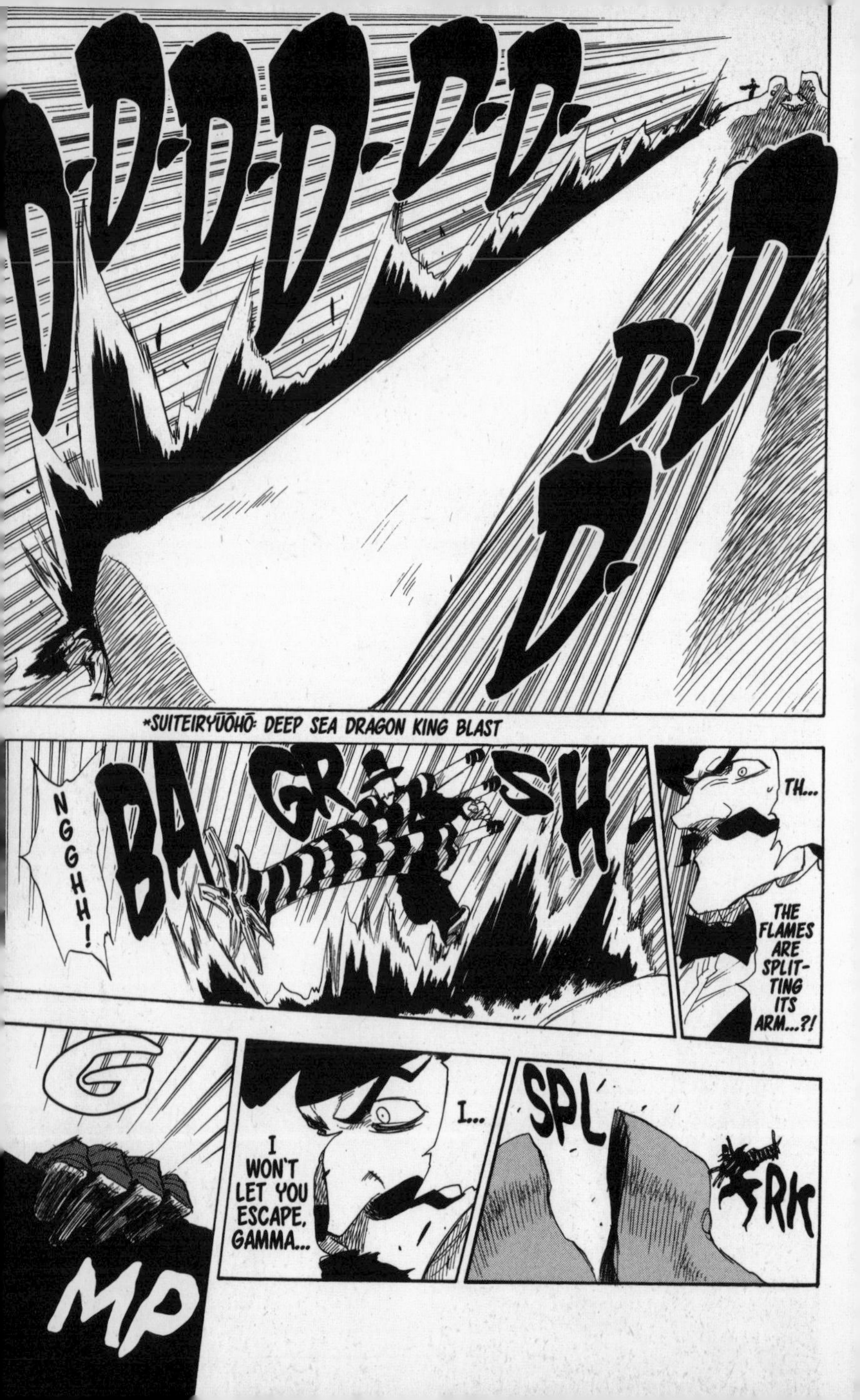
D-D-D-D-D-D-D-D-D-D
*SUITEIRYŪHŌ: DEEP SEA DRAGON KING BLAST
TH...
THE FLAMES ARE SPLIT-TING ITS ARM...?!
BA GR SH
NGGHH!
SPL
RK
I...
I WON'T LET YOU ESCAPE, GAMMA...
G
MP

IS THIS SHOULDER REAL?

AKUTABI...

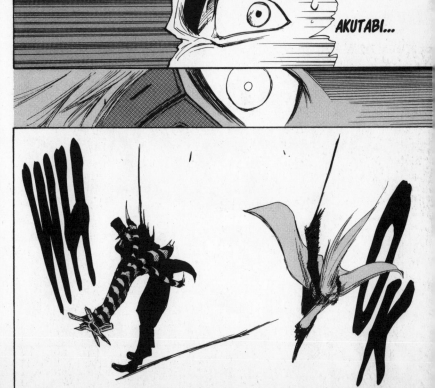

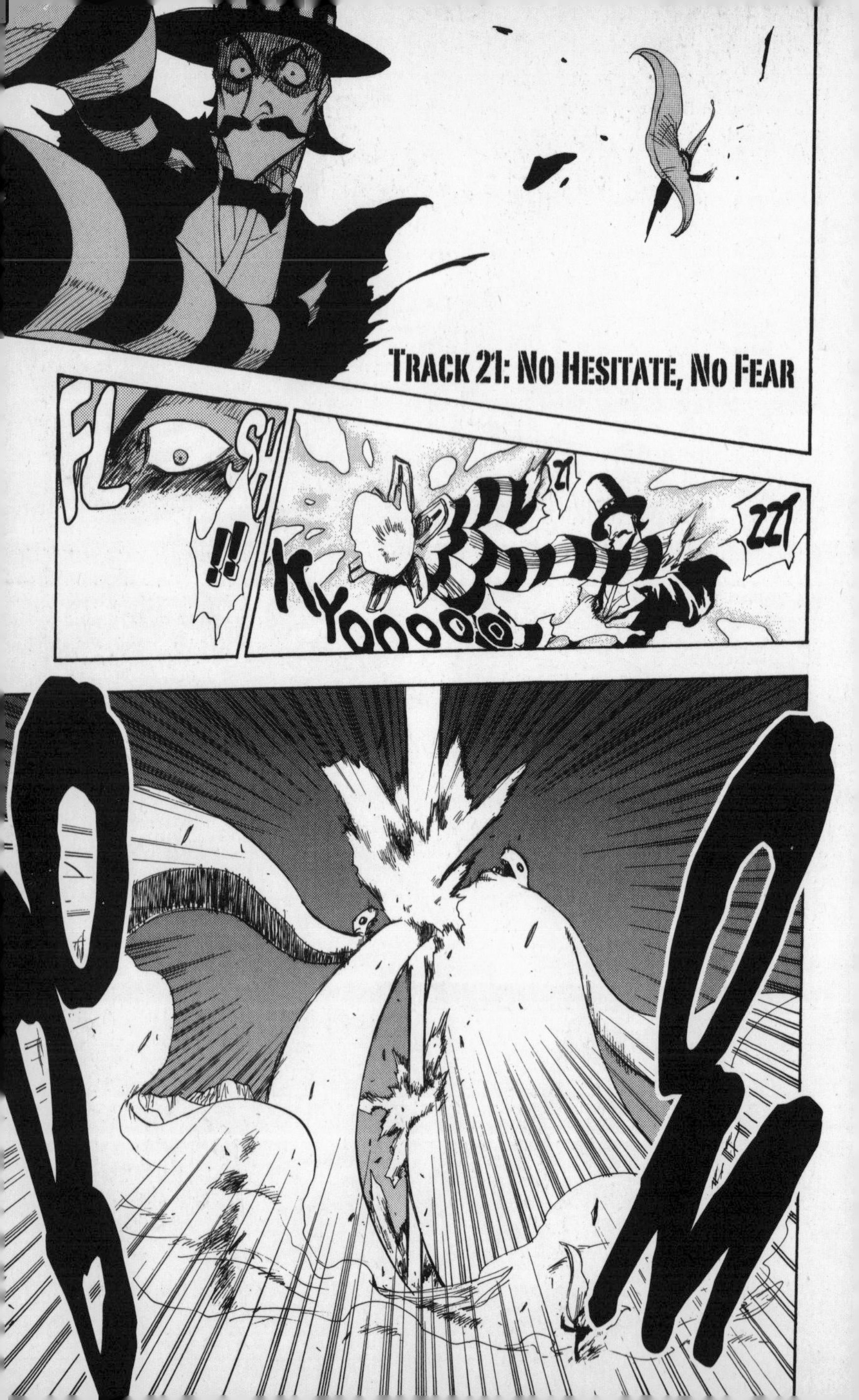
Track 21: No Hesitate, No Fear
ZZT
ZZT
KYOOOOO
FLASH
!!

TRACK 21: NO HESITATE, NO FEAR

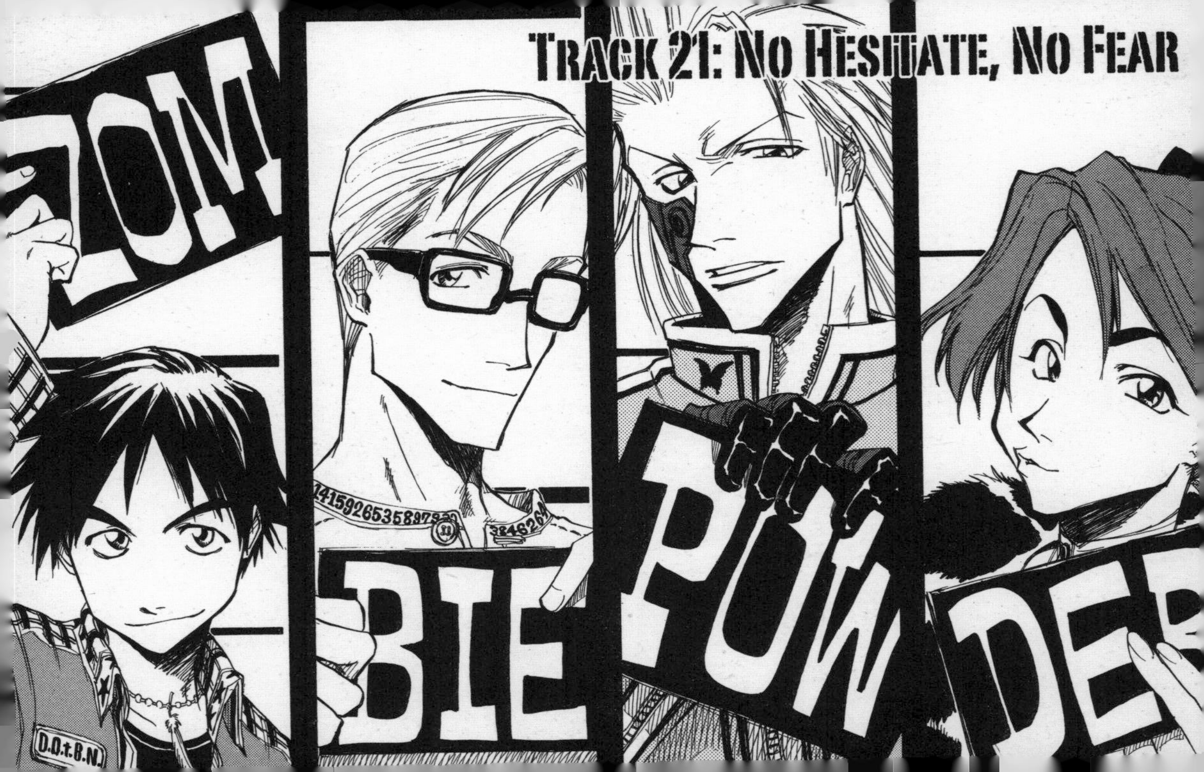
ZOM
BIE
POW
DER
D.O.t.B.N.

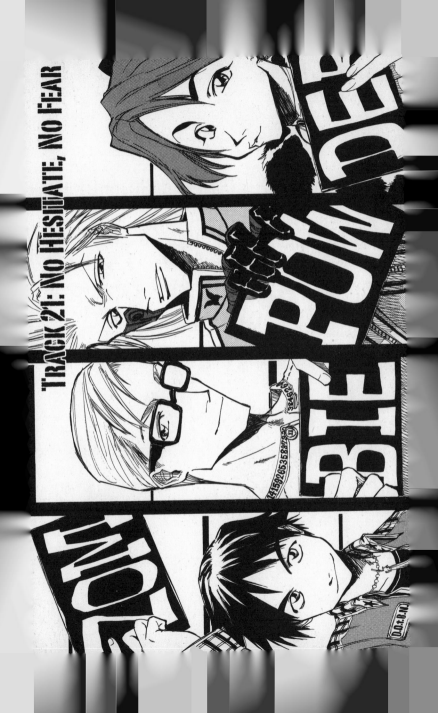

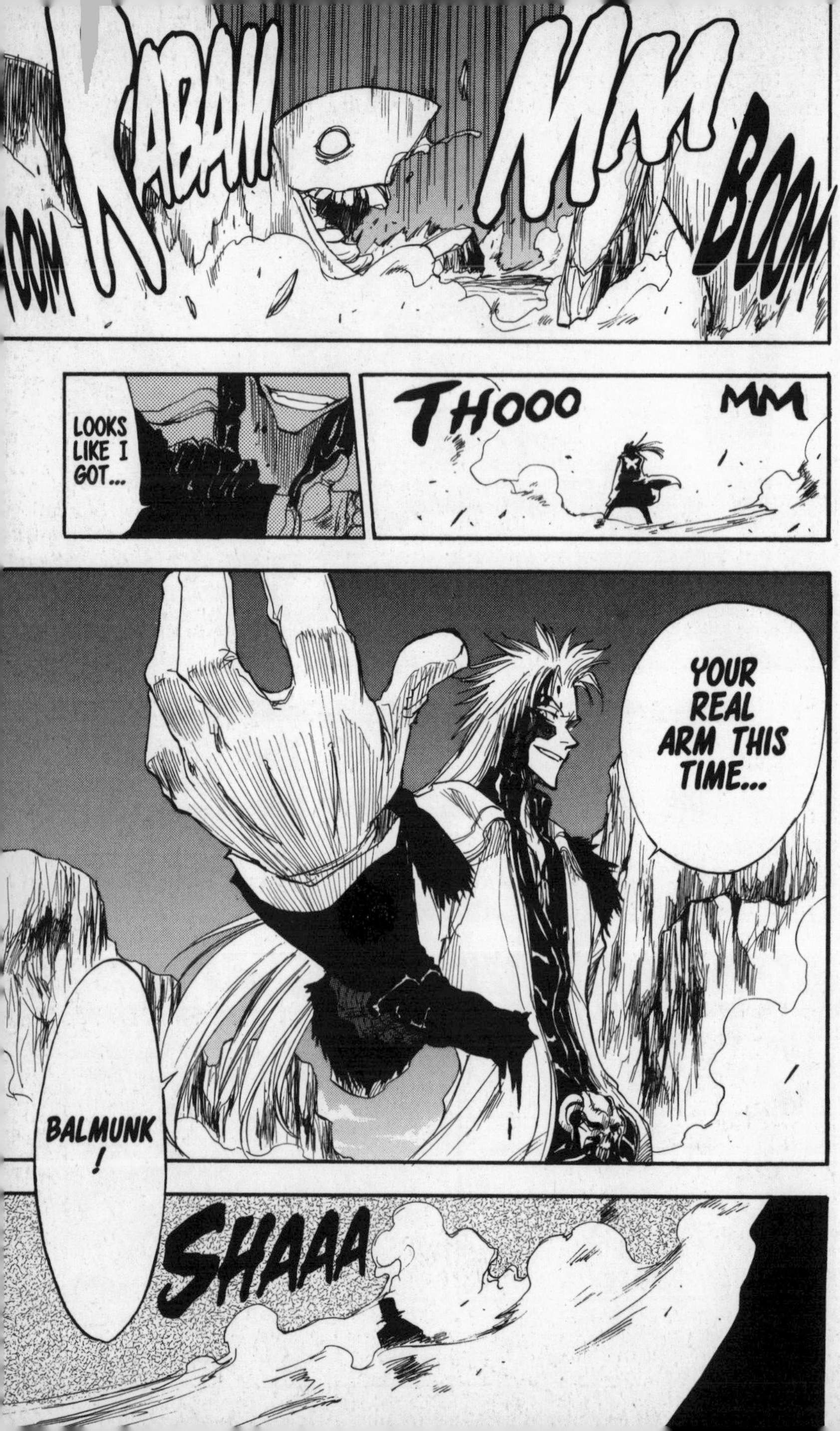

BOOM
KABAMMM
OOM
THOOO MM
LOOKS LIKE I GOT...
YOUR REAL ARM THIS TIME...
BALMUNK!
SHAAA

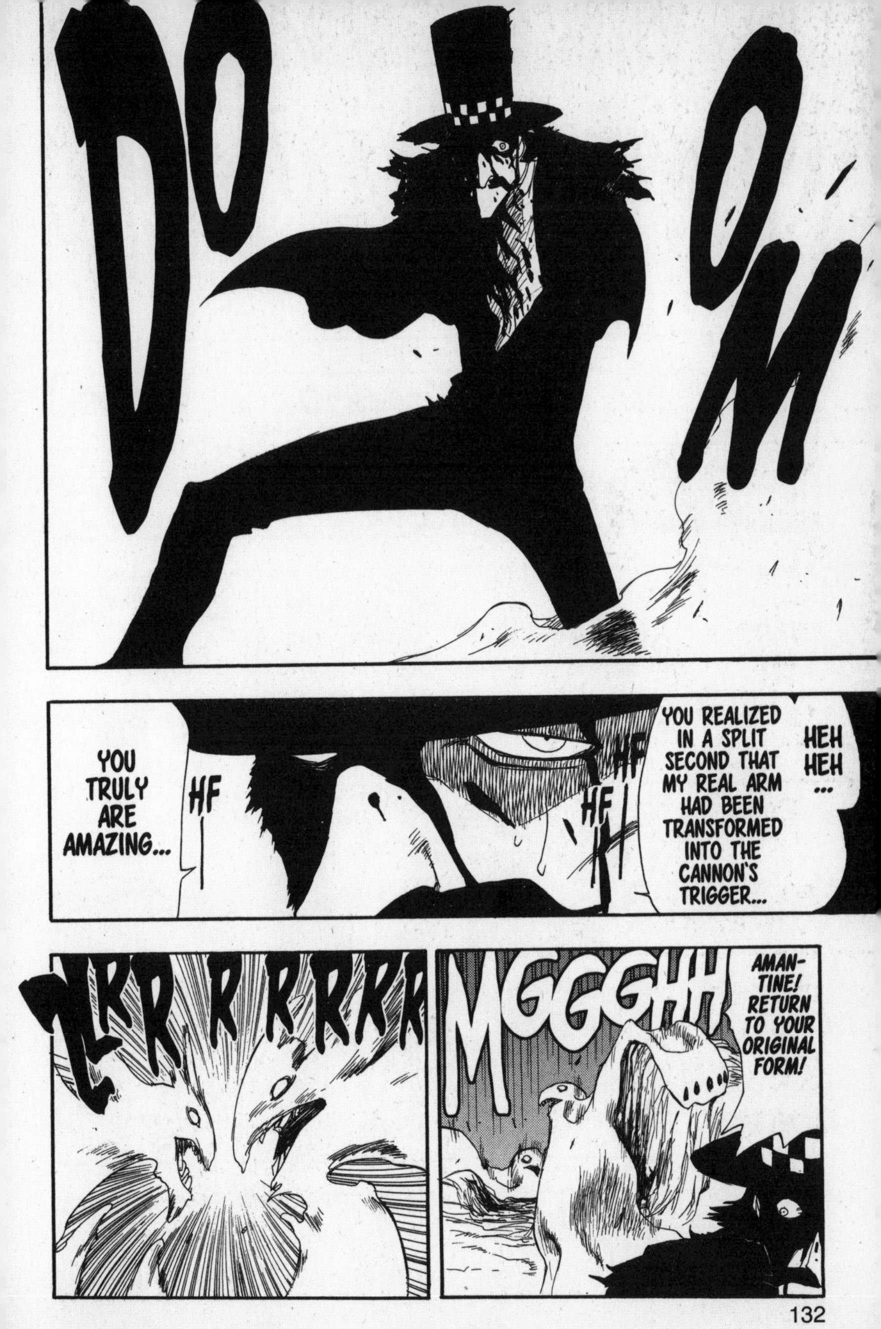
DOOM
HEH HEH...
YOU REALIZED IN A SPLIT SECOND THAT MY REAL ARM HAD BEEN TRANSFORMED INTO THE CANNON'S TRIGGER...
HF HF
HF
YOU TRULY ARE AMAZING...
AMAN-TINE! RETURN TO YOUR ORIGINAL FORM!
MGGGHH
RR R R RRR

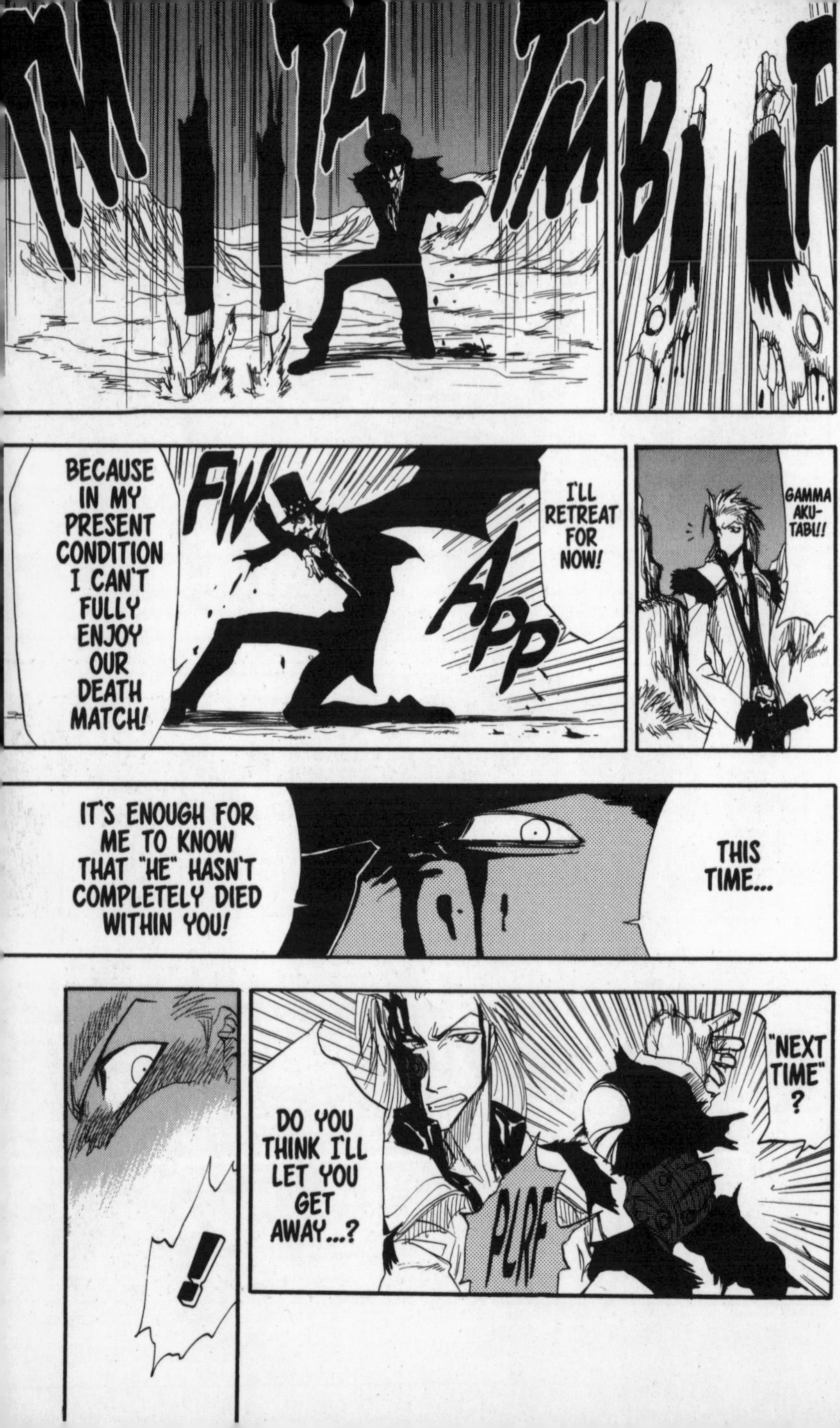
GAMMA AKU-TABI!!
I'LL RETREAT FOR NOW!
FWAPP
BECAUSE IN MY PRESENT CONDITION I CAN'T FULLY ENJOY OUR DEATH MATCH!
THIS TIME...
IT'S ENOUGH FOR ME TO KNOW THAT "HE" HASN'T COMPLETELY DIED WITHIN YOU!
"NEXT TIME"?
PLRF
DO YOU THINK I'LL LET YOU GET AWAY...?
!

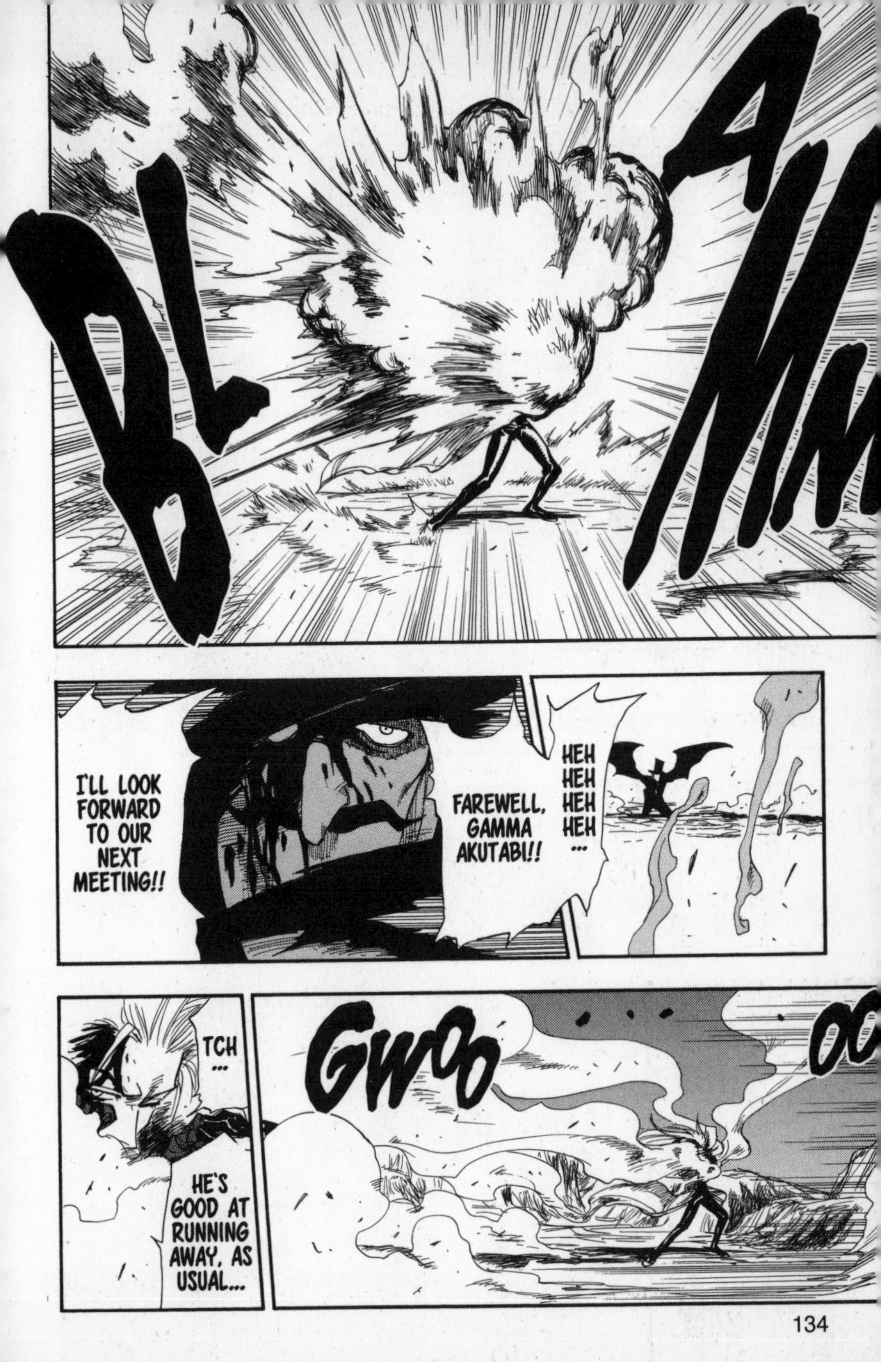
BL
AM
HEH HEH HEH HEH ...
FAREWELL, GAMMA AKUTABI!!
I'LL LOOK FORWARD TO OUR NEXT MEETING!!
GWOO OO
TCH ...
HE'S GOOD AT RUNNING AWAY, AS USUAL...

READ THIS WAY

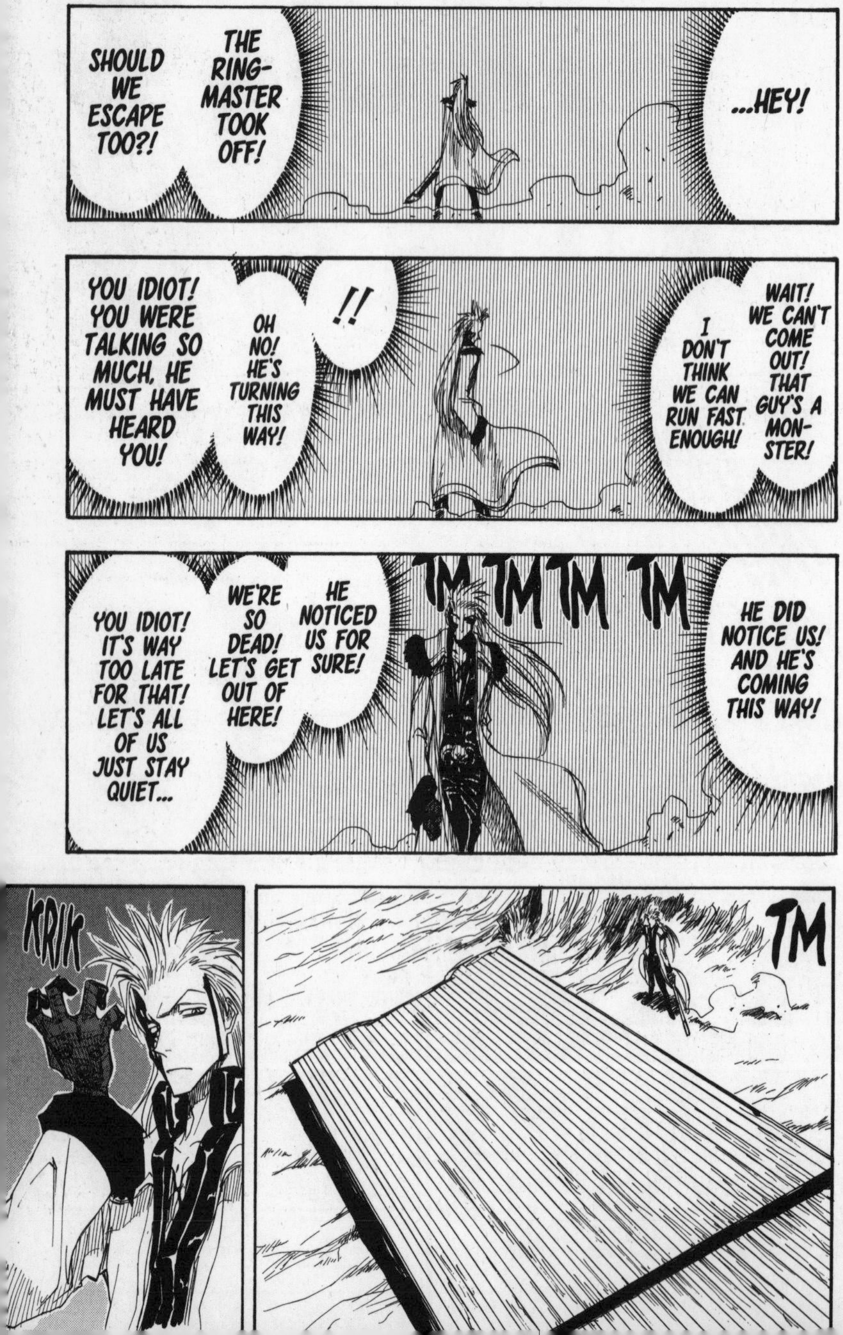
...HEY!
THE RING-MASTER TOOK OFF!
SHOULD WE ESCAPE TOO?!
WAIT! WE CAN'T COME OUT! THAT GUY'S A MON-STER!
I DON'T THINK WE CAN RUN FAST ENOUGH!
!!
OH NO! HE'S TURNING THIS WAY!
YOU IDIOT! YOU WERE TALKING SO MUCH, HE MUST HAVE HEARD YOU!
TM TM TM TM
HE DID NOTICE US! AND HE'S COMING THIS WAY!
HE NOTICED US FOR SURE!
WE'RE SO DEAD! LET'S GET OUT OF HERE!
YOU IDIOT! IT'S WAY TOO LATE FOR THAT! LET'S ALL OF US JUST STAY QUIET...
TM
KRIK

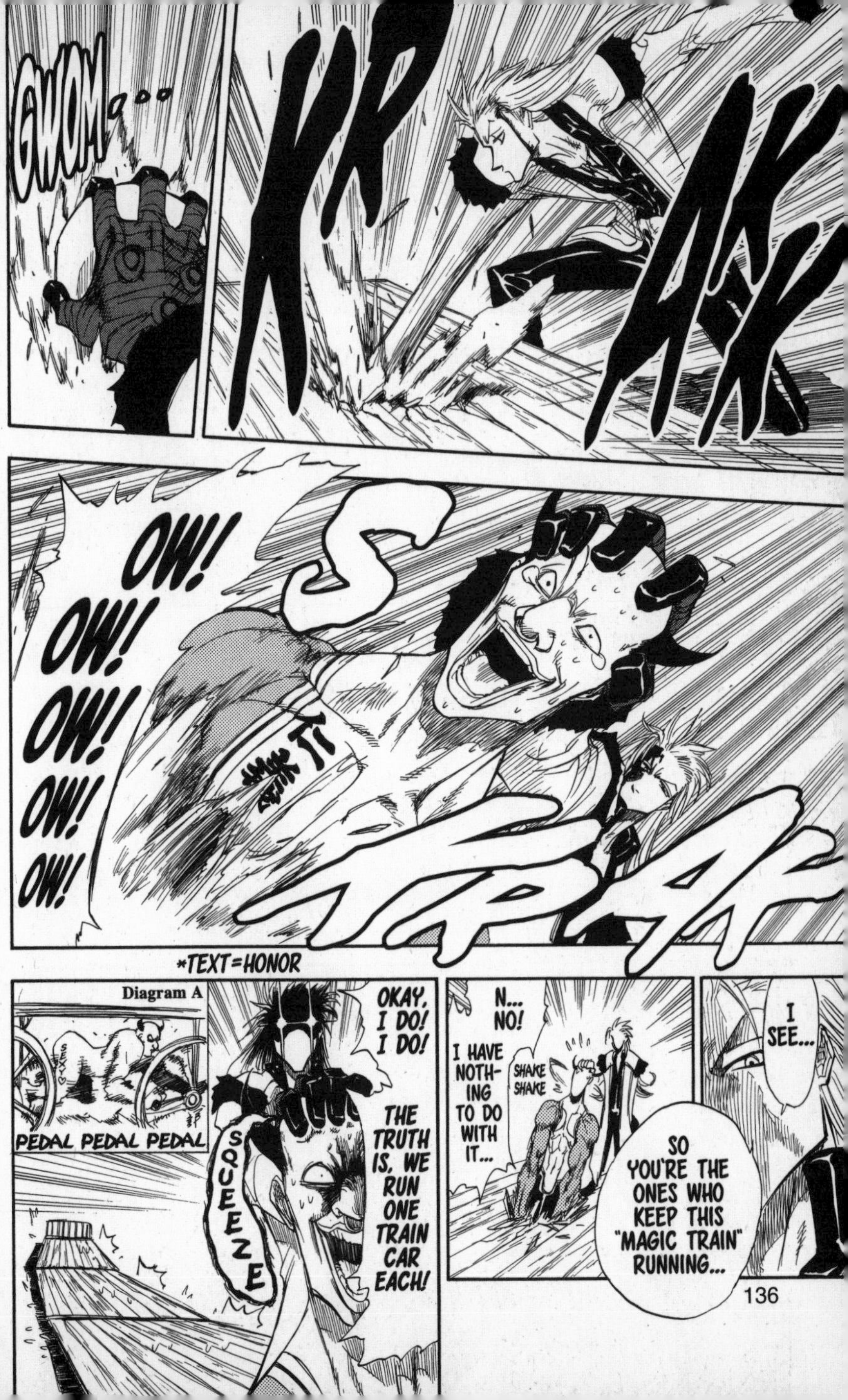
KRAK
GWOM...
STRAK
OW! OW! OW! OW! OW!
*TEXT=HONOR
I SEE...
SO YOU'RE THE ONES WHO KEEP THIS "MAGIC TRAIN" RUNNING...
N... NO!
I HAVE NOTHING TO DO WITH IT...
SHAKE SHAKE
OKAY, I DO! I DO!
THE TRUTH IS, WE RUN ONE TRAIN CAR EACH!
SQUEEZE
Diagram A
SEXY♡
PEDAL PEDAL PEDAL

READ THIS WAY

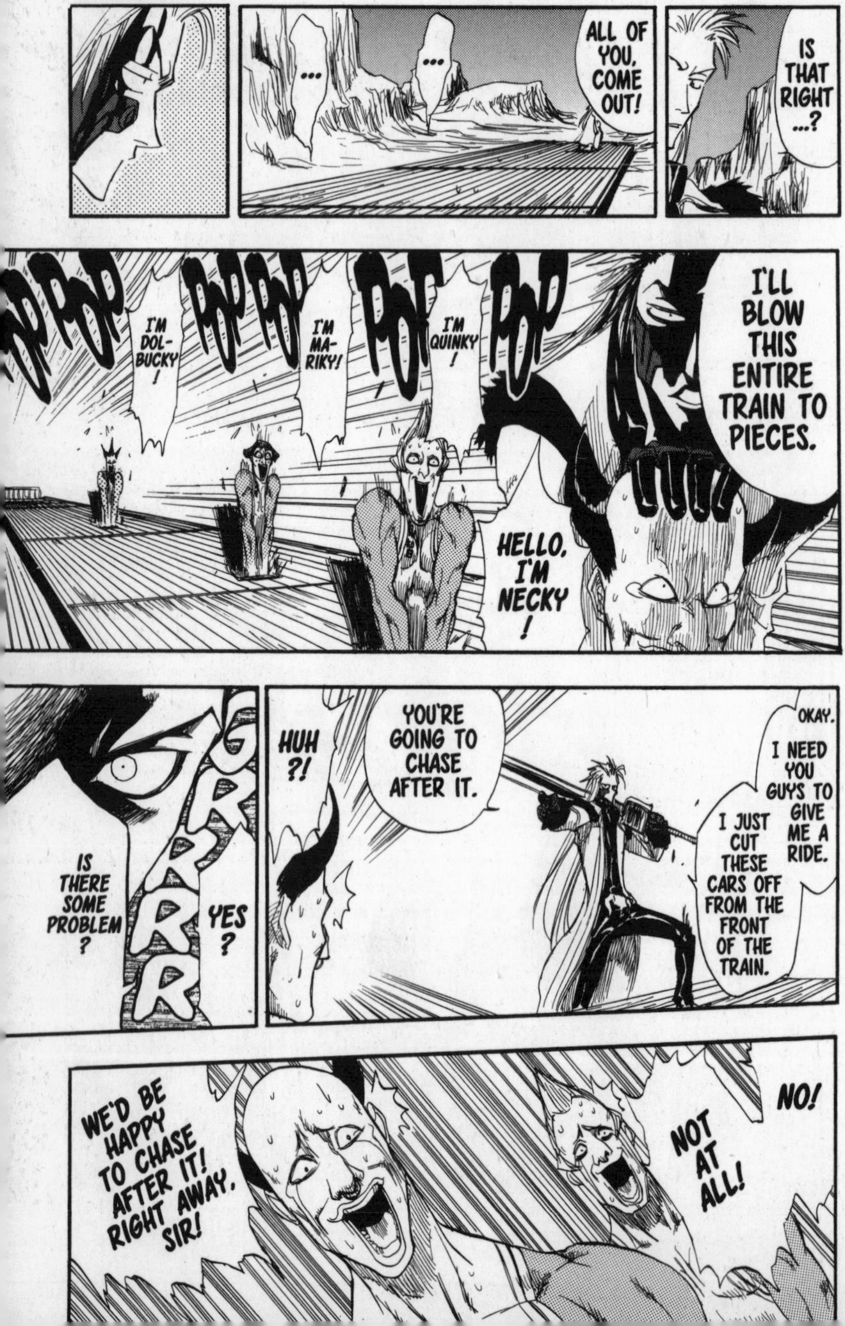
IS THAT RIGHT ...?
ALL OF YOU, COME OUT!
...
...
I'LL BLOW THIS ENTIRE TRAIN TO PIECES.
POP
HELLO, I'M NECKY!
POP
I'M QUINKY!
POP POP
I'M MA-RIKY!
POP POP POP
I'M DOL-BUCKY!
POP POP
OKAY. I NEED YOU GUYS TO GIVE ME A RIDE.
I JUST CUT THESE CARS OFF FROM THE FRONT OF THE TRAIN.
YOU'RE GOING TO CHASE AFTER IT.
HUH?!
YES?
GRRRRR
IS THERE SOME PROBLEM?
NO!
NOT AT ALL!
WE'D BE HAPPY TO CHASE AFTER IT! RIGHT AWAY, SIR!

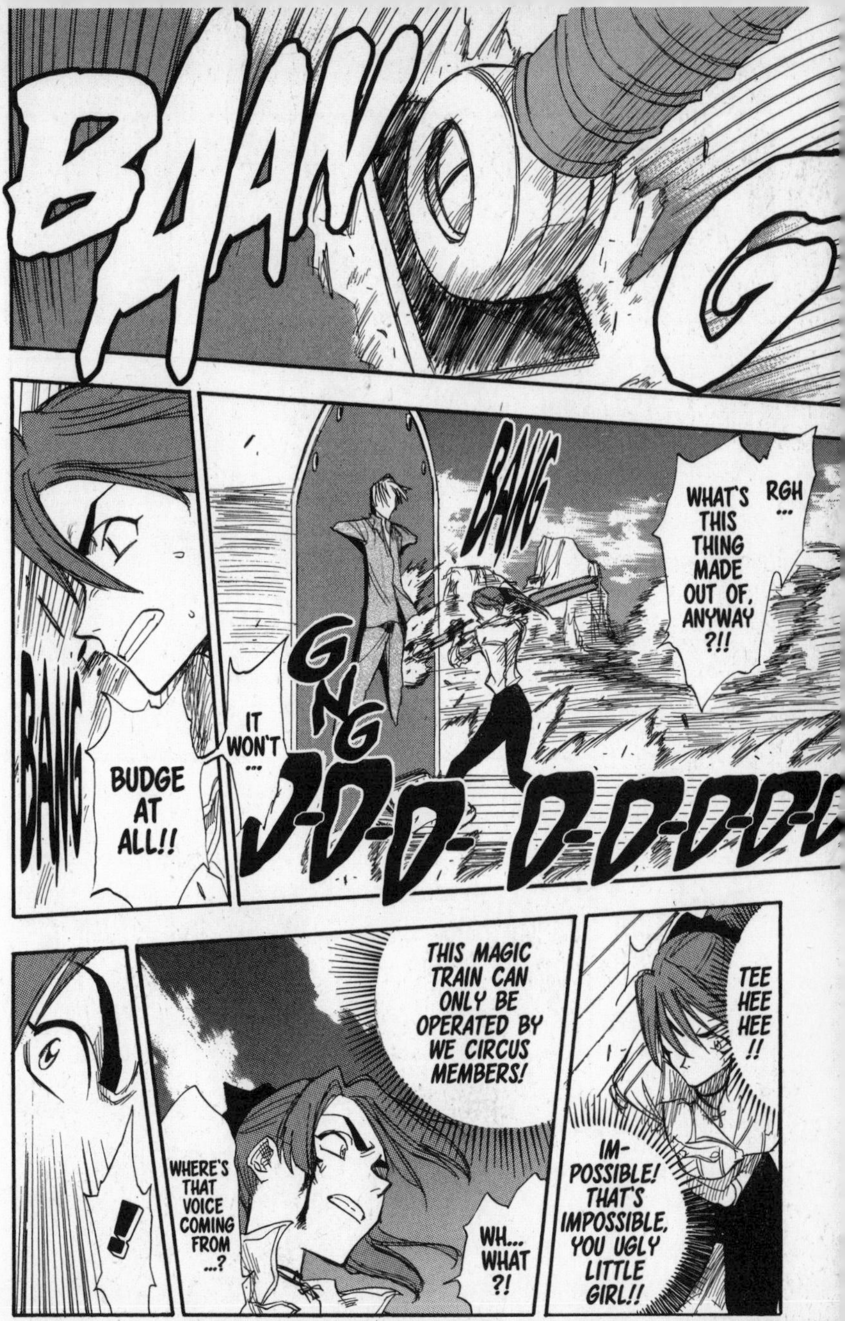
BAANG
RGH...
WHAT'S THIS THING MADE OUT OF, ANYWAY?!!
BANG
GNG
IT WON'T...
D-D-D-D-D-D-D-D
BANG
BUDGE AT ALL!!
TEE HEE HEE!!
IM-POSSIBLE! THAT'S IMPOSSIBLE, YOU UGLY LITTLE GIRL!!
THIS MAGIC TRAIN CAN ONLY BE OPERATED BY WE CIRCUS MEMBERS!
WH... WHAT?!
WHERE'S THAT VOICE COMING FROM...?
!

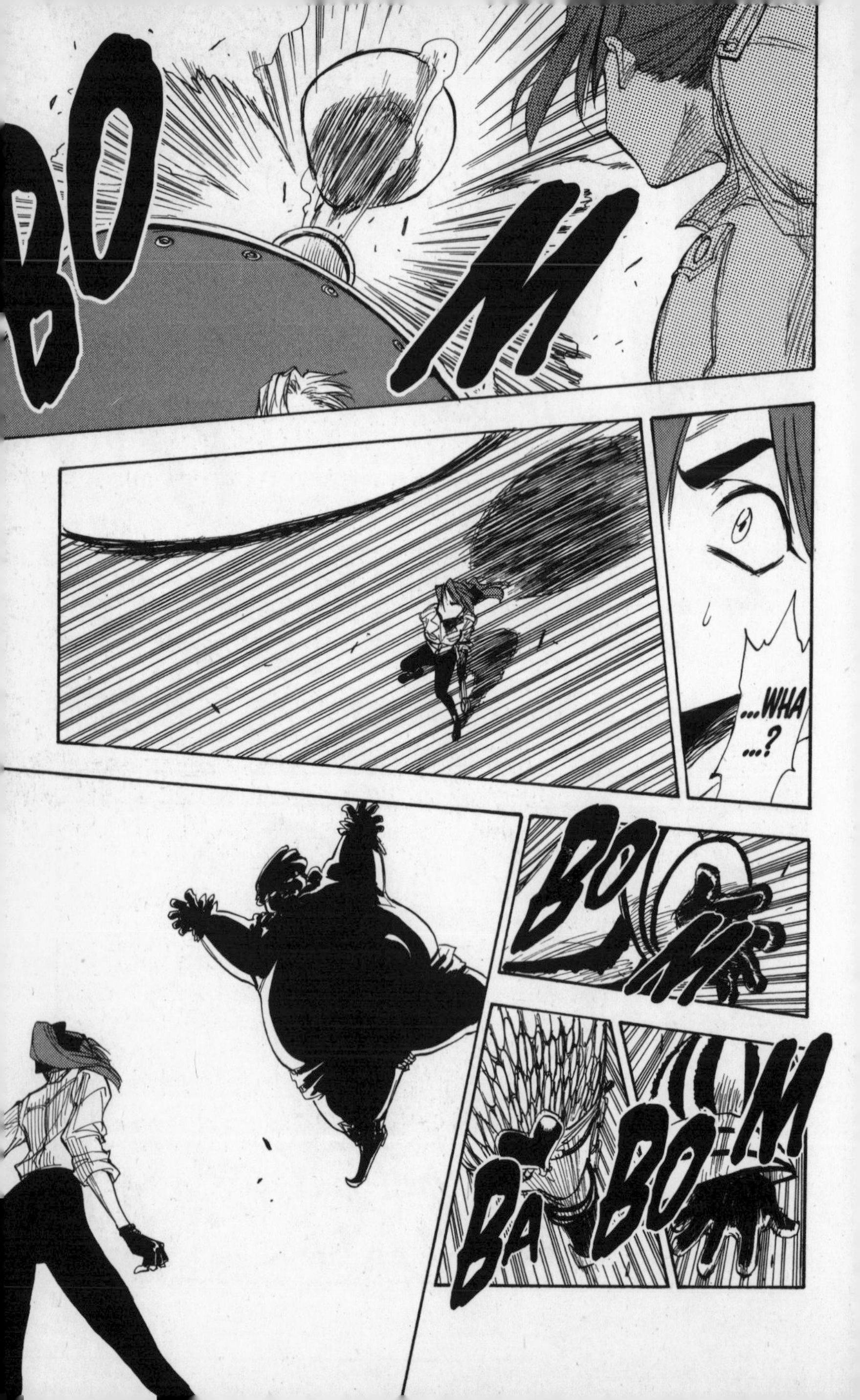
BOOM
...WHA ...?
BOOM
BA BOOM

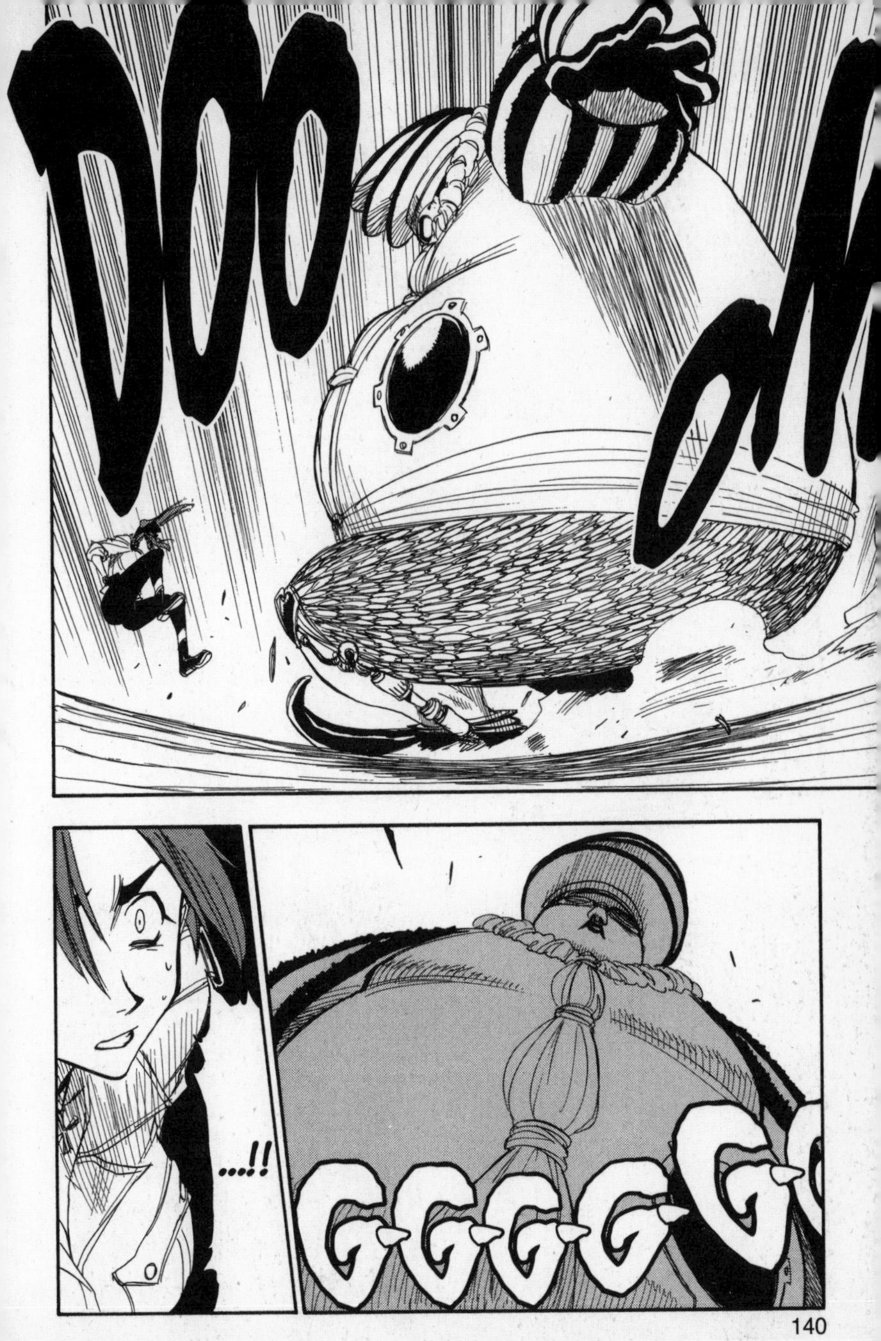
DOO
GGGGG
...!!

READ THIS WAY

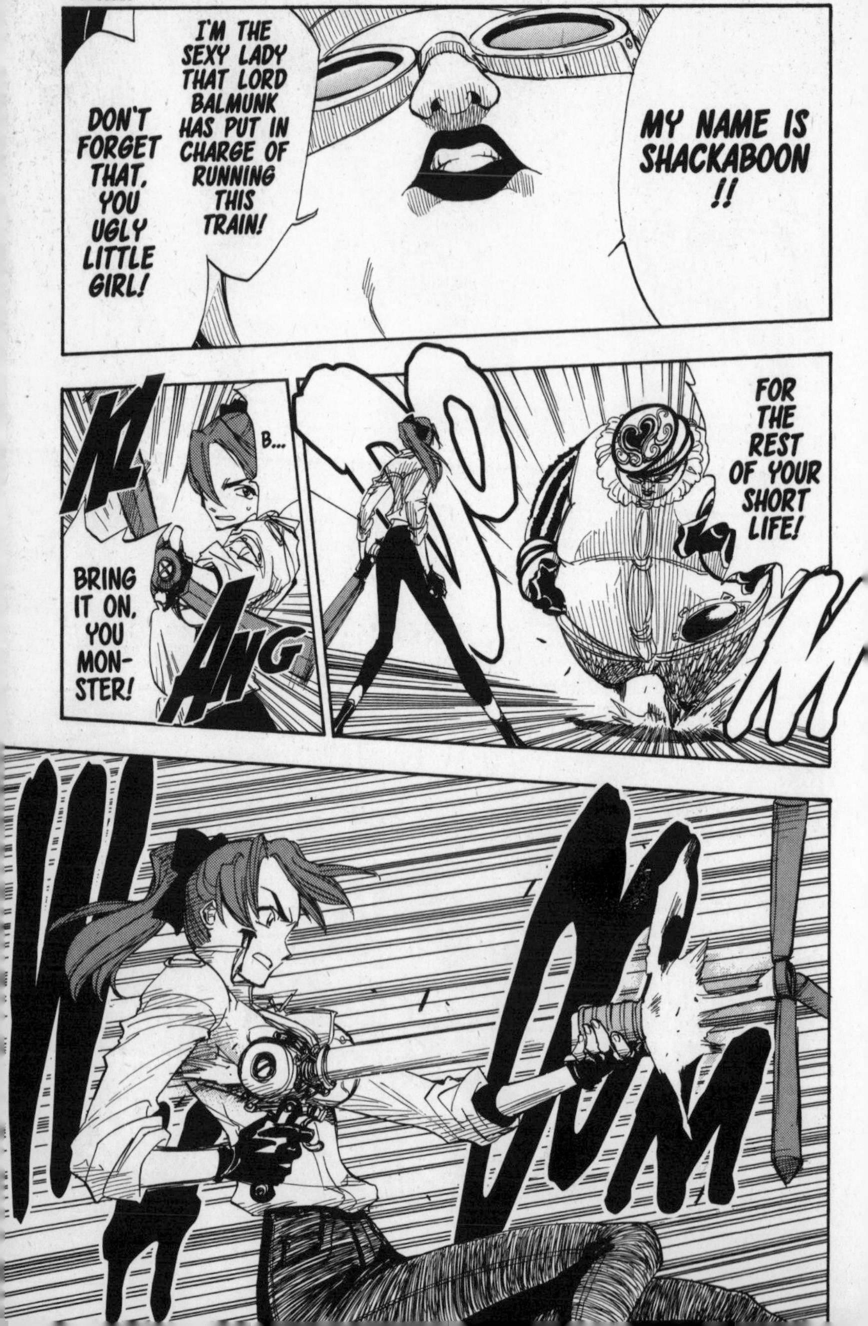
MY NAME IS SHACKABOON !!
I'M THE SEXY LADY THAT LORD BALMUNK HAS PUT IN CHARGE OF RUNNING THIS TRAIN!
DON'T FORGET THAT, YOU UGLY LITTLE GIRL!
FOR THE REST OF YOUR SHORT LIFE!
B...
BRING IT ON, YOU MONSTER!

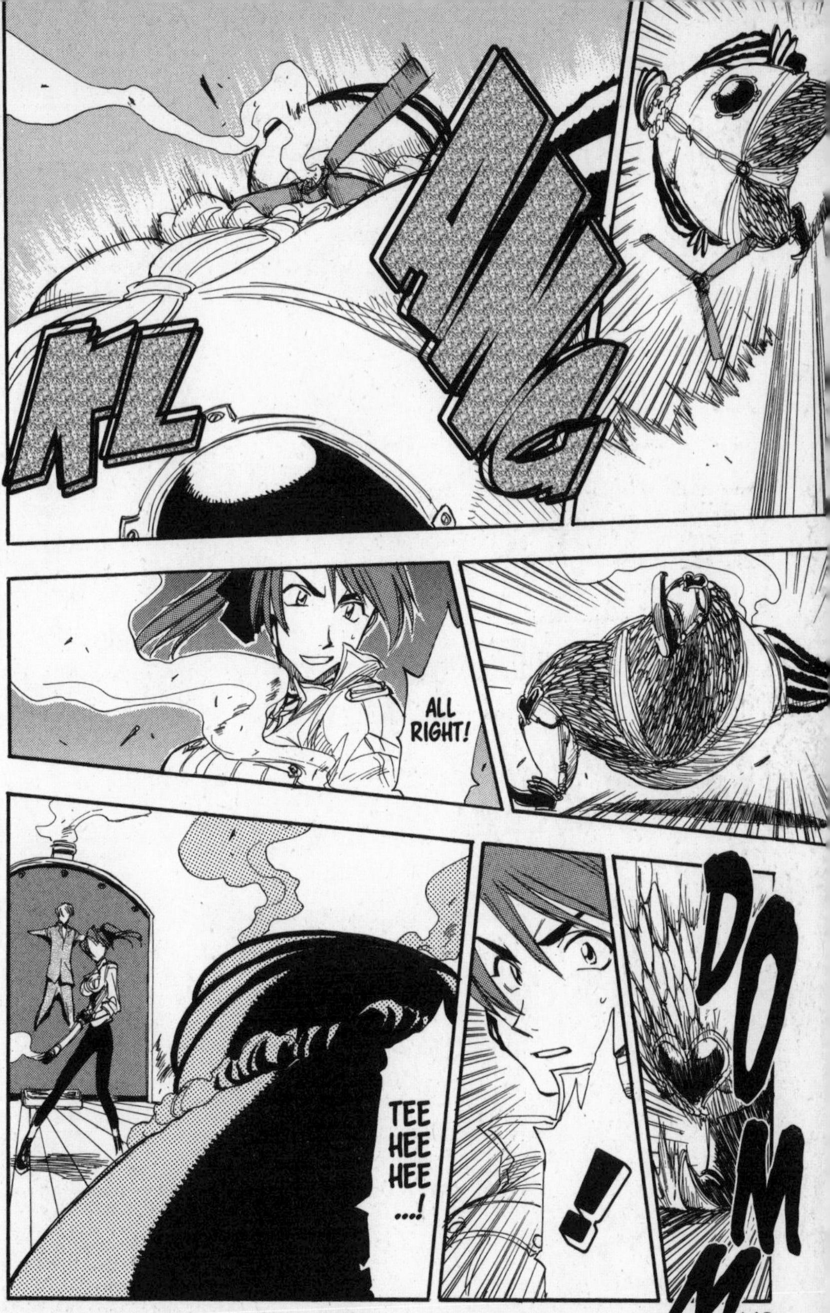
ALL RIGHT!
DOMM
!
TEE HEE HEE ...!

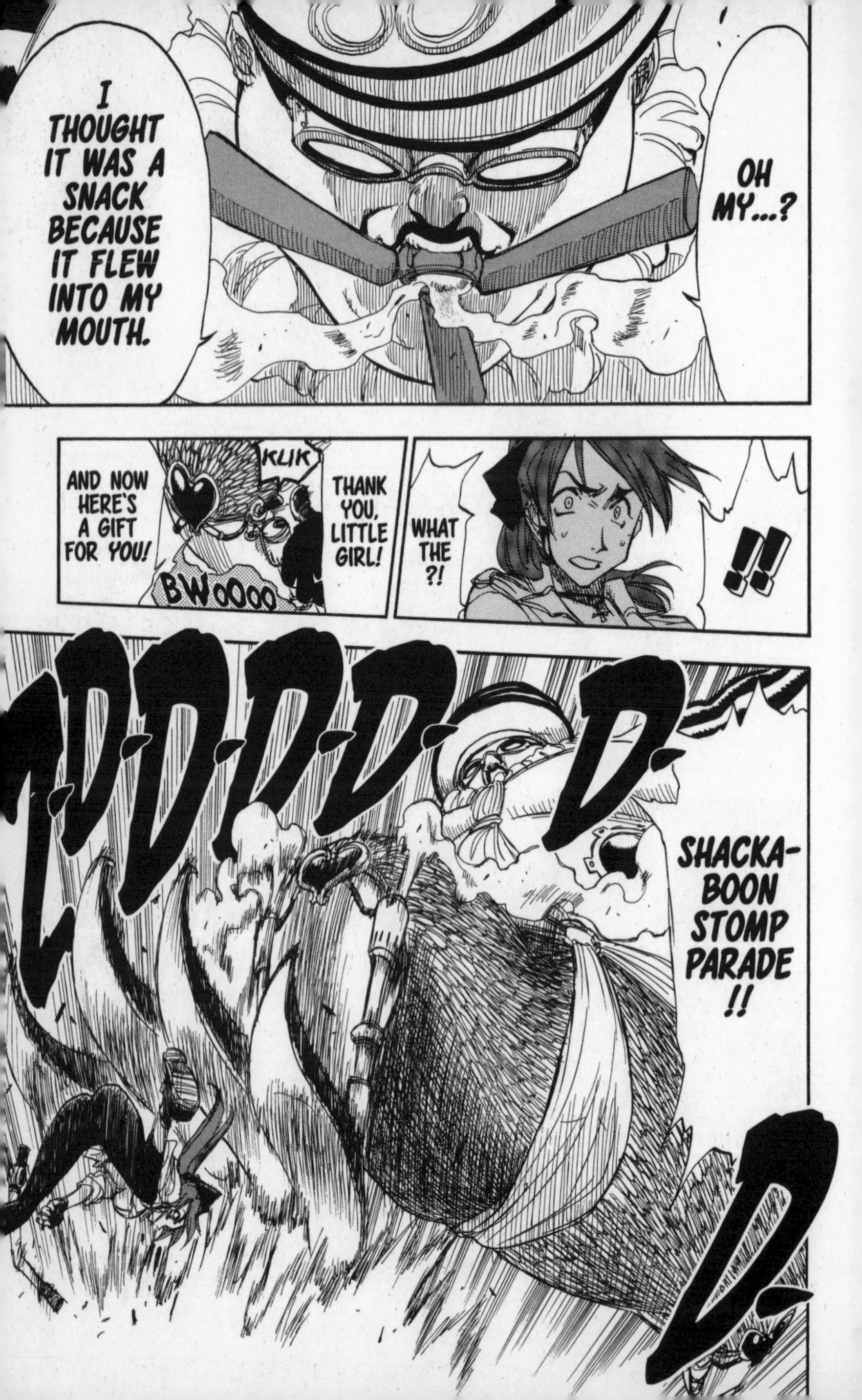
OH MY...?
I THOUGHT IT WAS A SNACK BECAUSE IT FLEW INTO MY MOUTH.
!!
WHAT THE ?!
THANK YOU, LITTLE GIRL!
KLIK
AND NOW HERE'S A GIFT FOR YOU!
BWOOOO
SHACKA-BOON STOMP PARADE !!

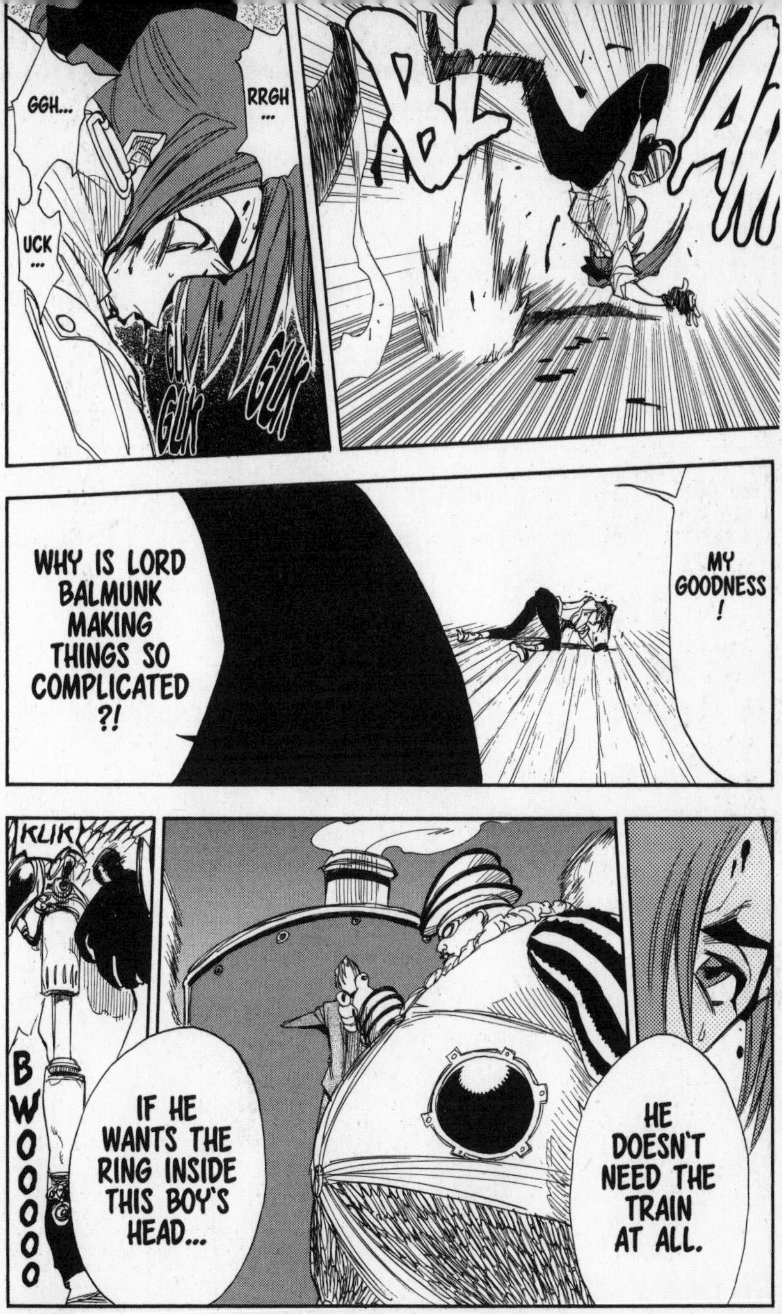
BLAM
RRGH...
GGH...
UCK...
GLK GLK GLK GLK
MY GOODNESS!
WHY IS LORD BALMUNK MAKING THINGS SO COMPLICATED?!
IF HE WANTS THE RING INSIDE THIS BOY'S HEAD...
HE DOESN'T NEED THE TRAIN AT ALL.
KLIK
BWOOOOOO

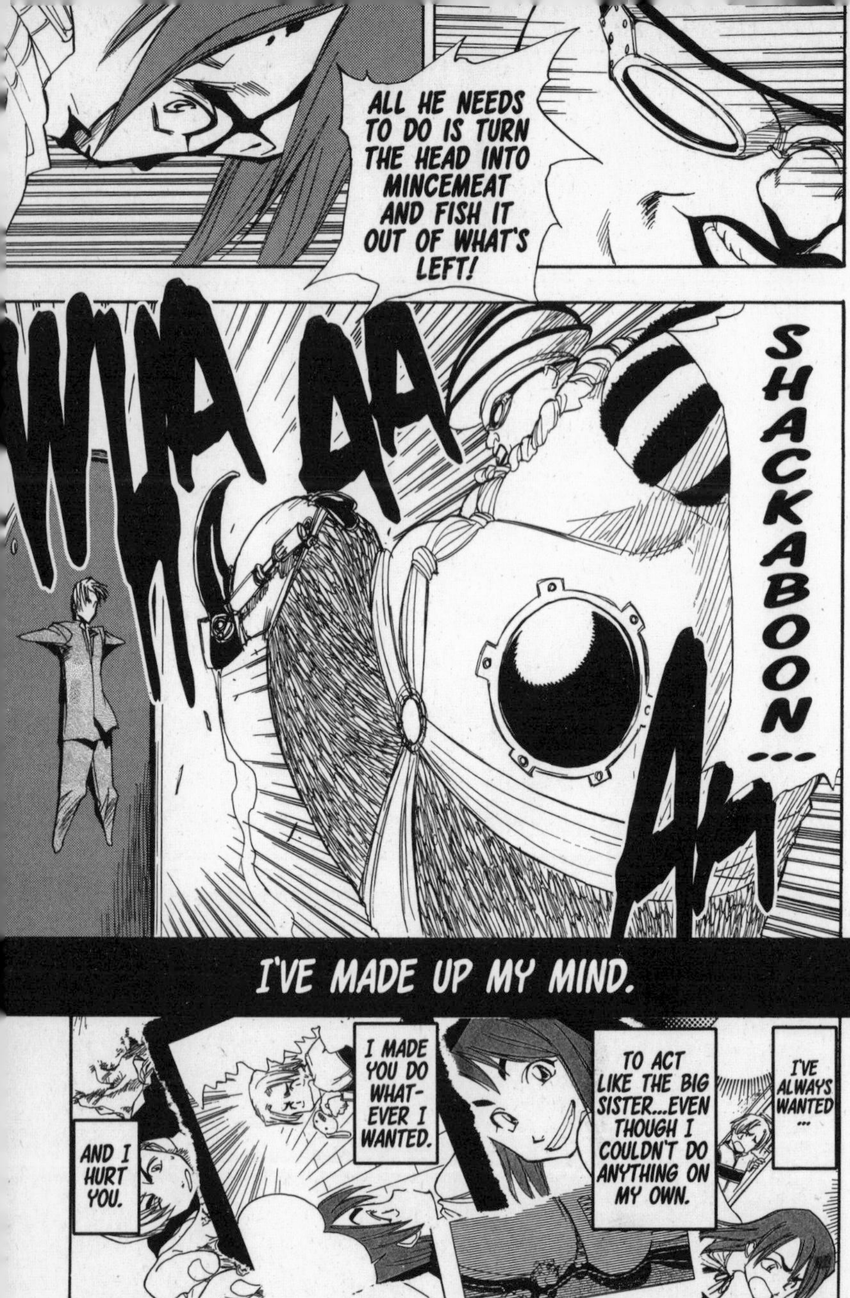
ALL HE NEEDS TO DO IS TURN THE HEAD INTO MINCEMEAT AND FISH IT OUT OF WHAT'S LEFT!
SHACKABOOON...
I'VE MADE UP MY MIND.
I'VE ALWAYS WANTED...
TO ACT LIKE THE BIG SISTER...EVEN THOUGH I COULDN'T DO ANYTHING ON MY OWN.
I MADE YOU DO WHATEVER I WANTED.
AND I HURT YOU.

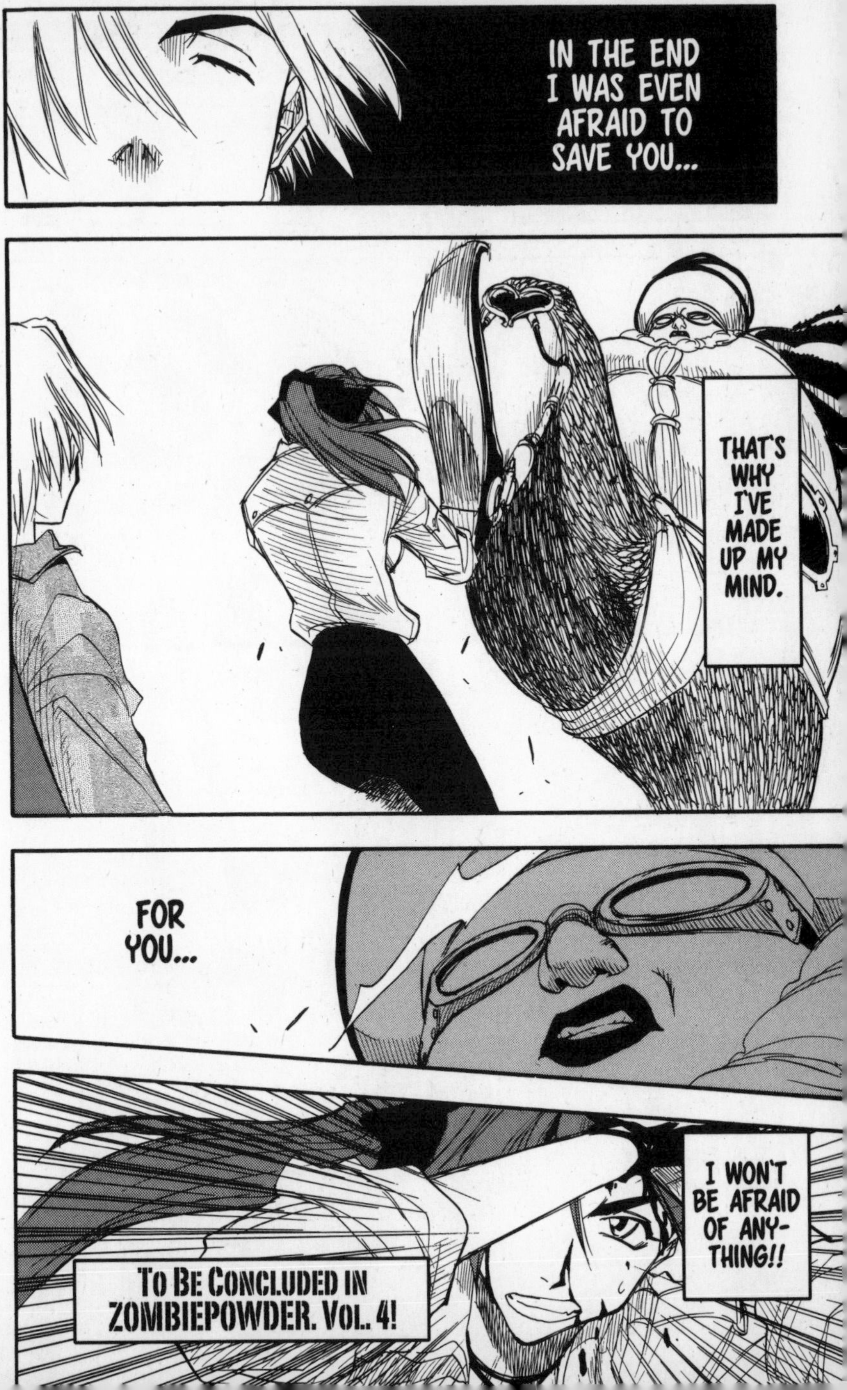
IN THE END I WAS EVEN AFRAID TO SAVE YOU...
THAT'S WHY I'VE MADE UP MY MIND.
FOR YOU...
I WON'T BE AFRAID OF ANY-THING!!
TO BE CONCLUDED IN ZOMBIEPOWDER. VOL. 4!

B-side NAKED MONKEYS 14.

Amantine
アマンティーヌ

Date of Birth: 1/3

Age: 3

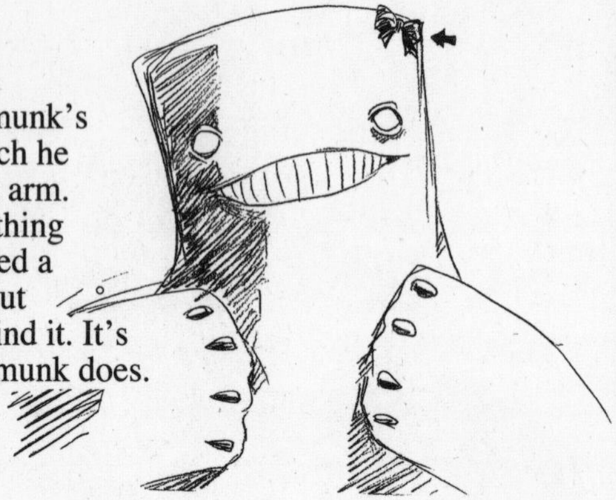

The crystallization of Balmunk's most powerful magic, which he created from his own right arm. By what logic could something like this be made? I received a lot of questions like this, but there's really no logic behind it. It's just another thing that Balmunk does. By the way, you might be able to tell from the name that it's a girl.

Shackaboon
シャカブーン

Height: 291cm

Weight: 355kg

Date of Birth: unknown

Age: 23 (allegedly)

Blood Type: AA

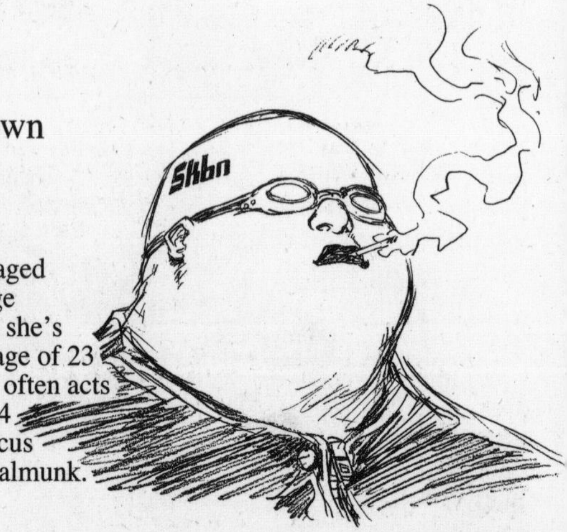
Skbn

A heavily made up middle-aged lady with a ridiculously large and heavy body. (Or maybe she's a young lady.) Her alleged age of 23 makes one wonder why she often acts so desperate. She's the No. 4 member of the Balmunk circus troupe and is in love with Balmunk.

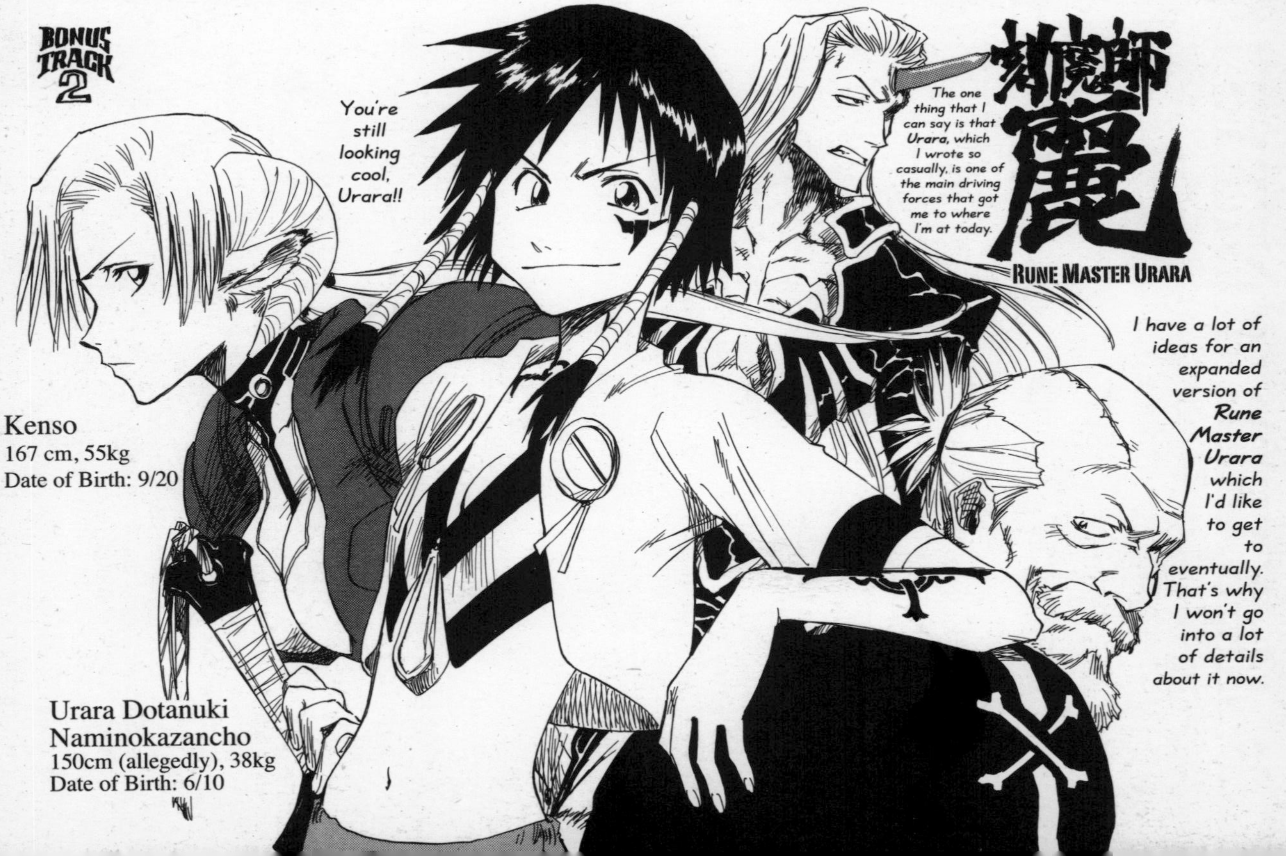
BONUS TRACK 2
RUNE MASTER URARA
The one thing that I can say is that Urara, which I wrote so casually, is one of the main driving forces that got me to where I'm at today.
I have a lot of ideas for an expanded version of Rune Master Urara which I'd like to get to eventually. That's why I won't go into a lot of details about it now.
You're still looking cool, Urara!!
Kenso
167 cm, 55kg
Date of Birth: 9/20
Urara Dotanuki Naminokazancho
150cm (allegedly), 38kg
Date of Birth: 6/10

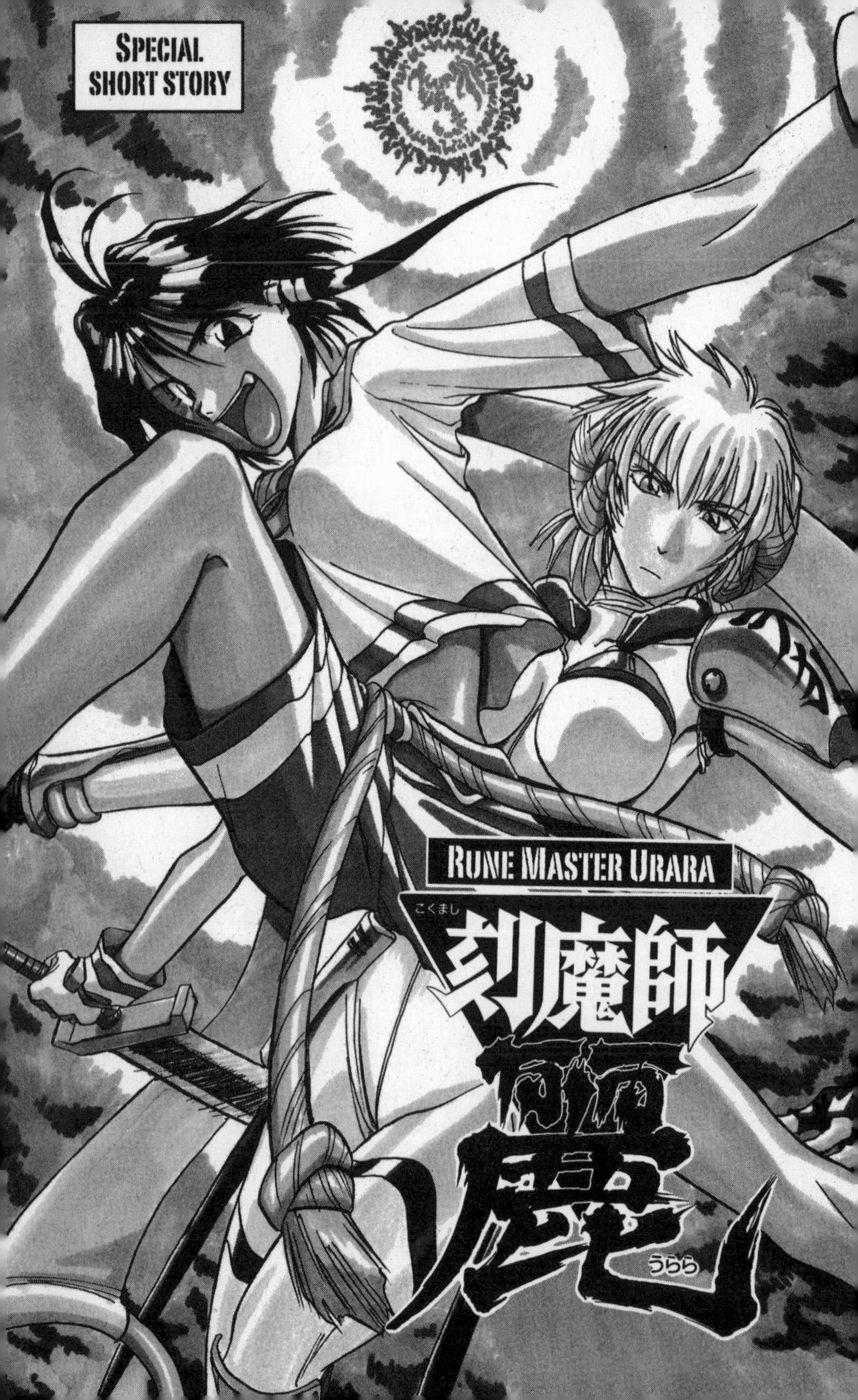
SPECIAL SHORT STORY
RUNE MASTER URARA
こくまし
刻魔師
麗
うらら

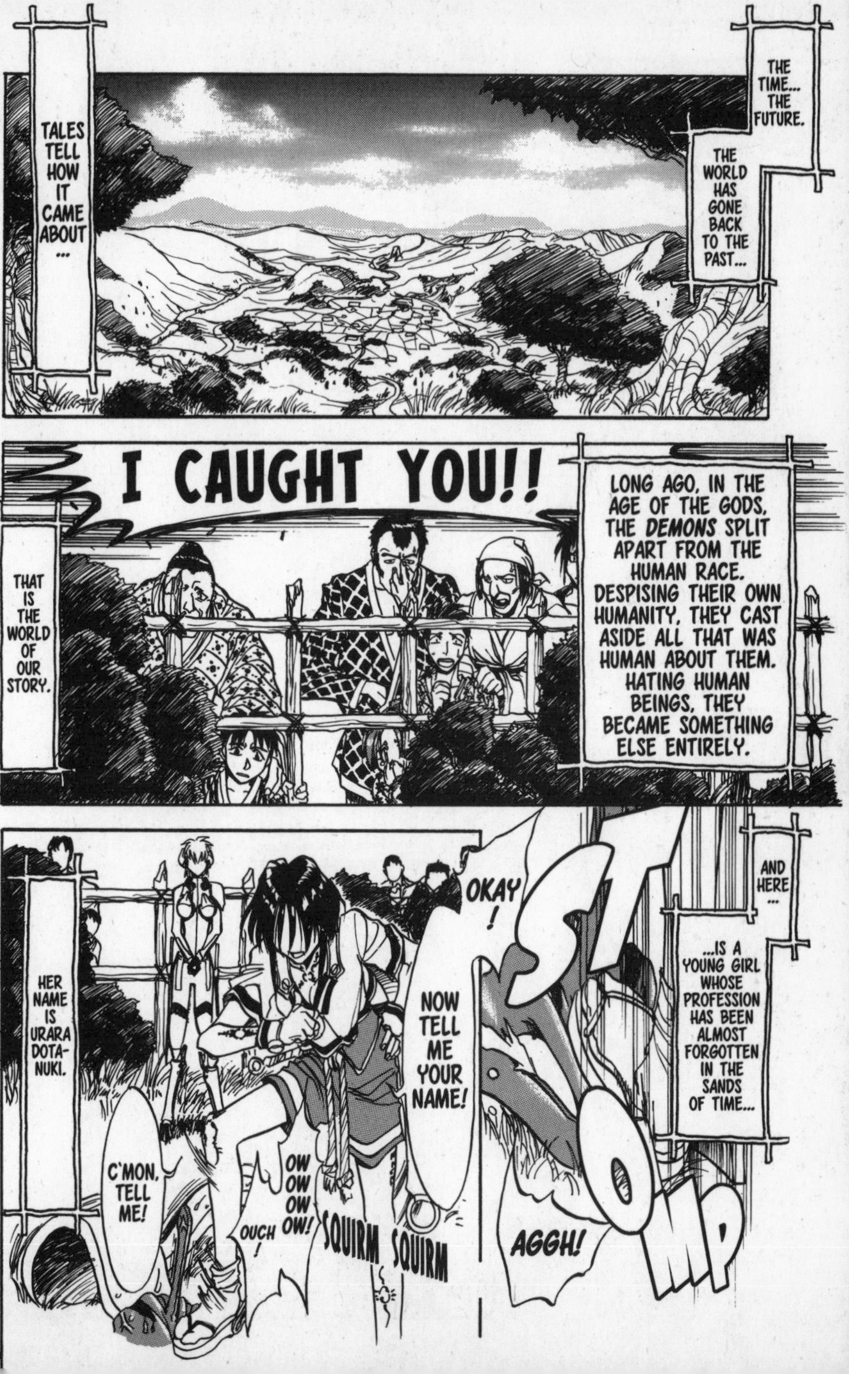
THE TIME... THE FUTURE.
THE WORLD HAS GONE BACK TO THE PAST...
TALES TELL HOW IT CAME ABOUT...
LONG AGO, IN THE AGE OF THE GODS, THE *DEMONS* SPLIT APART FROM THE HUMAN RACE. DESPISING THEIR OWN HUMANITY, THEY CAST ASIDE ALL THAT WAS HUMAN ABOUT THEM. HATING HUMAN BEINGS, THEY BECAME SOMETHING ELSE ENTIRELY.
I CAUGHT YOU!!
THAT IS THE WORLD OF OUR STORY.
AND HERE...
...IS A YOUNG GIRL WHOSE PROFESSION HAS BEEN ALMOST FORGOTTEN IN THE SANDS OF TIME...
OKAY!
STOMP
AGGH!
NOW TELL ME YOUR NAME!
HER NAME IS URARA DOTANUKI.
OW OW OW OW!
OUCH!
C'MON, TELL ME!
SQUIRM SQUIRM

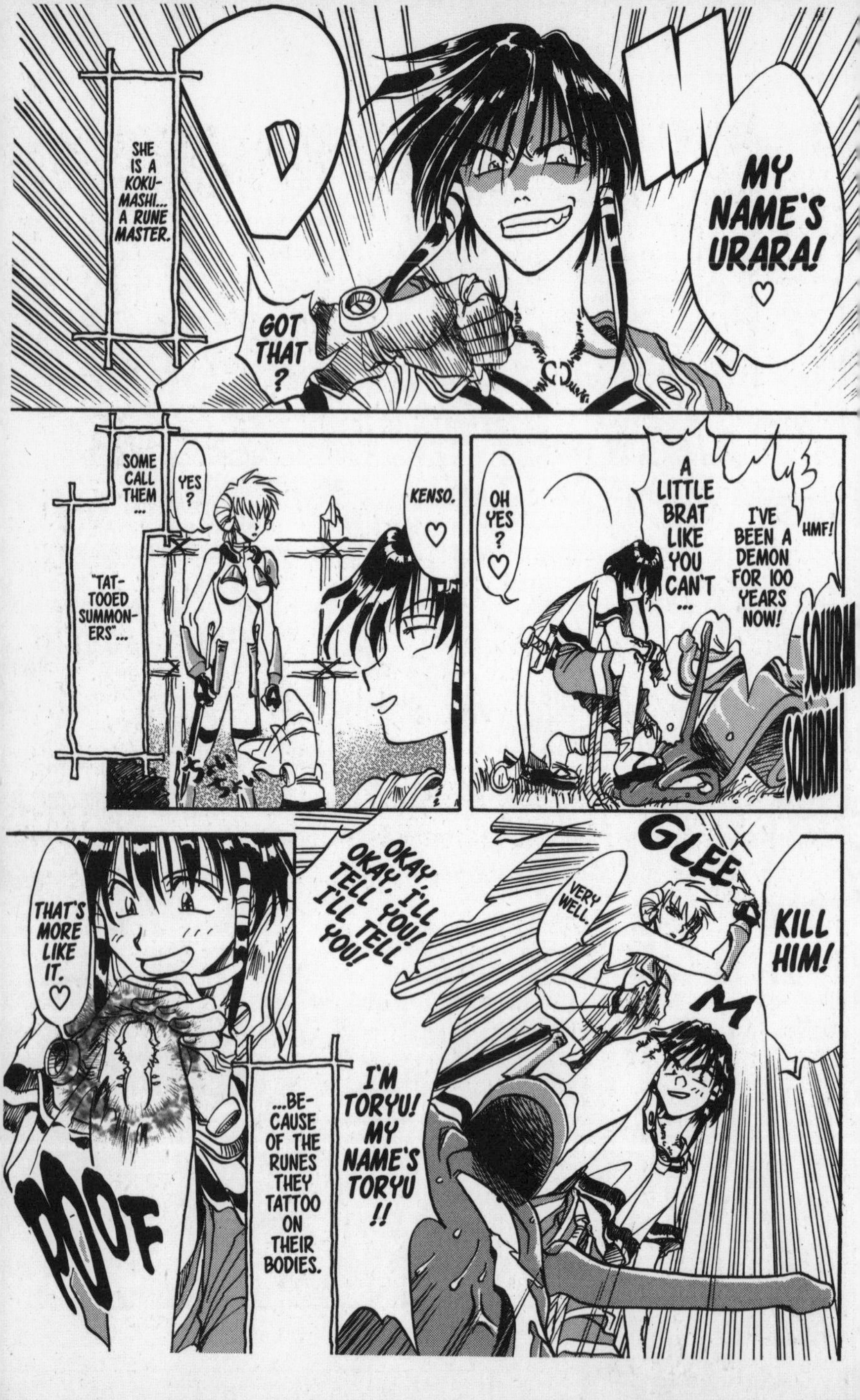
MY NAME'S URARA! ♡
GOT THAT?
SHE IS A KOKU-MASHI... A RUNE MASTER.
HMF!
I'VE BEEN A DEMON FOR 100 YEARS NOW!
A LITTLE BRAT LIKE YOU CAN'T ...
OH YES? ♡
SQUIRM
SQUIRM
KENSO. ♡
YES?
SOME CALL THEM ...
"TAT-TOOED SUMMONERS"...
KILL HIM!
GLEE
VERY WELL.
OKAY, OKAY, I'LL TELL YOU! I'LL TELL YOU!
M
I'M TORYU! MY NAME'S TORYU!!
...BE-CAUSE OF THE RUNES THEY TATTOO ON THEIR BODIES.
THAT'S MORE LIKE IT. ♡
POOF

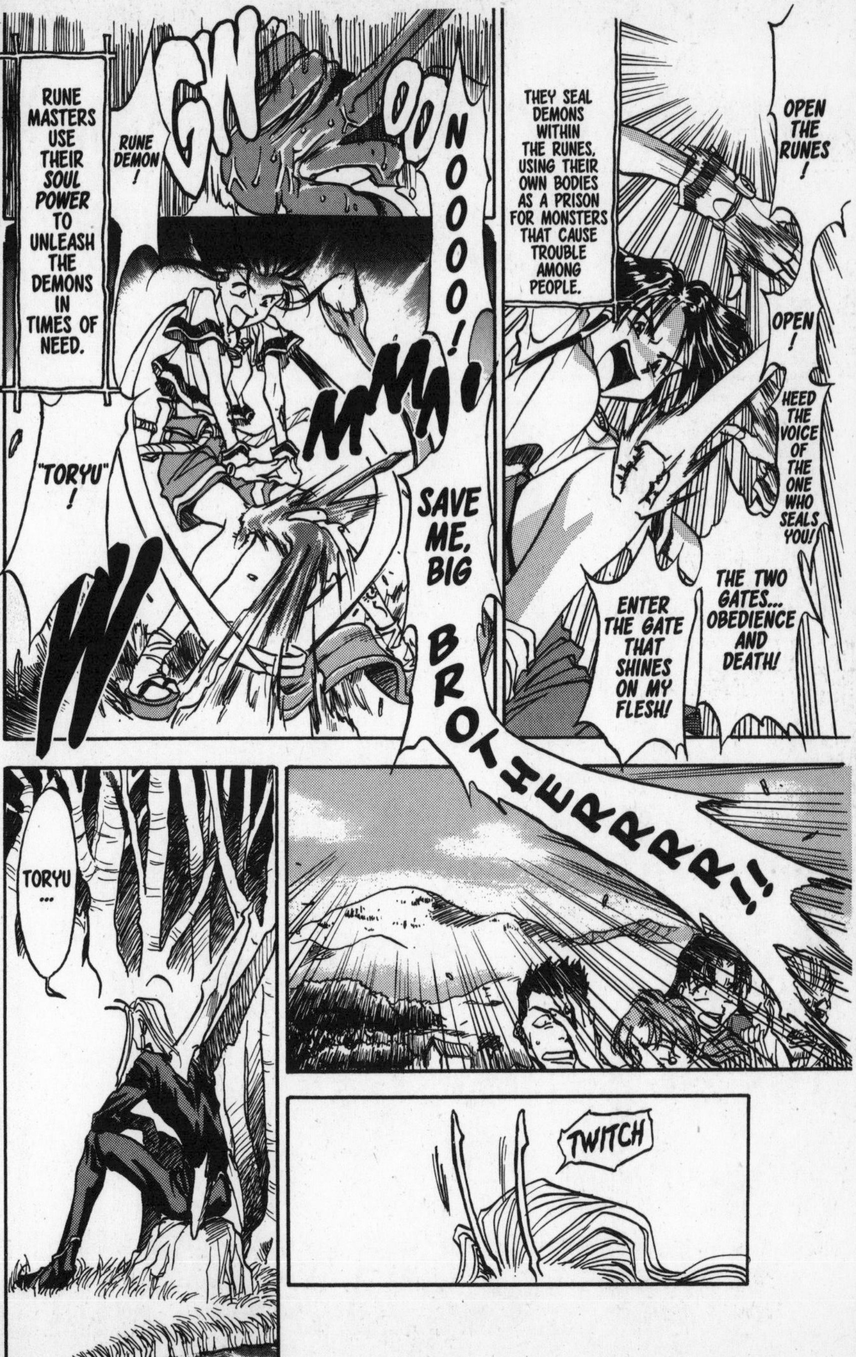
THEY SEAL DEMONS WITHIN THE RUNES, USING THEIR OWN BODIES AS A PRISON FOR MONSTERS THAT CAUSE TROUBLE AMONG PEOPLE.
OPEN THE RUNES!
OPEN!
HEED THE VOICE OF THE ONE WHO SEALS YOU!
THE TWO GATES... OBEDIENCE AND DEATH!
ENTER THE GATE THAT SHINES ON MY FLESH!
RUNE MASTERS USE THEIR SOUL POWER TO UNLEASH THE DEMONS IN TIMES OF NEED.
RUNE DEMON!
GN
OO
NOOOOO!
MMM
"TORYU"!
W
SAVE ME, BIG BROTHERRRR!!
TWITCH
TORYU...

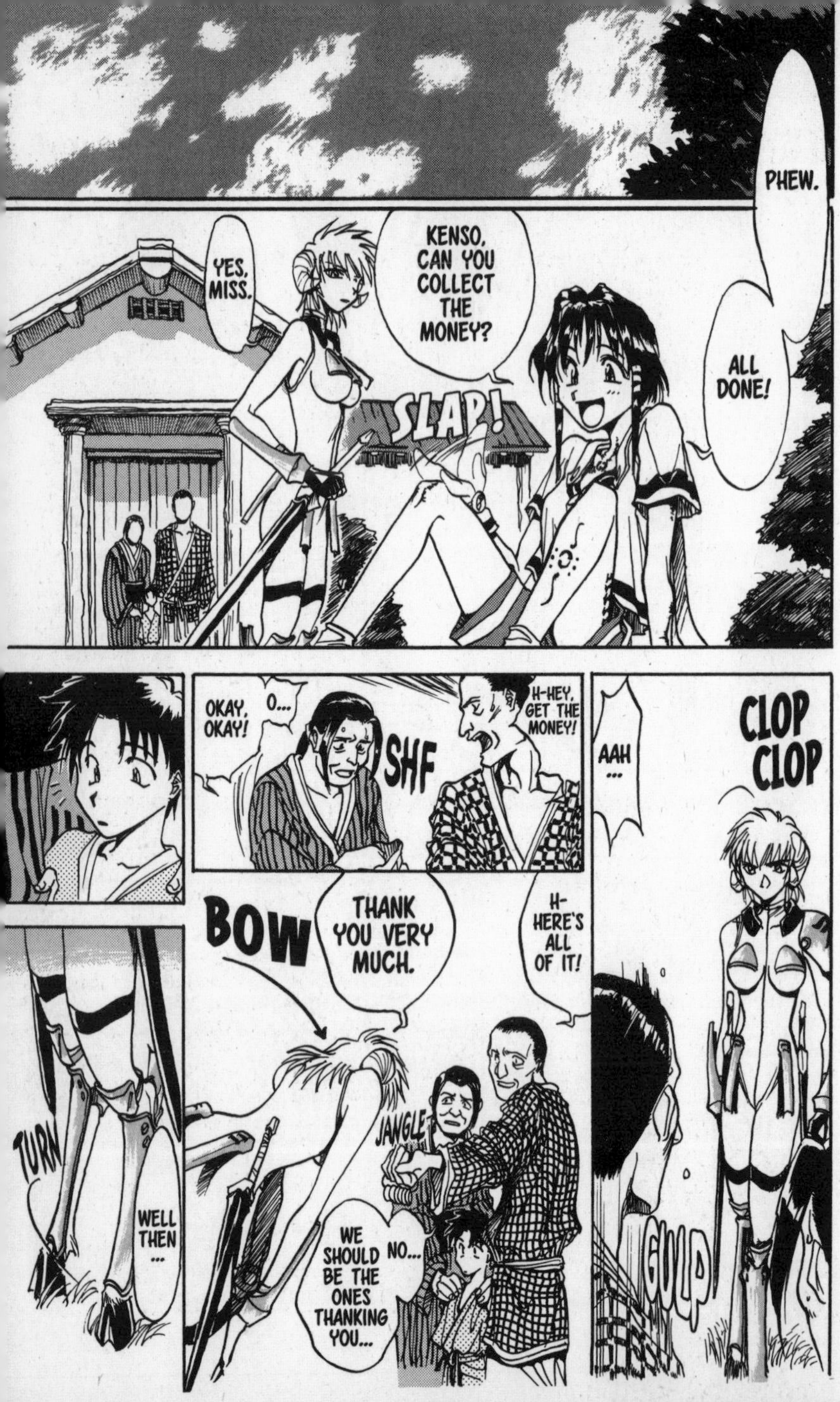
PHEW.
ALL DONE!
SLAP!
KENSO, CAN YOU COLLECT THE MONEY?
YES, MISS.
CLOP CLOP
AAH...
GULP
H-HEY, GET THE MONEY!
SHF
O...
OKAY, OKAY!
H-HERE'S ALL OF IT!
THANK YOU VERY MUCH.
BOW
JANGLE
NO...
WE SHOULD BE THE ONES THANKING YOU...
WELL THEN...
TURN

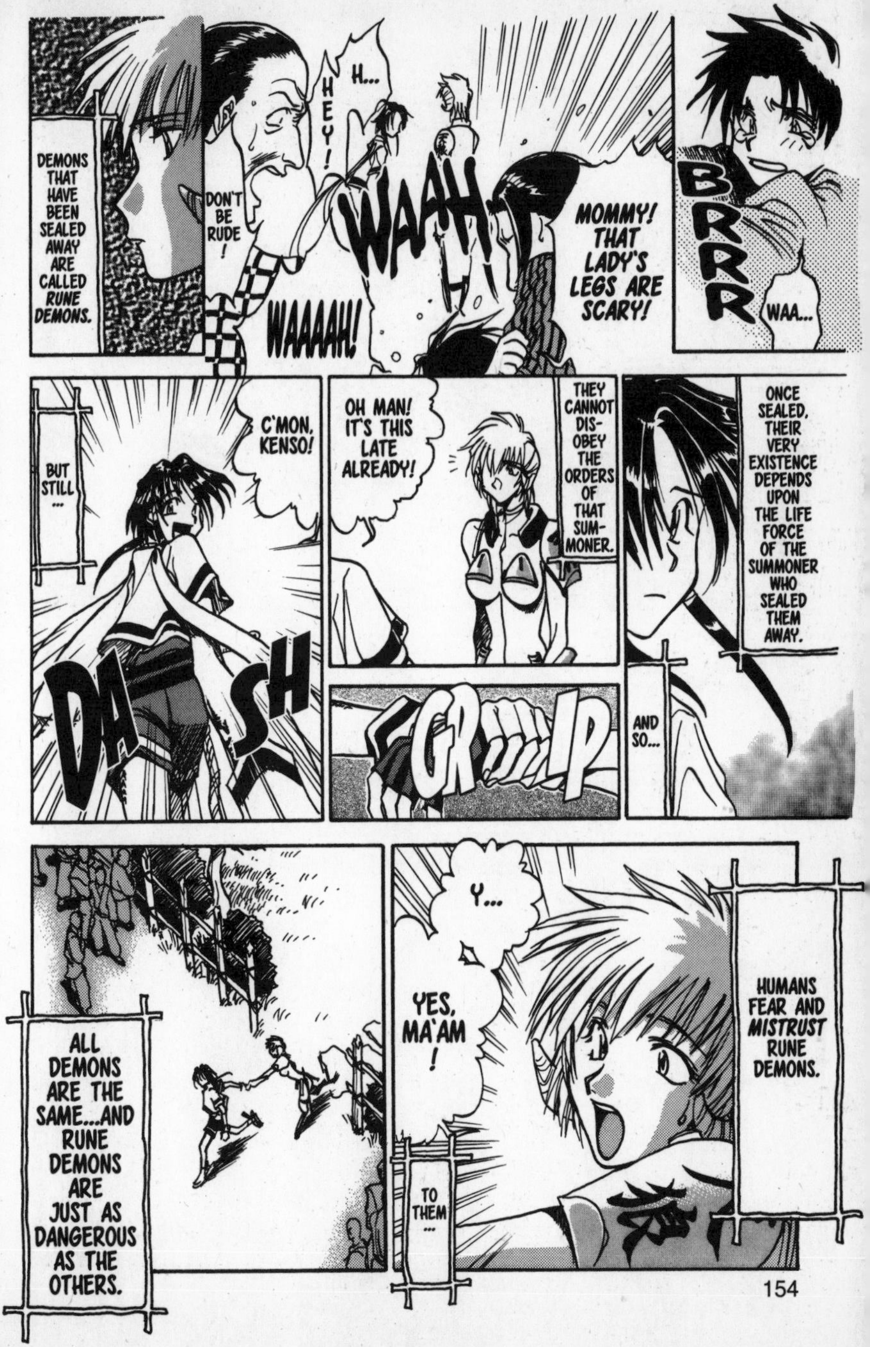
BRRR
WAA...
H...
HEY!
MOMMY! THAT LADY'S LEGS ARE SCARY!
WAAH
DON'T BE RUDE!
WAAAAH!
DEMONS THAT HAVE BEEN SEALED AWAY ARE CALLED RUNE DEMONS.
ONCE SEALED, THEIR VERY EXISTENCE DEPENDS UPON THE LIFE FORCE OF THE SUMMONER WHO SEALED THEM AWAY.
AND SO...
THEY CANNOT DIS-OBEY THE ORDERS OF THAT SUM-MONER.
OH MAN! IT'S THIS LATE ALREADY!
GR....IP
C'MON, KENSO!
BUT STILL...
DASH
HUMANS FEAR AND MISTRUST RUNE DEMONS.
Y...
YES, MA'AM!
TO THEM...
ALL DEMONS ARE THE SAME...AND RUNE DEMONS ARE JUST AS DANGEROUS AS THE OTHERS.

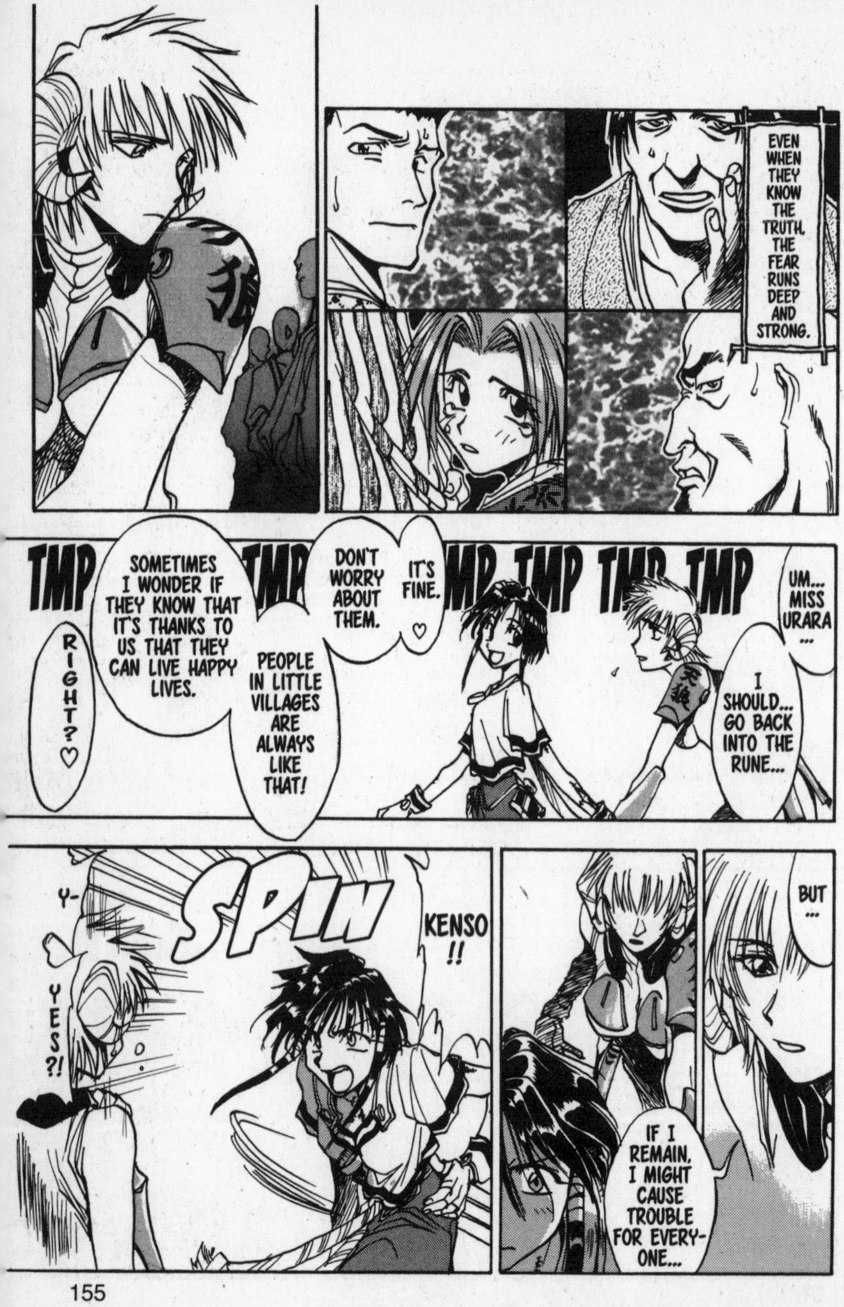
EVEN WHEN THEY KNOW THE TRUTH, THE FEAR RUNS DEEP AND STRONG.
UM... MISS URARA...
I SHOULD... GO BACK INTO THE RUNE...
TMP TMP TMP TMP TMP TMP
IT'S FINE. ♡
DON'T WORRY ABOUT THEM.
PEOPLE IN LITTLE VILLAGES ARE ALWAYS LIKE THAT!
SOMETIMES I WONDER IF THEY KNOW THAT IT'S THANKS TO US THAT THEY CAN LIVE HAPPY LIVES.
RIGHT? ♡
BUT...
IF I REMAIN, I MIGHT CAUSE TROUBLE FOR EVERYONE...
KENSO!!
SPIN
Y- YES?!

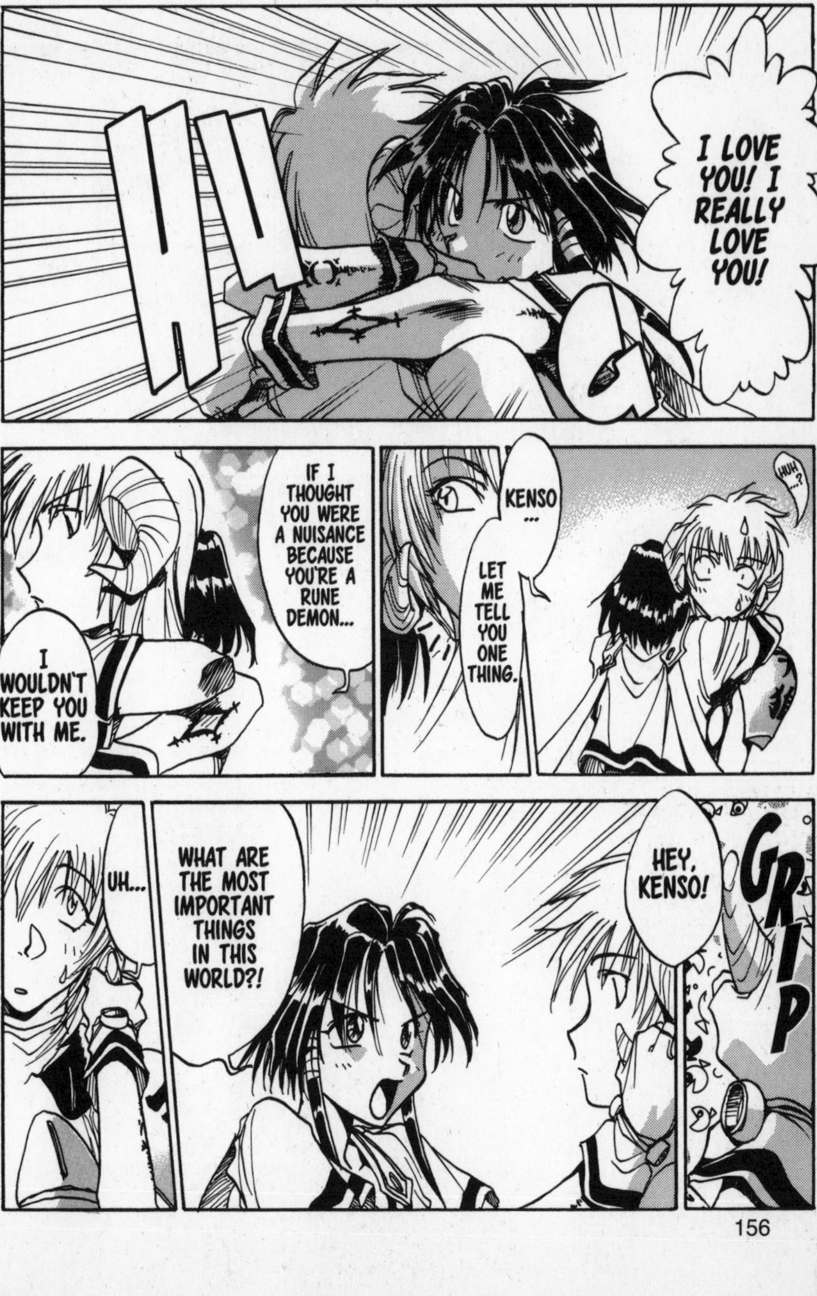
I LOVE YOU! I REALLY LOVE YOU!
HUG
HUH ...?
KENSO ...
LET ME TELL YOU ONE THING.
IF I THOUGHT YOU WERE A NUISANCE BECAUSE YOU'RE A RUNE DEMON...
I WOULDN'T KEEP YOU WITH ME.
GRIP
HEY, KENSO!
WHAT ARE THE MOST IMPORTANT THINGS IN THIS WORLD?!
UH...

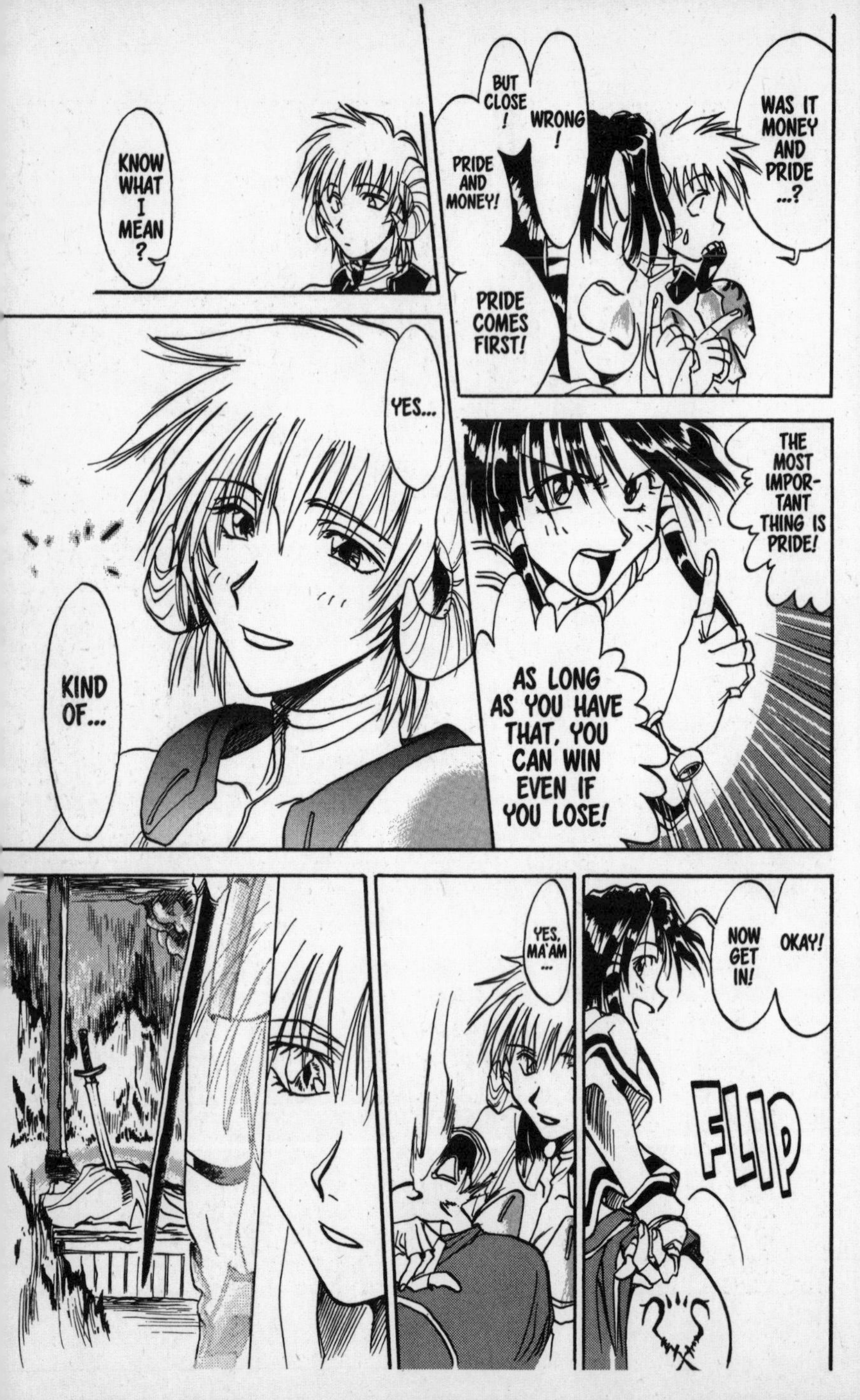
WAS IT MONEY AND PRIDE ...?
WRONG!
BUT CLOSE!
PRIDE AND MONEY!
PRIDE COMES FIRST!
KNOW WHAT I MEAN?
THE MOST IMPOR-TANT THING IS PRIDE!
AS LONG AS YOU HAVE THAT, YOU CAN WIN EVEN IF YOU LOSE!
YES...
KIND OF...
OKAY!
NOW GET IN!
FLIP
YES, MA'AM ...

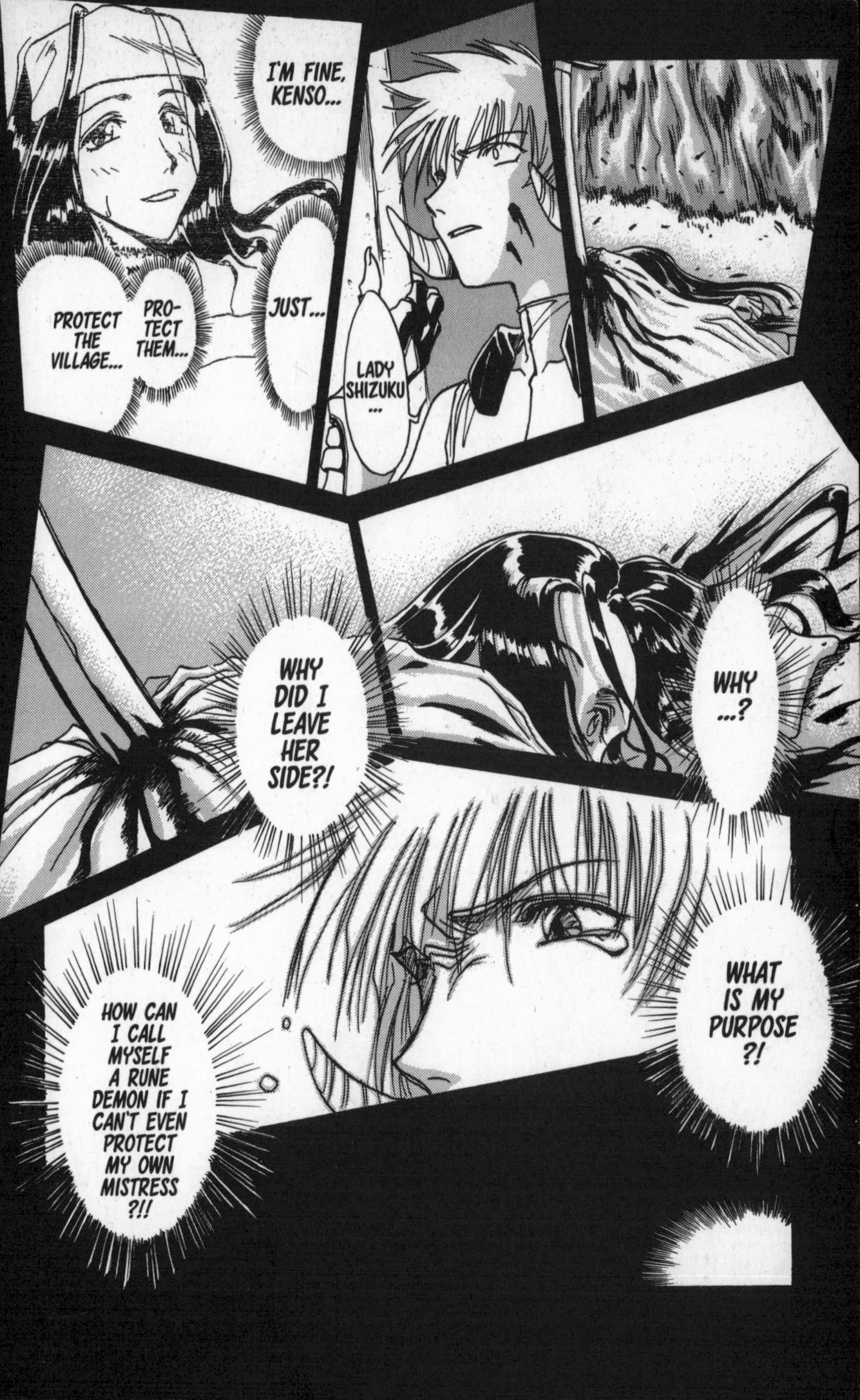
LADY SHIZUKU...
I'M FINE, KENSO...
JUST...
PROTECT THEM...
PROTECT THE VILLAGE...
WHY...?
WHY DID I LEAVE HER SIDE?!
WHAT IS MY PURPOSE?!
HOW CAN I CALL MYSELF A RUNE DEMON IF I CAN'T EVEN PROTECT MY OWN MISTRESS?!!

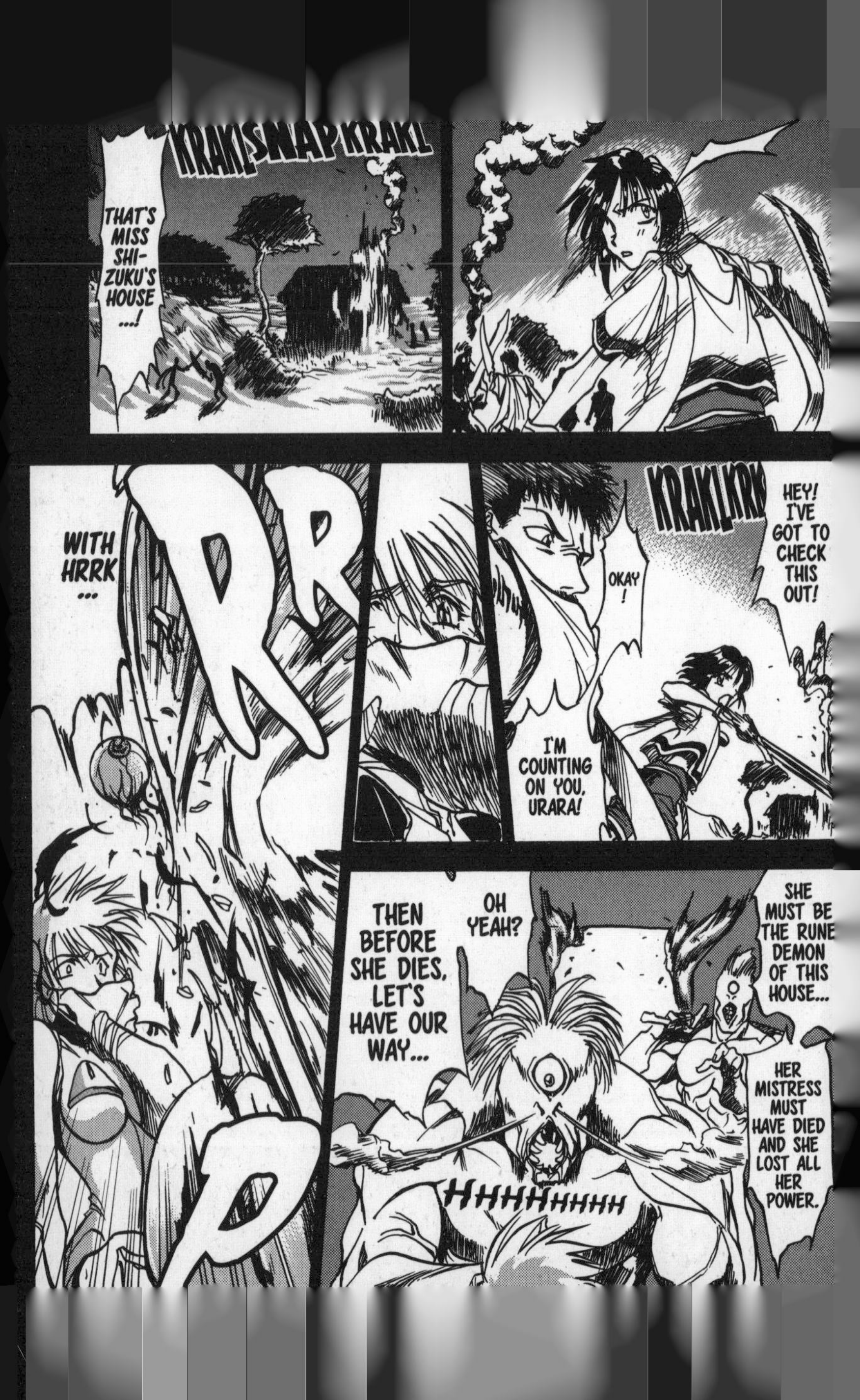
KRAK! SNAP KRAK!
THAT'S MISS SHI-ZUKU'S HOUSE ...!
KRAK! KRK
HEY! I'VE GOT TO CHECK THIS OUT!
OKAY!
I'M COUNTING ON YOU, URARA!
SHE MUST BE THE RUNE DEMON OF THIS HOUSE...
HER MISTRESS MUST HAVE DIED AND SHE LOST ALL HER POWER.
OH YEAH?
THEN BEFORE SHE DIES, LET'S HAVE OUR WAY...
HHHHHHHH
WITH HRRK ...
RR
P

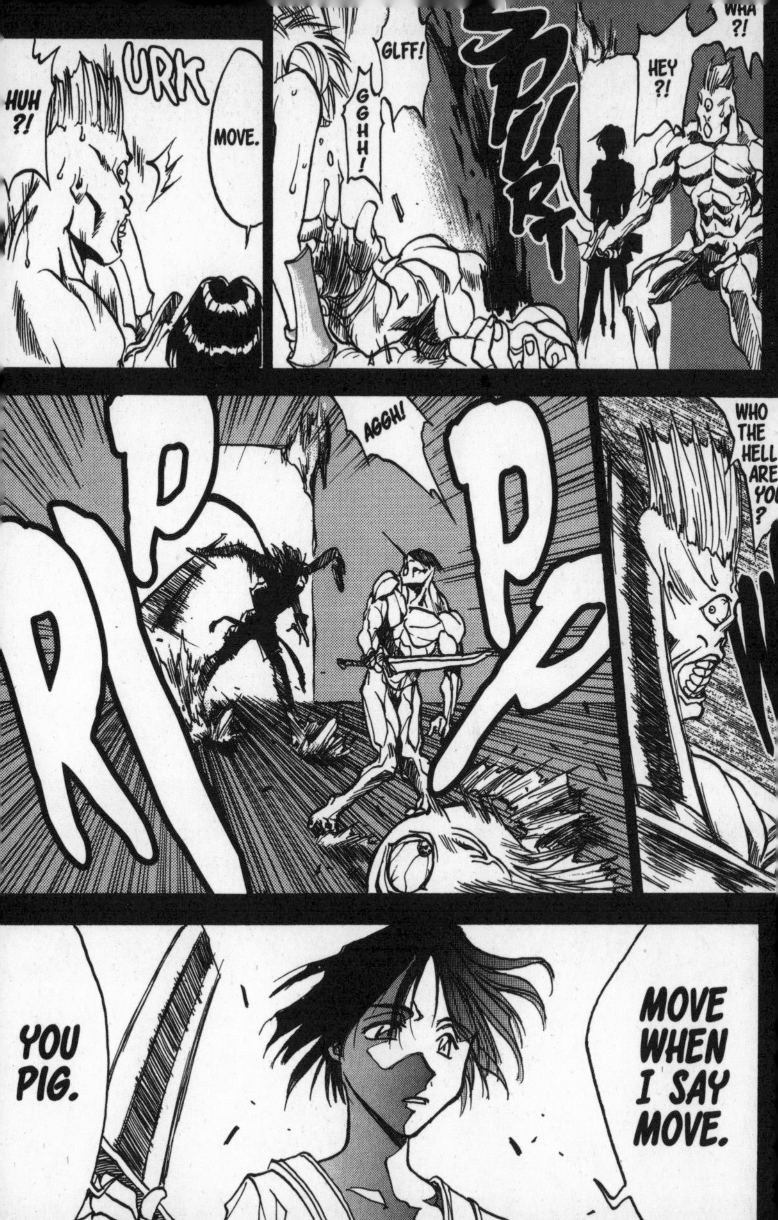
WHA ?!
HEY ?!
SPURT
GLFF!
GGHH!
MOVE.
URK
HUH ?!
WHO THE HELL ARE YOU?
RIPP
AGGH!
MOVE WHEN I SAY MOVE.
YOU PIG.

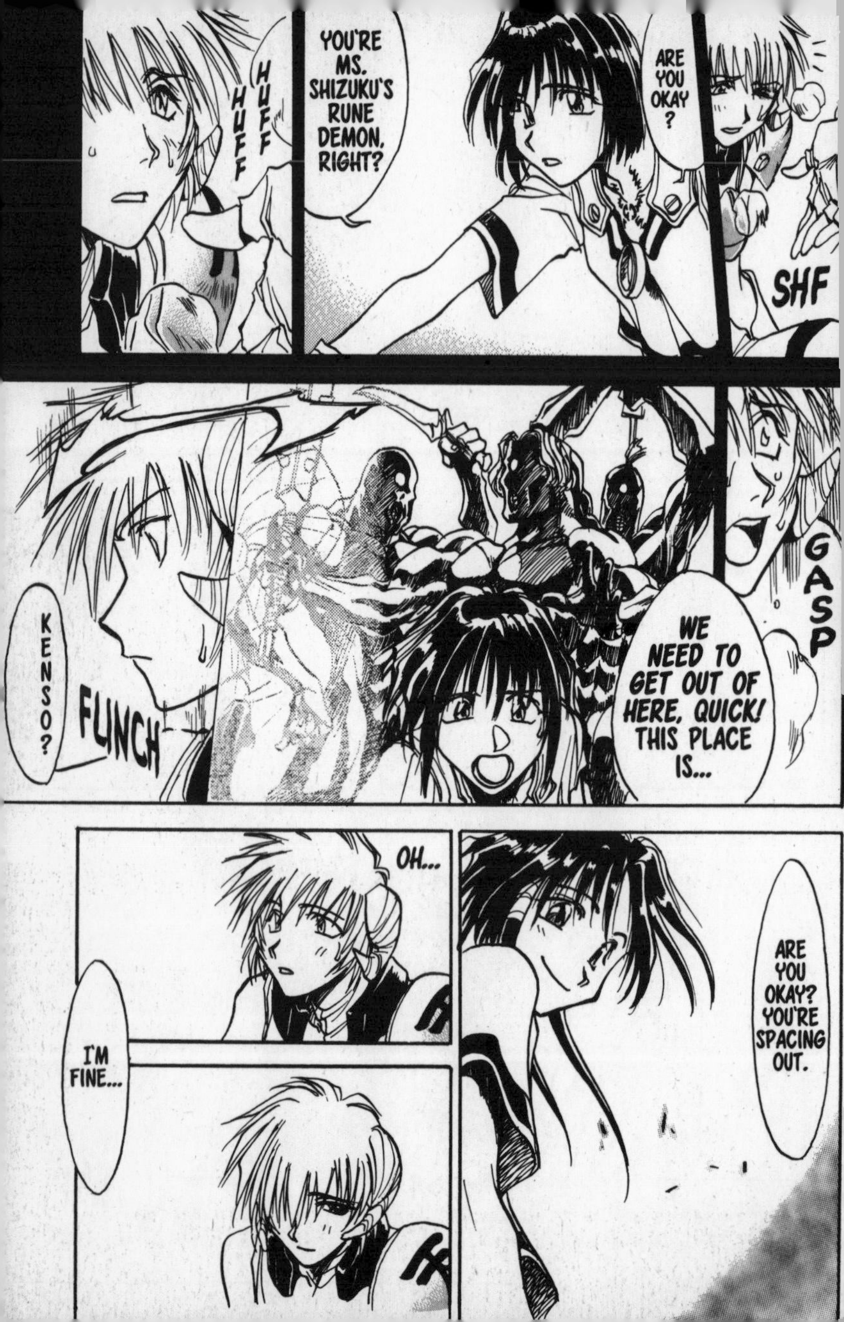
ARE YOU OKAY?
SHF
YOU'RE MS. SHIZUKU'S RUNE DEMON, RIGHT?
HUFF HUFF
GASP
WE NEED TO GET OUT OF HERE, QUICK! THIS PLACE IS...
FLINCH
KENSO?
ARE YOU OKAY? YOU'RE SPACING OUT.
OH...
I'M FINE...

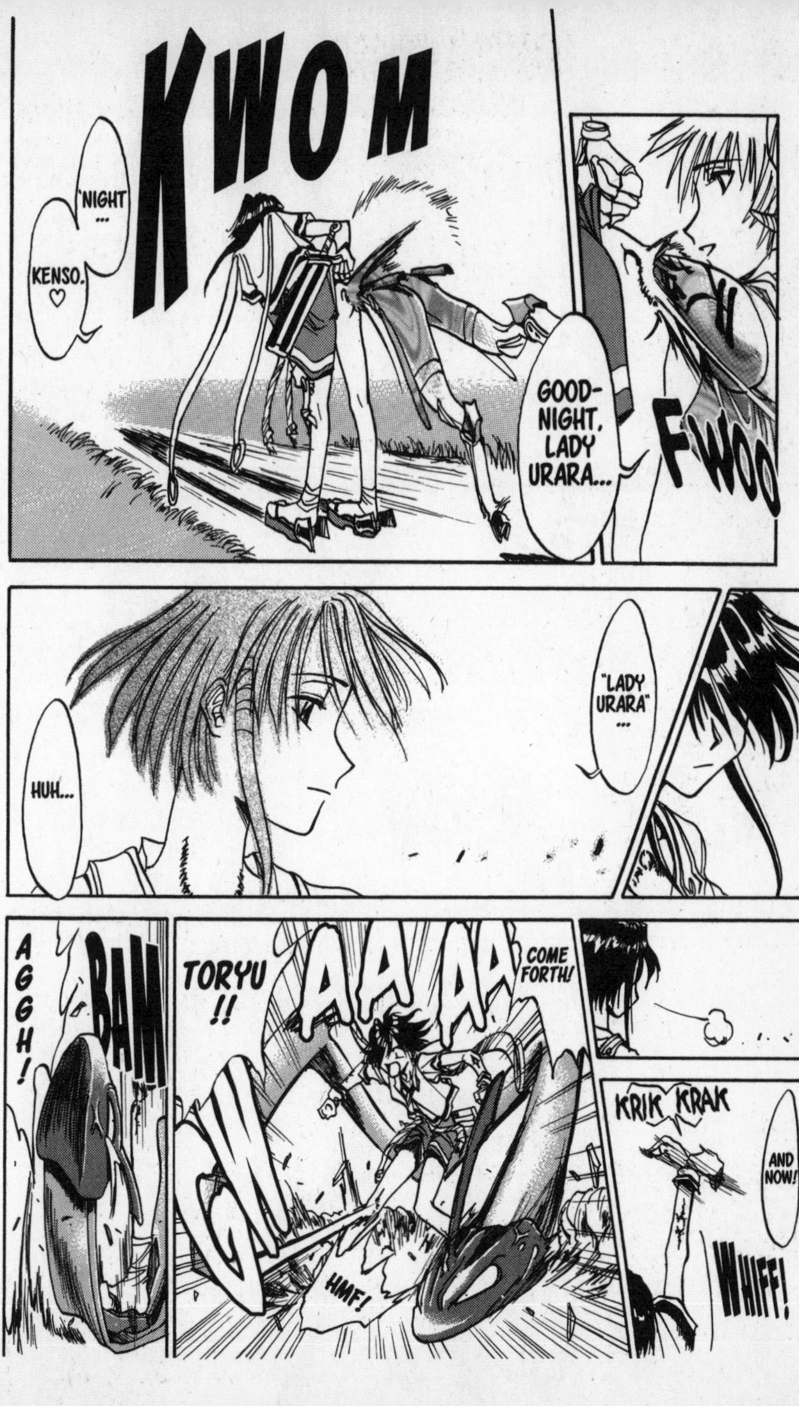
FWOO
GOOD-NIGHT, LADY URARA...
KWOM
`NIGHT... KENSO. ♡
"LADY URARA"...
HUH...
KRIK KRAK
AND NOW!
WHIFF!
COME FORTH!
AAAA
TORYU!!
HMF!
BAM
AGGGH!

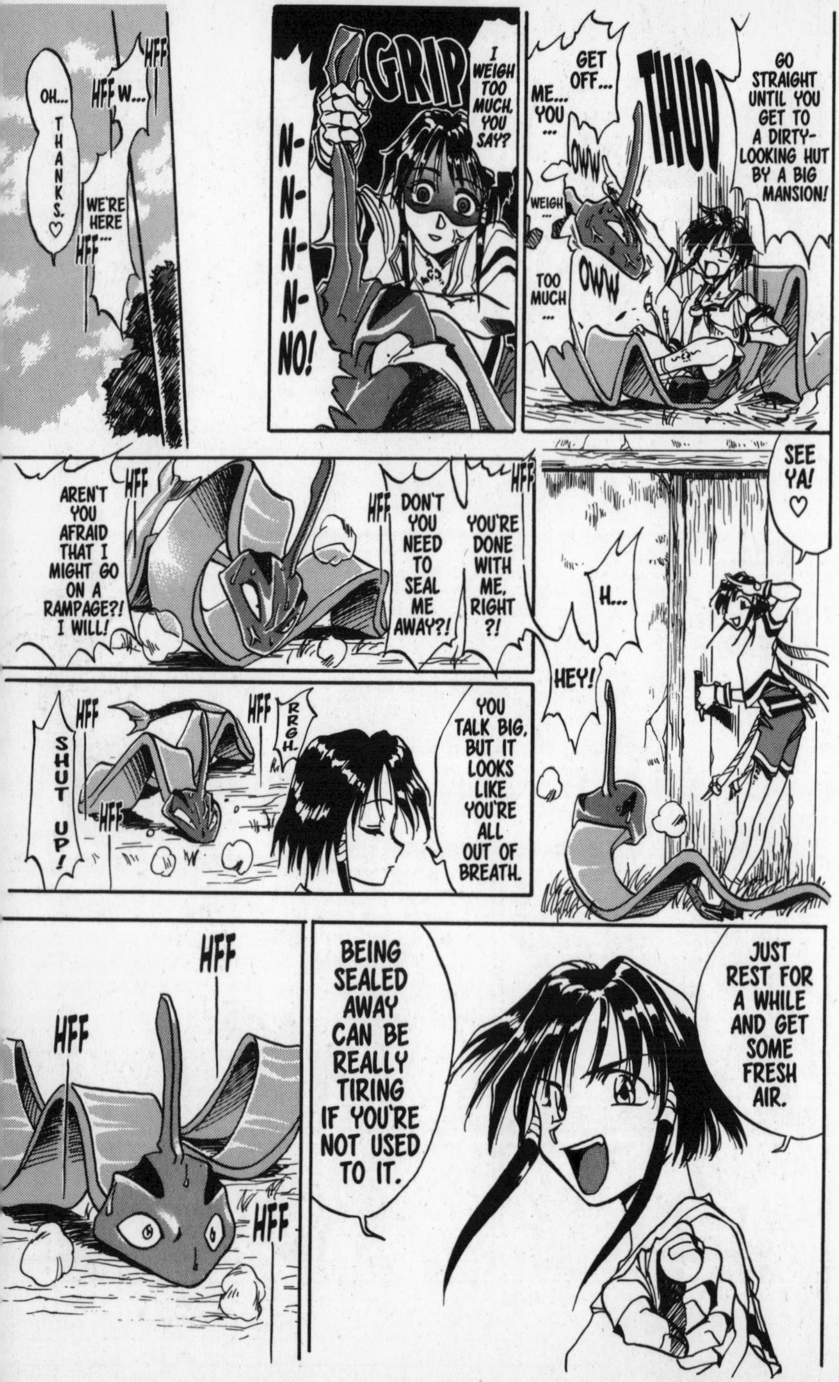
GO STRAIGHT UNTIL YOU GET TO A DIRTY-LOOKING HUT BY A BIG MANSION!
THUD
GET OFF...
ME... YOU ...
OWW
WEIGH ...
TOO MUCH ...
OWW
I WEIGH TOO MUCH, YOU SAY?
GRIP
N-N-N-N-NO!
HFF
HFF W...
OH... THANKS.♡
WE'RE HERE ...
HFF
SEE YA! ♡
H...
HEY!
HFF
YOU'RE DONE WITH ME, RIGHT ?!
HFF
DON'T YOU NEED TO SEAL ME AWAY?!
HFF
AREN'T YOU AFRAID THAT I MIGHT GO ON A RAMPAGE?! I WILL!
YOU TALK BIG, BUT IT LOOKS LIKE YOU'RE ALL OUT OF BREATH.
RRGH...
HFF
HFF
SHUT UP!
HFF
JUST REST FOR A WHILE AND GET SOME FRESH AIR.
BEING SEALED AWAY CAN BE REALLY TIRING IF YOU'RE NOT USED TO IT.
HFF
HFF
HFF

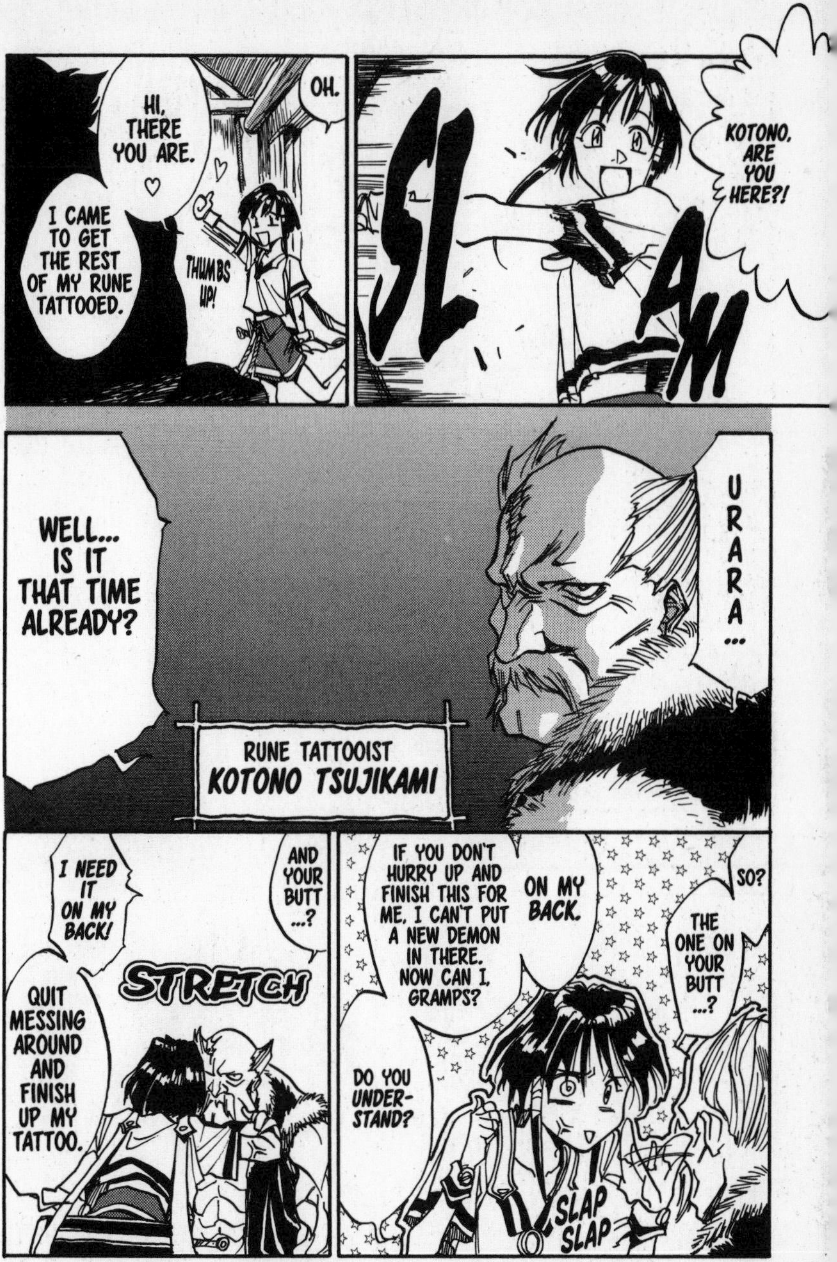
KOTONO, ARE YOU HERE?!
SLAM
OH.
HI, THERE YOU ARE.
I CAME TO GET THE REST OF MY RUNE TATTOOED.
THUMBS UP!
URARA...
WELL... IS IT THAT TIME ALREADY?
RUNE TATTOOIST KOTONO TSUJIKAMI
SO?
THE ONE ON YOUR BUTT ...?
ON MY BACK.
IF YOU DON'T HURRY UP AND FINISH THIS FOR ME, I CAN'T PUT A NEW DEMON IN THERE. NOW CAN I, GRAMPS?
DO YOU UNDER-STAND?
SLAP SLAP
AND YOUR BUTT ...?
I NEED IT ON MY BACK!
STRETCH
QUIT MESSING AROUND AND FINISH UP MY TATTOO.

↑BUTT ALIEN

READ THIS WAY

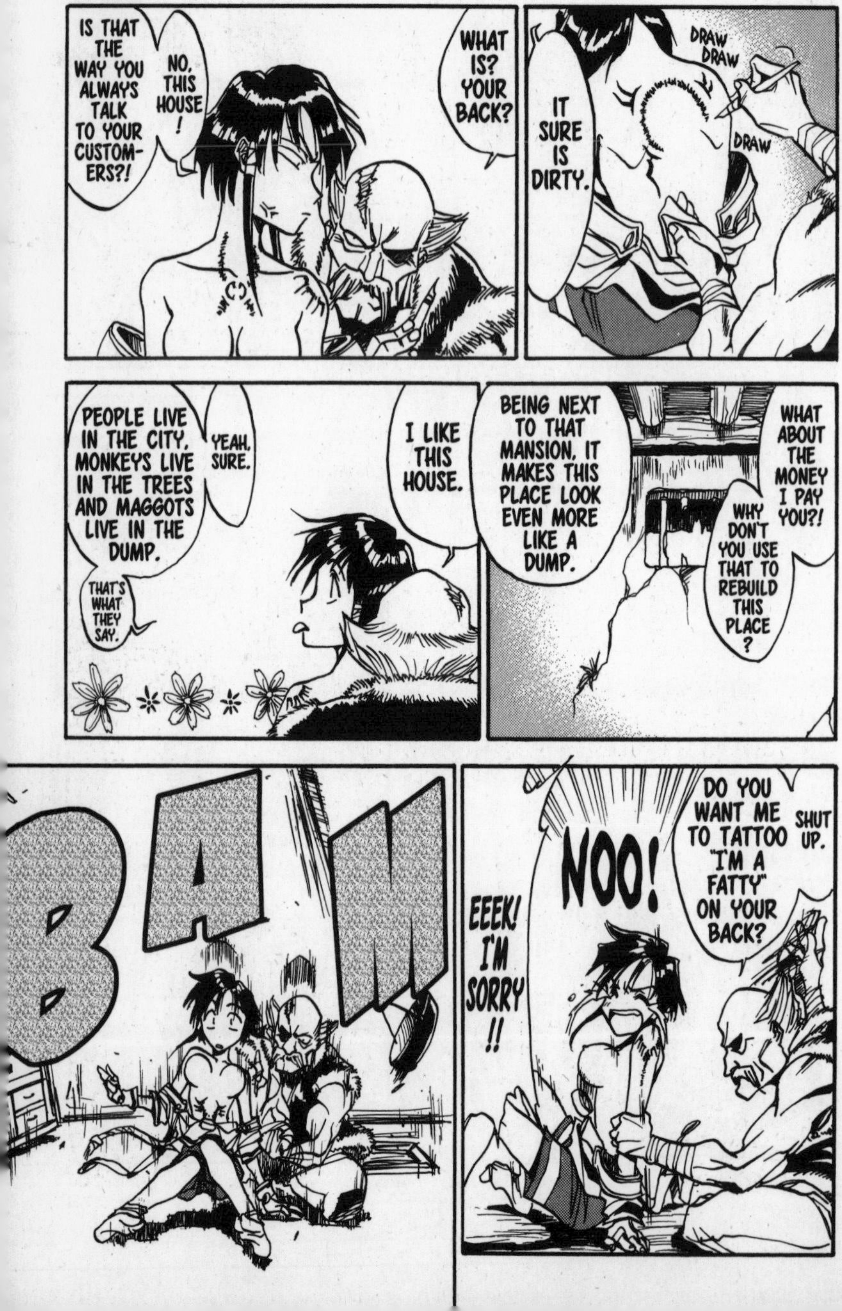
DRAW DRAW
IT SURE IS DIRTY.
DRAW
WHAT IS? YOUR BACK?
NO, THIS HOUSE!
IS THAT THE WAY YOU ALWAYS TALK TO YOUR CUSTOM-ERS?!
WHAT ABOUT THE MONEY I PAY YOU?!
WHY DON'T YOU USE THAT TO REBUILD THIS PLACE?
BEING NEXT TO THAT MANSION, IT MAKES THIS PLACE LOOK EVEN MORE LIKE A DUMP.
I LIKE THIS HOUSE.
YEAH, SURE.
PEOPLE LIVE IN THE CITY, MONKEYS LIVE IN THE TREES AND MAGGOTS LIVE IN THE DUMP.
THAT'S WHAT THEY SAY.
SHUT UP.
DO YOU WANT ME TO TATTOO "I'M A FATTY" ON YOUR BACK?
NOO!
EEEK! I'M SORRY!!
BAM

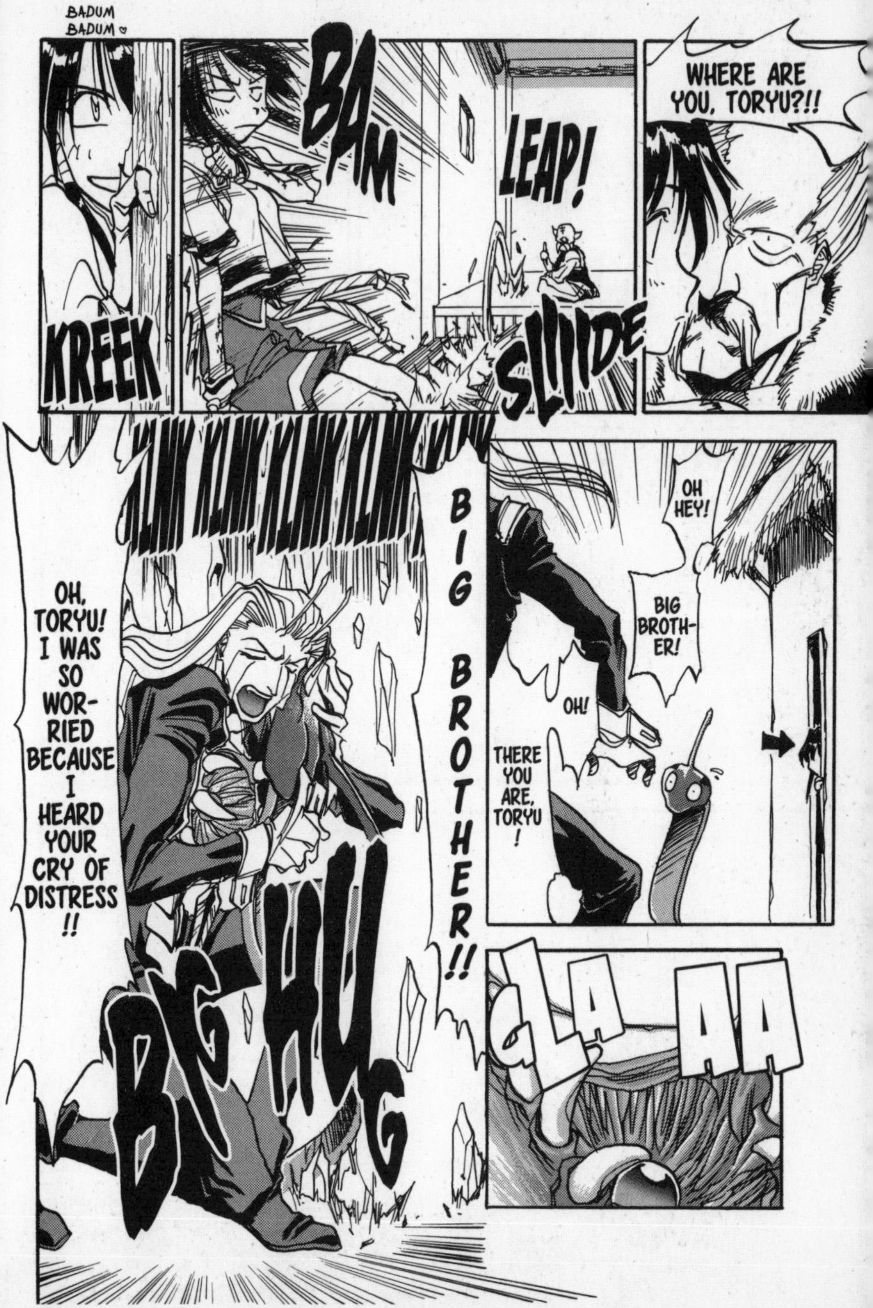
BADUM
BADUM
WHERE ARE YOU, TORYU?!!
BAM
LEAP!
SLIIIDE
KREEK
OH HEY!
BIG BROTH-ER!
OH!
THERE YOU ARE, TORYU!
GLA AA
BIG BROTHER!!
OH, TORYU! I WAS SO WOR-RIED BECAUSE I HEARD YOUR CRY OF DISTRESS!!
BIG HUG

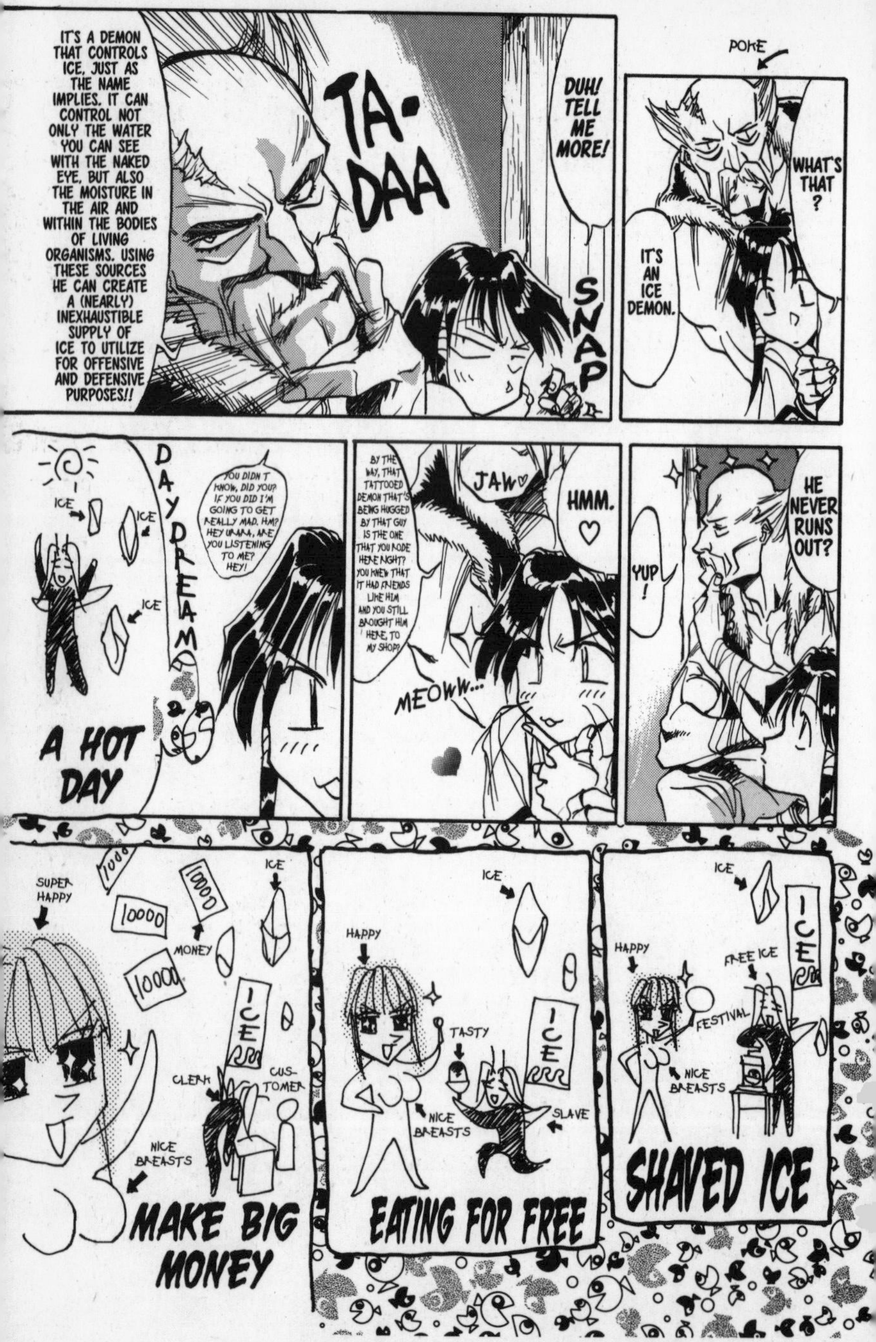
POKE
WHAT'S THAT?
IT'S AN ICE DEMON.
DUH! TELL ME MORE!
TA-DAA
IT'S A DEMON THAT CONTROLS ICE, JUST AS THE NAME IMPLIES. IT CAN CONTROL NOT ONLY THE WATER YOU CAN SEE WITH THE NAKED EYE, BUT ALSO THE MOISTURE IN THE AIR AND WITHIN THE BODIES OF LIVING ORGANISMS. USING THESE SOURCES HE CAN CREATE A (NEARLY) INEXHAUSTIBLE SUPPLY OF ICE TO UTILIZE FOR OFFENSIVE AND DEFENSIVE PURPOSES!!
SNAP
HE NEVER RUNS OUT?
YUP!
HMM. ♥
JAW♥
BY THE WAY, THAT TATTOOED DEMON THAT'S BEING HUGGED BY THAT GUY IS THE ONE THAT YOU RODE HERE RIGHT? YOU KNEW THAT IT HAD FRIENDS LIKE HIM AND YOU STILL BROUGHT HIM HERE, TO MY SHOP?
MEOWW...
YOU DIDN'T KNOW, DID YOU? IF YOU DID I'M GOING TO GET REALLY MAD. HM? HEY URARA, ARE YOU LISTENING TO ME? HEY!
DAYDREAM
ICE
ICE
ICE
A HOT DAY
ICE
ICE
FREE ICE
HAPPY
FESTIVAL
NICE BREASTS
SHAVED ICE
ICE
HAPPY
TASTY
ICE
NICE BREASTS
SLAVE
EATING FOR FREE
SUPER HAPPY
10000
10000
10000
ICE
MONEY
ICE
CLERK
CUS-TOMER
NICE BREASTS
MAKE BIG MONEY

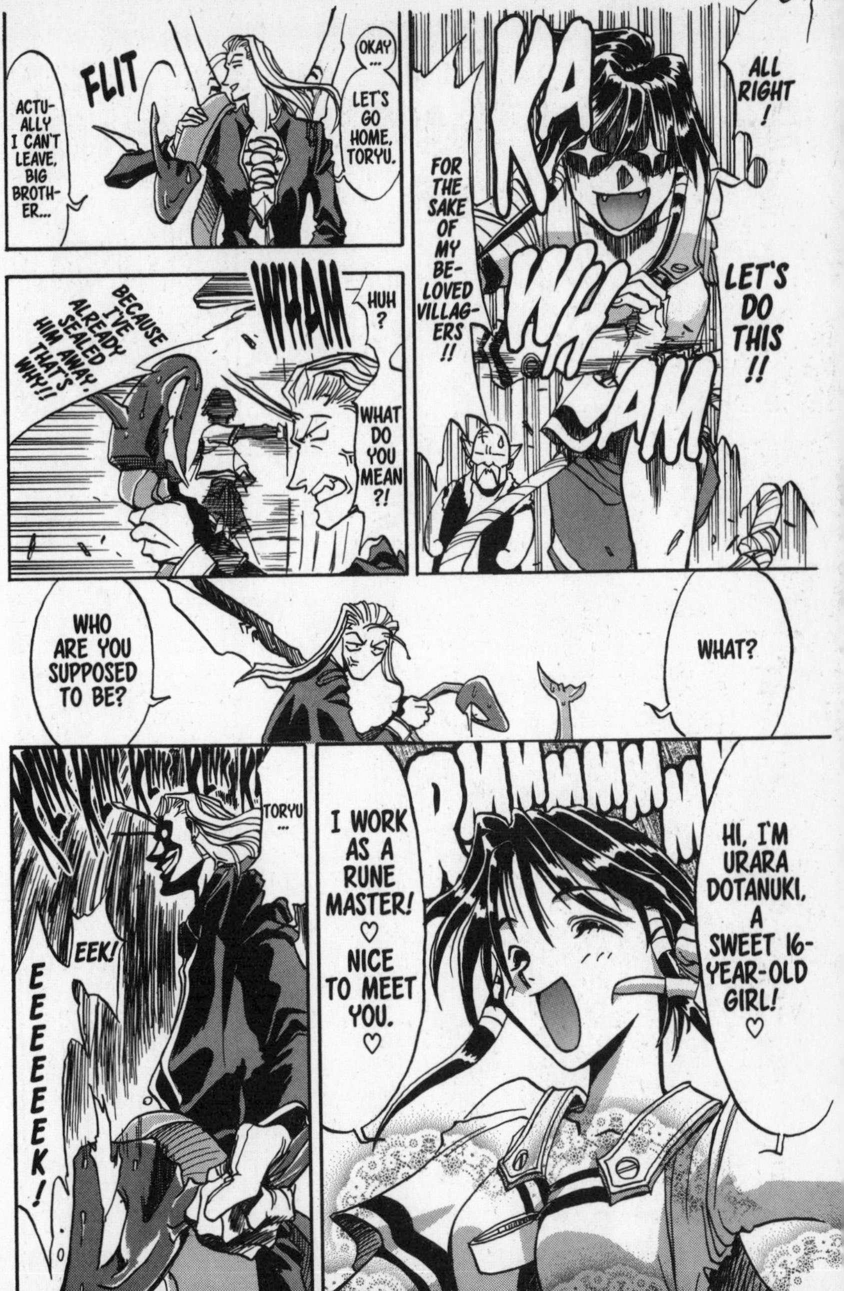
ALL RIGHT!
KA
WH
AM
LET'S DO THIS!!
FOR THE SAKE OF MY BELOVED VILLAGERS!!
OKAY...
LET'S GO HOME, TORYU.
FLIT
ACTUALLY I CAN'T LEAVE, BIG BROTHER...
WHAM
HUH?
WHAT DO YOU MEAN?!
BECAUSE I'VE ALREADY SEALED HIM AWAY, THAT'S WHY!!
WHAT?
WHO ARE YOU SUPPOSED TO BE?
HI, I'M URARA DOTANUKI, A SWEET 16-YEAR-OLD GIRL! ♡
I WORK AS A RUNE MASTER! ♡
NICE TO MEET YOU. ♡
TORYU...
EEK!
EEEEEEEEK!

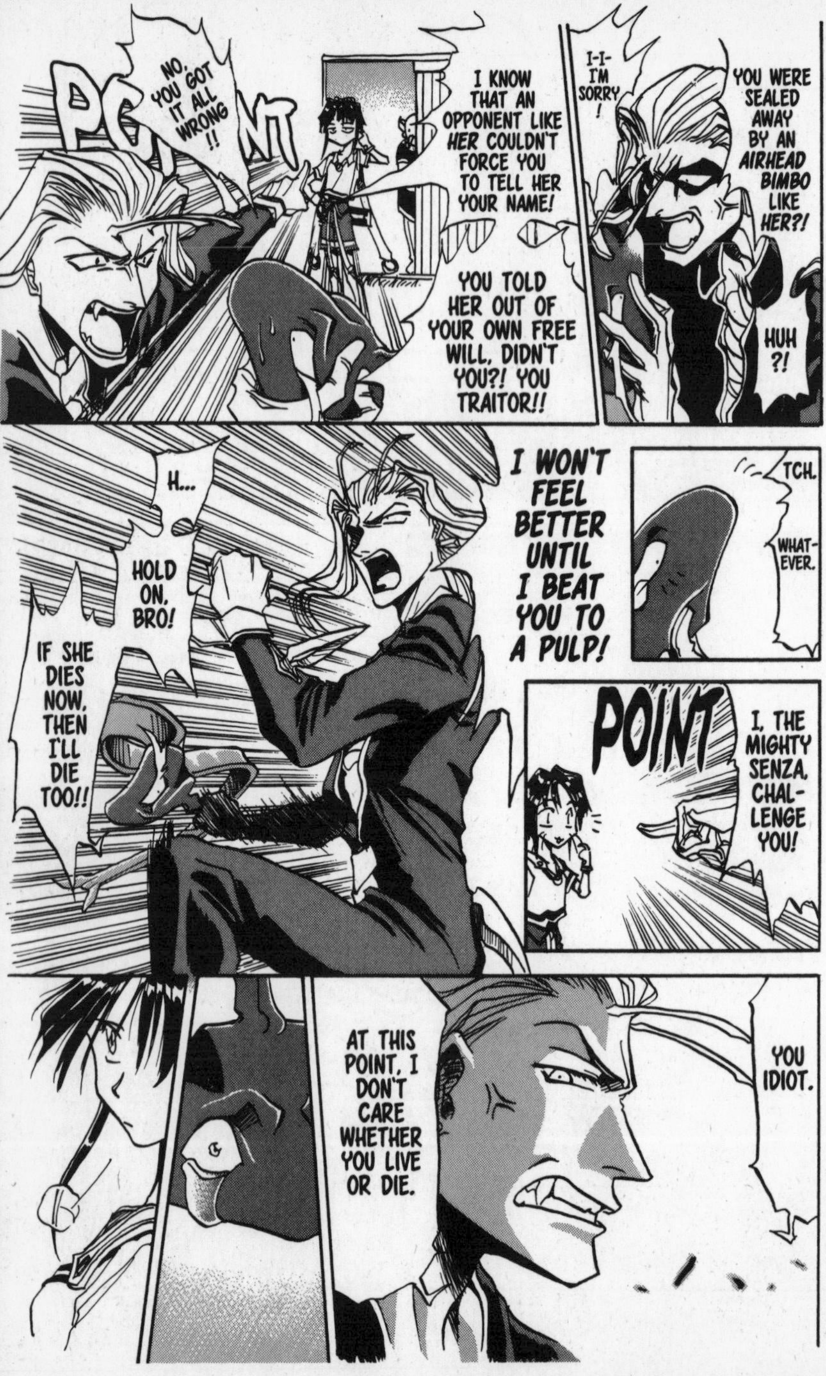
YOU WERE SEALED AWAY BY AN AIRHEAD BIMBO LIKE HER?!
I-I-I'M SORRY!
HUH?!
I KNOW THAT AN OPPONENT LIKE HER COULDN'T FORCE YOU TO TELL HER YOUR NAME!
POINT
NO, YOU GOT IT ALL WRONG!!
YOU TOLD HER OUT OF YOUR OWN FREE WILL, DIDN'T YOU?! YOU TRAITOR!!
TCH.
WHATEVER.
I, THE MIGHTY SENZA, CHALLENGE YOU!
POINT
I WON'T FEEL BETTER UNTIL I BEAT YOU TO A PULP!
H...
HOLD ON, BRO!
IF SHE DIES NOW, THEN I'LL DIE TOO!!
YOU IDIOT.
AT THIS POINT, I DON'T CARE WHETHER YOU LIVE OR DIE.

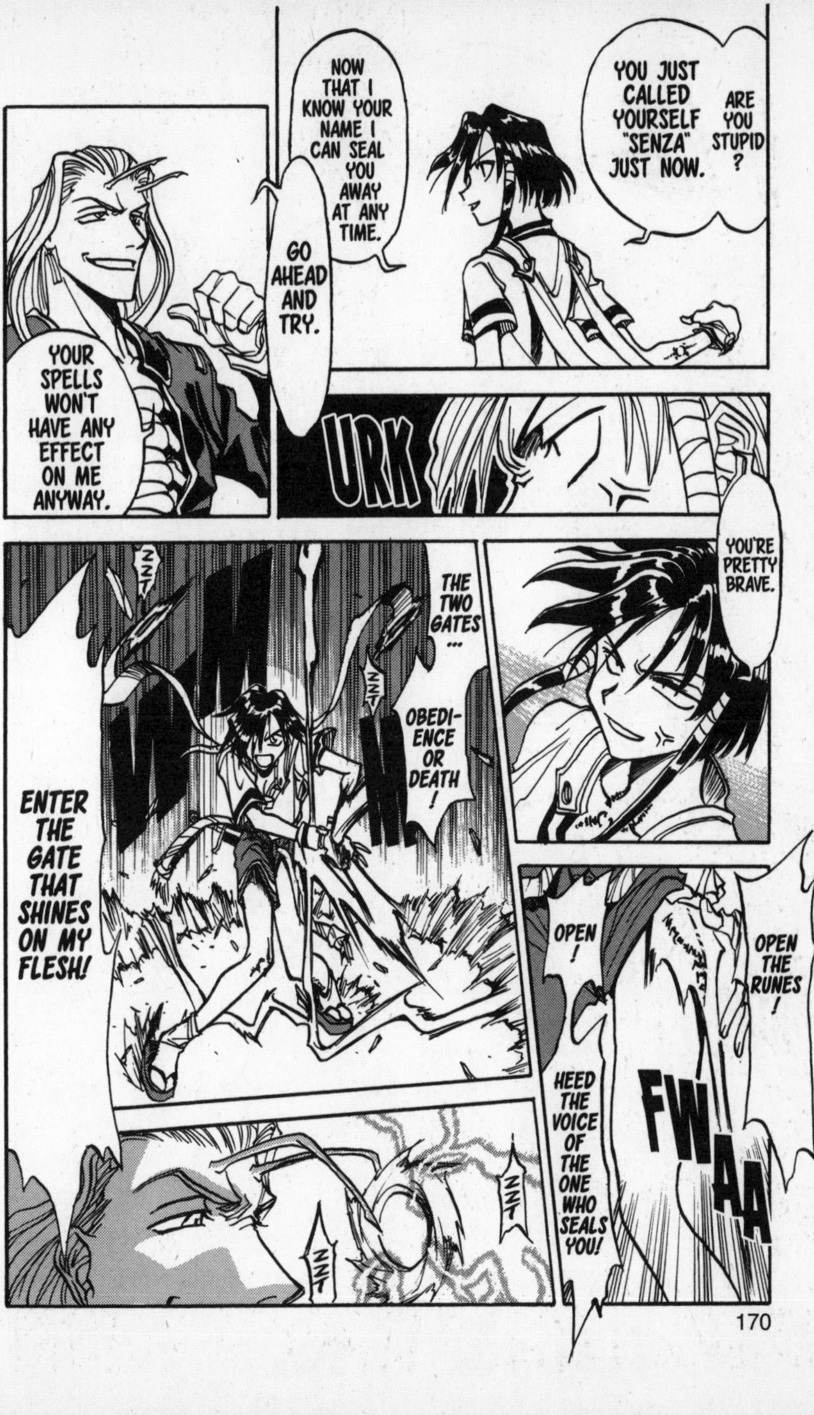

YOU JUST CALLED YOURSELF "SENZA" JUST NOW.
ARE YOU STUPID?
NOW THAT I KNOW YOUR NAME I CAN SEAL YOU AWAY AT ANY TIME.
GO AHEAD AND TRY.
URK
YOUR SPELLS WON'T HAVE ANY EFFECT ON ME ANYWAY.
YOU'RE PRETTY BRAVE.
THE TWO GATES...
ZZT
OBEDIENCE OR DEATH!
ZZT
ENTER THE GATE THAT SHINES ON MY FLESH!
OPEN THE RUNES!
OPEN!
HEED THE VOICE OF THE ONE WHO SEALS YOU!
FWAA
ZZT
ZZT

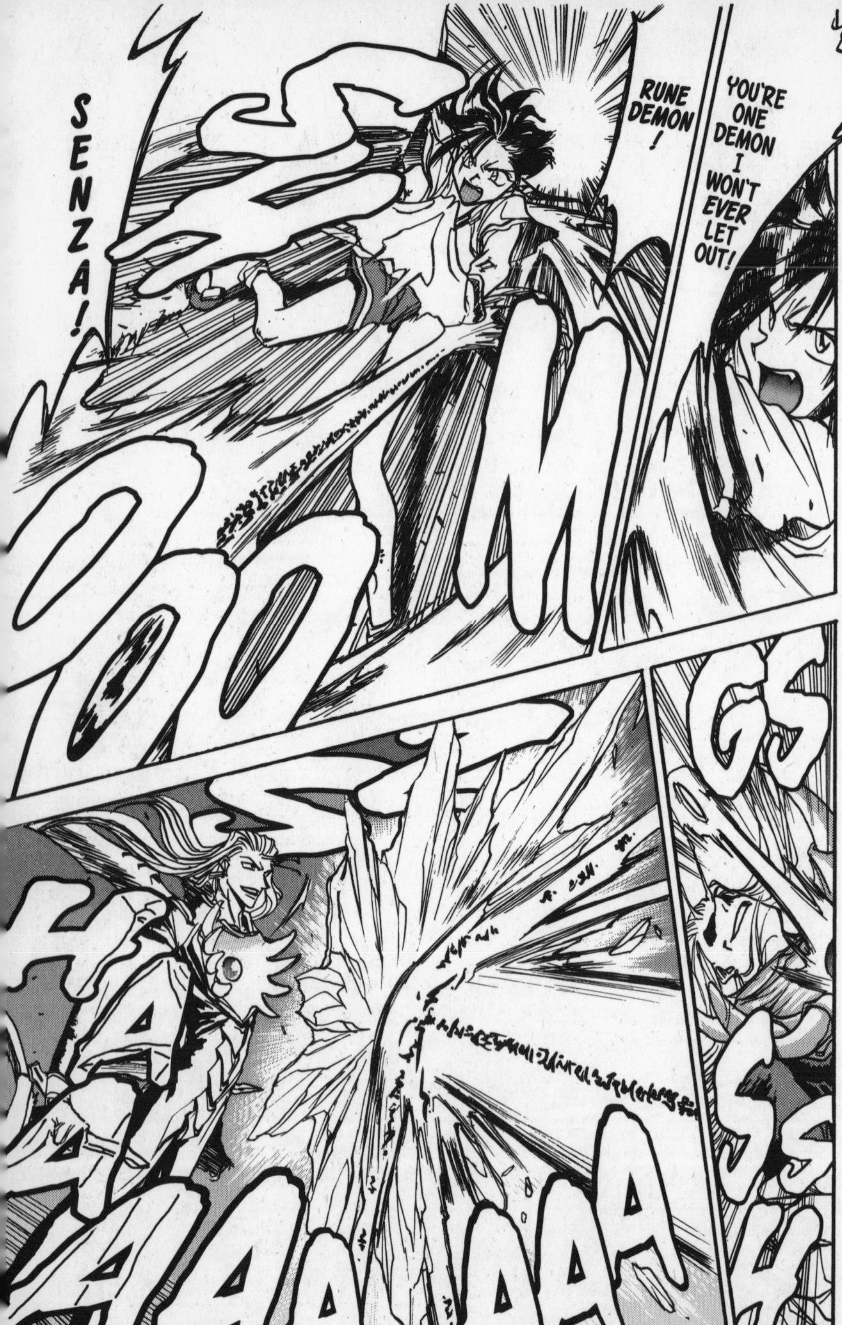

YOU'RE ONE DEMON I WON'T EVER LET OUT!
RUNE DEMON!
SENZA!
DOOM
GSS
SS
HAAAAAAA

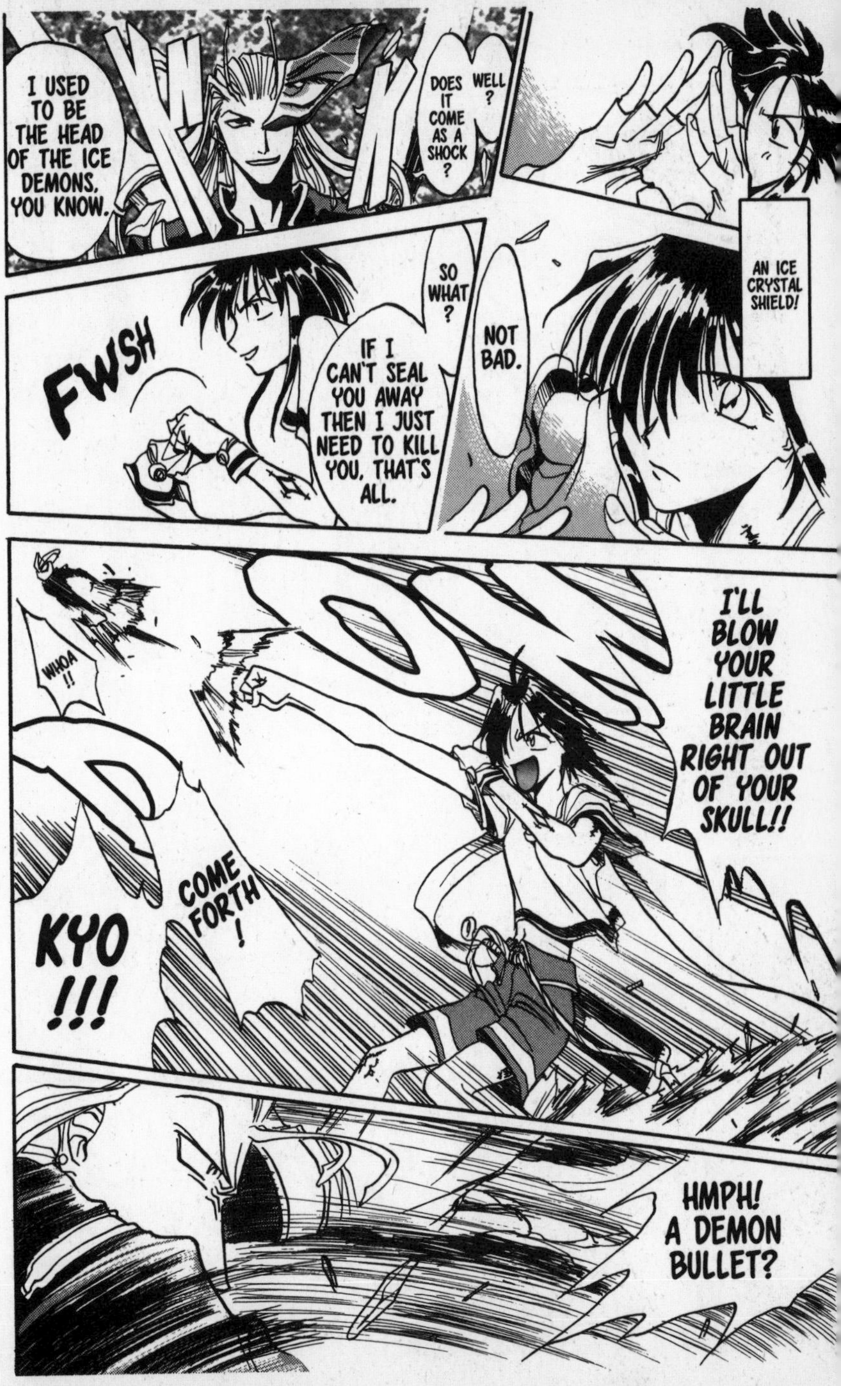
WELL?
DOES IT COME AS A SHOCK?
I USED TO BE THE HEAD OF THE ICE DEMONS, YOU KNOW.
AN ICE CRYSTAL SHIELD!
NOT BAD.
SO WHAT?
IF I CAN'T SEAL YOU AWAY THEN I JUST NEED TO KILL YOU, THAT'S ALL.
FWSH
I'LL BLOW YOUR LITTLE BRAIN RIGHT OUT OF YOUR SKULL!!
WHOA!!
COME FORTH!
KYO!!!
HMPH! A DEMON BULLET?

READ THIS WAY

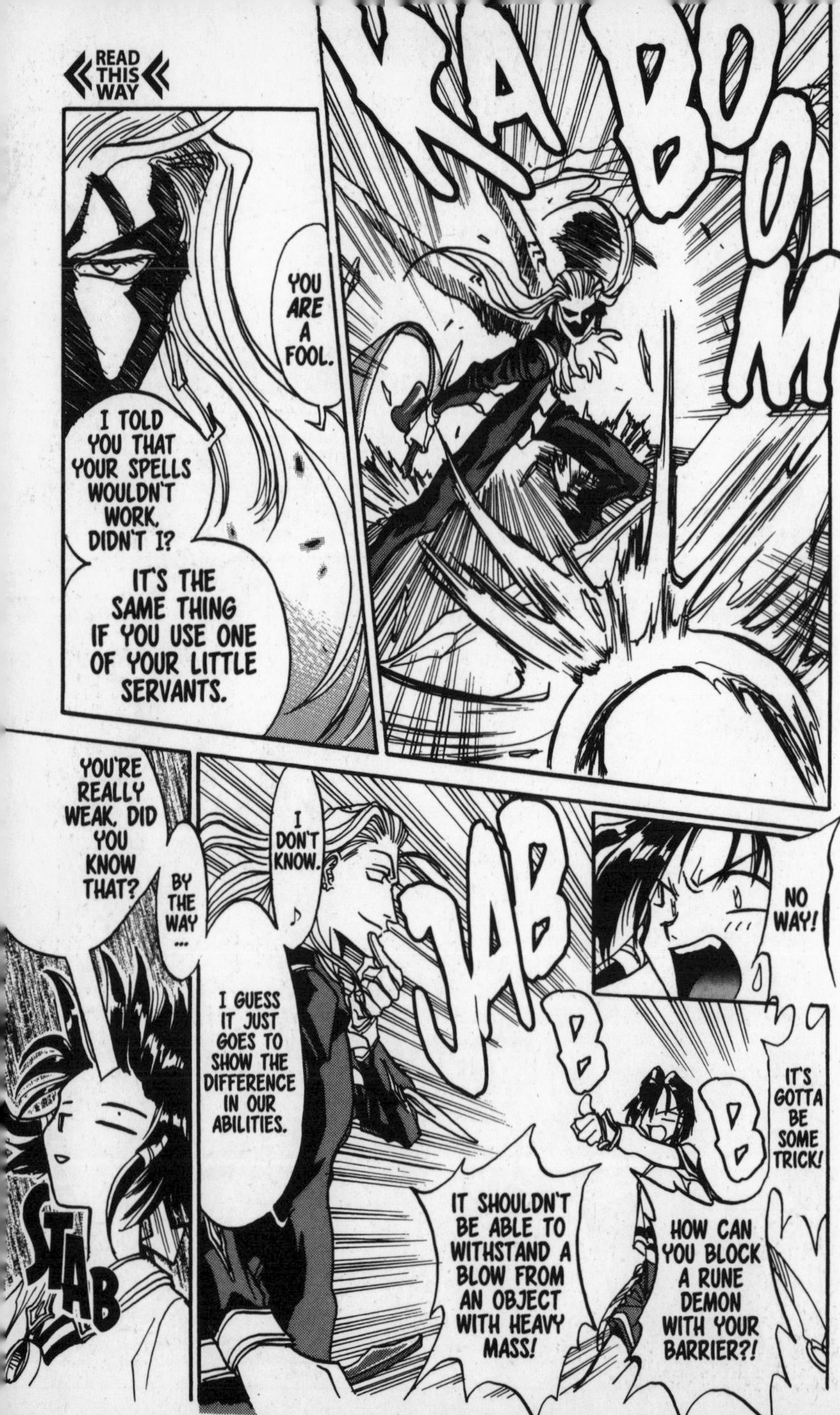
KABOOM
YOU ARE A FOOL.
I TOLD YOU THAT YOUR SPELLS WOULDN'T WORK, DIDN'T I?
IT'S THE SAME THING IF YOU USE ONE OF YOUR LITTLE SERVANTS.
NO WAY!
JABBB
IT'S GOTTA BE SOME TRICK!
HOW CAN YOU BLOCK A RUNE DEMON WITH YOUR BARRIER?!
IT SHOULDN'T BE ABLE TO WITHSTAND A BLOW FROM AN OBJECT WITH HEAVY MASS!
I DON'T KNOW.
BY THE WAY...
I GUESS IT JUST GOES TO SHOW THE DIFFERENCE IN OUR ABILITIES.
YOU'RE REALLY WEAK, DID YOU KNOW THAT?
STAB

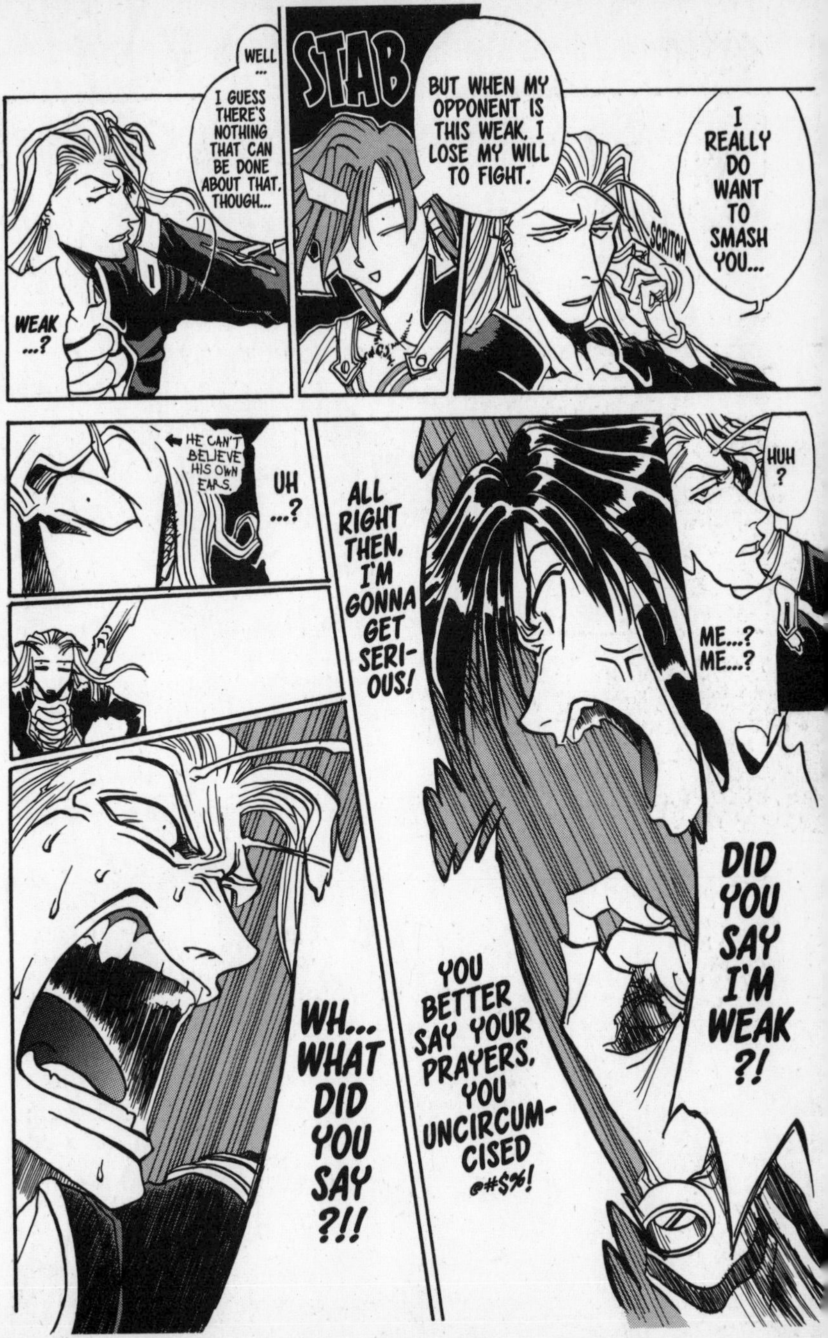
I REALLY DO WANT TO SMASH YOU...
SCRITCH
STAB
BUT WHEN MY OPPONENT IS THIS WEAK, I LOSE MY WILL TO FIGHT.
WELL ...
I GUESS THERE'S NOTHING THAT CAN BE DONE ABOUT THAT, THOUGH...
WEAK ...?
HUH ?
ME...? ME...?
DID YOU SAY I'M WEAK ?!
ALL RIGHT THEN, I'M GONNA GET SERI-OUS!
YOU BETTER SAY YOUR PRAYERS, YOU UNCIRCUM-CISED @#$%!
UH ...?
HE CAN'T BELIEVE HIS OWN EARS.
WH... WHAT DID YOU SAY ?!!

READ THIS WAY

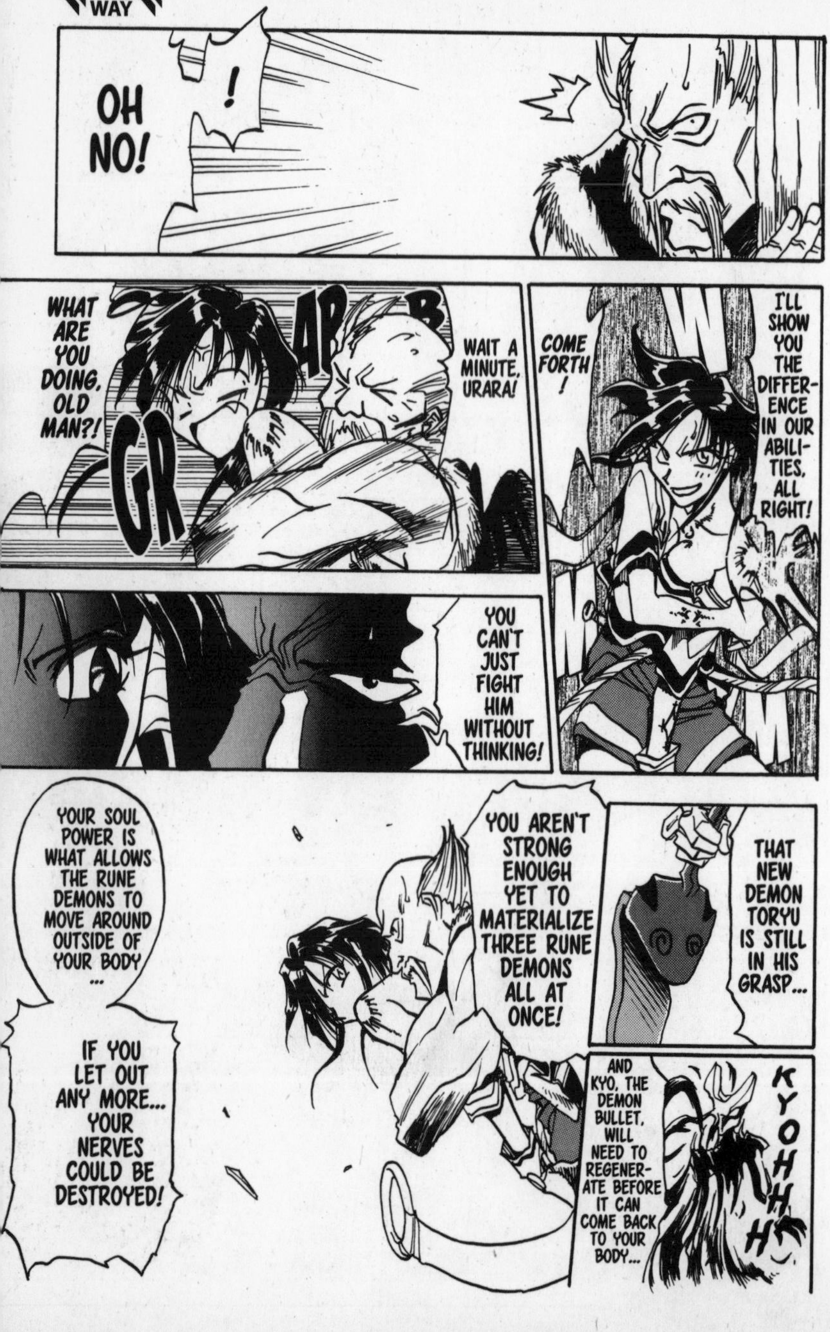
!
OH NO!
I'LL SHOW YOU THE DIFFERENCE IN OUR ABILITIES, ALL RIGHT!
COME FORTH!
WAIT A MINUTE, URARA!
WHAT ARE YOU DOING, OLD MAN?!
YOU CAN'T JUST FIGHT HIM WITHOUT THINKING!
THAT NEW DEMON TORYU IS STILL IN HIS GRASP...
AND KYO, THE DEMON BULLET, WILL NEED TO REGENERATE BEFORE IT CAN COME BACK TO YOUR BODY...
KYOHHHH
YOU AREN'T STRONG ENOUGH YET TO MATERIALIZE THREE RUNE DEMONS ALL AT ONCE!
YOUR SOUL POWER IS WHAT ALLOWS THE RUNE DEMONS TO MOVE AROUND OUTSIDE OF YOUR BODY...
IF YOU LET OUT ANY MORE... YOUR NERVES COULD BE DESTROYED!

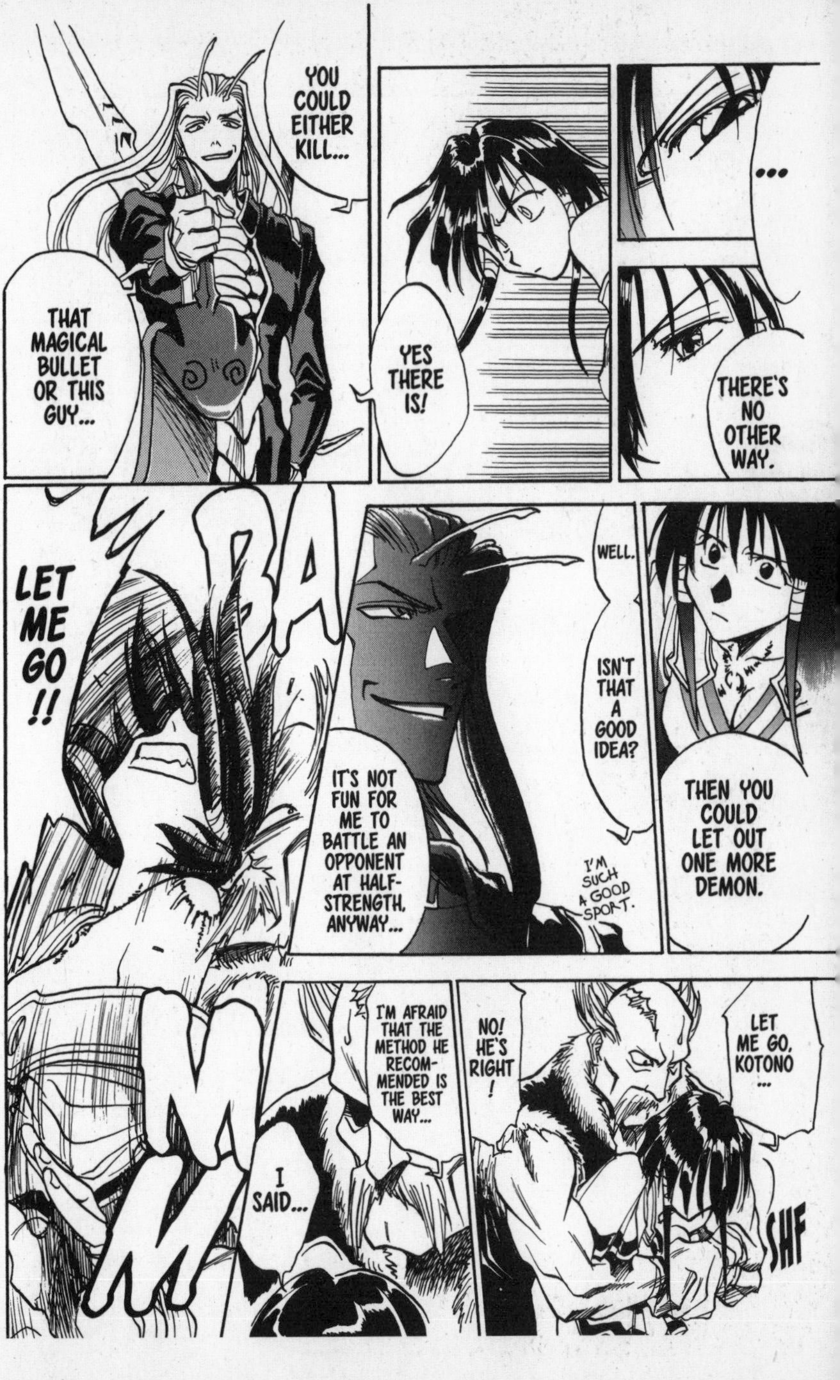
...
THERE'S NO OTHER WAY.
YES THERE IS!
YOU COULD EITHER KILL...
THAT MAGICAL BULLET OR THIS GUY...
THEN YOU COULD LET OUT ONE MORE DEMON.
WELL.
ISN'T THAT A GOOD IDEA?
IT'S NOT FUN FOR ME TO BATTLE AN OPPONENT AT HALF-STRENGTH, ANYWAY...
I'M SUCH A GOOD SPORT.
LET ME GO, KOTONO...
SHF
NO! HE'S RIGHT!
I'M AFRAID THAT THE METHOD HE RECOMMENDED IS THE BEST WAY...
I SAID...
BAM
LET ME GO!!

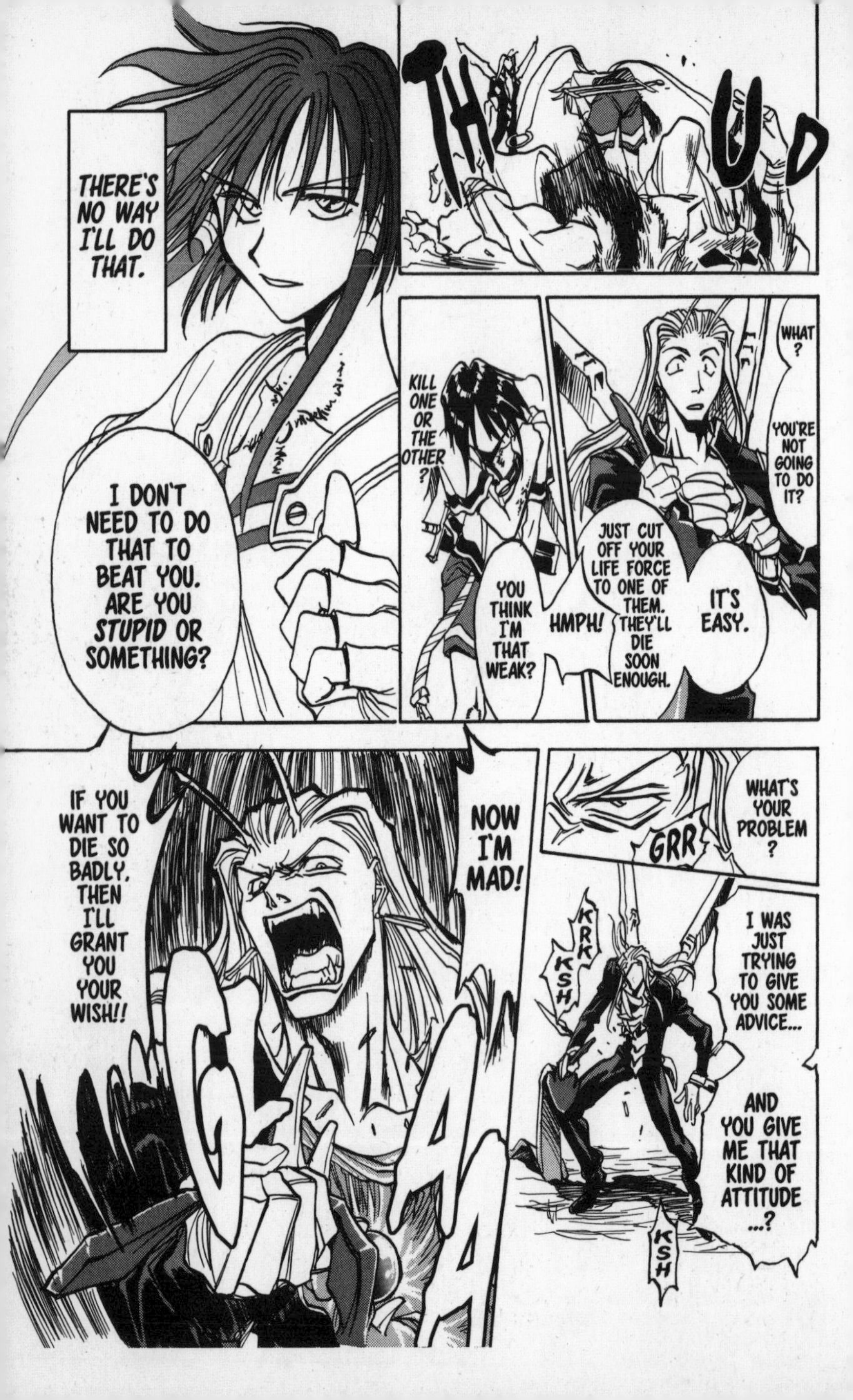
THUD
WHAT?
YOU'RE NOT GOING TO DO IT?
IT'S EASY.
JUST CUT OFF YOUR LIFE FORCE TO ONE OF THEM. THEY'LL DIE SOON ENOUGH.
KILL ONE OR THE OTHER?
HMPH!
YOU THINK I'M THAT WEAK?
THERE'S NO WAY I'LL DO THAT.
I DON'T NEED TO DO THAT TO BEAT YOU. ARE YOU *STUPID* OR SOMETHING?
WHAT'S YOUR PROBLEM?
GRR
I WAS JUST TRYING TO GIVE YOU SOME ADVICE...
AND YOU GIVE ME THAT KIND OF ATTITUDE...?
KRK
KSH
KSH
NOW I'M MAD!
IF YOU WANT TO DIE SO BADLY, THEN I'LL GRANT YOU YOUR WISH!!

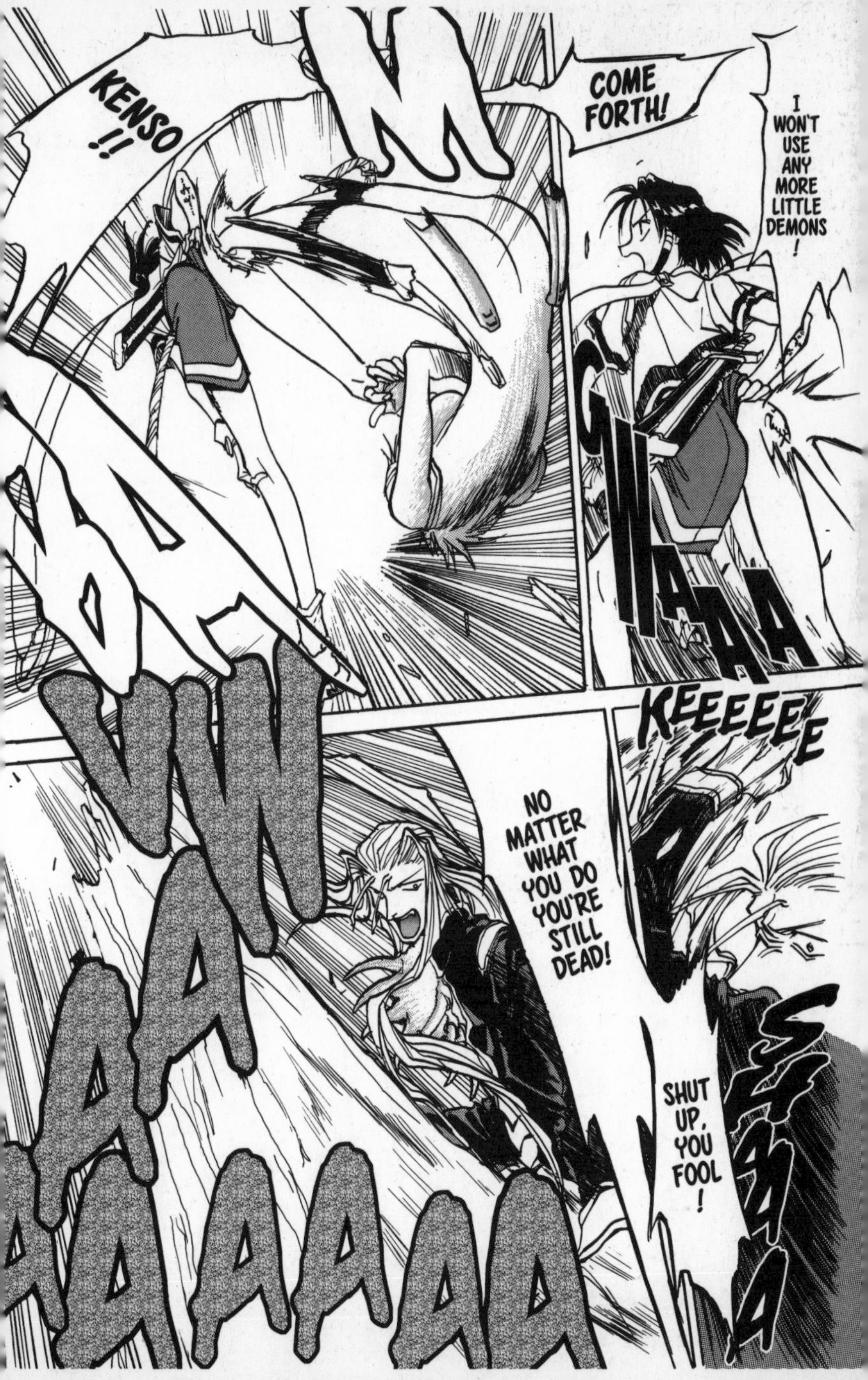
I WON'T USE ANY MORE LITTLE DEMONS!
COME FORTH!
KENSO !!
SHUT UP, YOU FOOL!
NO MATTER WHAT YOU DO YOU'RE STILL DEAD!

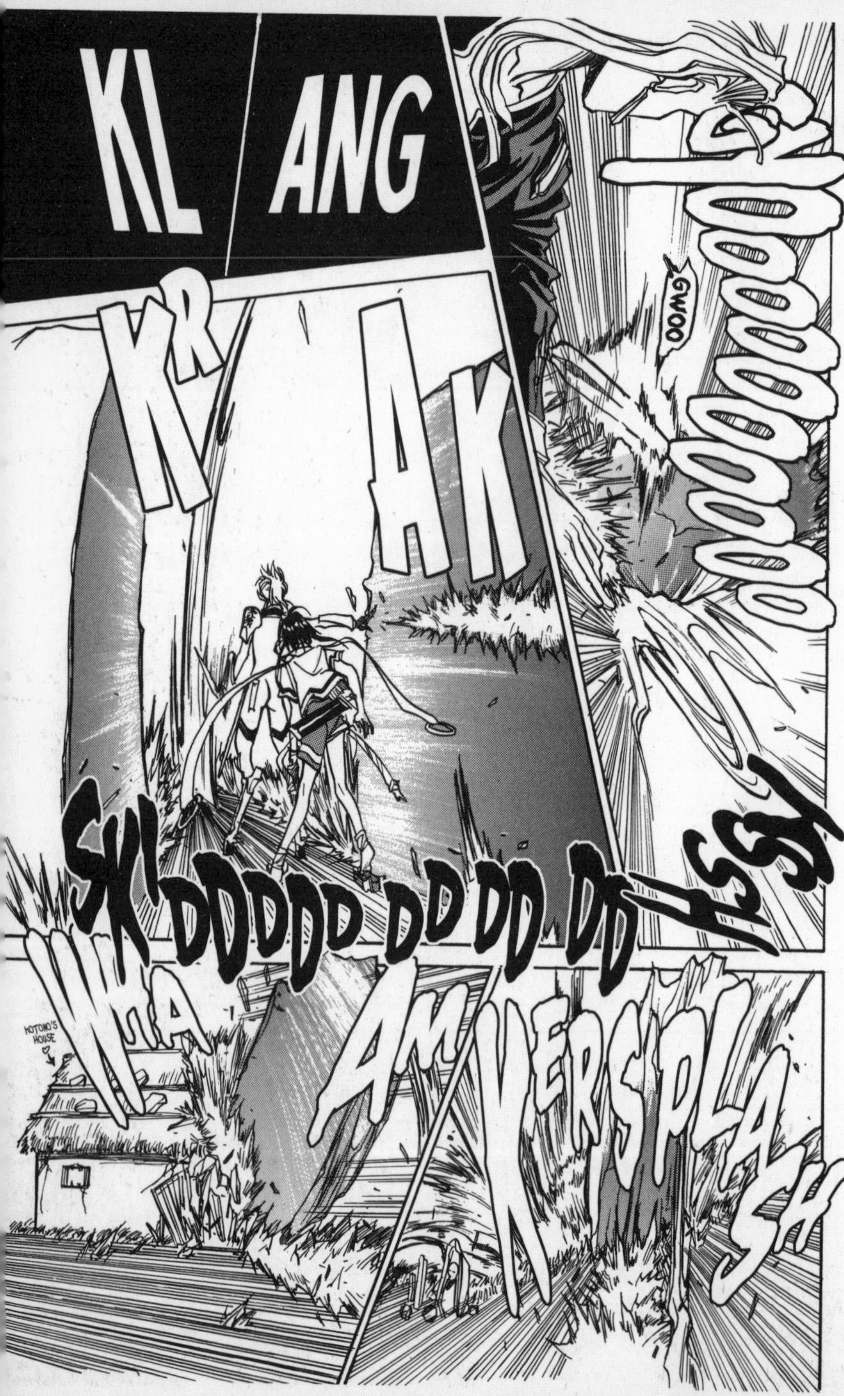
GWOOOOOOOOOOOOOOOOH
GWOO
KLANG
KRAK
SKIDDDDDD DDDD DD DDSH!
KERSPLASH
WHAAM
KOTONO'S HOUSE

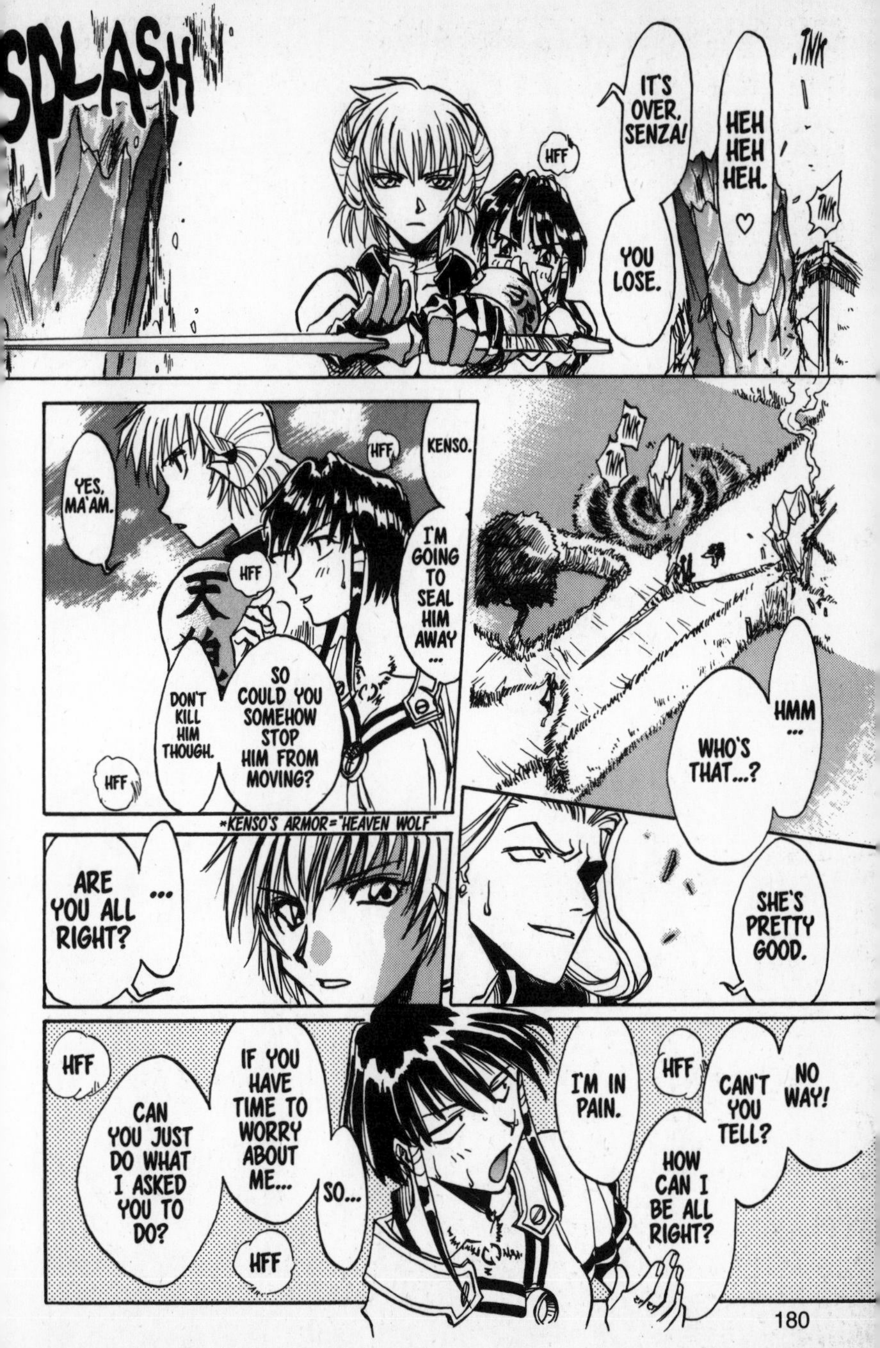
.TNK
HEH HEH HEH. ♥
IT'S OVER, SENZA!
YOU LOSE.
TNK
HFF
SPLASH
TNK
TNK
KENSO.
HFF
YES, MA'AM.
I'M GOING TO SEAL HIM AWAY...
HFF
SO COULD YOU SOMEHOW STOP HIM FROM MOVING?
DON'T KILL HIM THOUGH.
HFF
*KENSO'S ARMOR="HEAVEN WOLF"
HMM...
WHO'S THAT...?
SHE'S PRETTY GOOD.
...
ARE YOU ALL RIGHT?
NO WAY!
CAN'T YOU TELL?
HFF
HOW CAN I BE ALL RIGHT?
I'M IN PAIN.
SO...
IF YOU HAVE TIME TO WORRY ABOUT ME...
HFF
CAN YOU JUST DO WHAT I ASKED YOU TO DO?
HFF

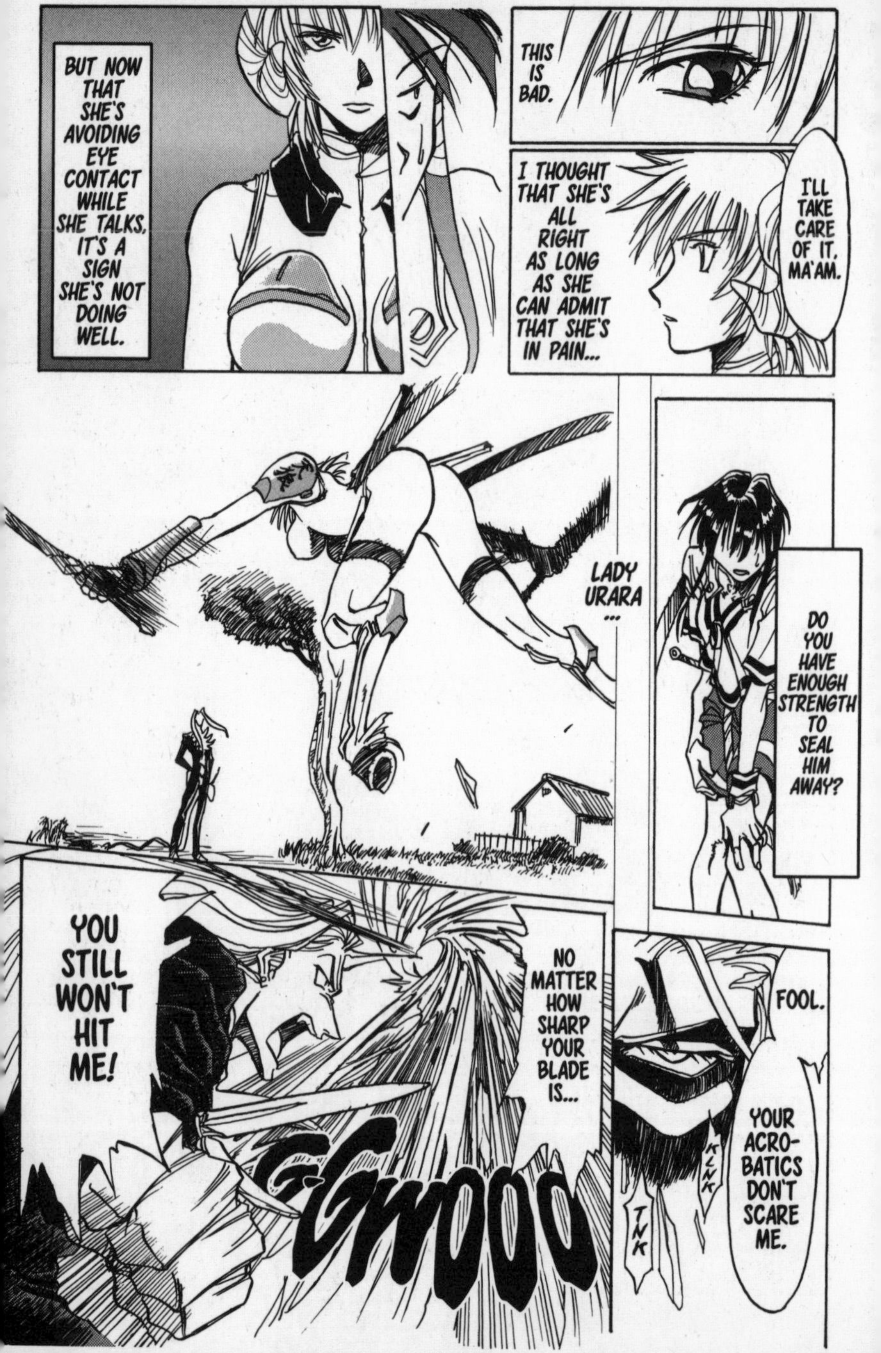
THIS IS BAD.
I'LL TAKE CARE OF IT, MA'AM.
I THOUGHT THAT SHE'S ALL RIGHT AS LONG AS SHE CAN ADMIT THAT SHE'S IN PAIN...
BUT NOW THAT SHE'S AVOIDING EYE CONTACT WHILE SHE TALKS, IT'S A SIGN SHE'S NOT DOING WELL.
DO YOU HAVE ENOUGH STRENGTH TO SEAL HIM AWAY?
LADY URARA...
FOOL.
YOUR ACROBATICS DON'T SCARE ME.
KLNK
TNK
NO MATTER HOW SHARP YOUR BLADE IS...
YOU STILL WON'T HIT ME!
GOWOOO

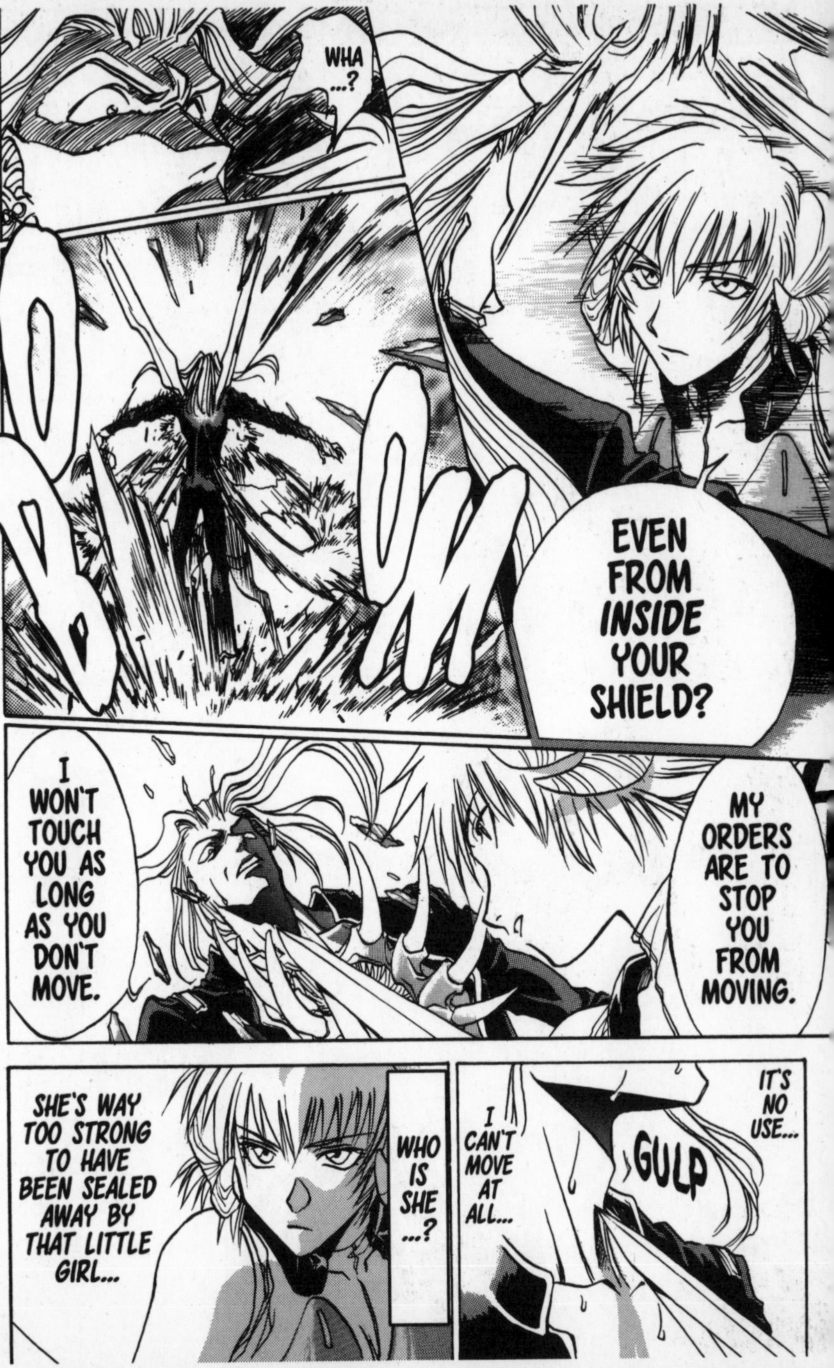
WHA ...?
BOOM
EVEN FROM INSIDE YOUR SHIELD?
MY ORDERS ARE TO STOP YOU FROM MOVING.
I WON'T TOUCH YOU AS LONG AS YOU DON'T MOVE.
IT'S NO USE...
GULP
I CAN'T MOVE AT ALL...
WHO IS SHE ...?
SHE'S WAY TOO STRONG TO HAVE BEEN SEALED AWAY BY THAT LITTLE GIRL...

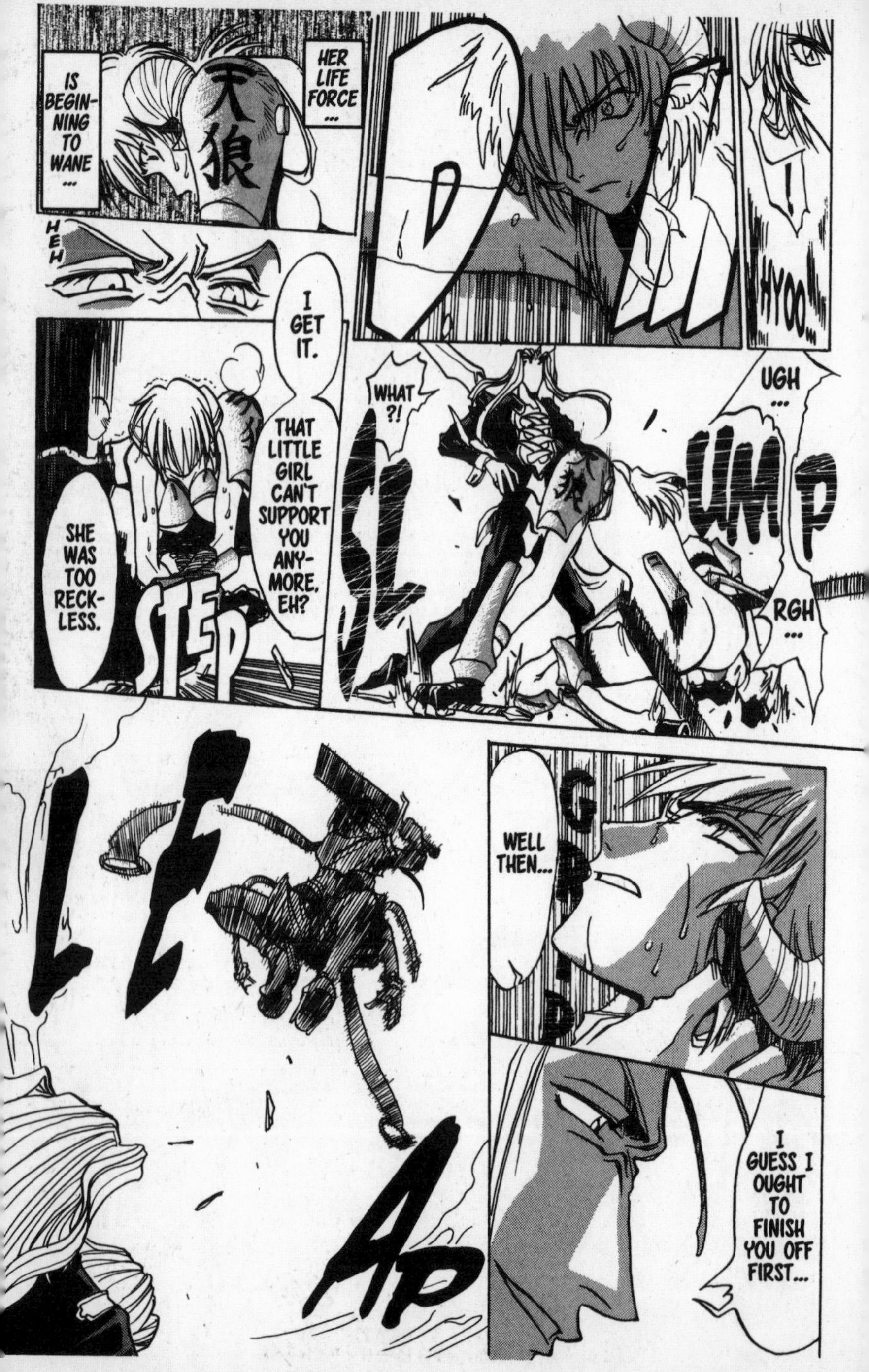
!
HYOO...
D
HER LIFE FORCE ...
IS BEGIN-NING TO WANE ...
HEH
I GET IT.
UGH ...
UMP
RGH ...
WHAT ?!
SL
THAT LITTLE GIRL CAN'T SUPPORT YOU ANY-MORE, EH?
SHE WAS TOO RECK-LESS.
STEP
WELL THEN...
I GUESS I OUGHT TO FINISH YOU OFF FIRST...
LEAP

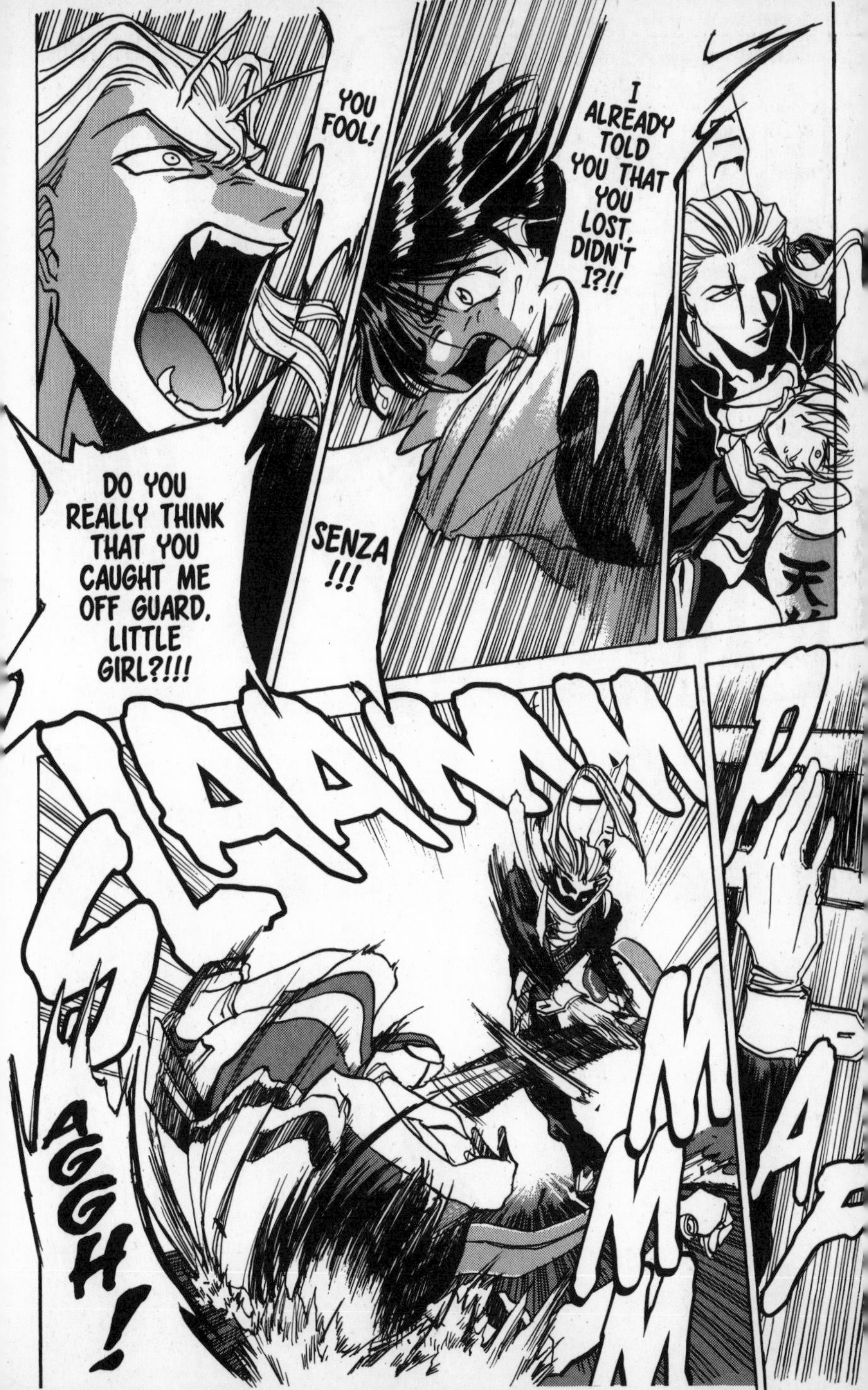
I ALREADY TOLD YOU THAT YOU LOST, DIDN'T I?!!
YOU FOOL!
SENZA!!!
DO YOU REALLY THINK THAT YOU CAUGHT ME OFF GUARD, LITTLE GIRL?!!!
AGGH!

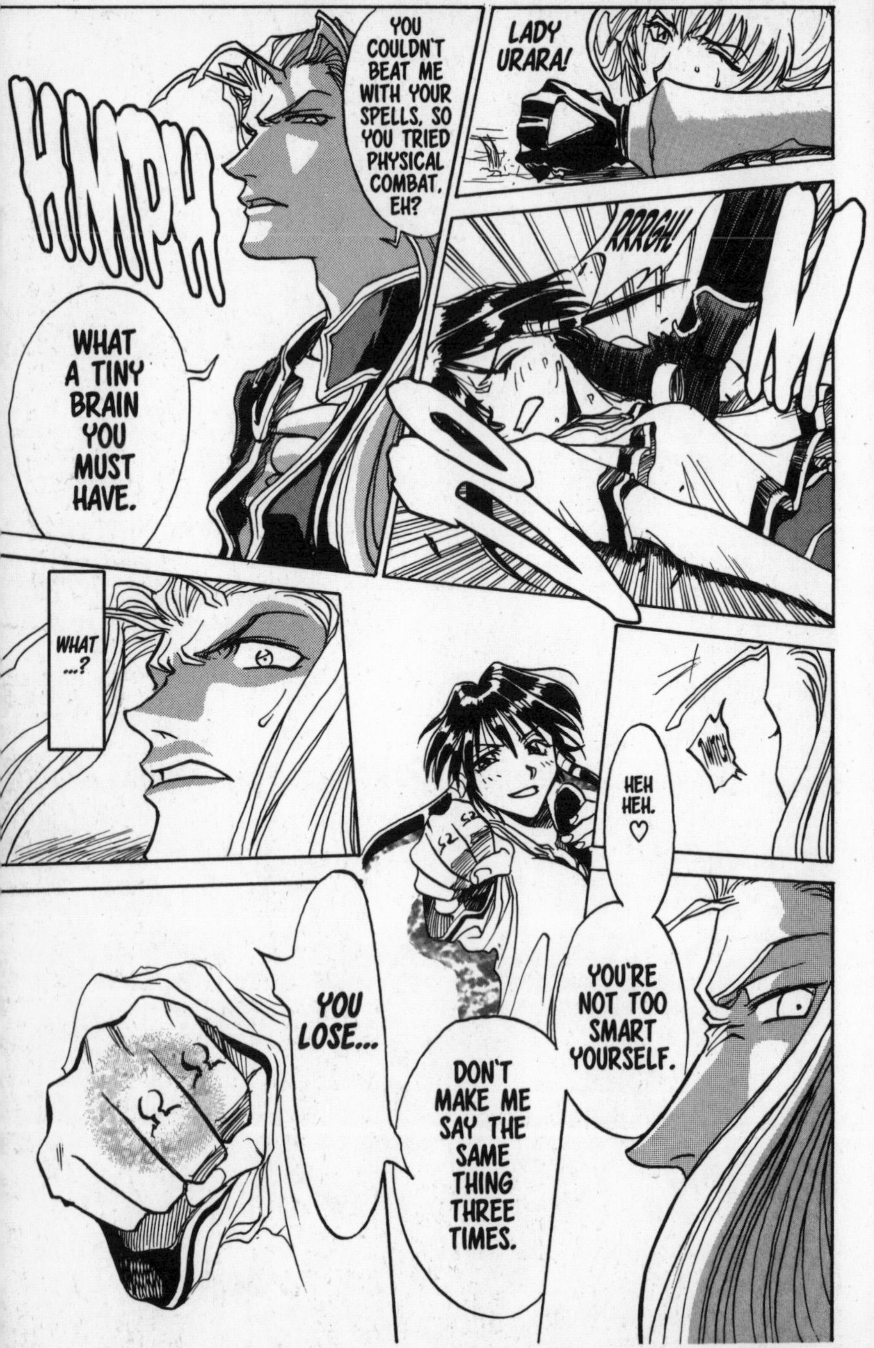
LADY URARA!
RRRGH!
YOU COULDN'T BEAT ME WITH YOUR SPELLS, SO YOU TRIED PHYSICAL COMBAT, EH?
HMPH
WHAT A TINY BRAIN YOU MUST HAVE.
TWITCH
HEH HEH. ♥
WHAT ...?
YOU'RE NOT TOO SMART YOURSELF.
DON'T MAKE ME SAY THE SAME THING THREE TIMES.
YOU LOSE...

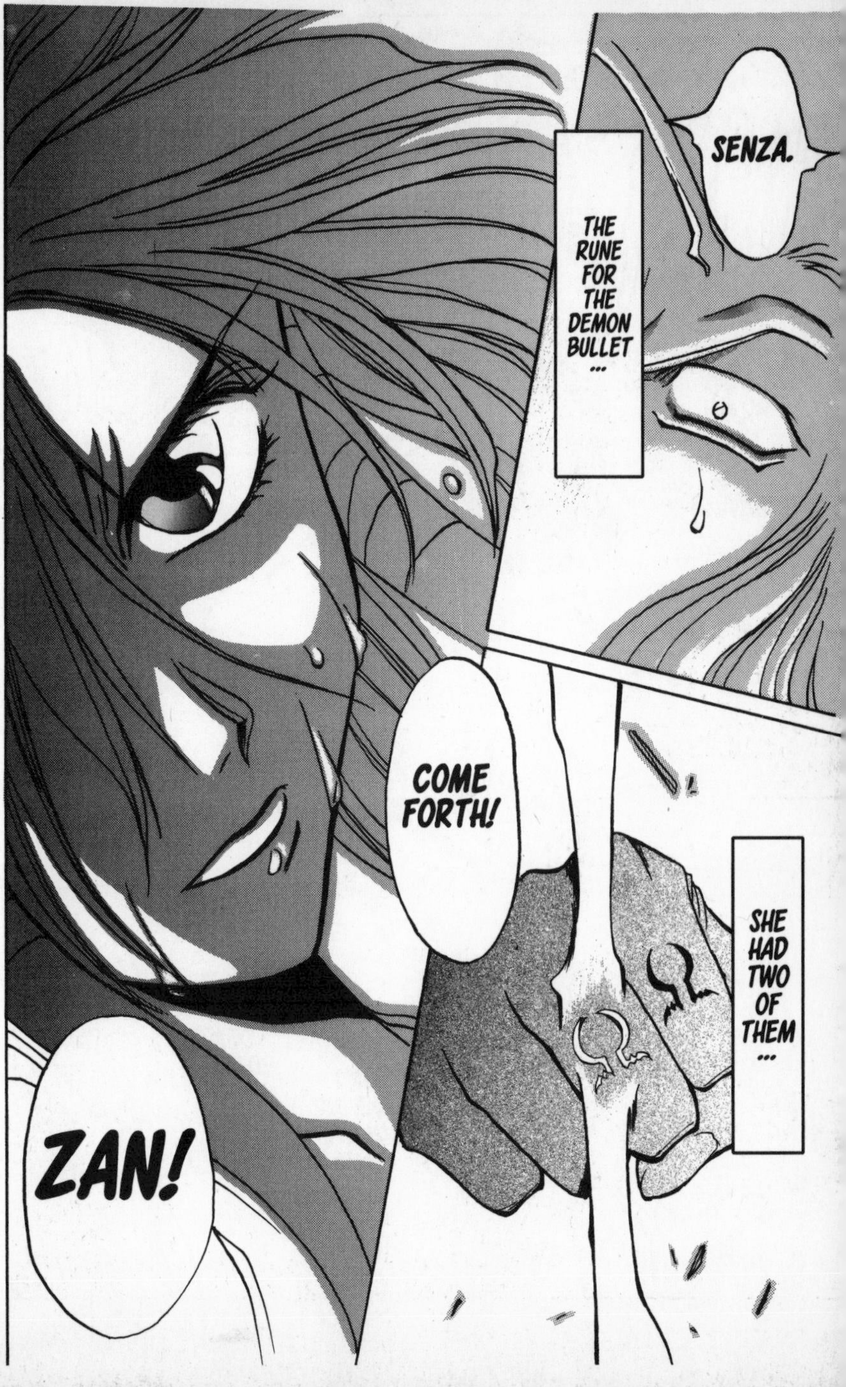
SENZA.
THE RUNE FOR THE DEMON BULLET...
SHE HAD TWO OF THEM...
COME FORTH!
ZAN!

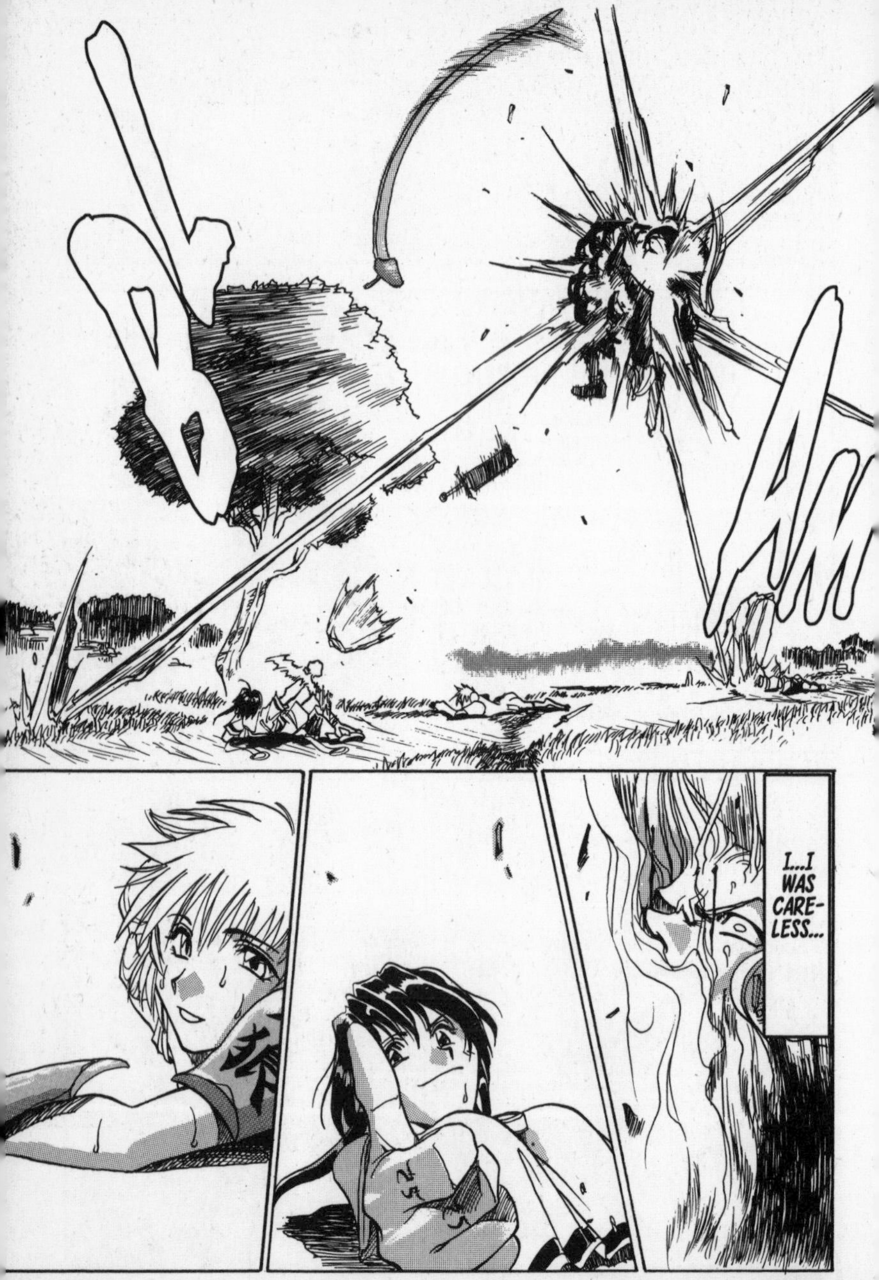
I...I WAS CARE-LESS...

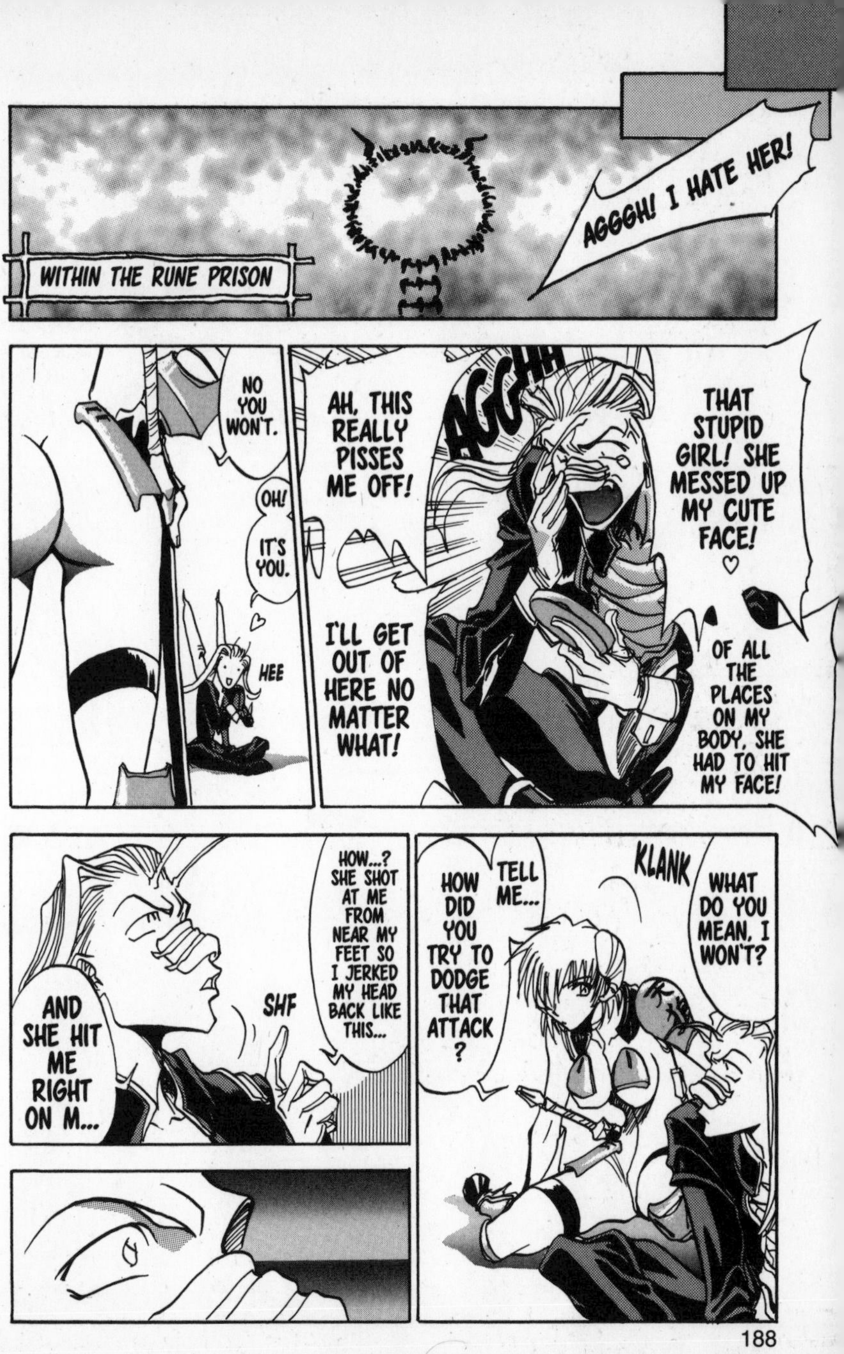
AGGGH! I HATE HER!
WITHIN THE RUNE PRISON
THAT STUPID GIRL! SHE MESSED UP MY CUTE FACE! ♡
AGGHH
AH, THIS REALLY PISSES ME OFF!
OF ALL THE PLACES ON MY BODY, SHE HAD TO HIT MY FACE!
I'LL GET OUT OF HERE NO MATTER WHAT!
NO YOU WON'T.
OH!
IT'S YOU.
HEE
KLANK
WHAT DO YOU MEAN, I WON'T?
TELL ME...
HOW DID YOU TRY TO DODGE THAT ATTACK?
HOW...? SHE SHOT AT ME FROM NEAR MY FEET SO I JERKED MY HEAD BACK LIKE THIS...
SHF
AND SHE HIT ME RIGHT ON M...

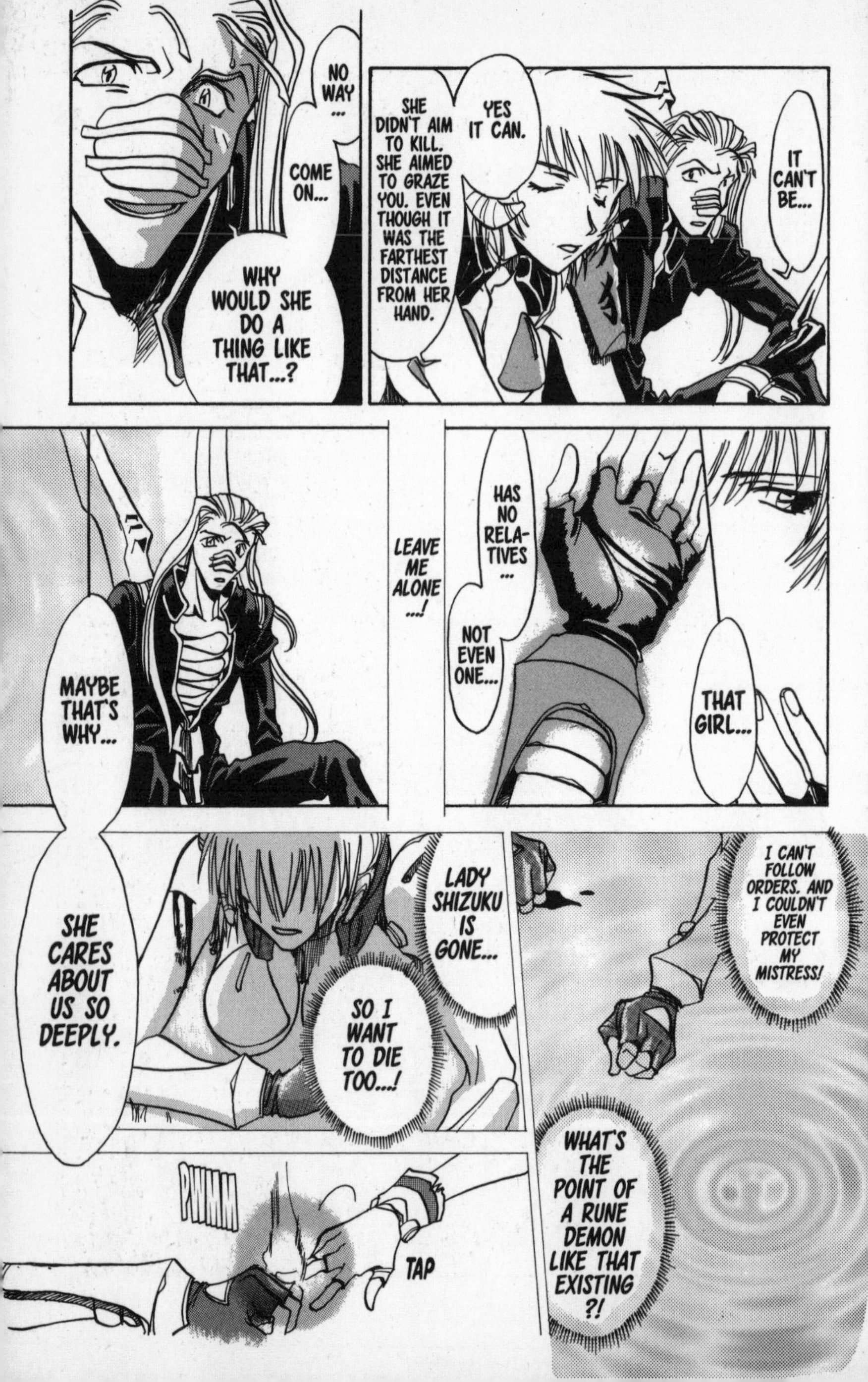
IT CAN'T BE...
YES IT CAN.
SHE DIDN'T AIM TO KILL. SHE AIMED TO GRAZE YOU. EVEN THOUGH IT WAS THE FARTHEST DISTANCE FROM HER HAND.
NO WAY...
COME ON...
WHY WOULD SHE DO A THING LIKE THAT...?
THAT GIRL...
HAS NO RELATIVES...
NOT EVEN ONE...
LEAVE ME ALONE...!
MAYBE THAT'S WHY...
SHE CARES ABOUT US SO DEEPLY.
I CAN'T FOLLOW ORDERS. AND I COULDN'T EVEN PROTECT MY MISTRESS!
WHAT'S THE POINT OF A RUNE DEMON LIKE THAT EXISTING?!
LADY SHIZUKU IS GONE...
SO I WANT TO DIE TOO...!
PWMM
TAP

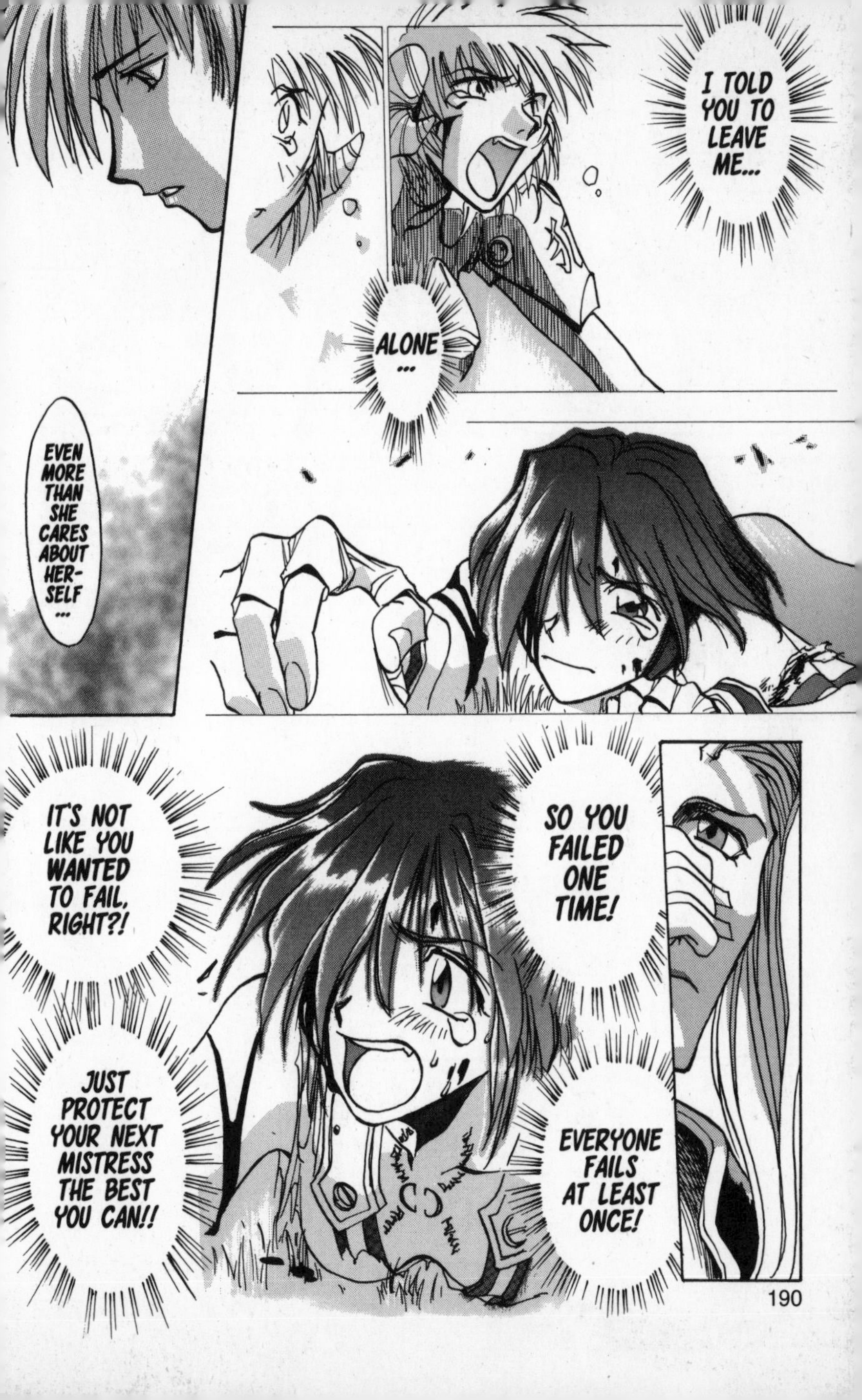
I TOLD YOU TO LEAVE ME...
ALONE ...
EVEN MORE THAN SHE CARES ABOUT HER-SELF ...
SO YOU FAILED ONE TIME!
EVERYONE FAILS AT LEAST ONCE!
IT'S NOT LIKE YOU WANTED TO FAIL, RIGHT?!
JUST PROTECT YOUR NEXT MISTRESS THE BEST YOU CAN!!

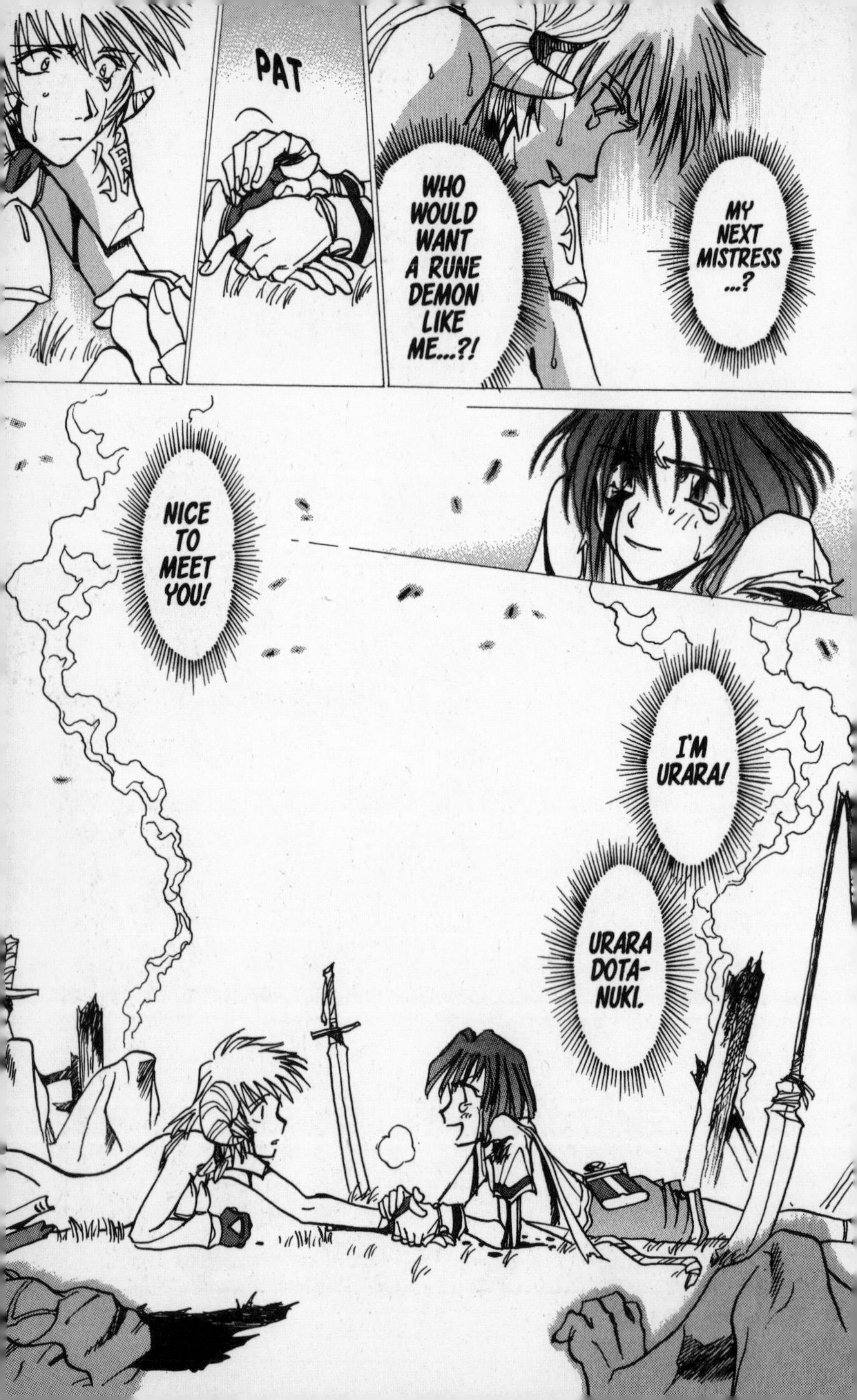
MY NEXT MISTRESS ...?
WHO WOULD WANT A RUNE DEMON LIKE ME...?!
PAT
NICE TO MEET YOU!
I'M URARA!
URARA DOTA-NUKI.

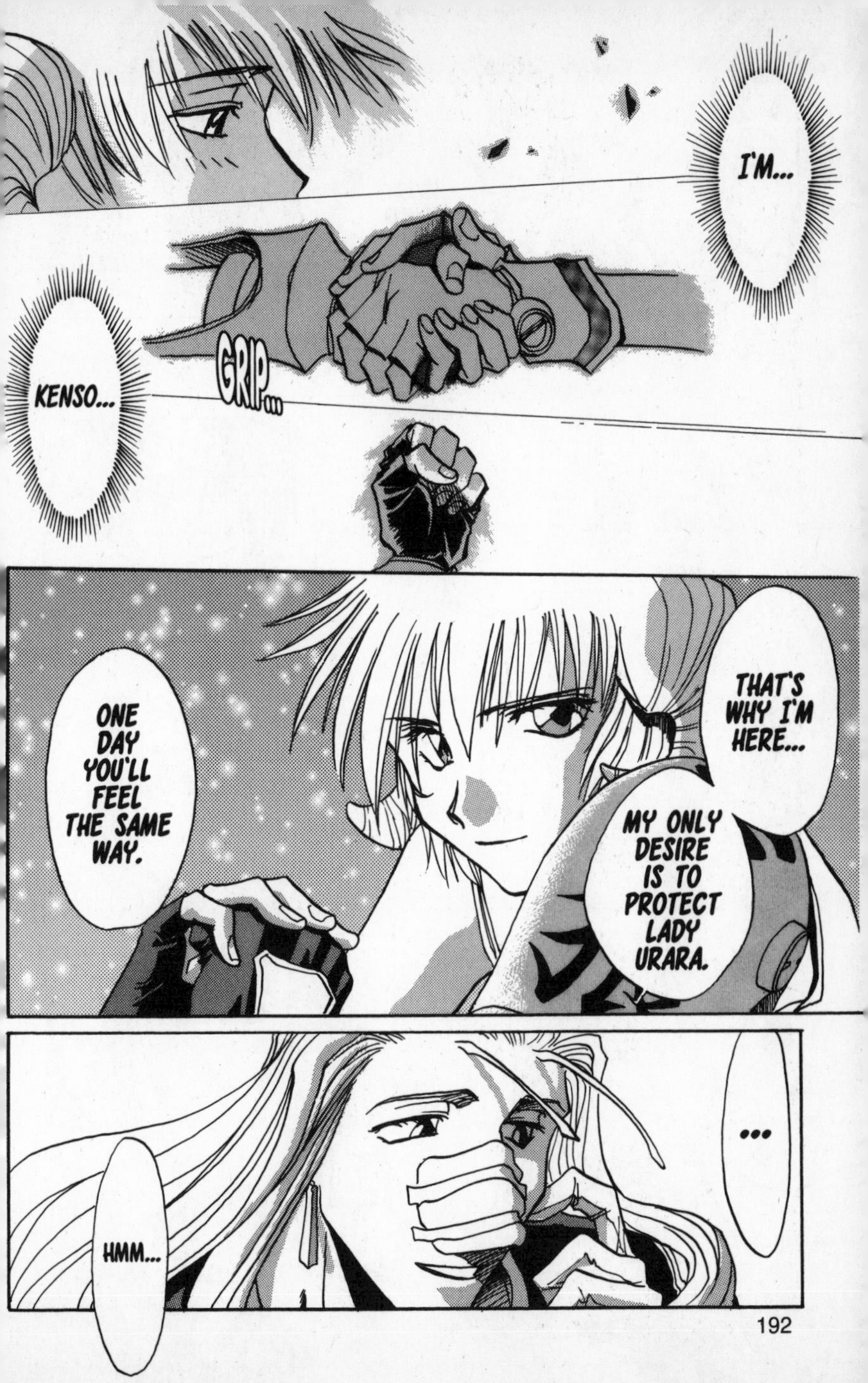
I'M...
KENSO...
GRIP...
THAT'S WHY I'M HERE...
MY ONLY DESIRE IS TO PROTECT LADY URARA.
ONE DAY YOU'LL FEEL THE SAME WAY.
...
HMM...

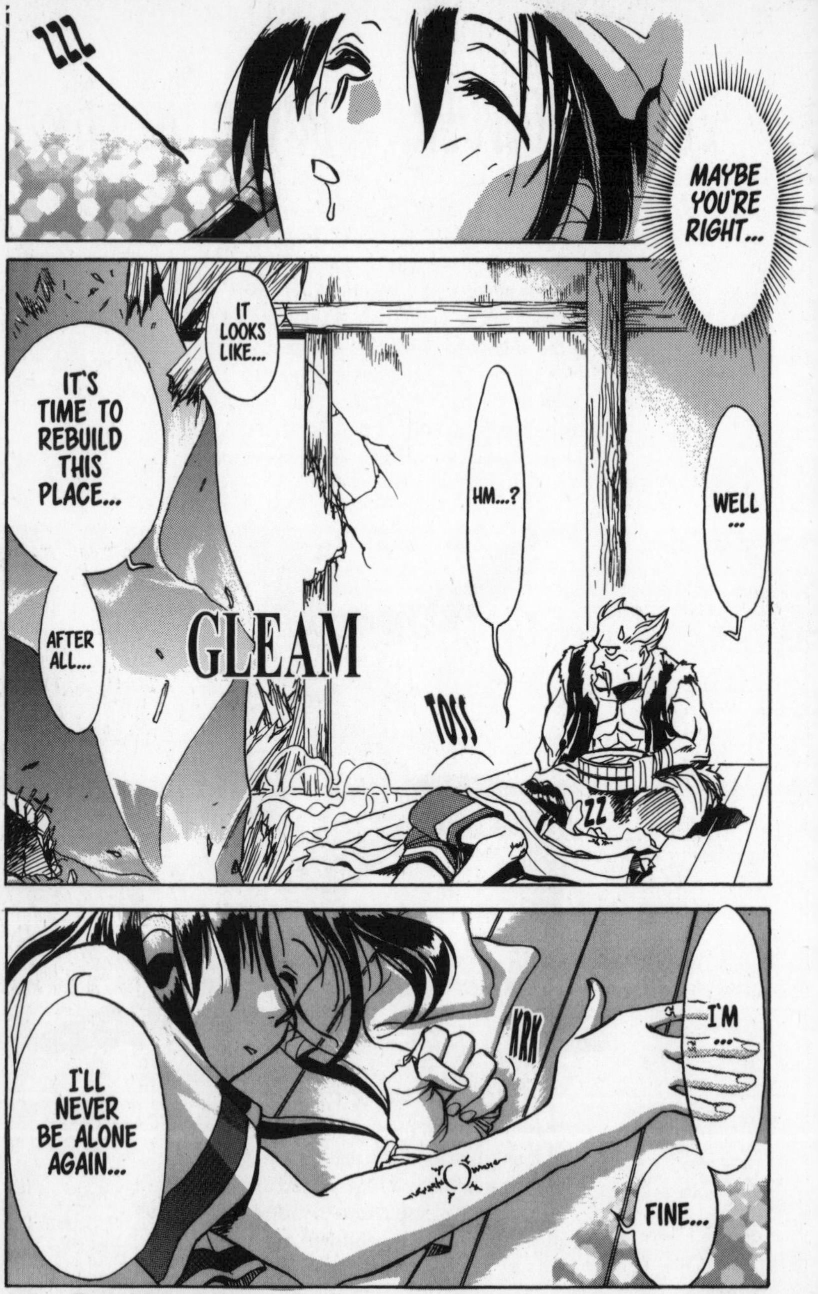
MAYBE YOU'RE RIGHT...
ZZZ
WELL...
HM...?
IT LOOKS LIKE...
IT'S TIME TO REBUILD THIS PLACE...
AFTER ALL...
GLEAM
TOSS
ZZ
I'M... FINE...
KRK
I'LL NEVER BE ALONE AGAIN...

ZOMBIEPOWDER.: A Day in the Life

In this section we will look at the lives of the
various characters. I, Balmunk the love
mystic, will be your guide. I say that, but this
is the only page in which I will appear. (Smile.)
Now, please step with me into this secret garden.
After that, please forget about me and peer into
the true personalities of the characters! And did
I mention that you should forget about me?

The Warning of Love

These pages will discuss characters from
all four volumes of the manga...*including
volume four!* If you haven't read all four
volumes yet, please return to this section
after volume four is published and reread it.

        -Balmunk

ELWOOD AND WOLFINA'S DAY

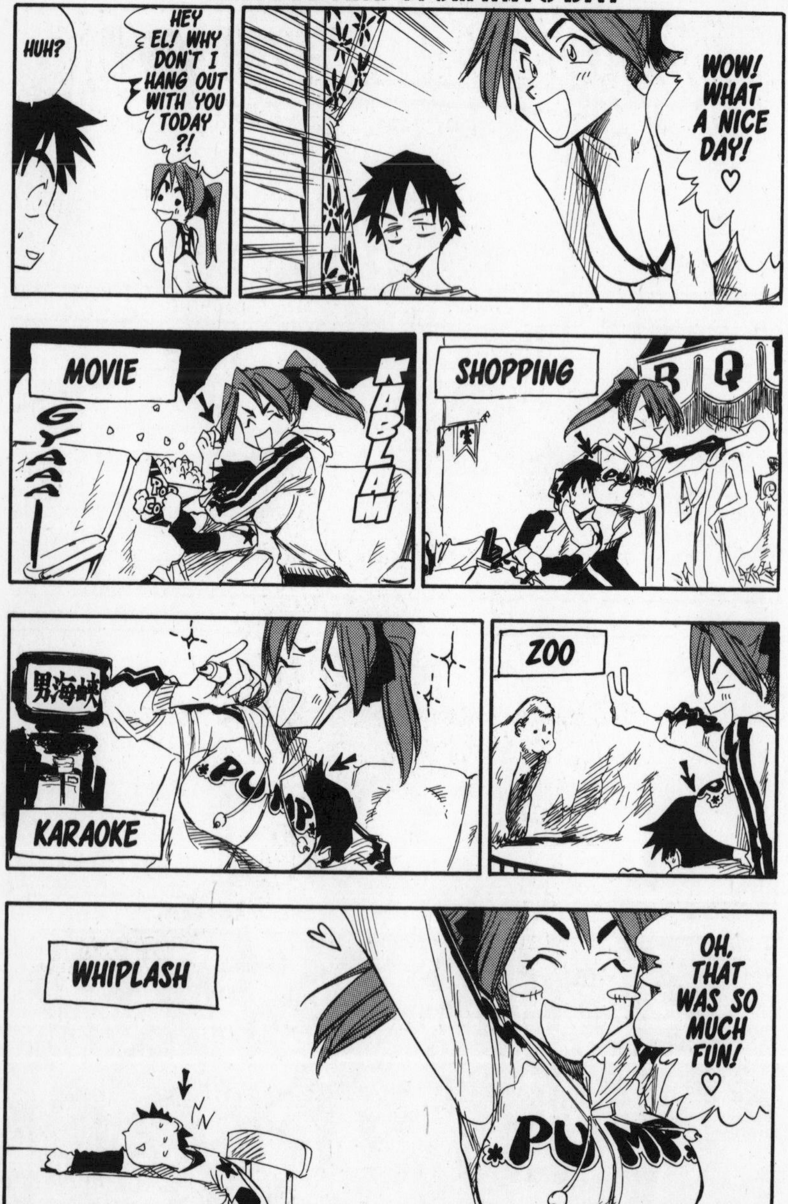
WOW! WHAT A NICE DAY! ♡
HEY EL! WHY DON'T I HANG OUT WITH YOU TODAY ?!
HUH?
SHOPPING
KABLAM
MOVIE
GYAAA
ZOO
男海峡
PUMP
KARAOKE
OH, THAT WAS SO MUCH FUN! ♡
WHIPLASH
PUMP

GAMMA'S DAY

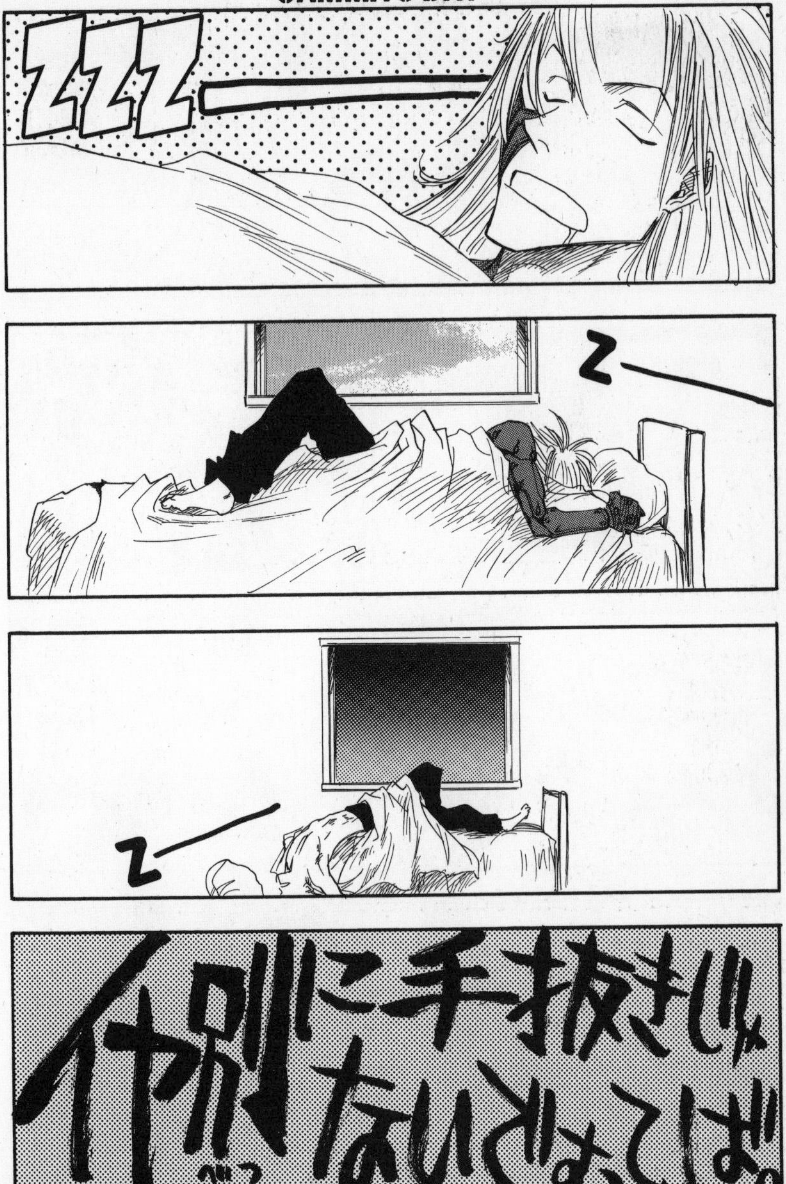
ZZZ
Z
Z
イヤ別に手抜きじゃないですってば。

"NO, I'M NOT SLACKING OFF OR ANYTHING."

NAZNA AND ANGEL'S DAY

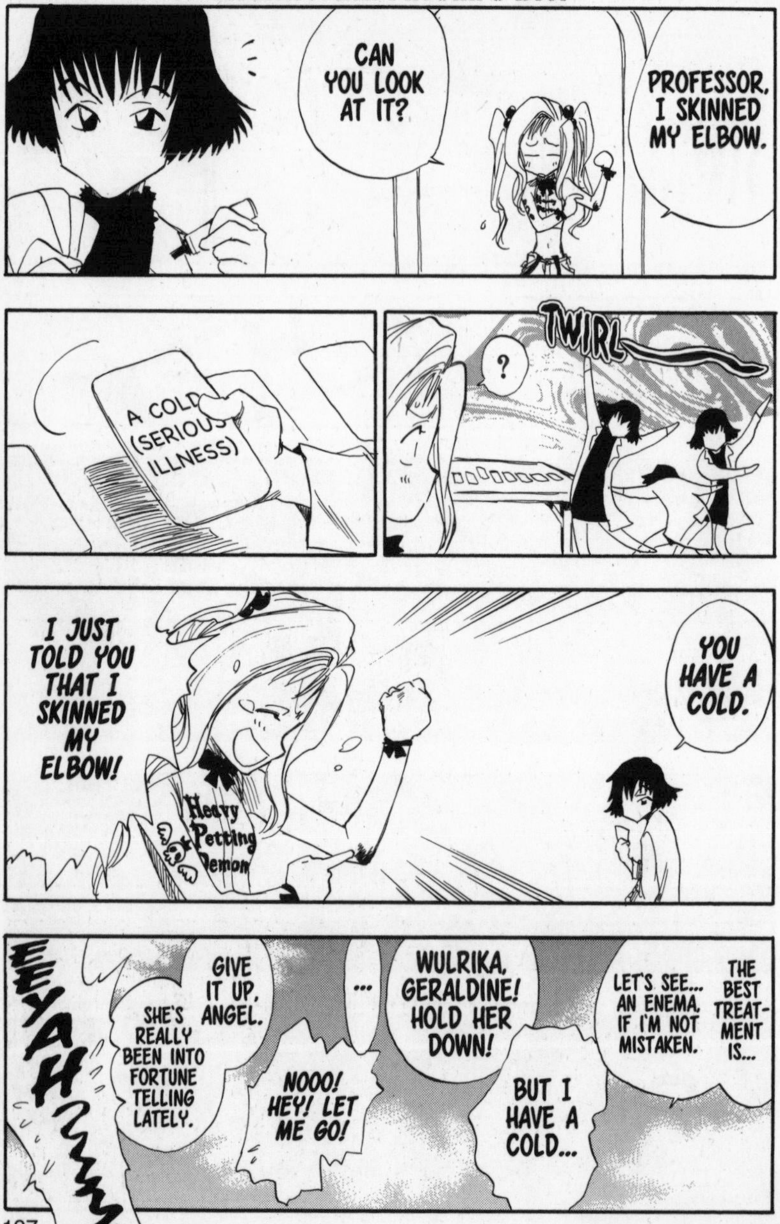

PROFESSOR, I SKINNED MY ELBOW.
CAN YOU LOOK AT IT?
TWIRL
?
A COLD (SERIOUS ILLNESS)
YOU HAVE A COLD.
I JUST TOLD YOU THAT I SKINNED MY ELBOW!
Heavy Petting Demon
THE BEST TREATMENT IS...
LET'S SEE... AN ENEMA, IF I'M NOT MISTAKEN.
BUT I HAVE A COLD...
WULRIKA, GERALDINE! HOLD HER DOWN!
...
NOOO! HEY! LET ME GO!
GIVE IT UP, ANGEL.
SHE'S REALLY BEEN INTO FORTUNE TELLING LATELY.
EEYAH

SMITH'S DAY

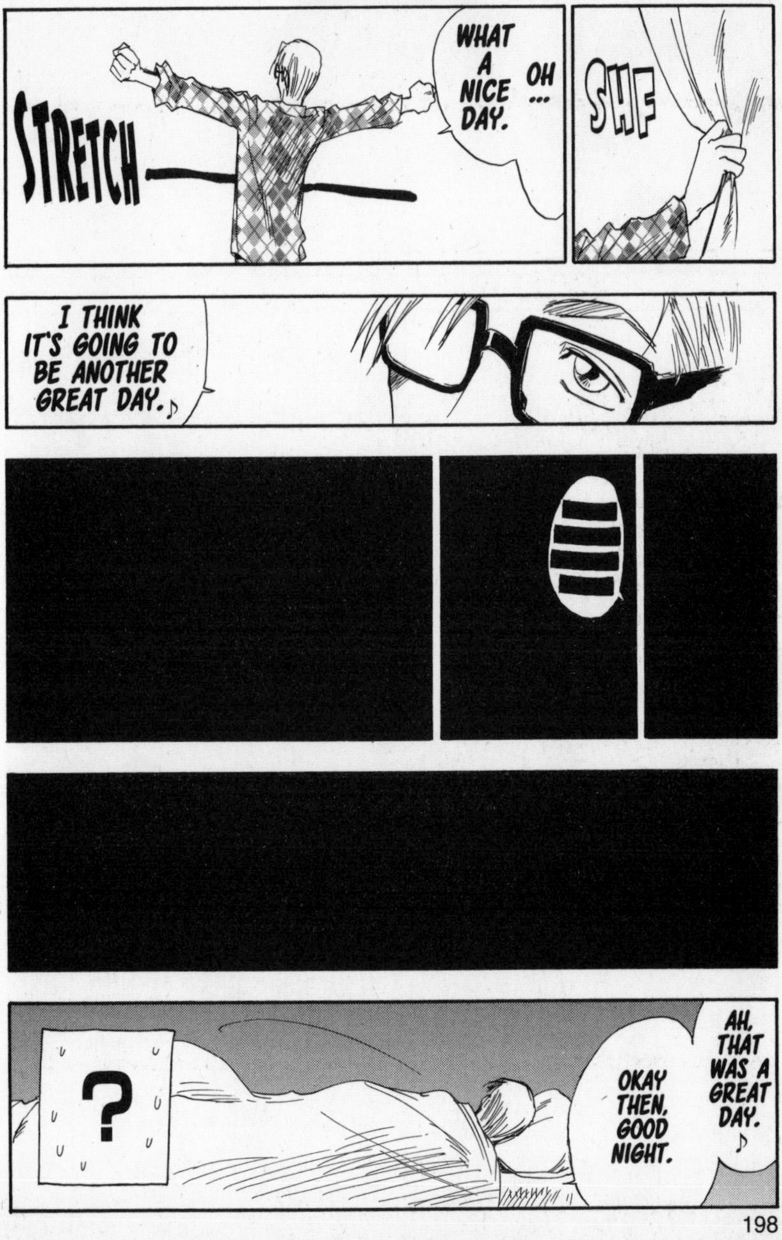
SHF
OH ...
WHAT A NICE DAY.
STRETCH
I THINK IT'S GOING TO BE ANOTHER GREAT DAY.♪
AH, THAT WAS A GREAT DAY. ♪
OKAY THEN, GOOD NIGHT.
?

IN THE NEXT VOLUME...

With the rest of the group nowhere in sight, Wolfina fights alone to save her brother from a fate worse than death! But can she defeat the brutal Shackaboon...and can anything get the ring from Emilio's body without triggering the monstrous hunger of the Ring of the Dead? At the end of the line is a woman who might have the answer...or might just have a lot of sharp cutting implements! Includes another one of Tite Kubo's early stories, "Bad Shield United"!

AVAILABLE NOW!

Zom
bie
pow
der.
4
.
.
june
2007
.
.
out

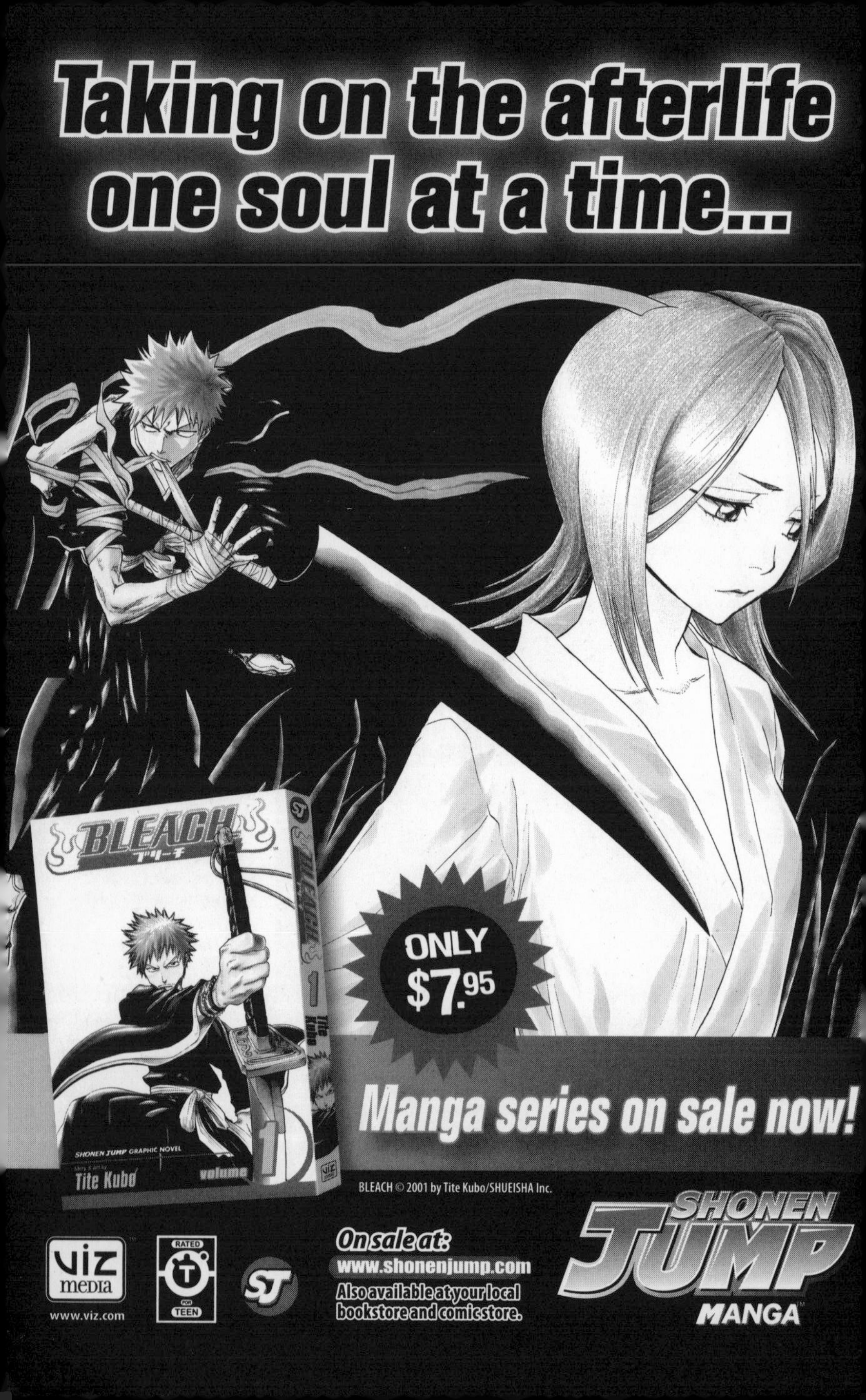

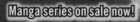

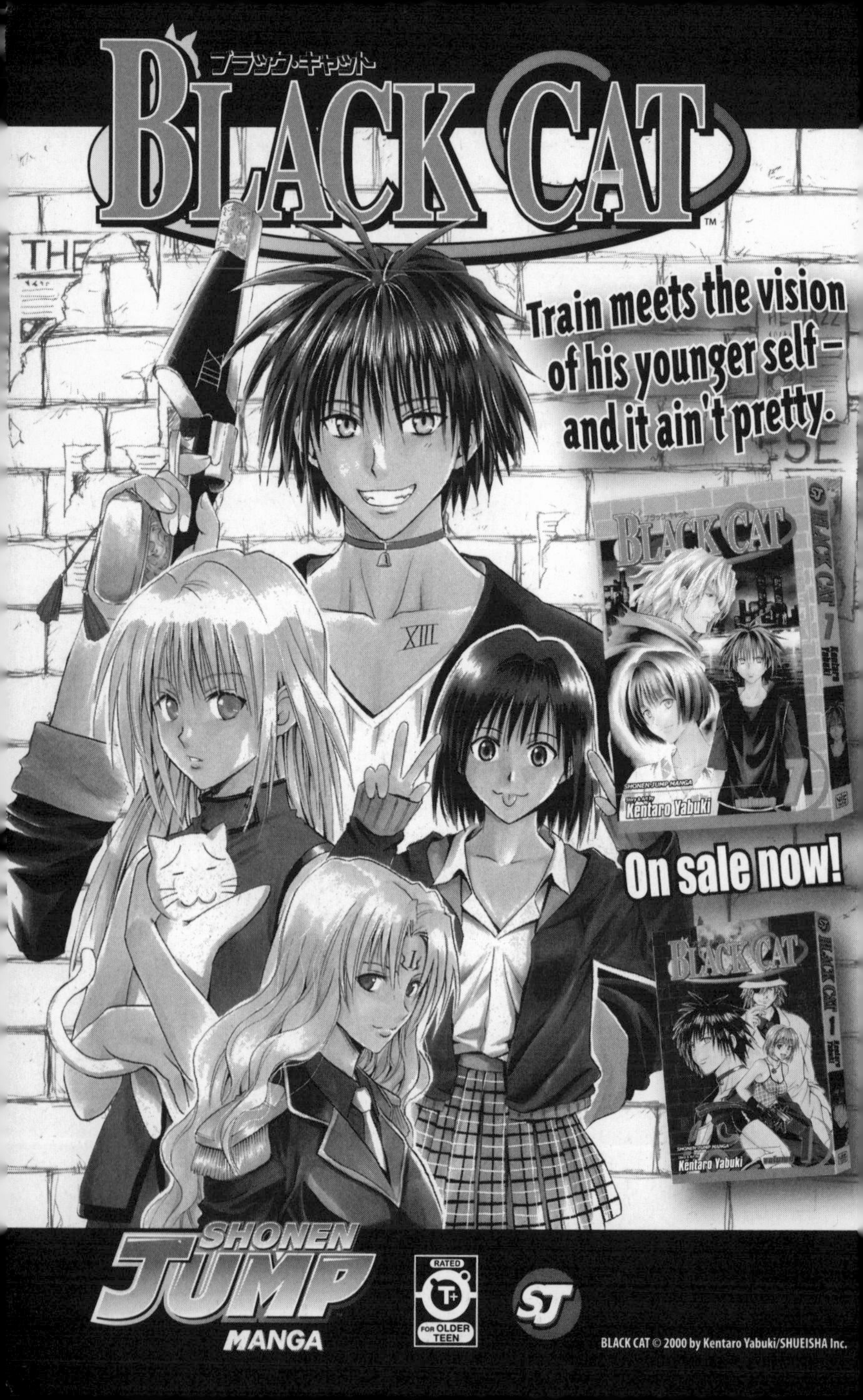
ブラック・キャット
BLACK CAT™
Train meets the vision of his younger self – and it ain't pretty.
BLACK CAT
SHONEN JUMP MANGA
Kentaro Yabuki
On sale now!
BLACK CAT
SHONEN JUMP MANGA
Kentaro Yabuki
SHONEN JUMP MANGA
RATED T+ FOR OLDER TEEN
SJ
BLACK CAT © 2000 by Kentaro Yabuki/SHUEISHA Inc.

ZOMBIEPOWDER. VOL. 3
The SHONEN JUMP Manga Edition

STORY AND ART BY
TITE KUBO

Translation/Akira Watanabe
Touch-up Art & Lettering/Stephen Dutro
Design/Sean Lee
Editor/Jason Thompson

Editor in Chief, Books/Alvin Lu
Editor in Chief, Magazines/Marc Weidenbaum
VP, Publishing Licensing/Rika Inouye
VP, Sales & Product Marketing/Gonzalo Ferreyra
VP, Creative/Linda Espinosa
Publisher/Hyoe Narita

Printed in the U.S.A.

Published by VIZ Media, LLC
P.O. Box 77010
San Francisco, CA 94107

SHONEN JUMP Manga Edition
10 9 8 7 6 5 4 3 2
First printing, March 2007
Second printing, August 2008

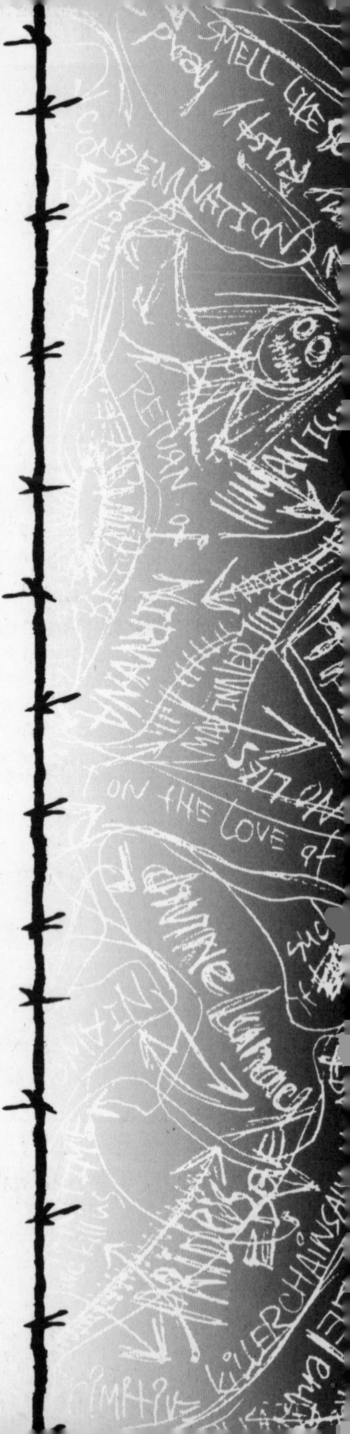
CONDEMNATION
ON THE LOVE of

For certain reasons, I was forced to start
ZOMBIEPOWDER. in a shaky emotional
state. In the beginning, I was so critical of
what I had drawn that I couldn't even bear
to look at the finished product. It's only
from the third volume onward that I've finally
been able to look at my work.
All right, read on! This is my manga!

–Tite Kubo, 2000

Tite Kubo is best known as the creator
of the smash hit *SHONEN JUMP*
manga series *Bleach*, which began
serialization in *Weekly Shonen Jump* in
2001. *ZOMBIEPOWDER.*, his debut
series, began serialization in 1999.